CREATIVITY IN TRANSITION

Material Mediations: People and Things in a World of Movement

Edited by **Birgit Meyer**, Department of Religious Studies and Theology, Utrecht University, and **Maruška Svašek**, School of History and Anthropology, Queens University, Belfast

During the last few years, a lively, interdisciplinary debate has taken place between anthropologists, art historians and scholars of material culture, religion, visual culture and media studies about the dynamics of material production and cultural mediation in an era of intensifying globalization and transnational connectivity. Understanding 'mediation' as a fundamentally material process, this series provides a stimulating platform for ethnographically grounded theoretical debates about the many aspects that constitute relationships between people and things, including political, economic, technological, aesthetic, sensorial and emotional processes.

Volume 1
Moving Subjects, Moving Objects
Transnationalism, Cultural Production and Emotions
Edited by Maruška Svašek

Volume 2
Growing Artefacts, Displaying Relationships
Yams, Art and Technology amongst the Nyamikum Abelam of Papua New Guinea
Ludovic Coupaye

Volume 3
Objects and Imagination
Perspectives on Materialization and Mediation
Edited by Øivind Fuglerud and Leon Wainwright

Volume 4
The Great Reimagining
Public Art, Urban Space, and the Symbolic Landscapes of a 'New' Northern Ireland
Bree T. Hocking

Volume 5
Having and Belonging
Homes and Museums in Israel
Judy Jaffe-Schagen

Volume 6
Creativity in Transition
Politics and Aesthetics of Cultural Production Across the Globe
Edited by Maruška Svašek and Birgit Meyer

Volume 7
Death, Materiality and Mediation
An Ethnography of Remembrance in Ireland
Barbara Graham

CREATIVITY IN TRANSITION

Politics and Aesthetics of Cultural Production Across the Globe

Edited by

Maruška Svašek and Birgit Meyer

berghahn

NEW YORK · OXFORD

www.berghahnbooks.com

Published in 2016 by
Berghahn Books
www.berghahnbooks.com

© 2016 Maruška Svašek and Birgit Meyer

Library of Congress Cataloging-in-Publication Data

A C.I.P. cataloging record is availabe from the Library of Congress

British Library Cataloguing in Publication Data

A catalogue record for this book is available from the British Library

ISBN 978-1-78533-181-7 hardback
ISBN 978-1-78533-183-1 paperback
ISBN 978-1-78533-182-4 ebook

Contents

List of Figures   vii

Acknowledgements   xii

Introduction
Creativity and Innovation in a World of Movement   1
Maruška Svašek

1. African Lace: Agency and Transcontinental Interaction in
Textile Design   33
Barbara Plankensteiner

2. Heads Against Hands and Hierarchies of Creativity: Indian
Luxury Embroidery Between Craft, Fashion Design and Art   61
Tereza Kuldova

3. The Social Life of *Kottan* Baskets: Craft Production,
Consumption and Circulation in Tamil Nadu, India   86
Kala Shreen

4. Art and the Making of the Creative City of Chennai, India   107
Amit Desai

5. Approximation as Interpretive Appropriation: Guaraní-Inspired
Ceramics in Misiones, Argentina   131
Arnd Schneider

6. Positioned Creativity: Museums, Politics and Indigenous Art
in British Columbia and Norway   158
Øivind Fuglerud

7. 'We Paint Our Way and the Christian Way Together':
   Transforming Yolngu and Ngan'gi Art through Creative
   Ancestral-Christian Practice   185
   Fiona Magowan and Maria Øien

8. Undoing Absence through Things: Creative Appropriation
   and Affective Engagement in an Indian Transnational Setting   218
   Maruška Svašek

9. 'The Eye Likes It': National Identity and the Aesthetics of
   Attraction Among Sri Lankan Tamil Catholics and Hindus   245
   Stine Bruland

10. Narratives, Movements, Objects: Aesthetics and Power in
    Catholic Devotion to Our Lady of Aparecida, Brazil   267
    João Rickli

11. The Art of Imitation: The (Re)Production and Reception of
    Jesus Pictures in Ghana   290
    Rhoda Woets

Afterword
   Creativity in Transition   312
   Birgit Meyer

Index   319

Figures

1.1 Samples of contemporary 'Up and Down' styles on the cover of the fashion magazine *Designers Delight* (Issue 24, 2010). 36

1.2 Contemporary male outfit designed by the well-known Lagos designer Goodwin Mekuye. Photo: Moussa Moussa, © Austrian Embroidery Association. 37

1.3 Lady's suit, Nigeria c. 1975. Industrial guipure embroidery with cotton yarn. Collection Weltmuseum Wien. Photo: Alex Rosoli. 38

1.4 Men's suit, Nigeria, early 1970s. Cotton fabric with industrial eyelet embroidery. Collection Weltmuseum Wien. Photo: Alex Rosoli. 44

1.5 Lace outfits paraded at a party of the elites in Lagos in 2010. In this case, the seventieth birthday celebration of Chief Alhaji Rasaq Okoya, a renowned business 'mogul' posing with the *Oloris* (Queens) of Lagos (*Ovation*, issue 118: 23). 51

1.6 Austrian embroidery exporters dressed in lace together with Nigerian colleagues and friends at the title taking party for Chief Modupe Obebe (middle) in Abeokuta 1979. Second from right stands Olusegun Obasanjo, who like the other male guests wears a precious lace *agbada* outfit. Photo: Studio 22, Fritz Hagen; courtesy Oswald Brunner. 53

2.1 Rolls-Royce Phantom II 'Star of India' (1934) built for the Maharaja of Rajkot, the only Rolls-Royce ever executed in saffron (*bhagwa*), the sacred colour of Hinduism, paradoxically also representing renunciation of material gains. Photo: www.vccci.com, 2012 62

2.2 The aesthetic return to feudalism is reflected in current popular visual culture, fashion and film that increasingly portray a clearly hierarchical feudal world of royals, their subjects and servants, pointing to the role of royal aesthetics in reflecting contemporary concerns. Backstage at India couture week 2014, collection by Rohit Bal. Photo: courtesy Nitin Patel Photography.   63

2.3 Designer Samant Chauhan posing with a model in a village setting with the family of one of his weavers in the background. Photo: courtesy Vineet Modi, 2012.   65

2.4 Producing chikan embroidery, traditionally white-on-white embroidery from Lucknow, the nostalgic capital of the precolonial opulent and mythologized district of Awadh, known for the lavish lifestyles of its Nawab rulers. Photo: Tereza Kuldova, 2011.   70

2.5 Chikan embroiderers laughing while working, Lucknow, Uttar Pradesh. Photo: courtesy Arash Taheri, 2012.   80

3.1 *Kottan*s reproduced in silver in different sizes at the showroom of a silverware retailer in central Chennai. Photo: Kala Shreen.   89

3.2 *Kottan*s reproduced as innovative turmeric and vermillion holders at a Chennai-based silverware retailer. Photo: Kala Shreen.   90

3.3 Reproduction of an award-winning *kottan* in brightly coloured chemical dyes. Photo: Kala Shreen.   95

3.4 *Kottan* weaves, glass framed and hung on the wall at the *kottan* exhibition. Photo: Kala Shreen.   98

3.5 *Kottan* exhibits, neatly labelled with taxonomies and pertaining descriptions Photo: Kala Shreen.   99

3.6 *Kottan* delegate kits at the World Crafts Summit, which innovatively combined jute and *kottan* weaving. Photo: Kala Shreen.   101

4.1 Main museum and gallery building, Cholamandal Artists' Village. Photo: Amit Desai.   111

4.2 A sculpture by Cholamandal artist Nandagopal in the home of a Chennai collector who has presented it surrounded by 'traditional' representations of the god Ganesh. Photo: Amit Desai.   123

5.1 Guaraní pipe, partly restored, Museo Provincial Andrés
Guacurarí, Posadas, Misiones, Argentina. Photo: Arnd
Schneider. 135

5.2 Historic Guaraní funerary urns (*yapepó*) on view at the
Museo Regional Aníbal Cambas, Posadas, Misiones,
Argentina; two small re-creations in the foreground. Photo:
Arnd Schneider. 138

5.3 Guillermo Cribb showing a recreation of a funerary urn
(*yapepó*) with lid. Photo: Arnd Schneider. 141

5.4 A variety of re-creations of Guaraní ceramics, by Stella Maris
Muñoz de Cribb and Guillermo Cribb, Posadas. Photo: Arnd
Schneider. 141

5.5 Partial View of Installation *Identidade* (Group C),
Universidade Comunitária Regional de Chapecó (Santa
Catarina State), Brazil (from Dutra 2005: 185; also Nunes
and Dutra 2015). Photo: courtesy Eduardo Dutra. 146

5.6 Pottery from the ceramics workshop in Santa Ana, Misiones.
Photo: Arnd Schneider. 149

6.1 Robert Davidson, *Sgaan Sgaanwee*. Photo: courtesy Robert
Davidson. 159

6.2 MoA's Great Hall. Photo: Øivind Fuglerud. 164

6.3 Bill Reid, Raven design in gold, carving 1971. Photo: courtesy
MoA. 172

6.4 Bill Reid, *The Spirit of Haida Gwaii* carved bracelets 1997.
Photo: courtesy MoA. 174

6.5 Iver Jåks, *Gudenes Dans* (Dance of the Gods), relief, wood
and concrete 1972. Photo: courtesy RidduDuottar Museat. 175

6.6 Iver Jåks, *Kvinnene* (The Women). Photo: courtesy
RidduDuottar Museat. 176

6.7 Iver Jåks, *Oppadstrebende samekultur* (Sami culture striving
upwards), perishable sculpture 1994–1996. Photo: courtesy
RidduDuottar Museat. 178

6.8 Eirik Wuohti, *Spor* (Traces). Photo: courtesy RidduDuottar
Museat. 179

6.9 Synøve Persen, *Labyrint II*. Photo: courtesy RidduDuottar
Museat. 180

6.10 Geir Tore Holm, *Parabol* ('dish antenna'), assemblage 1993.
Photo: courtesy RidduDuottar Museat.   180

7.1 Gali Gurruwiwi exhibition at the Rebecca Hossack Gallery,
15 July–10 September 2010. Two large Morning Star poles
(centre). Photo: Fiona Magowan.   196

7.2 Gali Gurruwiwi's completed Banumbirr poles at the Rebecca
Hossack Gallery, 15 July 2010. Photo: Fiona Magowan.   197

7.3 Sketch by Gali Gurruwiwi of the interrelationship between
the Morning Star and Christian theology. Photo: Fiona
Magowan, Galiwin'ku, 22 November 2010.   199

7.4 Patricia Marrfurra, *Welcome to Country*, 1991. Photo:
courtesy Eileen Farrelly.   203

7.5 Miriam-Rose Ungunmerr Baumann, *Both Ways to Heal the
Spirit*, 1987. Photo: courtesy Eileen Farrelly.   206

8.1 The *puja* room in Manika's house. Photo: Maruška Svašek.   219

8.2 Manika fills a lamp with ghee. Photo: Maruška Svašek.   226

8.3 Curatorial play: placement of two Ganesha figures. Photo:
Maruška Svašek.   229

8.4 Wooden Ganesh, bought in Belfast. Photo: Maruška Svašek.   231

8.5 Lighting a candle in front of photographs of deceased kin.
Photo: Maruška Svašek.   232

8.6 Bronze standard depicting the symbols *Om* and *Swastik*.
Photo: Maruška Svašek.   233

8.7 A photograph of the main deity in Radharamana temple.
Photo: Maruška Svašek.   236

9.1 Malar circling incense clockwise during her Friday morning
prayer. Photo: Stine Bruland.   253

9.2 Hindu God with flower garland. Photo: Stine Bruland.   257

9.3 The *Matha* arriving at Suganthy's home. Photo: Stine Bruland. 259

9.4 The *Matha* with flowers, light, dress and incense. Photo: Stine
Bruland.   260

10.1 View of the Basilica. Photo: João Rickli.   275

10.2 *Ex-votos*. Photo: João Rickli.   277

10.3 View of the *ex-voto* room. Photo: João Rickli.   278

10.4 Official image with certificate of authenticity and view of
images displayed in a shop. Photo: João Rickli. 284

10.5 A second official image with certificate of authenticity and
view of images displayed in a shop. Photo: João Rickli. 285

11.1 Poster-seller, Accra, June 2011. Photo: Rhoda Woets. 291

11.2 Kobina Bucknor (1968), title unknown, acrylic polymers on
board. Christ the King Church in Accra. Photo: Rhoda Woets. 297

11.3 Rikki Wemega-Kwawu (1981) *What More Could I Have
Done for You … ?* pastel on pastel paper. Photo: Rhoda Woets. 300

11.4 Bernard Akoi-Jackson (2002–2003), *Wobole Kutu Wokpe*
(Together We Sit to Eat) acrylic on canvas. Photo: courtesy
Bernard Akoi-Jackson. 303

11.5 Two Christ paintings by Kwame Akoto, both made in 1990.
Photo: courtesy Atta Kwami. 306

ACKNOWLEDGEMENTS

This book is one of the outcomes of the collaborative research project Creativity and Innovation in a World of Movement (CIM), which brought together researchers from universities and research institutions in Austria, Norway, the United Kingdom and the Netherlands. As editors we would like to express our sincere thanks to all the persons we encountered and worked with in various field sites in India, Ghana, Brazil, Sri Lanka, Argentina, Australia, Canada, Norway, France and the United Kingdom, without whose assistance the chapters assembled in this book could never have been written.

CIM was financially supported by the HERA Joint Research Programme Cultural Dynamics, which was co-funded by AHRC, AKA, DASTI, ETF, FNR, FWF, HAZU, IRCHSS, MHEST, NWO, RANNIS, RCN, VR and the European Community FP7 2007–2013, under the Socio-economic Sciences and Humanities programme. We would like to thank all involved for their generous financial and organizational support, and Julia Boman from HERA for her willingness to answer endless questions with exceptional expertise and patience. We are also very grateful for support given by the research offices of our collaborating institutions, including Queen's University Belfast, Vrije Universiteit Amsterdam, Utrecht University, the Open University (Milton Keynes), Manchester Metropolitan University, the Museum of Cultural History (Oslo) and Weltmuseum Wien.

This volume is based on two conferences held by our project in Belfast in February 2010 and in Utrecht in 2012. The chapters were discussed intensely among the contributors. We would like to thank André Bakker, Markus Balkenhol, Heike Becker, the late Martha Blassnigg (our esteemed colleague in the larger HERA Cultural Dynamics initiative whose sudden death in September 2015 shocked us deeply), Christiane Brosius, Marleen de Witte, Raj Isar, Wayne Modest, George Petitjean and Irene Stengs for their stimulating comments on earlier versions of the contributions assembled in this book and two anonymous reviewers for offering insightful and constructive suggestions for improvement. Marion Berghahn and the production team at Berghahn Books deserve equal thanks for their competent help and efficient guidance. Last but not least, we express our appreciation to Gordon Ramsey for his excellent editorial input and his overall engagement in the preparation of the manuscript for publication.

—Amsterdam and Belfast, February 2016, Birgit Meyer and Maruška Svašek

INTRODUCTION

Creativity and Innovation in a World of Movement

―――•:◆:•―――

Maruška Svašek

'It was ridiculous what they taught us!' exclaimed the Ghanaian artist Amon Kotei (1915–2011) in 1989, talking about his time at Achimota Art College in the 1940s. During that period, the Gold Coast was part of the British Empire and Kotei's European teachers had expected him, in addition to learning the basics of 'Western' techniques such as drawing in perspective, to work in a style that was 'traditionally African'. The artist's expression of indignation concluded with his account of how, one day, while making a figurative clay portrait of a female model, his teacher, Vladimir Meyerowitz, had suddenly shouted at him for idling away his time by 'copying European art' (Svašek 1997: 32).

Born in 1900 in St Petersburg as the son of Russian and German parents, Meyerowitz had been trained as a woodcarver at the *Kunstgewerbeschule* in Berlin. Interested in 'traditional African design', he had moved to South Africa, teaching art and crafts at the University of Capetown. Invited by the deputy director of education of the Gold Coast colony, he took up the job of arts and crafts master at Achimota College. The director had been worried about the quality of arts and crafts produced by school pupils, and Meyerowitz agreed that they were in danger of losing the skills of their ancestors. His advice to Kotei was that in his three-dimensional work, he should rather stick to 'African' traditions (Woets 2011: 98–99). It was ironic, said Kotei, that his teacher had condemned his interest in European sculpture while applauding the efforts of European artists like Picasso who took inspiration from African masks. In Kotei's view, it seemed unfair that European appropriations of African visual elements were celebrated as valuable artistic innovations, and African appropriations of European elements were disparaged as acts of mindless copying. The irony, however, was lost on Meyerowitz.

Kotei's insight captures the main theme of this book: the dynamics of cultural production and creativity in an era of intensifying globalization and transnational connectivity. The approach of the volume is informed by an argument made by Tim Ingold and Elizabeth Hallam (2007) against a limited understanding of creativity as pure innovation, an understanding that derives from a limited, typically modernist view that seeks to assess the 'originality' of end products, ranking them on a scale from (inferior, mechanistic) imitations to (superior, creative) innovations. This perspective of creativity as innovation (marked as Creativity, with a capital C, by Birgit Meyer in the afterword to this book) erroneously offers a 'backwards reading of creativity [that] lies outside time' and fails to acknowledge the ongoing improvisational dynamics of product manufacture and use, as well as of human life in more general terms (Ingold and Hallam 2007: 10). This volume argues that practices of copying and reproduction should not be placed in opposition to creativity, but conceptualized as part and parcel of the creative process. As Arjun Appadurai (1986) and Fred Myers (2001) have pointed out, circulating within and across different regimes of value, images actively coproduce concrete contexts. Whether replicated or not, there is always uniqueness in artefacts and pictures; produced or used in new situations, they are necessarily drawn into specific temporal or spatio-temporal situations. It is this process of active people-thing dynamics that is at the centre of this book. Its contributors pay particular attention to processes of authentication and authorization that shape creative practices. As Kotei's case highlights, cultural producers do not create in a social vacuum, and are confronted with expectations that stipulate what kind of products are appropriate, correct or pleasing and which are not. Direct or indirect demands and desires are communicated, and in some cases strongly enforced in wider fields of practice, including institutional settings (such as schools, museums, religious organizations), markets (for example, of art, fashion or religious artefacts), and political regimes (in national, colonial and postcolonial settings) (Fuglerud and Wainwright 2015: 5; MacClancy 1997). As the example of Kotei illustrates, while such demands do not necessarily dictate what is actually produced, they need to be taken into consideration if we wish to understand the creative process in its full depth. The perspective of improvisation helps us to bring the process of *creating* into focus, and allows us to explore the force of specific expectations within different fields of creative practice. As Rob Pope (2005: 38) pointed out: 'An emphasis upon the creat*ed* rather than the creat*ing* aspects of production ... underwrites an aesthetics and a politics of fixed (not fluid) form and absolute (not relative) value.'

The creativity-as-improvisation perspective featured in this book emphasizes the fluidity of material and visual production, demonstrating that values are actively produced through artefact-focused discourses, practices and embodied experiences.

The Temporal Dimension: A Sidestep to Jazz

In 2001, John Liep edited a volume on creative practice that conceptually separated 'improvisation' from 'cultural creativity'. He identified the former as 'a more conventional exploration of possibilities within a certain framework of rules', opposing it to creativity that involved 'the acceptance of the novel in a social environment' (2011: 2).[1] By contrast, and for reasons that will be outlined below, this book uncouples notions of creativity and the unconventional, agreeing with Ingold and Hallam (2007: 3) that processes of improvisation are 'not conditional upon judgments of the novelty or otherwise of the forms [they yield]'. From this perspective, both copying and innovation are central aspects of creative processes.

To assess the suitability of the creativity-as-improvisation perspective for the analysis of material production, it is enlightening to consider recent debates in the field of music that similarly question the repetition-innovation dichotomy. Scholars such as Ryan McCormack (2012) have criticized the idea that improvisation in Jazz should be considered the unrestricted free creation of unanticipated sonic flows, signifying endless newness.[2] Representations of Jazz as an entirely impulsive, unrestrained form of music-making have disregarded the impact of embodied learning on subsequent musical practice, ignoring a longer-term temporal perspective (Faulkner and Becker 2009; Stanbridge 2004a; 2004b). Sara Ramshaw (2013: 6) has pointed out that 'the distinction between a planned or described act and improvisation is always already unsettled'. This impossibility of absolute singularity on the one hand, and of isolated newness on the other, means that neither those who aim to make exact reproductions of existing forms (whether sonic or material), nor those who strive to invent entirely new ones, can escape the intertwining of past, present and future (Derrida 2001). As Kirsten Hastrup (2007: 200) has similarly argued: 'Creativity is not cut loose from the world (in which case it would register as madness), nor is it simply a competent response to anticipated outcomes (putting it on a par with agency). For "creativity" to retain a separate meaning, it must comprise both the unexpected and the recognizable, both newness and anticipation.'

This statement raises many crucial questions explored in this book. How are experiences of the recognizable and the unexpected produced, orchestrated and judged in different social settings? How do cultural producers, both individuals and institutions including museums, governmental organizations and religious authorities, create, value and control the tensions between desired anticipation and unwelcome surprise? And how does the appropriation of specific visual and material forms inform processes of identification in an interconnected, highly diverse world? As in the case of Kotei, conflicts over the ownership of certain images or styles can be indicative of complex histories of oppression and resistance, and central to claims to national identity and independence.

To further assess the analytical possibilities of the perspective of improvisation to explore such issues, let us focus on the ways in which two British Jazz musicians have approached questions of newness and repetition. As music is, by definition, a temporal, performative phenomenon, the comparison will help us to think further about material production as a transformational force in people's experiences of subjectivity and identity claims. In the summer of 2011, I was present at a workshop that formed part of the International Summer School for Pianists at Chetham's Music School in Manchester. During this workshop, Jazz musicians Steve Berry and Les Chisnall enacted and commented on the workings of musical improvisation. Les started off asking the participating musicians to raise their hands if they had any previous experience in improvisation. When only a third of the audience responded, he commented that, in fact, everybody should have done so. He stated:

> People improvise all the time. Take me as an example. Here I am, talking to you, but I don't know exactly what I am going to say to you next. I don't have a pre-written script in front of me, I know vaguely what I want to talk about, but the words really come to my mind as I am speaking. This is normal; we do not, when we wake up, have a completely planned schedule for the day, and we need to adjust our plans all the time as we respond to situations.

Chisnall's point resonates with Ingold and Hallam's (2007: 9) argument that 'far from being a strategic planner, aloof from the material world upon which its designs are inscribed, the mind is in practice a hotbed of tactical and relational improvisation'. For the following five minutes, Les and Steve talked about the rigidity of much music tuition, in which students expect to follow a set curriculum, mostly playing technical exercises and preset scores. To demonstrate the possibilities of what they saw as a more humanistic approach to music, Les sat down behind the piano and Steve took hold of his contra-bass. What followed was a minimalist performance where the two players alternated playing single notes. It was fascinating to follow their musical dialogue, to see the anticipation on their faces, and to experience with them how expected and unexpected musical sequences generated and resolved sonic and emotional tensions. What stood out was the playfulness of the process; the sense that they were teasing each other, withholding and giving in, creating and blocking flows.

Especially remarkable was the intense emotional involvement of the audience members (including myself), who listened in excited expectancy, and laughed when surprising musical responses were given. They also responded to the musicians' body language and facial expressions; the nods, smiles and frowns that marked their interaction. Next, Les asked the audience to actively imagine which note would come next, and raise hands whenever an *expected* note was played. An interesting dance of hands followed; at times almost everybody put their hands up, less often only a few hands were raised. Reflecting on the result, he explained that during improvisation sessions it was crucial to not just play random notes; this would result in uninteresting chaos that nobody would be able to make sense of.[3]

Rather, he suggested, in responding to notes, the improvising musician should listen very carefully to unfolding sound sequences, imagining different possible developments. Conscious or less conscious choices should then be made between 'more' and 'less' predictable alternatives. His earlier point about the rigidity of much musical tuition was not that classically trained students did not improvise at all, which was, in his view, logically impossible (cf. Barber 2007: 32; Cook 1990: 113), but, rather, that their musical imagination was not sufficiently stimulated, and that they were not made aware of potential alternative approaches to set scores.

The central argument of this book is that the tension between experiences of (un)predictability and (restricted) choice, a tension central to creative practice, can only become analytically visible when attention is given to the temporal dimension, by taking a processual approach. Improvisation must, therefore, not just be understood as working within the boundaries of existing 'cultural repertoires' (Tilley 1995): it entails practices of repetition as well as practices of 'repertoire-building' that emerge in dynamic processes of performance (Faulkner and Becker 2009: 194). Returning to the session with Les and Steve, the musical alternatives (which note to play, which sequence to repeat or break up) could not be fully predicted at the very start of the musical dialogue, but arose in the process of musicking. The options were generated in the interactive process between the musicians as they produced and responded to each other and developed melodic lines, and as they responded musically to the reactions of the public. In this dynamic emotional process, they not only challenged each other, but also surprised themselves and the audience members, as they constituted themselves as players in an affective field. The surprise element lay as much in unexpected repetition as in the creation of new configurations. Past and present were intertwined, since new musical routes could only be explored because earlier renderings were actively remembered.

Importantly, Les reminded workshop participants that, since he had often improvised with Steve, some sequences that sounded less predictable to most audience members were routine to them, a phenomenon Robert Faulkner and Howard Becker (2009:187) call 'network-specific repertoires'. These repertoires expanded through rehearsal and repetition. Through their creative practice, certain notions of creative subjectivity were also reinforced. As established artists, Les and Steve worked in wider professional infrastructures in which discourses of improvisation, that regarded the aim to surprise as a signifier of individuality, were promoted and shared (Becker 1983). Thus, their particular view of creative practice produced its own expectations. While this approach competed with more dominant classical music tuition traditions taught at the school, their classes were equally part of an accepted curriculum, and linked to an existing subsection of the music industry.

So why is the discussion of musical improvisation relevant to this book? Like musical fragments that are reproduced and expanded in succeeding performances, visual fragments and stylistic features are also recycled, reconfigured and recombined – in new times, places and infrastructures, the last of which may include the religious, the artistic or the museological. As such, copies are truly reproductions; they are actively made in new times and spatial settings, gaining situationally specific functions, meanings and appeal. In the words of Patricia Spyer and Mary Margaret Steedly (2013: 31), this means we have to investigate '[to] what extent mages [can] "leap" across media to travel beyond their originally imagined audience and, in conjunction with other factors, produce unanticipated publics and counter-publics elsewhere? In what ways does media technology itself transform the "message" of the image?'

Like musicians who work with and against expectations within musical fields, visual image producers and users also create expanding and changing visual and material repertoires, producing material and pictorial forms in expected and unexpected ways (Mall 2007; Nakamura 2007). The question whether specific instances of imitation are positively or negatively valued, then, is not a query into the supposed levels of creativity of those engaged in replication. Instead, it critically explores the underlying discourses that set specific expectations regarding the design and use of material products in and across particular sociohistorical and geographical settings. The creativity-as-improvisation framework, in other words, investigates not just occurrences of people-thing interactions, but acknowledges that 'what is accepted or not, and accorded value or not, is decided in social settings where market forces and power are at play' (Fuglerud, chapter 6, this volume).

Interconnected Localities and Overlapping Fields of Practice

The contributors to this volume explore the 'who, what, where and why' of material production in different localities that are globally connected to other localities in distinct ways. Several questions are crucial. First, how are the production of objects and images and the institutional management and evaluation of such cultural production shaped by divergent, implicit and explicit understandings of creativity? Second, how does transnational interaction trigger both expected and surprising forms of creative production? And third, how do the processes of authentication and authorization that dominate particular infrastructures of production and consumption influence creative interactions and experiences? The chapters present case studies from a broad selection of locations in Asia, Africa, Australia, Europe and the Americas, challenging conceptions of creativity that regard 'art' as the ultimate domain of innovative creation, opposing it to conventional, repetitive 'craft', and separating it from 'religion'. While the book shows that such views, established in Europe as part of specific modernist ideologies in the late nineteenth century, have been reproduced in certain settings outside Europe, it argues that the dichotomies they reproduce are highly problematic. Crucially, the chapters in this volume examine the circulation and appropriation of cultural forms within and across a diversity of emergent and interconnected markets of art and fashion, religious spaces and museums of art and ethnology, and show that creative activities that at first appear local in dimension are more often than not part of translocal, 'transcultural' chains of production (Brosius and Wenzheimer 2010).[4] In some cases these processes involve actors embedded in numerous institutional fields, for example as professional artists, ritual actors and protectors of heritage. The complexity of the translocal movement of people, things and images reinforces the need for a global approach that critically explores, rather than reifies, exclusivist notions of art and aesthetics (Svašek 1997: 4 Belting and Buddensieg 2009; Harris 2011; Kaur and Mukherji 2014: 1; Marcus and Myers 1995; Spyer and Steedly 2013).

Three related notions that underpin – more or less explicitly – the analyses in this book are transit, transition and transformation (cf. Svašek 2010, 2012b). Highlighting the mobility of people, things, images and ideas underlying cultural production, they provide a useful perspective on artefact-focused improvisational dynamics in a world of movement. 'Transit' refers generally to the movement of people, objects and images across space and time, a process that is influenced by changing technologies of transportation and communication. New media technologies, for example, that mediate images in new ways, have strongly increased people's access to visual cultures produced in faraway locations, creating new possibilities of appropriation in locations across the globe (Brosius and Butcher 1999; Ramaswamy 2003). Relatively cheap flights, affordable to some, though not all, travellers, have also expanded exposure to distant human and material environments, stimulating the production of artefactual commodities that can be moved to, and recontextualized in, various new locations. The second notion of 'transition' describes how artefacts and images that are taken to and reproduced in new spatial and/or temporal contexts, gain new significance, value and appeal. As pointed out earlier, this is not an automatic, unmediated process:

> Global flows are neither frictionless nor ubiquitous; they depend on particular media platforms and their infrastructures, which regulate and restrict the direction and transmission of information; they face interruptive forces, including institutional forms of censorship or the requirements of capitalization or the routine degradation of technological capacities; they generate static as much as signal; they create novel aesthetic experiences and replicate or revamp existing ones. (Spyer and Steedly 2013: 23)

Examples of transition through movement to new geographic locations are artefacts bought at pilgrimage sites and taken home to become an object of personal devotion (Huyler 1999); and design elements printed from websites and used locally or integrated into existing designs (Buchloh 2006). Transition also describes how artefacts that remain in the same location can become meaningful and effective in new ways. Examples are the changing significance of a political monument under a new regime (Svašek 1995) or the rearrangement of a permanent museum collection, reflecting new curatorial intentions (Stocking 1985).

The third term, 'transformation', refers to the dynamic ways in which cultural producers experience and perform subjectivity as they create and relate to material environments. This perspective rests on an understanding of human subjectivity as a relational process of social performance and experience that is partially influenced by internalized cultural norms and social habitus (Bourdieu 1977). In this conceptualization, subject-object relationships are mutually constitutive (see Miller 1987: 33) and subjectivity emerges as a dynamic of repetition and change (Hastrup 2010: 195).[5] Situationally specific transformations can be transient, for example when a person dresses up for a birthday party and the costume marks the ritual occasion, or when a Catholic enters a church to pray for a sick friend in front of a statue of Mary. Transformation, in these cases, is directly related to transition (Svašek 2012b: 5). Taken out of the wardrobe, changing the outer appearance of its owner, the party dress helps to increase the celebratory mood, or at least this is the intention. During prayer, the statue gains personal meaning and emotional efficacy as the worshipper senses closeness to God. Transition-transformation can also describe more lasting social changes, for example when a queen is crowned or a Muslim convert starts wearing a headscarf, their attires marking their new status and identity.

While these examples describe instances of transformation/transition that are relatively conventional and unsurprising, engagement with artefacts and visual forms can also be less predictable. Arnd Schneider (2003, 2006) has used the term 'appropriation' to explore transitioning cultural forms in unfamiliar places and social settings. As Schneider argues, appropriation entails an active process of interpretation, and thus changes the outlook of the appropriating agents. As this book will show, such transformations do not only happen through hermeneutic practice, but also through active emotional and sensorial engagement with objects and images. Evidently, the different political conditions of appropriation need to be taken into account: there is a vast difference, for example, between the incorporation of 'homeland' religious icons in new diasporic settings (Plasquy 2012: 86) and looting in contexts of war (Davis 1997: 153).

A Case of Creative Transition and Transformation

The following case study of a temporary exhibition in Worthing, UK, illustrates in more detail how a focus on transit, transition and transformation can help to elucidate creative processes across times, spaces and social fields. In the spring of 2015, Worthing Museum and Art Gallery, situated in East Sussex, opened the exhibition 'East Meets West'. The show had been conceptualized by Kalamandalam Barbara Vijayakumar, a British textile artist who, after her degree at Winchester School of Art, had also undergone training in traditional performance art in India. Two exhibition spaces on the first floor displayed costumes, photographs and other objects related to five quite different themes: Kathakali theatre, Bharathanatyam theatre, Morris dancing, Romani Gypsy art and culture and the culture of the Downland shepherds. Linked to the overall theme of 'East Meets West', the artefacts were recontextualized and presented in a familiar ethnographic format, placed in groups and accompanied by labels and explanatory texts. An intended balance between surprise and recognition characterized the creative curatorial process.

As a person with a particular life trajectory, Barbara herself embodied the notion of 'East meets West'. As she explained in the exhibition catalogue, her title Kalamandalam signified that she had completed her training in traditional makeup techniques at the Kerala Kalamandalam, a famous school that taught Kathakali, a form of traditional Hindu theatre that itself had 'evolved from a variety of sacred temple and folk arts of Kerala' (Vijayakumar 2015: 5; cf. Nair and Paniker 1993; Zarrilli 2000). Together with her husband, Kalamandalam Vijayakumar (VJ), who had been trained as an actor at the same institute, Barbara had established the Kala Chethena Kathakali Company in Southampton, appropriating the tradition in new ways. The Company organized both traditional performances adapted to UK audiences, and offered a variety of workshops to schools and community groups, tweaking the format in response to different aims and circumstances (Svašek 2012b: 25). Between 2007 and 2015, I participated in numerous workshops at different venues, witnessing the ways in which the traditional theatre techniques were used for different purposes. In 2007, for example, anthropology students at Queen's University Belfast explored questions around the performativity of emotions during a week of workshops, lectures and a final performance by VJ. They learnt to recognize, and tried to copy, some of the dramatic facial expressions conveying basic emotions that are central to the Kathakali acting style. By contrast, in 2011 Kathakali was framed as 'religious theatre' at a secondary school in England, where students learnt about Kathakali as part of their religious education. The emphasis was now on the transformation of actors into divine beings, Hindu mythology, and the sacredness of Kathakali performance.[6] At the 'East meets West' exhibition, the focus was on the Kathakali costume tradition. A text in the catalogue (Svašek 2012b: 3) referred to a photograph of VJ as a female character and a photograph of a 150-year-old wooden headdress, asserting that: 'from the pictures ... we can tell that *the arts* in Kerala used fine materials, were financially supported, were considered important, jacquard looms were used, carpenters, silversmiths, weavers, tailors and costume workers were highly skilled, had good tools and enough time to carry out their work' (my emphasis). The use of the term 'the arts' was deliberate. Avoiding the term 'crafts', the items were 'artistic', and thereby highly valued.

Entering the museum in Worthing, visitors were confronted with a large poster that advertised the display. The title 'East Meets West' communicated the idea of movement, encounter and interaction. As Indian art forms, Kathakali and Bharathanatyam stood for 'East', but were linked to the United Kingdom. During one of her talks, Barbara explained that migrants 'had brought the art forms with them'. The sections on Morris dancing, the history of the Downland shepherds, and the Romani Gypsy community represented 'West'. More precisely, West meant West Sussex, where the groups, and the museum itself, were situated. The Gypsy part of the display also signified movement from East to West. The catalogue noted that the '[ancestors of] the West Sussex Gypsy community ... left India around 1,500 years ago' (ibid.: 2).

Spatially and discursively recontextualized in processes of 'enframement' (Spyer and Steedly 2013: 9) and 'refocalisation' (Morris 2013), the costumes were presented as celebrations of human expression, commitment and skill. The catalogue framed the items as follows:

> For thousands of years our ancestors depended on nature to survive. As people evolved we made dances, costumes, poems, stories and music to express our eternal link with the world in which we lived. These are some of the remarkable traditions that have existed for centuries and carry the story of the people who preserved them. (Vijayakumar 2015: i)

> [The making of the costumes] require[d] passion, commitment and skill. They were also created, preserved and nurtured within agricultural communities that share a common respect for the land. (Ibid.: 1)

The transit of the costumes to the museum space, and their transition as exhibits in the 'East Meets West' display can be usefully explored through the lens of creativity-as-improvisation. As Barbara was making different curatorial decisions, the meaning and function of the objects changed: they no longer covered moving bodies, but instead became static museum pieces to be quietly looked at, appreciated and compared. In the catalogue, similarities and differences were mapped in a table, and several references were made to their status as 'heritage'.[7] The focus on heritage was consistent with the agenda of the funders, the Heritage Lottery Fund, a body that aims to 'demonstrate the value of heritage to modern life'.[8]

Developing ideas for the exhibition, Barbara had worked separately with various individuals and organizations that represented the participating groups, selecting artefacts for the display. Heritage production was clearly a 'negotiated process potentially involving numerous players and as expressive of more complex relationships with the past' (MacDonald 2008: 51). The concept was not a ready-made product, but evolved out of the cooperative process. In the resulting exhibition, the Morris dancers' section included both black-and-white outfits and colourful rag jackets, cross baldrics and decorated straw hats. The catalogue mentioned that they were part of 'an English folk tradition', first recorded in the fifteenth century (Vijayakumar 2015: 18). The Downland shepherds section included nineteenth-century smocks that had been taken from the museum's permanent collection and were presented, in the 'East Meets West' display, as objects that had 'evolved from an ancient culture' (ibid.: 37). Colourful Bharatanatyam attires were contextualized as 'exquisite costumes' that '[take] us back more than 2,000 years when this classical dance emerged from the Dravidian Hindu temples of Tamil Nadu' (ibid.: 15). Interestingly, the Romany Gypsy section was dominated by unique individual outfits that had been produced by the academically trained artist Delaine Le Bas. It was important, Barbara told me, to undermine stereotypical and negative images of Gypsy history and culture, as these had led to persecution, slavery, torture and discrimination (ibid.: 23). By including works of a successful contemporary artist, who had been accepted by the mainstream art world, Barbara hoped to communicate an alternative view of 'her Gypsy culture'.[9] Reifying a bounded notion of Gypsy culture, she wrote that the works of Le Bas:

> incorporate the use of embroidery, fabrics and costume to create large multimedia installation work with sound, photographic and moving images. They include motifs *from her culture* and imagery depicting the 'other', different ways, of seeing and working that *stretch back across time* and many countries that ties her contemporary artworks with the present context, *history and heritage of her people* and those who find themselves on the 'outside'. (Ibid.: 28, my emphasis)

The only other artist who was represented through several works was Barbara herself. On display were the colourful abstract costumes that she had made in the 1970s for Centre Ocean Stream Performance Art Company. This was a time, she told me, when she had taken a prominent position as director, costume producer and choreographer, in a collaborative artistic project. By contrast, in the world of Kathakali, she held a relatively low position in a hierarchical order of actors (most valued), musicians (one rank below) and (below that) producers of costumes and makeup. Barbara strongly objected to this ranking system. In her view, Kathakali actors could only act effectively when wearing the right attire, so the input of makeup artists and costume makers should have been equally valued. The 'East Meets West' exhibition countered the common actor-focused spotlight on Kathakali by placing the costume design and makeup techniques centre stage.[10]

Barbara and VJ also organized a Kathakali Costume Conservation Workshop that was attended by some of the people who had helped to create the exhibition.[11] Like the exhibition, the concern of the workshop was with 'heritage', and it particularly focused on 'heritage protection'. The alignment of this focus with the agenda of the funding body, the Heritage Lottery Fund, was emphasized by the participation of a representative from the organization, sent to assess the project. Participants were given the task of repairing jewellery worn on stage by the Kathakali characters, sticking pieces of gold leaf on the wooden material. On one of the last pages, the exhibition catalogue stated: 'The people involved are very proud of their heritage and pass knowledge from one generation to the next to ensure that their customs survive' (ibid.: 37).

As Barbara saw it, heritage development had to be open to experimentation and change. This idea was also communicated on the very last page of the catalogue. Under the heading 'The traditions of Southern India and

West Sussex', three photographs were printed. The first showed a close-up of the legs of a Morris dancer from Sompting Village, wearing trousers decorated with bells. In the second photograph, Kalamandalam Nelliyod Ashan performed a Hindu *puja* (ritual) to 'bless the 2006 Kathakali UK tour'. The third showed a boy wearing a self-made, Kathakali-inspired paper mask. The caption said: 'The future – our children *take inspiration* from the traditions around them, *make something of their own* and *our heritage is made*' (ibid.: 39, my emphasis).

The case shows that heritage, so often claimed to be a stable property of a particular national, ethnic or religious group, is in fact actively, and creatively, produced. The artefacts, reclassified in the museum context, crossed fluid boundaries of 'craft', 'art' and 'culture', gaining new appeal as products of 'human dexterity' and 'heritage'. The curatorial process involved reproduction and reconfiguration, and was influenced by institutional expectations and individual choice. In Barbara's case, her strong belief in creative cooperation and her dislike of social hierarchies was reflected in her curatorial decisions.

Discourses of Creativity and Cultural Value

Stressing the temporal and relational dimension of creativity, Ingold and Hallam (2007: 19) have argued that creative acts are 'intrinsic to the very processes of social and cultural life'. Taking a stance in the long-standing debate concerning the extra/ordinariness of creativity (Pope 2005: 53), their model emphasizes the ordinariness of everyday being and becoming in the world. Like Bakhtin (1990), who has taken a performative approach to language as a dialogic, anticipatory process, Ingold and Hallam's understanding of creative cultural production assumes that people draw on elements from the past as they improvise and experiment in emerging environments. Conceptualized as improvisation, creativity can thus be regarded as a common aspect of cultural production. As already pointed out, this means that it is necessary to explore 'the extent to which cultural forms are produced and reproduced, rather than merely replicated and transmitted, through the active and experimental engagement over time and in generation of persons within their social and material environments' (http://www.theasa.org/conferences/asa05/theme.shtml, last accessed 02/03/2015).

In contrast, I will now turn the focus to the more limited notions of Creativity that, historically, have produced the problematic dichotomies of art-craft, art-religion and art-culture. As we will see, such conceptions were developed in Europe, and selectively circulated to other parts of the world.

Art-religion

The separation of 'art' and 'religion' is a relatively recent phenomenon, and is not common throughout the world (Elkins 2004: 5). Different religious traditions have promoted different views of creativity (Czikszentmihalyi 1996: 5), and these ideas have influenced the production of paintings, statues and other artefacts. Early Judeo-Christian understandings claimed that creativity stemmed from acts of divine creation of which human creativity was another product (Kruse 2003).[12] This perspective has been visualized in numerous religious representations, for example in fourth-century mosaic depictions of Old and New Testament scenes in the church of Santa Costanza in Rome.

In Europe the idea of the *human* creator was initially developed within the Christian paradigm (Prior 2002). It was central to the development of a separate professional field of 'fine arts' in Europe, a process that started in fifteenth-century Italy when painters and sculptors like Michelangelo and Leonardo da Vinci set up their own art studios, distinguishing themselves from artisans who worked collectively through guilds. Michelangelo's early sixteenth-century fresco in the Sistine Chapel, for example, did not only depict the creative power of a (human-looking) Almighty God, but also indexed human artistic creativity, defined as a capacity of inspired genius or extraordinary being. Classified by critics as works of timeless, universal beauty, products of 'fine art' were incorporated in a new field of 'art history', pioneered by Giorgio Vasari (Hauser 1968[1951]; Kempers 1992[1987]). They included paintings with Christian themes that were commissioned by rich and powerful art patrons who held positions of authority in European courts. These artworks were placed in churches and royal galleries, where they not only mediated God's presence, but also increased the status of their producers and commissioners.

Art patronage elevated the status of the artistic genius while relegating the artisan to the status of less creative but skilled technician (Baxandall 1972). This perspective underplayed the importance of relational sociality and collaboration to productive processes and failed to acknowledge that discourses, practices and embodied experiences of creativity are entangled with changing politics of value that take place in specific times and places.

The idea of human creativity was further informed by a discourse of personhood that evolved in seventeenth- and eighteenth-century Europe and construed people as clearly bounded bodies with innate talents and personal responsibilities (Hirsch and Macdonald 2007: 186; Stallybrass and White 1986). Fine artists in Europe had also started to 'enjoy a degree of professional and financial stability', which, towards the end of the eighteenth century, led to their works and creativity being viewed through a non-religious prism (Prior 2002: 17; Elkins 2004: 7). Walter Benjamin (1936) coined the terms 'cult value' and 'exhibition value' to indicate an emerging distinction between the valuation of *religious* artefacts that were placed in sacred places such as churches, and *artistic* objects that circulated in worlds of art. Fields of artistic and religious practice were slowly disentangled, a process characteristic of Western modernity (Belting 1994; Blumenberg 1983). The relation of 'art' and 'religion' has, however, remained complex, not only because the former emerged from the latter, but also because many artistic and religious ideologies are based on a belief in the aesthetic or spiritually uplifting transformative power of beauty or the divine (Elkins 2004). The resulting experience is often mediated through engagement with artefacts, a process either denied or hypercognized in different religious traditions (Belting 2001; Meyer 2010, 2012; Morgan 1998, 2010).

In the globalizing context of colonial empire building, religious and artistic notions of material production and creativity that were dominant in Europe entered other parts of the world, including Africa and India. When the British began colonizing India, systems of royal and religious patronage characterized professional art production. As in pre-Renaissance Europe, the artist's status was 'humble and traditionally defined, irrespective of the caste they belonged to' (Mitter 1994: 13). While specific individual producers, renowned for their skills, were in high demand, individual artists did not sign their work and there was no elaborate discourse of individual artistic creativity (Levy et al. 2008: 18).[13] Hindu temple artefacts, for example, were manufactured by hereditary professionals, such as bronze casters and stone sculptors. They learnt the skills from older family members and improvised within the boundaries of specific rules of measurement, form and design, stipulated by the Shilpa Shastras (Dye 2001: 71).[14] There were no clear-cut distinctions between fields of 'art' and 'religion'.

Driven by a belief in the superiority of their religious convictions, Christian missionaries fiercely opposed the belief systems they encountered. A primitive mindset, they argued, manifested itself through superstition and irrational fears of the 'fetish'.[15] The production and worship of 'cult objects' was deemed blasphemous and uncultured (Meyer 2010; Mitter 1977). Influenced by Darwin's biological evolutionism, nineteenth- and early twentieth-century anthropologists like Edward B. Tylor and Lewis H. Morgan constructed theories of social evolution that projected an image of European civilized 'culture', opposing it to the primitive 'nature' of non-European social forms. Colonial administrators also attempted to impose specific discourses of productivity on colonial subjects through educational policies, as already discussed at the beginning of this introduction. The British, for example, while admiring the artefacts produced by skilled artisans in India, ridiculed classical temple art, disparaging depictions of Hindu gods as weird monstrosities.[16] Some praised them as exotic pieces of 'oriental art', while still classifying them as examples of repetitive 'tradition'.

Art-Culture

From the eighteenth century onwards, creative hierarchies were also reproduced in Europe in newly established museums of art and ethnography. The
transitionary process revalued exhibits that had appeared in sixteenth- and
seventeenth-century curiosity cabinets and princely collections, and classified new acquisitions (Clifford 1988; Karp and Lavine 1991; Prior 2002;
Impey and MacGregor 1985; Svašek 2007: 123–153). In national art museums, selected works by European fine artists were displayed in particular
spatial arrangements to display the genius of the imagined nations (Duncan
191; Honour 1979). In ethnographic museums, first established during the
first half of the nineteenth century, artefacts taken from non-European contexts were recontextualized as examples of 'tribal cultures' that were less developed than those of the colonizing powers (Fabian 1983, 1998; Chapman
1985; Stocking 1985). The art-culture dichotomy had clear political aims,
justifying colonial domination (Clifford 1988). The classification not only
sustained the false idea that creativity signified a higher state of human evolution, it also ignored the fact that non-European artists consciously strove for
newness, and found inspiration in places across the globe. In nineteenth-century India, Ravi Varma, for example, appropriated European romantic painting styles, and Tagore was inspired by Japanese visual genres (Mitter 1994).

From the end of the eighteenth century onwards, the idea of human creative imagination was increasingly linked to the ability to produce 'something new or novel in contradistinction to the "imitation" of something old'
in industrializing Europe (Pope 2005: 38; Hall 2010: ix). New production
methods enabled relatively cheap, large-scale reproduction of goods that
were affordable to larger consumer groups. The abundance of mass-produced
identical or similar-looking items fed a cult of artistic originality and authenticity, a process that was reinforced by the invention of cheap photo-
graphic reproduction in the nineteenth century (Benjamin 1955).

Partly as a consequence of the cult of the unique, in Europe and the United
States many fine artists began to perceive the reproduction of religious imagery as unimaginative practice. They either moved away from religious themes
or strongly diverged from genres typically found in church settings, instead
creating works that were 'inimical to ordinary liturgical use' (Elkins 2004:
11).[17] This did not mean that Christian devotional pictures disappeared
from public life (Freedberg 1989; Elkins 2004: 7), but rather that artistic
and religious infrastructures were far less intertwined than they had been
before. This was not the case in nineteenth- and twentieth-century colonial
India where, despite the collapse of the traditional patronage system, much
image production remained closely tied to religious frames of value, from
bronze-making (Levy et al. 2008) to calendar art (Jain 2007).[18] Working for
new consumer groups, many printmakers, painters and sculptors, whether

self-made or those trained in the newly established art academies, depicted religious themes, both in response to market demands and as contributions to identity politics (Jain 2003; Mitter 1994; Ramaswamy 2003).

From the nineteenth century onwards, industrialization intensified and increasingly resulted in tensions between ideals of originality and the demand for cheaply manufactured products. In a world perceived by some social commentators to be increasingly tainted by capitalist values, binding people into chains of interdependence, fine artists in Europe were idealized as the last bastions of freedom, imagined as independent individuals who, through their creative acts, had direct access to a realm of artistic transcendence (Wolff 1981, 1983; Zolberg 1990). Various discourses replicated this view, opposing the superior creative abilities of fine artists to the supposedly inferior activities of commercial industrial manufacturers, skilled craftspeople and immoral producers of pornography and kitsch (Svašek 2007: 154–190). While the more successful European fine artists were thus given a quasi-religious status as free creators of 'authentic' culture, their products, nevertheless, remained embedded in interrelated processes of production and consumption, as they gained or lost appeal and value within the economic frameworks of developing art markets. The 'commodity potential' (Appadurai 1986) of specific artistic styles thus influenced the 'social lives' (ibid.), of particular works.[19]

Creation-Production

In the late nineteenth century, socialist and communist paradigms began to challenge the myth of artistic freedom by exposing the binding mechanisms of capitalist economies that, in their view, only served the interest of a cosmopolitan bourgeoisie (Marx and Engels 1967[1848]: 83). Marxist scholars argued that artists should stop subscribing to a mystifying, alienating ideology of creativity (Fischer 1959; Jícha 1950). Instead of making elitist, formalist art, they should reject the class-based system, identify themselves as workers, and actively propagate Communism through their visual work. The reframing of art production as work of equal value to other types of labour clearly served a political goal, aimed at the transformation of both individuals and society as a whole (Wolff 1981). State-controlled and -censored institutional structures in the Communist Eastern Bloc, Cuba and China were used to sponsor and authorize the activities of artists who took on the new paradigm. As with the so-called free, individual artists in the capitalist West, they were heralded as propagators of a higher political truth (Svasek 1996: 61). Not surprisingly, art, understood as 'creation' or 'production', became an important ideological battlefield in Cold War politics, played out across the world (Lindey 1990; Craven 1999). Several chapters in this book explore the politicization of art, particularly in contexts of nationalism, colonialism and postcolonialism, showing how artefacts and images in transit can gain specific political meaning and impact.[20]

Since the 1980s, as a result of the introduction neoliberal economic policies across the world, the discourse of 'creativity and innovation' has become a political mantra, and the related category of 'creative industries' has been used by numerous governments to mobilize workers and industry, for example by promoting market-driven cultural production and flexible working practices (Bharucha 2010; Garnham 2005; Lofgren 2001). Educational policies have similarly promoted the creation of 'flexible and creative individuals' who must continuously adapt to a rapidly changing world resulting from technological development (Leach 2007: 109). The trope of the creative and innovative producer has once again been questioned, this time by critical commentators and scholars who object not to change, but who question the claim that change itself has inherent transformative value. Siding with these scholars, this book seeks to contribute to this debate, drawing critical attention to changing and conflicting discourses of creation and creativity that authorize and authenticate specific modes of being. Providing a global perspective on the improvisational dynamics of material production, it aims to highlight the complex political, economic, institutional and technological conditions that shape not only the actual products, but also the underlying ideologies of practice. Undermining the association of creativity with individual, 'artistic' genius and novelty, and imploding dichotomies of art-craft, art-religion and art-culture, the chapters demonstrate that both imitation and change are part and parcel of creative improvisation. They show that reproduction and remediation of existing forms and styles take place within dynamic chains of local and translocal interaction.. This perspective allows for critical analysis of regimes of value that vest cultural forms with a particular appeal, and draws attention to the conflicts that ensue when certain objects, particularly those considered sacred, enter alternative spheres of representation. Also key here is the link between sensation and emotion: how people feel about, and feel through engagements with material objects (Meyer 2006; Mitchell 1997; Morgan 2009; Svašek 2012a); how they produce, manage, control and subvert specific expectations in unique temporal-spatial situations, improvising within the context of certain constraints, be they 'temporal, material, technical, genre-specific, linguistic, cultural, or societal' (Landgraf 2011: 17; MacClancy 1997).

The Chapters of This Book

The contributors explore creative processes of (re)production and ideologies of creativity in overlapping fields of fashion, craft, art, museum curation and religious practice. The first two chapters focus on the fashion industry. In chapter 1, Barbara Plankensteiner disentangles the long history of dealings between Austrian industrial manufacturers of lace and Nigerian buyers of the product. Considered by many Nigerians as a traditional African fabric, African lace is the product of a dynamic process of transcontinental, multi-local productivity with a (pre)history of several centuries. Clearly showing that 'traditions' are always in the making, Plankensteiner traces the movements of creative ideas and their back-and-forth appropriation across continents, arguing that the end products epitomize the interlaced nature of global relationships. In the production process, raw materials from Asia, exported to the west Austrian town of Vorarlberg, have turned into luxury fabrics, used to create Nigerian 'national costumes'. The designs, products of trial and error, are based on older hand embroidery techniques and weaving styles apparent in Turkey, Austria, southern Nigeria and the coastal areas of the Congo. Newly introduced production processes have stimulated the remediation of older patterns and the production of new designs, thus catering for customers who desire products that are both recognizably 'African lace' and 'refreshing'. The improvisational process ends with the consumers, who create and manage social identities through dress, playfully combining specific garments and using lace as part of their everyday performance of self. The case of African lace shows that 'creativity' cannot be reduced to the activities of one individual, or even to the activities of people within one geographical region, as the agency of Austrian designers and manufacturers *and* of Nigerian importers and consumers have had an important impact on the final product and its development over the years.

Chapter 2, by Tereza Kuldova, brings to light how, despite the interdependency of designers and makers in the creative process of fashion production, a dichotomous concept of creativity has operated in the contemporary Indian fashion industry. An ideology of high art versus low craft has shaped relationships and distinctions between New Delhi–based designers and embroiderers from Lucknow, thus bringing two categories of 'artist-designers' and 'craftspeople' into being. Traditional Indian crafts are essential in the work of most contemporary Indian fashion designers, and the perfectly crafted embroideries and embellishments are often the unique selling point of these garments. On the part of the designers, however, the idea of individual creativity as an intellectual endeavor, has often served as a legitimization of existing hierarchical relations in which producers of crafts are represented as mere manual workers. The creativity of the latter is effectively denied and power relations are perpetuated; craft workers are seen as frozen in a static traditionalist framework in which they are incapable of innovation and therefore unworthy of being called creative in the modern sense of the word, a perception criticized by various embroiderers in Lucknow. At the same time, craft producers are idealized in the narratives of the fashion designers as representative of the 'real' India, associated with romanticized village life, becoming therefore an ambiguous subject.

In chapter 3, Kala Shreen further explores the image of craft production as static tradition, focusing on recent developments in Tamil Nadu. Agreeing with Ingold and Hallam's objection to the conceptualization of creativity as pure newness, she does however share Liep's (2001) interest in the production of designs that have new forms and functions. Her emphasis on innovative production is directly related to her intention to critically question the 'dynamic art – static craft' opposition. The chapter investigates how plaited palm leaf basket designs, traditionally produced by a particular south Indian ethnic group and used in ritual contexts, have been executed in more permanent materials such as silver. Appropriating different style elements, a wide range of non-ritual artefacts has emerged. Identifying a growing clientele base, Shreen demonstrates that visiting migrants and foreign tourists, who have taken the items to other continents, have changed the products' meaning and impact in new social contexts, such as lounges and office spaces. Shreen also considers the transformative potential of heritage policies aimed at the women who produce these innovative products for new markets. Participating in competitions and demonstrating their skills at craft fairs, several craftswomen have emerged as individual creators, a process that blurs the classificatory boundaries of contemporary art and traditional craft. Digital media have also reframed the designs as works of a superior aesthetic quality, presenting them as works of art to anyone accessing the websites from localities around the globe.

In chapter 4, Amit Desai is also concerned with creative production in Tamil Nadu in the light of global audiences. He scrutinizes activities in three sites in the state capital of Chennai, where places are made creative in different ways, with different intentions: Art Chennai, Cholamandal and Dakshinachitra. In the process, artistic people and institutions in the city negotiate and reconstitute different meanings of creativity and innovation, with the aim to transform the city into a 'world-class' place. Art Chennai intends to be a global art event, branding the city as a space on a par with other major cities around the world that house international art fairs and bienniales. The history of the nearby art village of Cholamandal that was established in the 1960s, unveils a complexity of artistic practices, where artists of different backgrounds and generations take different and changing positions in the production of selves as postcolonial subjects, rooted in local place but taking inspiration from globally circulating styles. In Dakshinachitra, an open-air museum, politics of heritage are played out, in an ethnographic style common in other countries around the world. Desai's analysis shows how, through a politics of urban space intending to attract international investment, artists and their products are framed as signifiers of global quality.

In chapter 5, Arnd Schneider investigates practices of appropriation from indigenous cultures among urban-based potters in Posadas, the capital of Misiones province in northeast Argentina, and Santa Ana, a small nearby town, and former Jesuit Mission. His analysis builds on earlier work (Schneider 2003, 2006; Schneider and Wright 2006), in which he argued that appropriation is best understood as an interpretive hermeneutic practice that goes beyond a simple act of taking cultural forms out of context and transplanting them into a new one. Appropriation entails a learning process, and thus requires active cognitive engagement. The potters and ceramicists in Schneider's study were inspired by the ancient pottery of the Guaraní indigenous people and experimented with different techniques, aiming to get similar results through the learning process. As such, they positioned themselves as close to, but different from, the indigenous Other, preferring the term 'approximation' to 'appropriation' in evaluating their actions. Reproduced in new times, the designs gained new significance and emotional appeal, framing the makers as Argentinians, interested in, and thereby producing the idea of, local history and culture. The process was influenced by social imaginaries of multicultural nationhood and heritage, ideas with a global circulation.

Chapter 6 by Øivind Fuglerud explores intertwining processes of local, national and transnational material production through the perspective of 'positioned creativity'. Fuglerud is critical of a notion of creativity-as-improvisation that does not pay attention to the institutional and political forces that shape the possibilities and limitations of cultural production. Creativity, he argues, is always 'positioned' in the sense that it plays out in dynamic social and political fields. The chapter focuses particularly on the impact of large-scale political forces on artefact-focused institutional practice. Based on a comparison between British Columbia in Canada, and Norway, and the respective roles played by the Museum of Anthropology, Vancouver, and the Museum of Cultural History in Oslo, his chapter scrutinizes the interaction and interchange between museums and their social surroundings, conceptualizing them as historical agents that contribute to the formation of society through visualizing technologies. Addressing historically specific creative ideologies that have opposed 'art' to 'craft' and 'primitive' to 'developed' production in both contexts, he provides a fascinating comparative analysis of political constructions and curatorial framings of 'native art'. Pointing out that artistic and curatorial practices have been linked to ideologies of nationhood, he explores how the two museums have shaped the understanding of what constitute authentic national treasures worthy of display. His analysis also highlights the appropriating strategies by native artists in both geographical settings, who in the Canadian case often draw on designs considered to be traditionally native, but in the Norwegian case are less likely to position themselves through recognizably 'indigenous' visual repertoires.

In chapter 7, Fiona Magowan and Maria Øien turn the focus to the interface of art, politics and religion, exploring the production of Aboriginal art in the nexus between Christian aesthetics and Ancestral painting conventions. The authors discuss the impact of denominational differences between Catholic and Protestant doctrine and practice on Aboriginal Christian faith, belief, aesthetic practice and subjectivity. Their analysis compares and contrasts the work of artists living in two remote mission-based communities, Nauiyu and Galiwin'ku in the Northern Territory. Locating their activities within historical infrastructures of centuries of missionary activity, they discuss the changing creative opportunities and constraints offered in globally connected sites. The chapter argues that expressions of Christian Aboriginal art and belief are embodied in processual states of becoming, created in an intersection of Christian aesthetics and Ancestral painting conventions. The entanglements raise questions about continuities and discontinuities of personhood, religiosity, denominational practice and collective rights in art. The chapter further locates Christian Aboriginal artistic expressions within the Australian art market and shows how this context has provided Aboriginal communities with recognition, income and a voice in the Australian nation-state, while potentially limiting output and productivity due to art critics' perceptions of Christian Aboriginal art as syncretic or inauthentic.

The remaining four chapters explore sensorial and emotional aspects of transition-transformation dialectics, examining how artefacts come to mediate religious authority when appropriated in specific public and private spaces, such as home shrines, churches and temples. They show that, circulating through local, national and transnational networks, specific sacred images gain value and appeal as they come to make up the religious life worlds of people in different locations. As in the earlier chapter by Magowan and Øien, historical processes of religious configuration and transnational authorization have influenced these contemporary improvisations. In chapter 8, by Maruška Svašek, the central focus is on pictures and statues in the homes of Hindu families in Northern Ireland who are of Indian descent. The artefacts include depictions of Hindu gods, photographs of relatives and gurus, wedding cards and other items. Svašek explores how absent gods, kin and the sacred homeland are given affective presence through material objects in a process of transition and transformation. The chapter shows that tradition is a dynamic process whereby familiar images are mediated and remediated in sometimes unexpected ways, afforded by new technologies. Examining the shrine of one family, the analysis explores the meaning and impact of material artefacts and images, examining how their earlier social lives and creative curatorial decisions have shaped their significance within the home shrine context. The question addressed is to what extent individual improvisational performances of careful ritual attention are informed, not only by affective and religious regimes that stretch across the globe, but also by playfulness and notions of beauty.

In chapter 9, Stine Bruland also discusses traditional practices of religious ritual engagement in people's homes. The chapter zooms in on sensorial practices and the use of sacred artefacts across the religious divide between Hinduism and Catholicism among Sri Lankan Tamils residing in Paris, showing that religious practices in the Tamil diaspora are closely linked to traditions in Sri Lanka. She argues that, in a political situation in which processes of religious identification (as Buddhists, Muslims, Hindus and Christians) have tended towards ethnification and have informed the escalation of violence, shared religious aesthetics among Tamil Hindus and Tamil Catholics in Sri Lanka and Paris reflect the absence of tensions and violence between these two Tamil groups. Their shared aesthetics include ritual practices such as the clockwise circulation of incense, the use of flower garlands and the worship of Mother Mary, all part of Tamil Catholic and Tamil Hindu prayers. Rather than classifying these practices into religious categories to confirm bounded religious traditions, she argues for a need to examine how such practices come to be shared. By employing a material approach to religious aesthetics that recognizes that material things are active and have agency, affecting how we sense and thus experience our world, she contends that the use of the same or similar objects and practices should be understood as a creative process of achieving crucial experiences and emotions in prayer, rather than being written off as religious syncretism. In both cases, the aesthetic elements are able to produce strong feelings of religiosity, mediating a sense of closeness to the divine.

João Rickli also addresses the theme of material mediation and religiosity in chapter 10, in his analysis of the shrine of Our Lady of Aparecida, the patron saint of Brazil. Pilgrimage to this shrine is one of the most popular devotional practices of Brazilian Catholicism, attracting millions of devotees every year. The chapter investigates dynamics of creativity and innovation involved in the production, circulation and consumption of religious objects and images, and explores their aestheticization as mediators of the divine. Rickli follows the century-long transitions of the 'original' image found in 1717, as it became a powerful sensational form that is able to mobilize a large number of believers and articulate different national and transnational forces. The chapter also explores the transit of people and objects as part of the devotional tradition. Taking the shrine as the centre of extensive networks of devotees and devotional objects, the author identifies two main directions of circulation: on the one hand, the centripetal flux of people and artefacts from different parts of the country and the world, towards the shrine; on the other hand, the centrifugal spread of objects, images, values, religious power and people from Aparecida's shrine to the whole of Brazil and beyond. The chapter also analyses the politics of authenticity and persuasiveness implicated in the material production and circulation of devotional objects, arguing that the production and reproduction of such objects depends on constant and continuous interactions between official and popular beliefs and practices.

In the final chapter, Rhoda Woets addresses the omnipresence of depictions of Jesus in Ghana's public and private spheres in the form of both mass-produced and hand-painted posters, stickers, billboards, screensavers, cement statues, plastic crucifixes and rosaries. These objects and pictures, often based on a renowned eighteenth-century painting of the Sacred Heart, are bought, commissioned, displayed and used by Christians of all denominations, who imbue them with spiritual power through the senses and body. In so doing, they draw on historically grounded uses of religious objects and modes of interaction with the divine. This means that Jesus pictures are more than a medium that provides access to the supernatural; when charged with spiritual power, they become part of sensations of supernatural immediacy. In transit and transition, the objects thus move from the profane to the sacred through touch, intense prayer, blessing and particular bodily regimes. This dynamic encounter between believers and religious objects is embedded in historical relations of power and authority.

The tournaments of competing values (Appadurai 1986) surrounding creative production and appropriation are marked by histories of interaction and technologies of mediation that link times, venues and people in complex ways. As we shall see in all the chapters that follow, cultural producers always work in situations that offer possibilities and pose constraints. Disagreements and contestations about creativity often betray underlying social inequalities that need to be critically examined. Only through careful ethnographic research and analysis can the intertwined politics and poetics of creative improvisation become visible. As the contributors to this book will show, such analysis requires a global perspective that acknowledges the complexities of local and translocal movements, and critically questions discourses of art, craft, tradition, modernity, heritage and culture.

Acknowledgements

I would like to thank Birgit Meyer for her excellent feedback on earlier drafts of this introduction that pushed me to give it a clearer focus. I am also grateful to Yudhishthir Raj Isar for his encouraging and critical comments on the Creativity in a World of Movement HERA project at a workshop in Belfast in 2010. I also thank the two anonymous reviewers for their constructive comments, and Gordon Ramsey for his perceptive editorial input.

Maruška Svašek is reader in anthropology at the School of History and Anthropology, Queens University, Belfast. Her main research interests include material culture, art, migration and emotional dynamics. Major publications include *Anthropology, Art and Cultural Production* (2007), *Emotions and Human Mobility: Ethnographies of Movement* (2012), *Moving Subjects, Moving Objects: Transnationalism, Cultural Production and Emotions* (2012). She is coeditor of the Berghahn Books series Material Mediations: People and Things in a World of Movement.

Notes

1. Mihaly Csikszentmihaly (1996: 107) also defined creativity as process leading to newness, defining it as 'any act, idea or product that changes an existing domain, or that transforms an existing domain into a new one'.
2. Those criticizing Jazz for this supposed lack of constraint saw this impulsiveness as a sign of unsophisticated subjectivity. See for example, Schuller 1968. These views have reinforced a loaded notion of uncontrolled primitive Otherness, opposing it to the idea of the highly civilized European Classical composer (Gilroy 1995; Townsend 2000: 8; Gabbard 2004). McCormack (2012: 1) has argued that the discourse on the 'transcendental improvising subject' is based on American ideologies of individuality and freedom, a view that ignores diversities of Jazz practice around the world (cf. Gebhardt 2001: 134). With regard to Indian classical music, the trope of improvisation as magical route to transcendence and spiritual freedom has been widespread since the 1960s (Napier 2006: 3).
3. His viewpoint also undermined a dichotomous understanding of 'improvisation versus composition', in which composition is valued as a mental act of thinking and constructing, superior to the supposedly uncontrolled bodily act of improvisation. See also McMullen (2010) concerning the privileging of 'mind-over-body' models in Western music, and Friedman (2001: 60) on creativity as a 'negentropic', as opposed to 'entropic', phenomenon.
4. Christiane Brosius and Rolan Wenzhuemer (2011) have employed the term 'transcultural image flows' to describe the reproduction and remediation of visual images, producing new image configurations. The resulting products, made up of images taken from cultural settings around the world, materialize the very idea of global movement across times and places, and across artistic, religious and other cultural spheres.
5. Drawing on Bakhtin (1993), Hastrup (2010: 195) has used the term 'eventness of being' to make this point.

6. I also played a role in this 'religious' contextualization, as Barbara and VJ had asked me to give an additional talk to the pupils on migration and religious artefacts.

7. The Kathakali and Bharatanatyam costumes were comparable because both were 'sacred'; the actors/dancers who wore them represented Hindu gods. The use of bells to highlight rhythm was another similarity, connecting Kathakali, Bharatanatyam and Morris dance performers. By contrast, Downland shepherds tied bells to their sheep. The table also identified 'gold' and 'jewellery' as material linking Kathakali, Bharatanatyam and Gypsy traditions.

8. 'From the archaeology under our feet to the historic parks we love, from precious memories to rare wildlife ... we use money raised by National Lottery players to help people across the UK explore, enjoy and protect the heritage they care about' (http://www.hlf.org.uk/about-us#.VTvsus0h2ok, last accessed 20 April 2015).

9. Le Bas has also used sound, photography and moving images in multimedia installations that were not part of the exhibition.

10. Images of Kathakali acting were, however, present, shown on a video in the exhibition space, and on several occasions when VJ performed in full attire for different audiences.

11. Several Morris dancers, descendants of Downland shepherds, and three Romani Gypsy artists, including Delaine Le Bas, participated in the event.

12. This is reflected in the following biblical texts: 'In the beginning was the Word, and the Word was with God, and the Word was God. He was in the beginning with God. All things were made through him, and without him was not any thing made that was made' (John 1:1–3). 'By faith we understand that the universe was created by the word of God, so that what is seen was not made out of things that are visible' (Hebrews 11:3). By contrast, according to various Hindu sources, the universe has been created by the sacred sound of '*om*'. As outlined in the Vedas, this sound is the manifestation of an omnipresent, immaterial divine energy that can be made immanent through devotional practices. In this view, creation is regarded as a phase in an endless cycle of creation, preservation and destruction, embodied in the divine figures of Brahma, Vishnu and Shiva (Flood 2004; Huyler 1999).

13. The recent rise of temple building in India and abroad, and the construction of websites by bronze casters, stone carvers and other producers of Hindu icons as part of their business strategies has made them less anonymous, emphasizing the significance of personal artistic skills in individually crafted or cocreated works in a global arena (Waghorne 2004).

14. Specific Sanskrit concepts formulated in the Hindu Vedas have construed humans as fluid elements in cycles of creation and destruction. The notion of reincarnation (*samsara*), refers to this process of energy flow, a transformational cycle that can be broken through salvation (*moksa*), which is realized when *atman,* the essence of self, dissolves in the divine essence of the universe (*brahman*) (Flood 84-6). Devotees can actively aim to experience the Divine through meditation and God image worship, the latter becoming 'the central liturgical program for public religion in India' by the eighth century (Davis 1997: 37).

15. As Bruno Latour (2010) has pointed out, the idea of the fetish was part of a series of dichotomies central to Modernist discourse, opposing primitive to modern, passion to reason, fiction to fact, false belief to true reality, constraint to freedom, subjectivity to objectivity and object agency to subject agency.
16. Comments by eighteenth century traveller J. Ives after his trip to India illustrate how art-craft oppositions were used to reinforce notions of European artistic superiority. He noted: 'The Indian mechanics are by no means deficient in the handicraft arts, yet their talents seem to be only of a second rate kind. In many respects they certainly do not seem to come up to the dexterity of European artists, particularly in those works where great accuracy is required. They likewise labour under a poverty of genius which makes them dull at invention' (Ives 1773: 53, quoted by Marshall 1990: 57 and Svašek 2007: 98).
17. Elkins (2004: 11) referred to the forms that Christianity took in the work of nineteenth-century painters such as Friedrich, Runge, William Blake, the Pre-Raphaelite Brotherhood and Samuel Palmer.
18. This collection of Sanskrit and Tamil texts, written for those working in artistic professions, is still being used today, for example by the bronze sculptors in Tamil Nadu (Levy et al. 2008: 18).
19. Making similar arguments, other terms used to describe this are 'careers' (Zolberg 1990) or 'cultural biographies' (Kopytoff 1986).
20. See the chapters by Fuglerud, Desai and Woets, this volume.

References

Appadurai, A. (ed.). 1986. *The Social Life of Things: Commodities in Cultural Perspective*. Cambridge: Cambridge University Press.

Asad, T. 1993. *Genealogies of Religion: Discipline and Reasons of Power in Christianity and Islam*. Baltimore and London: John Hopkins University Press.

Bakhtin, M. 1990. *Art and Answerability: Early Philosophical Works* (edited by M. Holquist and V. Liapunov). Austin: University of Texas Press.

———. 1993. *Towards a Philosophy of the Act*. Austin: University of Texas Press.

Barber, K. 2007. 'The Art of Making Things Stick', in E. Hallam and T. Ingold (eds), *Creativity and Cultural Improvisation*. Oxford: Berg, 25–41.

Baxandall, M. 1972. *Painting and Experience in Fifteenth-Century Italy*. Oxford: Oxford University Press.

Becker, H. 1982. *Art Worlds*. Berkeley: University of California Press.

Belting, H. 1994. *An Anthropology of Images: Picture, Medium, Body*. Princeton: Princeton University Press.

Belting, H., and A. Buddensieg. 2009. *The Global Contemporary and the Rise of New Art Worlds*. Cambridge, MA: MIT Press.

Benjamin, W. 1968[1936]. *Illuminations: Essays and Reflections* (edited by Hannah Arendt, translated by Harry Zohn). New York: Schocken Books.

Bharucha, R. 2010. 'Creativity: Alternative Paradigms to the "Creative Economy"', in Y. R. Isar and H. K. Anheier (eds), *Cultural Expression, Creativity and Innovation*. Los Angeles: Sage.

Blumenberg, H. 1983. *The Legitimacy of the Modern Age* (translated by Robert Wallace). Cambridge, MA: MIT Press.

Bourdieu, P. 1977. *Outline of a Theory of Practice* (translated by Richard Ice). Cambridge: Cambridge University Press.

———. 1984[79]. *Distinction: A Social Critique of the Judgement of Taste.* London and New York: Routledge and Kegan Paul.

Brosius, C., and M. Butcher (eds). 1999. *Image Journeys: Audio-Visual Media and Cultural Change in India.* New Delhi: Sage.

Brosius, C., and R. Wenzlhuemer (eds). 2011. *Transcultural Turbulences: Towards a Multi-Sited Reading of Image Flows.* Berlin: Springer Verlag.

Buchloh, B. H. D. 2006. 'Allegorical Procedures: Appropriation and Montage in Contemporary Art', in A. Alberro and S. Buchmann (eds), *Art After Conceptual Art.* Cambridge, MA: MIT Press, 27–53.

Chapman, W. R. 1985. 'Arranging Ethnology: A.H.L.F. Pitt Rivers and the Typological Tradition', in G. W. Stocking (ed.), *Objects and Others: Essays on Museums and Material Culture.* Madison: University of Wisconsin Press.

Clifford, J. 1988. *The Predicament of Culture: Twentieth-century Ethnography, Literature and Art.* Cambridge, MA: Harvard University Press.

Cook, N. 1990. *Music, Imagination and Culture.* Oxford: Oxford University Press.

Craven, D. 1999. *Abstract Expressionism as Cultural Critique: Dissent during the McCarthy Period.* Cambridge: Cambridge University Press.

Czikszentmihalyi, M. 1996. *Creativity: Flow and the Psychology of Discovery and Invention.* New York: Harper Perennial.

Dye, J. M. 2001. *The Arts of India.* Virginia: Virginia Museum of Fine Arts.

Derrida, J. 2001. *Deconstruction Engaged: The Sydney Lectures* (edited by P. Patton and T. Smith). Sydney: Power Publications.

Duncan, C. 1991. 'Art Museums and the Ritual of Citizenship', in I. Karp and S. D. Lavine (eds), *Exhibiting Cultures: The Poetics and Politics of Museum Display.* Washington, DC, and London: Smithsonian Institution, 88–103.

Elkins, J. 2004. *On the Strange Place of Religion in Contemporary Art.* New York: Routledge.

Faulkner, R. R., and H. S. Becker. 2009. *'Do You Know … ?' The Jazz Repertoire in Action.* Chicago: University of Chicago Press

Fabian, J. 1983. *Time and the Other: How Anthropology Makes its Object.* New York: Columbia University Press.

———. 1998. *Moments of Freedom: Anthropology and Popular Culture.* Charlottesville: University of Virginia Press.

Fischer, E. 1963[1959]. *The Necessity of Art.* New York: Penguin Books.

Flood, G. 2004. *An Introduction to Hinduism.* New Delhi: Cambridge University Press India.

Freedberg, D. 1989. *The Power of Images.* Chicago: University of Chicago Press.

Friedman, J. 2001. 'The Iron Cage of Creativity', in J. Liep (ed.), *Locating Cultural Creativity.* London: Pluto, 46–61.

Fuglerud, O., and L. Wainwright 2014. 'Introduction', in O. Fuglerud and L. Wainwright (eds), *Objects and Imagination: Perspectives on Materialization and Meaning.* New York and Oxford: Berghahn Books.

Gabbard, K. 2004. 'Improvisation and Imitation: Marlon Brando as Jazz Actor', in D. Fischlin and A. Heble (eds), *The Other Side of Nowhere: Jazz, Improvisation, and Communities in Dialogue*. Middletown: Wesleyan University Press, 298–318.

Garnham, N. 2005. 'From Cultural to Creative Industries: An Analysis of the Implications of the "Creative Industries" Approach to Arts and Media Policy Making in the United Kingdom', *International Journal of Cultural Policy* 11(1): 15–29.

Gebhard, N. 2001. *Going for Jazz: Musical Practices and American Ideology*. Chicago: University of Chicago Press.

Gilroy, P. 1995. '"… To Be Real": The Dissident Forms of Black Expressive Culture', in C. Ugwu (ed.), *Let's Get It On: The Politics of Black Performance*. London: ICA.

Hall, S. 2010. 'Foreword', in Y. R. Isar and H. K. Anheier (eds), *Cultural Expression, Creativity and Innovation*. Los Angeles: Sage.

Harris, J. (ed.). 2011. *Globalization and Contemporary Art*. Oxford: Wiley-Blackwell, 1–16.

Hastrup, K. 2001. 'Othello's Dance: Cultural Creativity and Human Agency', in J. Liep (ed), *Locating Cultural Creativity*. London: Pluto, 31–44.

Hastrup, K. 2007. 'Performing the World: Agency, Anticipation and Creativity', in E. Hallam and T. Ingold (eds), *Creativity and Cultural Improvisation*. Oxford: Berg, 193–206.

Hirsch, E., and S. Macdonald. 2007. 'Part III Introduction', in E. Hallam and T. Ingold (eds), *Creativity and Cultural Improvisation*. Oxford: Berg, 185–92.

Hauser, A. 1968[1951]. *The Social History of Art*. London: Routledge and Kegan Paul.

Honour, H. 1979. *Romanticism*. London and New York: Penguin Books.

Huyler, S. P. 1999. *Meeting God: Elements of Hindu Devotion*. New Haven: Yale University Press.

Ingold, T., and E. Hallam. 2007. 'Creativity and Cultural Improvisation: An Introduction', in E. Hallam and T. Ingold (eds), *Creativity and Cultural Improvisation*. Oxford: Berg, 1–24.

Impey, O., and A. MacGregor (eds). 1985. *The Origins of Museums: The Cabinet of Curiosities in Sixteenth-Century Europe*. Oxford: Clarendon Press.

Ives, J. 1773. *A Voyage from England to India, in the Year 1754*. London: Edward and Charles Dilly.

Jain, K. 2007. *Gods in the Bazaar: The Economies of Indian Calendar Art*. Durham: Duke University Press.

Jain, J. 2003. 'More than Meets the Eye: The Circulation of Images and the Embodiment of Value', in S. Ramaswamy (ed.), *Beyond Appearances: Visual Practices and Ideologies in Modern India*. New Delhi: Sage, 33–70.

Jicha, V. 1950. 'Na novou cestu', *Výtvarné Umění* 1(1): 1–2.

Kaur, R., and P. Dave-Mukherji. 2014. *Arts and Aesthetics in a Globalizing World*. London: Bloomsbury.

Karp, I., and S. B. Lavine (eds). 1991. *Exhibiting Cultures: The Poetics and Politics of Museum Display*. Washington, DC: Smithsonian Institution.

Keane, W. 2007. *Christian Moderns: Freedom and Fetish in the Mission Encounter.* Berkeley: University of California Press.

Kempers, B. 1992[1987]. *Painting, Power and Patronage: The Rise of the Professional Artist in the Italian Renaissance.* London: Allen Lane.

King, F. E. 2010. *Material Religion and Popular Culture.* New York: Routledge.

Kopytoff. I. 1986. 'The Cultural Biography of Things: Commoditization as Process', in A. Appadurai (ed.), *The Social Life of Things: Commodities in Cultural Perspective.* Cambridge: Cambridge University Press, 64–91.

Kruse, C. 2003. *Wozu Menschen malen: historische Begründungen eines Bildmediums.* Munich: Wilhelm Fink.

Landgraf, E. 2011. *Improvisation as Art: Conceptual Challenges, Historical Perspectives.* New York and London: Continuum.

Leach, J. 2007. 'Creativity, Subjectivity and the Dynamic of Possessive Individualism', in E. Hallam and T. Ingold (eds), *Creativity and Cultural Improvisation.* Oxford: Berg, 99–118.

Levy, T. E., et al. 2008. *Masters of Fire: Hereditary Bronze Casters of South India.* Bochum: Deutsches Bergbau-Museum.

Lindey, C. 1990. *Art in the Cold War: From Vladiwostock to Kalamazoo, 1945–1962.* Berkeley: Amsterdam Books.

Liep, J. 2001. *Locating Cultural Creativity.* London: Pluto.

Lofgren, O. 2001. 'Celebrating Creativity: The Slanting of a Concept', in J. Liep (ed.), *Locating Cultural Creativity.* London: Pluto Press.

MacClancy, J. (ed.). 1997. *Contesting Art: Art, Politics and Identity in the Modern World.* Oxford: Berg.

MacDonald, S. 2008. 'Museum Europe: Negotiating Heritage', *Anthropological Journal of European Cultures* 17: 47–65.

Mall, S. A. 2007. 'Structure, Innovation and Agency in Pattern Construction: The Kolam of Southern India', in E. Hallam and T. Ingold (eds), *Creativity and Cultural Improvisation.* Oxford: Berg, 55–78.

Marcus, G. E., and F. R. Myers (eds). 1995. *The Traffic in Culture: Refiguring Art and Anthropology.* Berkeley: University of California Press.

Marshall, P. J. 1990. 'Taming the Exotic: The British and India in the Seventeenth and Eighteenth Centuries', in G. S. Rousseau and R. Porter (eds), *Exoticism in the Enlightenment.* Manchester: Manchester University Press, 46–65.

Marx, K., and F. Engels. 1967[1848]. *The Communist Manifesto.* Harmondsworth and New York: Penguin Books.

McCormack, R. S. 2012. 'Outside of the Self: Subjectivity, the Allure of Transcendence, and Jazz Historiography', *Critical Studies in Improvisation* 8(1): 1–11.

McMullen, T. 2010. 'Subject, Object, Improv: John Cage, Pauline Oliveros, and Eastern (Western) Philosophy in Music', *Critical Studies in Improvisation* 6(2), http://www.criticalimprov.com/article/view/851/1918, last accessed 20 May 2015.

Miller, D. 1987. *Material Culture and Mass Consumption.* Oxford: Basil Blackwell.

Mitchell, J. P. 1997. 'A Moment with Christ: The Importance of Feelings in the Analysis of Belief', *Journal of the Royal Anthropological Institute* (n.s.) 3(1): 79–94.

Mitter. P. 1977. *Much Maligned Monsters.* Oxford: Claredon Press.

————. 1995. *Art and Nationalism in Colonial India 1850–1922: Occidental Orientations*. Cambridge: Cambridge University Press.

Mitter, P. 2003. 'Mechanical Reproduction and the World of the Colonial Artist', in Sumathi Ramaswamy (ed.), *Beyond Appearances: Visual Practices and Ideologies in Modern India*. New Delhi: Sage 1–32.

Meyer, B. (ed.). 2006. *Religious Sensations: Why Media, Aesthetics and Power Matter in the Study of Contemporary Religion*. Amsterdam: Vrije Universiteit.

————. 2010. '"There is a Spirit in that Image": Mass Produced Jesus Pictures and Protestant Pentecostal Animation in Ghana', *Comparative Studies in Society and History* 52(1): 100–130.

————. 2012. *Mediation and the Genesis of Presence: Towards a Material Approach to Religion*. Utrecht: Universiteit Utrecht.

Morgan, D. 1998. *Visual Piety: A History and Theory of Popular Religious Images*. Berkeley: University of California Press.

————. 2009. 'The Look of Sympathy: Religion, Visual Culture, and the Social Life of Feeling', *Material Religion* 5(2): 132–155.

———— (ed.). 2010. *Religion and Material Culture: The Matter of Belief*. London: Routledge.

Morris, R. C. 2013. 'Two Masks: Images of Future History and the Posthuman in Postapartheid South Africa', in P. Spyer and M. M. Steedly (eds), *Images That Move*. Sante Fe: SAR Press.

Myers, F. (ed.). 2001. *The Empire of Things: Regimes of Value and Material Culture*. Santa Fe: SAR Press. 2001.

Nair, D. A., and K. A. Paniker (eds). 1993. *Kathakali: The Art of the Non-wordly*. Mumbai: Marg Publications.

Nakamura, F. 2007. 'Creating or Performing Words? Observations on Contemporary Japanese Calligraphy', in E. Hallam and T. Ingold (eds), *Creativity and Cultural Improvisation*. Oxford: Berg, 79–98.

Napier, J. 2006. 'A Subtle Novelty: Repetition, Transmission and the Valorisation of Innovation within North Indian Classical Music', *Critical Studies in Improvisation* 1(3): 1–17.

Pope, R. 2005. *Creativity: Theory, History and Practice*. London: Routledge.

Prior, N. 2002. *Museums and Modernity: Art Galleries and the Making of Modern Culture*. Oxford: Berg.

Ramaswamy, S. (ed.). 2003. *Beyond Appearances? Visual Practices and Ideologies in Modern India*. New Delhi: Sage.

Ramshaw, S. 2006. 'Deconstructin(g) Jazz Improvisation: Derrida and the Law of the Singular Event', *Critical Studies in Improvisation* 2(1), http://www.critical improv.com/article/view/81/188, last accessed 20 May 2015.

Robbins, J. 2004. *Becoming Sinners: Christianity and Moral Torment in a Papua New Guinea Society*. Berkeley: University of California Press.

Schneider, A. 2003. 'On "Appropriation": A Critical Reappraisal of the Concept and its Application in Global Art Practices', *Social Anthropology* 11(2): 215–229.

————. 2006. *Appropriation as Practice: Art and Identity in Argentina*. New York: Palgrave.

Schneider, A., and C. Wright (eds). 2006. *Appropriations: Contemporary Art and Anthropology*. Oxford: Berg.

Schuller, G. 1968. *Early Jazz: Its Roots and Musical Development*. Oxford: Oxford University Press.

Spyer, P., and M. M. Steedly. 2013. 'Introduction: Images that Move', in P. Spyer and M. M. Steedly (eds), *Images That Move*. Sante Fe: SAR Press.

Stallybrass, P., and A. White. 1986. *The Politics and Poetics of Transgression*. London: Methuen.

Stocking, G. W. (ed.). 1985. *Objects and Others: Essays on Museums and Material Culture*. Madison: University of Wisconsin Press.

Svašek, M. 1995. 'The Soviets Remembered: Liberators or Aggressors?' *Focaal. Journal of Anthropology* (25): 103–124.

———. 1996. 'Styles, Struggles and Careers. An Ethnography of the Czech Art World, 1948–1992', PhD dissertation, University of Amsterdam.

———. 1997. 'Identity and style in Ghanaian artistic discourse', in J. MacClancy (ed.), *Contesting Art: Art, Politics, and Identity in the Modern World*. Oxford: Berg, 27–61.

———. 2007. *Anthropology, Art and Cultural Production*. London: Pluto.

———. 2010. 'Improvising in a World of Movement: Transit, Transition and Transformation', in Y. R. Isar and H. K. Anheier (eds), *Cultural Expression, Creativity and Innovation*. Los Angeles: Sage.

——— (ed.). 2012a. *Moving Subjects, Moving Objects: Transnationalism, Cultural Production and Emotions*. New York and Oxford: Berghahn Books.

———. 2012b. 'Affective Moves: Transit, Transition and Transformation', in M. Svašek (ed.), *Moving Subjects, Moving Objects: Transnationalism, Cultural Production and Emotions*. Oxford: Berghahn.

Tilley, C. 1995. *Popular Contention in Great Britain, 1758–1834*. Cambridge, MA: Harvard University Press.

Townsend, P. 2000. *Jazz in American Culture*. Edinburgh: Edinburgh University Press.

Vijayakumar, B. 2015. *East Meets West*. Southampton: The Kala Chethena Kathakali Company.

Waghorne, J. P. 2004. *Diaspora of the Gods: Modern Hindu Temples in an Urban Middle-Class World*. Oxford: Oxford University Press.

Woets, R. 2011. '"What is This?" Framing Ghanaian Art from the Colonial Encounter to the Present', PhD dissertation, University of Amsterdam.

Wolff, J. 1981. *The Social Production of Art*. London: Macmillan.

———. 1983. *Aesthetics and the Sociology of Art*. London: Allen and Unwin.

Zarrilli, P. 2000. *Kathakali Dance-Drama: Where Gods and Demons Come to Play*. London: Routledge.

Zolberg, V. 1990. *Constructing a Sociology of Art*. Cambridge: Cambridge University Press.

1

AFRICAN LACE
AGENCY AND TRANSCONTINENTAL INTERACTION IN TEXTILE DESIGN

Barbara Plankensteiner

Over the last fifty years a colourful fabric popularly known as 'lace' has come to define the public appearance of Nigerians at home and in the Diaspora. The industrially produced and largely imported fabric is commonly considered in Nigeria today as 'traditional' material and has become an essential feature of festive and official clothing. From an outsider's perspective, 'lace' seems to characterize the 'national' costume of Nigerians if something of this kind exists in such a varied, populous and multiethnic society. Indeed, the fabric can be seen to connect the diverse cultural landscape of the country, as it is tailored into differing ethnic clothing styles and thereby becomes the thread that acts as a common denominator, weaving together the external appearances of the people.[1] In essence an 'invented tradition' (Hobsbawm and Ranger 2009), the newly introduced fabric forms the ideal base material for clothing styles that have become an expression of postcolonial Nigerian-ness: a marker for a new and prospering nation.[2]

The term 'African Lace' is borrowed from the business world within which production companies and resellers clearly differentiate between embroidery products targeting Euro-American and African markets. African Lace is a specific product that has developed over the last fifty years and has been constantly readapted to changing fashion trends in Nigeria, which is the largest African outlet for this kind of material. As such, its history of production and consumption exemplifies the movement and appropriation of creative ideas across continents.

The Origin of African Lace

In Nigeria the term 'lace' denotes what, from a technological point of view, are industrially produced embroideries. The misleading term came into use for early products made of guipure (chemical lace) or eyelet embroidery that closely resembled real laces. Real laces are produced by braiding on bobbins or by crocheting work, both techniques producing a fabric just by intertwining yarn. In the specific guipure embroidery technique mentioned, the ground textile is chemically dissolved, thereby producing a similar effect.

Industrial embroidery production has its roots in Switzerland. Inspired by the hand-embroidery skills of Turkish women, Swiss merchants introduced the craft to the region around St Gallen during the mid-eighteenth century (Längle 2004). From there it soon spread to the neighbouring Austrian province of Vorarlberg. The invention of the chain-stitch machine and, in the late nineteenth century, the shuttle embroidery machine allowed the expansion of production and created a specific product that inspired European fashion at the turn of the twentieth century.[3] The small market town of Lustenau, close to the Swiss border, soon became the centre of the Austrian embroidery industry and competed by producing goods at a lower price range than their Swiss neighbours.

The major product of the industry in the late nineteenth and early twentieth century was whitework embroidery used for underwear, women's clothing, handkerchiefs or home textiles. The industry had always been export-driven and was constantly looking for new markets in Europe and the world.[4] In the late 1950s, the Vorarlberg embroiderers developed an interest in Africa and reached Nigeria in the early 1960s, where a newly established Austrian trade representation offered support services.[5] Probably from the 1930s on, women in Nigeria had been using industrial embroideries for white blouses worn with wraparound skirts made of locally woven fabrics. Such whitework embroideries in European designs were imported by British, German, Dutch, Lebanese or Indian trading houses located on the Niger Coast and sold through retailers across the country. Products from Austria probably already figured among their assortment, as large quantities were sold to export companies in Great Britain and the Netherlands. However, the Austrian manufacturers were not aware of the final destination of these exports.

After Nigerian independence, Austria opened a diplomatic mission in Lagos in 1962-1963 and created the office of a trade delegate within the embassy, seeing the wealth of the new country as an opportunity for the Austrian economy. By coincidence, the first trade commissioner, Heinz Hundertpfund, was native of the westernmost region of Austria, Vorarlberg, where the embroidery industry was located. He observed the use of white lace for blouses in Nigeria and alerted embroiderers in his home region about a possible business opportunity. This was further facilitated by the introduction of direct flights to Lagos by Lufthansa and Swiss Air in the early 1960s. On the Nigerian side, independence not only favoured the establishment of a wealthy middle class, but also spawned other developments that facilitated international business contacts.[6] Nigerian merchants increasingly took the initiative to circumvent commercial agencies established during the colonial era from which they had, until then, bought their goods. They preferred to establish direct contact with producers in Europe in order to increase profits and exert control over the design and quality of the goods.[7]

Thus, the origin of African Lace can be traced back to Switzerland where, by appropriation of an embroidery technique of Turkish origin, a European fashion was born. As a result of technological innovation, part of the production was moved to Austria in the search for cheaper labour. There, a competitive industry developed that finally reached out to postcolonial Africa, where a new and promising market evolved. New flight connections relativized spatial distance and enabled closer transnational ties between production centre and market outlet. All these processes, characteristic of globalization (Eriksen 2007), had a crucial impact on the creation of the final product, as will be shown in this chapter. Over more than fifty years, the transnational connections between Austrian manufacturers and Nigerian patrons further intensified with accelerated communication culminating with the spread of Internet access and mobile phone connections, leading to a further compression of time and space that shapes creative outcomes.

Nigerian Clothing Traditions: A History of Transformation

In everyday parlance in Nigeria a broad distinction is made today between 'African' and 'European' styles of dress. Since the early twentieth century, European clothing has become ever more widespread in daily life, and in certain office professions, such as banking, it remains the obligatory dress code. Nevertheless, so-called traditional clothing continues to dominate the overall image of urban life. The term 'traditional' in relation to clothing is used in Nigeria to refer to what are conceived to be non-European dress styles. It references something precolonial or something grounded in local traditions as opposed to foreign appropriations. As will be outlined in this chapter, much of what is understood as traditional today was actually inspired in the past by foreign models or materials. So in a sense we can speak here of a myth of tradition that actually defines modernity because 'modern styles' of dress can also be tailored in 'traditional' materials, such as hand-woven narrow-strip textiles or locally dyed *adire* fabrics, which may be seen as both modern and traditional at the same time. There is no strict opposition between the two, no unilinear process of movement from one to another, but rather, a contemporaneity with complex ramifications (see also Ferguson 1999).

Within the sphere of contemporary 'traditional' clothing, certain types of fabrics are commonly associated with specific styles of dress, but such conventions are in constant flux, triggered, not least, by the creative reinterpretations of well-known fashion designers. Everyday women's attire in what they usually refer to as 'African' or 'traditional style' consists in general of three pieces: a tailored blouse with a skirt that extends to the ankle, dubbed 'up and down', and a head tie of the same material (see fig. 1.1).

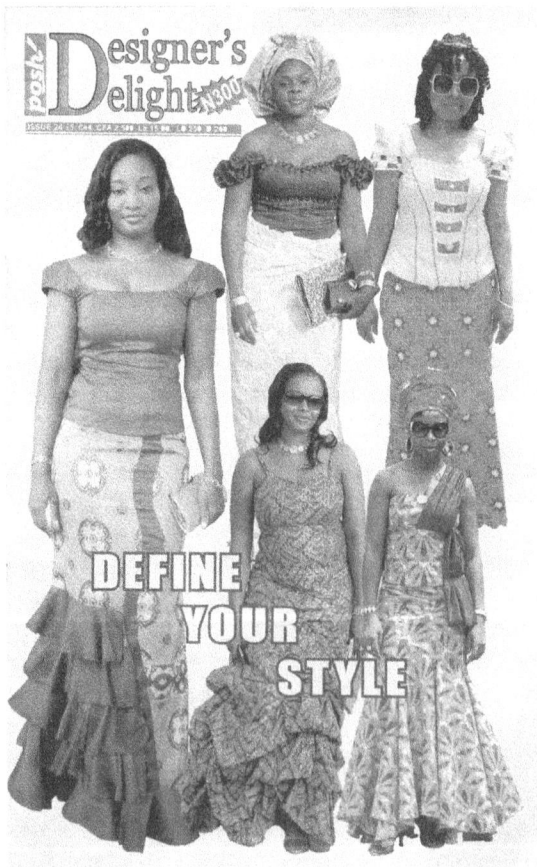

Figure 1.1. Samples of contemporary 'Up and Down' styles on the cover of the fashion magazine *Designers Delight* (Issue 24, 2010).

The close-fitted blouses and skirts are fashioned in a variety of styles following the current fashion or suiting personal taste. Industrially printed cotton material (*ankara*)[8] and resist-dyed cloth (*adire*) are predominantly used for such ensembles. The male counterpart in Nigerian dress consists of the *sokoto*, a long pair of trousers, and *buba*, a waist-length shirt with round collar (see fig. 1.2).[9]

The collar is usually bordered by delicate machine embroidery and has a short button panel. Muslims prefer to wear this shirt in a longer version reaching the lower leg. This style, dubbed 'Senegal' in the south, is also worn by non-Muslims according to personal preference or occasion. This variety of everyday attire for men is made of *ankara* or *adire,* but also from certain fabrics whose qualities are considered as characteristic of 'male materials' that are not usually worn by females. In the north, imported cotton damask (called *brocade* or, more specifically, *Guinea brocade,* in Nigeria) in white or pastel colours, such as light blue, beige and light green, is favoured for

Figure 1.2. Contemporary male outfit designed by the well-known Lagos designer Goodwin Mekuye. Photo: Moussa Moussa, © Austrian Embroidery Association.

this outfit. In the south of the country, a variety of lightly structured cotton cloths are employed in the same restrained tones, sometimes also finely striped or delicately patterned in designs similar to those commonly used for male western shirts.[10] This Nigerian dress in airy male-style materials is favoured by urban businessmen and politicians; it is well adapted to the local climate and cherished by many as an elegant alternative to the European business suit.

On special occasions, what is categorized as traditional clothing takes another form, and differs from everyday dress in cut. For festive events, women wear a wide, straight-cut blouse with round collar and long sleeves, a long wrapper and a matching headdress.[11] The cut of this ensemble has remained identical for almost a century, so it could be categorized as a 'classic style', occupying a similar position to a woman's suit in a Euro-American context. Although it can be made of *ankara* or *adire,* for festive occasions in southern Nigeria it is tailored in *aso oke,* a hand-woven narrow strip cloth, or more often in imported embroidery textiles, the so-called lace (see fig. 1.3).

Figure 1.3. Lady's suit, Nigeria c. 1975. Industrial guipure embroidery with cotton yarn. Collection Weltmuseum Wien. Photo: Alex Rosoli.

The matching head tie needs to be made from a stiff material, either new styles of *aso oke* or colourful damask called *brocade* in Nigeria, and tied in a manner to achieve voluminous proportions. Older ladies will supplement the ensemble with an *iborun,* a cloth made out of the same material as the headdress. This cloth is folded over one shoulder, draped over the lower arm or wrapped around the waist. Men's suits are of the same cut as those for everyday use, but are made predominantly of industrial embroideries. On official or special occasions, men of higher social status or age will wear an additional robe over the ensemble of shirt and pants. This voluminous gown in the Hausa style, known among the Yoruba of the south as *agbada,* and in the north as *babban riga,* is made of the aforementioned materials or of damask, the so-called *Guinea brocade,* and is usually decorated on the front and around the neckline with elaborate hand or machine embroidery. Completing the outfit is a cap, the *fila,* which in the south is made of *aso oke* or the stiff damask matching the women's headdresses, and among the Hausa is adorned with characteristic embroideries. The expensive industrial embroideries are tailored in such 'classical' styles because these are regarded as more long-lasting, thus justifying the expense.

The quantity of cloth used for festive attires and draped around the body amplifies the wearer's physical presence and enhances his or her social status. For this purpose, stiff materials that lend the garments a sculptural dimension are favoured. This predilection may relate to body ideals of fullness and plenty that also define age and associated higher status in society. At the same time, the voluminous gowns of men, with their pleats and heavy embroidered decoration, emphasize their elevated position in society, as family head or wealthy individual. The magnificent clothes also define their wearer's movements: the adjustment and repeated tying of the wraparound skirt or energetic flinging back of the heavy fabric over the shoulder pertain to a subtle performance and staging of the self, in itself a creative act (Borgatti 1983).

While these 'traditional' forms of dress are common throughout Nigeria, they coexist with ethnic or local styles that clearly denote the wearer's origins. These local styles are mainly worn at festive and official occasions and are often made of lace. Edo men, for example, wear a two-piece suit consisting of a shirt with stand-up collar and a long puffed-out skirt, while traditional women's dress is composed of a wrapper that is tied above the breast and a wig decorated with agate or coral beads. Dress styles in the Nigerian south are characterized by their hybrid nature and by the use of a variety of materials ranging from locally produced hand-woven or -coloured materials to a variety of imported fabrics and styles, all of which contribute to the constitution of what is considered as distinctively Nigerian. These dress styles, connoted in Nigeria as 'traditional', assumed their present form only after the country's independence, that is, since the 1960s. Yet, although there is little documentary evidence of the history of precolonial clothing traditions in Nigeria, we know that such practices of appropriation are not new or a result solely of colonization, but relate to trade interactions that go back over centuries.

Long before the Portuguese reached the West African coast on their way to India in the late fifteenth century, trade relationships had connected Europe and Africa through the Sahara.[12] The trans-Saharan and later the Atlantic trade brought a huge variety of fabrics of North African, European and Indian manufacture to West Africa. The coastal trade was initiated by Portuguese seamen in the late fifteenth century and continued with Dutch and British merchants from the seventeenth and eighteenth centuries. From the time of the first trade contacts, European traders adapted their selection to suit the taste of African customers (Kriger 2006: 34). Most sought after were fabrics unknown locally, such as linens, fine silks or expensive woollens. Textile traders – whether Portuguese or from the trading nations that followed them – catered to both mass and luxury markets. The import of European fabrics was not just a question of scarcity or lower prices. Rather the interest in novel exotic goods drove demand in West Africa as elsewhere in the world.

The concept of assembling exotic and rare things to enhance power and hierarchy in the European royal art cabinets of the Renaissance is well known. It was not only Western ruling classes that adopted such strategies, however. Marshall Sahlins (2000) aptly lays out how the Chinese elite from the emperor down cherished a passion for the exotic, using foreign treasures to signify their imperial dignity as the centre of the universe, or how Hawaiian rulers at the turn of the nineteenth century searched for distinction by ownership of European commercial goods, as did King Chulalongkorn of Siam – venerated to this day as a great modernizer (Stengs 2012). Similarly, in West Africa, luxury fabrics became an essential mark of status for the elite. The use of imported textiles was often strictly regulated and reserved for certain classes of society. Social status was indicated not only by the quality of the fabric, but also by the number of simultaneously worn pieces. While commoners were limited to one piece, the rich would layer as many as four, and they made sure that the design of each was visible. This practice, in regard to expensive imported textiles, was observed in both the Benin Empire and Allada (Kriger 2006: 37).

Despite the profusion of imported fabric over the centuries, weaving centres located in West Africa did not lose their importance, and their rich variety of products remained a vital element of the local wardrobe. Nineteenth-century travellers from Europe frequently reported the ingenious ways in which European, African, and Indian fabrics were mixed, the specific combination differing depending on the occasion or the wearer's rank and sex. In the late nineteenth century, cosmopolitan cities arose along the

West African coast that turned into fascinating melting pots of foreign and local dress styles. In Lagos, for example, the local Yoruba met with migrants from the surrounding rural areas or from the north, with European merchants and missionaries, British colonial officials, as well as with freed slaves returning from Brazil, and immigrants from Sierra Leone. In this multicultural ambiance, clothing became an essential marker of one's ethnic or group affiliation or of one's social status. Depending on the occasion, the choice was made between European dress – then in Victorian style – or regional garments, a practice that continues today.[13]

In the 1870s and 1880s, a British-influenced society life had developed in Lagos. A black elite, mostly immigrants from Sierra Leone, known as 'Saro', were educated in England, enjoyed British food, engaged in the kinds of cultivated conversation practiced in English drawing rooms, played European music and wore the latest European fashions (Euba 1987: 148f.). While European dress was customary for festive occasions, at home or in everyday life the characteristic attire of this elite combined European and African elements. Both the European-style suit and the Hausa-style gown, under Christian and Islamic influence acquired symbolic value denoting high status.

Over the centuries and in countless ways, imported fabrics were thus assimilated into West African clothing traditions, becoming characteristic components of what is commonly understood as 'traditional dress'. Clothing traditions in West Africa are closely interlinked with the global textile market. The embroidered textiles from Austrian Vorarlberg, as well as Switzerland, exported to Nigeria since the 1960s, therefore constitute only a recent chapter in a centuries-long history of cultural and economic exchange. Just like the wax prints that, from the early twentieth century on, left a deep imprint on everyday African wear, industrial embroideries became an essential component of Nigerian identity.

The pursuit of novelty, exemplified by elite consumption of imported fabrics over the centuries, engendered new styles of clothing whose origins and history are no longer evident in common perceptions. It is particularly the ceremonial and festive category of clothing that lends itself as the ideal motor for the introduction of new materials. In the following section, I will explore how innovation and creativity are interlinked in industrial design and manufacture within the framework of transnational economic exchange, and how it affected identity politics of postcolonial Nigeria.

The Creative Process: A Hidden Interaction

Conversations with witnesses involved in early production and trade of African Lace between Nigeria and Austria reveal a multilayered creative process.

The designs are defined by the contingencies of the industrial production technology, together with the creative work of the artist, itself guided by inputs from trends arising among both producers and distributors, while ultimately, it is the end-consumer wearing the finished product in a personal way, within a specific environment or social context, that itself generates a creative performative act.

In Vorarlberg and Switzerland, specialized designers create the patterns for the embroideries. Their training covers both technical knowledge of the production process and creative pattern development. Producer and patron are both equally involved in the design process, as the manufacturers in Vorarlberg and Switzerland identify trends through exchange with their Nigerian customers and follow their advice. This information is then passed on to the designers, either as suggestion or requirement. Based on his research on the origins of wax-print textiles' patterns in Great Britain, John Picton noted: 'It is evident from their various archives, firstly that these developments were contingent upon a local agency with a far greater determining role than has hitherto been realized, and secondly that the employees of these firms are kept in employment by African patronage' (1995: 25).

The same applies to the production of lace for the Nigerian market. Unlike research on the history of wax prints, which is limited to the information contained in archives, in the case of the embroidery industry it was possible to interview contemporary witnesses. The agency of the Nigerian patrons is indirect but decisive: their input was and is transferred by Austrian factory owners to the specialized designers located in Vorarlberg or in neighbouring St Gallen. These designers, in the past, developed their patterns without any direct contact with Nigerian clients and still today few direct encounters take place, the factory owners serving as a crucial channel of communication.

During the colonial era, when lace appeared for white ladies' blouses out of eyelet embroidery or guipure, no specific production for Africa existed: the same goods sold in Europe were traded to Nigeria. European embroidery firms primarily in Switzerland, in the Vorarlberg region of Austria and in Italy had fabricated so-called whitework since the nineteenth century. The factories could rely on a pattern reservoir that had been expanded and developed for decades. It was samples from this traditional assortment that the first Vorarlberg embroiderers travelling to Nigeria offered for sale there. Very soon, however, they started developing new product lines as they interacted with local importers.

In the beginning, the producers simply adapted the usual patterns of European whitework by enlarging them and by producing coarser versions. To this day, whitework patterns represent an important source of inspiration and are used time and again for African Lace in a multiplicity of variations.

These roots in whitework explain the different aesthetic of African Lace from that of wax prints: in the embroideries, floral motifs, paisley shapes and abstract patterns abound that are quite distinct from the textile patterns otherwise common in Africa. While the latter tend to be multicoloured, often figurative large-format motifs, the former are small in scale, mostly geometrical or floral, and rarely occur in large renderings. One reason for this is the cost of production, as machine embroidery of large motifs is more expensive than the production of small-format patterns. Colour ranges differ markedly from the bold hues usual in the hand-woven and printed cotton textiles popular in West Africa. By contrast, the costly lace textiles are preferred in subdued tones, the so-called cool colours that are considered in Nigeria to be more classic and long lasting.[14]

Initially, in the early 1960s, white all-over eyelet embroidery was the main product sold in Nigeria, but soon it also became available in various pastel colours.[15] According to Mobolaji Shittu, a large-scale importer, in about 1967 in addition to these plain laces, companies started producing bicoloured textiles. At his suggestion, fabrics in various base colours were embroidered with yarn in a different colour. He first selected patterns used in Europe for blouse fronts and suggested replicating these. These first bicoloured textiles were not embroidered all over, but rather had the appearance of assembled borders. In the 1960s, Austrian companies used sturdy cotton as their base material: first cambric and then sateen. The light, finer cotton voile fabrics still used today were not introduced until the 1970s.

In the early 1970s, heavy, multicoloured eyelet embroidery textiles came into fashion; their main feature was different colours aligned vertically, often resulting in a wave-like pattern along the length of the fabric. This feature also resulted from the production technique, because the needles only had to be threaded once, and the basic pattern of the all-over embroidery remained the same for the entire fabric. Because of the stitch density, this type of embroidery was expensive. With its lively pastel colours it set the tone for fashion in the early 1970s in Nigeria (see fig. 1.4). The fact that many of the stars of Juju music chose to have their stage outfits tailored from this material gives further evidence of their popularity, and lace remains the material of choice for Nigeria's rich party culture.

The yarn used for this kind of eyelet embroidery was mercerized cotton, while today primarily rayon is utilized. In the mid-1970s, looser embroidered cotton voile fabrics with large hand-cut perforations came into fashion. During the era of the oil boom, materials with fancy figurative motifs became popular and were produced in large quantities. In addition to the previously typical floral patterns, the motifs now embraced animals, fruit and everyday objects, as well as prestige items such as high-heeled shoes, watches, brand logos ranging from luxury cars to airlines, and even dollar

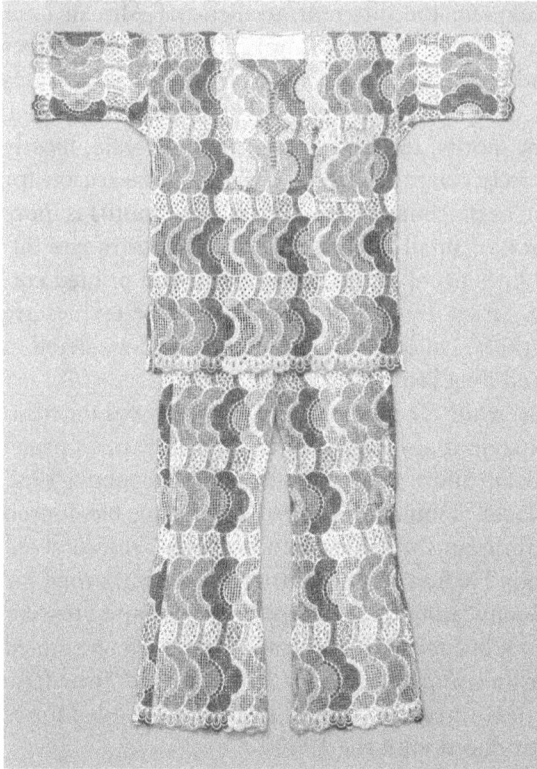

Figure 1.4. Men's suit, Nigeria, early 1970s. Cotton fabric with industrial eyelet embroidery. Collection Weltmuseum Wien. Photo: Alex Rosoli.

bills. These elaborate textiles were mainly crafted from cheap cotton weaves with loose stitching, and astonishing quantities of them were sold. At the end of the 1970s, the so-called etching boom occurred when heavy guipure fabrics became particularly popular. They were extremely costly because of the elaborate production process and the large amount of yarn used.

In the 1970s, producers started adding another effect to the fabric by applying Swarovski crystals. Initially, these stones were affixed to the material with metal claws. Later, after the Swarovski firm developed a new technique, the stones could be bonded to the fabric with adhesive, enabling smaller stones to be used. Fabrics with rhinestones are an essential feature of African Lace to this day, the sparkling effect being considered a very desirable feature. In the 1980s, lurex embroidery came into fashion, and polyester satin was a popular base material, sometimes with application embroideries. All-over embroidered cotton voile textiles gradually gained a foothold in the market and have remained popular to this day. Only the colour combinations and embroidery patterns have changed since the 1990s. Then, vibrant colours were popular, while later muted colours were preferred; now, shiny lurex embroidery and flashy colours are again in vogue. In the mid-1970s, the company HOH (Hofer Hecht Embroideries) introduced embroidered organza. When their general manager travelled to Nigeria for the first time in 1975, he took some of their 'Arabian' samples with him: organza with applied, hand-cut flowers and stones targeted for the Saudi Arabian market. When he showed his materials to importer Chief Obebe, she was excited by the 'Arabian' organza and placed an initial order. Silk, or the more common polyester organza, are sheer fabrics generally used as a base for sequin embroidery. Embroidered organza gained a wider market presence during the late 1990s and is now extremely fashionable for ladies' wear. Initially, only a single layer of fabric was embroidered, whereas now double organza, i.e. two layers, is more common. The doubling gives the end product more stiffness, which is especially desirable in Nigeria for cultural reasons explained above. Although colour trends and ideas of patterns, colour combinations and materials are conveyed or requested by the Nigerian business partners, giving them a critical role in the development of the embroideries both in the past and the present, the actual pattern designers still reside in Vorarlberg and Switzerland.

The memories of Helmut Ritter in Lustenau are particularly illuminating. He was one of the designers who created the first 'Africa patterns' for the company Lustima, designing literally thousands of fabrics during the heyday of the business. When I interviewed him in 2009 he claimed that, when he started working for this market, his clients did not brief him with clear instructions on the kind of patterns they desired. He had never seen African fabrics himself or received any for inspiration, and had never been to Africa. When he started creating designs for the newly acquired Nigerian market in the 1960s, he just tried to come up with designs that he thought would work. He started out using whitework patterns and adapted paisley shapes in larger formats. Another motif that he elaborated into a variety of versions was an oval, called the egg design in Nigeria, which became a bestseller and was issued by a number of companies based on patterns drawn from various designers. He drew his inspiration from his personal pattern archive and his assumptions of what Nigerian clients would like.[16] On this basis, and with the help of suggestions from his clients, he created countless patterns, but never studied African culture, textiles or iconography.

In the mid-1970s, on the basis of his own intuition, Ritter developed a design featuring an apple, laying the foundation for the fancy motifs that followed. Initially no one wanted to embroider the apple pattern, but he finally persuaded Kurt Nachbauer, from Lustima, who achieved sweeping success with the design. The other early patterns were scissors, a cat, an umbrella and finally the Mercedes star. Soon other designers and embroiderers adopted this idea, and mass production that was to last several years got underway. These figurative designs were an absolute novelty in Nigeria and with their depiction of consumer goods or prestige items seemingly met the tastes of the period of prosperity, peace and optimism that followed the terrors of the Biafra Civil War (1967–1970). The designs themselves were at once funny and self-ironic, a subtle way to comment on the influx of goods to the oil-rich country at the time.

Whereas in the European and American fashion business, trend agencies define certain seasonal colours and fashion themes, upon which textile producers then base their collections, trend scouting does not really exist for the African market. The common practice is still to simply try out what might prove successful – a method essentially based on trial and error. Decisions are made based on instinct, not on market research. Major Nigerian importers who are considered to have good fashion sense continue to exercise significant influence. Their advice and suggestions are willingly accepted and put into practice, as it is, after all, precisely these businesswomen and their customers set the fashion when they attend major events where they are photographed and thereafter appear in society and fashion journals. Lace often inspired a trend when worn as an *aso ebi*[17] at a party hosted by an influential Lagosian family. Today it is primarily society magazines such as *Ovation* in which these events and the wardrobes of the rich and beautiful are documented, so fashions are now launched through the media. International events also play a role. For example, the yellow lace suit that Michelle Obama wore to the inauguration of her husband as president of the United States prompted increased demand for guipure fabrics in pastel colours; in Lustenau and Lagos this was called the Obama effect. Some big importers also follow international fashion trends and request fabrics in relating styles and colours.

While during the boom, when Ritter Senior was active, it seemed almost anything could be sold, today the situation appears radically different.[18] Members of the contemporary generation of designers, such as Ritter's son, first of all have to take account of production costs in their designs and must develop them based on the cost factor of stitch density combined with the amount of material. In other words, they must be artist, technician and accountant at the same time. Only a few larger firms employ their own designers; most manufacturers purchase their patterns from freelance designers. These maintain their anonymity, and companies do not like to reveal from whom they buy their patterns. The sales agents in the lace companies normally decide which kind of designs should be developed, then brief the designers regarding limits on fabric costs, whether they want a floral, ornamental, or graphic motif, what the base material for the embroidery should be, and which technique, all-over embroidery, guipure, sequin or cord lace, should be used. Sometimes, sales agents bring materials from Nigeria for inspiration. The designers also suggest different colour combinations with each design and present up to twenty new creations at a time from which their patron can choose. A designer creates around three thousand patterns a year. Sometimes negotiations are also conducted with major Nigerian customers, who give feedback on the designs and offer suggestions. It is common today for Nigerian importers to create their own designs based on existing samples, which they adapt to suit their taste. Particularly for wedding *aso ebi*, for which orders may include fabric for several hundred persons, affluent brides prefer to order a new and unique style. Interaction between Nigerian patrons and Austrian manufacturers has become much closer today through the use of email, digital photography and smartphones. Within a few hours, a factory in Austria can suggest a pattern with several colour options to a Nigerian distributor, incorporate feedback and alter the initial proposal to suit the customer's taste.

Lace in the Crossfire: Politics, Social Morality and Aesthetic Appeal

Since its introduction into Nigerian public life, its swift path to success and spectacular popularity, lace has been a contested fabric entangled in politics and societal disputes: adored and celebrated by many, criticized and rejected by others. In a sense, lace mirrors Nigerian society and the ditch cutting across it, separating those profiting from a corrupt system from those suffering from it. Ironically, those on the losing end may dream of crossing over to the other side and therefore sustain the system.[19]

To understand the ambiguity of African Lace in Nigerian culture, Bruno Latour's concept of 'iconoclash' is useful, as it refers to comparable processes in the world of images.[20] 'Iconoclasm is when we know what is happening in the act of breaking and what the motivations for what appears as a clear project of destruction are; iconoclash, on the other hand, is when one does not know, one hesitates, one is troubled by an action for which there is no way to know, without further enquiry, whether it is destructive or constructive' (Latour 2002:16).

The concept helps to underscore the uncertainty about, and conflicting interpretations of, the impact of this newly introduced fabric on Nigerian dress culture and its level of integration into so-called traditional culture. Lace provides an exemplary moment of iconoclash, leaving Nigerians themselves in disagreement as to whether the material should be considered Nigerian or not, whether it is modern or traditional, a Yoruba or a national fashion, elitist or mainstream, local or global, contested or adored, decent or indecent, sexy or immoral, fashionable or outdated, just to list a few discrepancies in common associations with the material. Let us elaborate on these associations, then, by turning back to history.

Following the spread of European-style clothes in the British Protectorate at the end of the nineteenth century, critical voices were raised against this fashion based on anticolonial sentiments. John Payne Jackson, publisher of the *Lagos Weekly Record,* condemned such clothes as unsuited to the climate and regarded them as a symbol of the mental submission of those who wore them (Euba 1987: 155). From 1900 to 1939, European attire continued to predominate at festive occasions such as weddings, naming ceremonies, baptisms, house-warming parties, funerals and memorial services (Wass 1979).[21] In 1940–1959, a decisive change occurred. While earlier, Western dress indicated educated urban, Christian affiliations, these meanings changed as the call for independence became louder (ibid.: 339). In the late 1930s political parties had been formed in Lagos. They fought for self-determination and advocated a return to local cultural traditions. The use of local styles of dress by the educated classes became more common and native and European clothes began to be worn equally on special occasions. With Independence in 1960, a conscious adoption of local forms of dress, in part newly interpreted or invented, took hold. From this time on, everybody received the right to wear local clothing styles at work in both the public and private sectors, a choice people did not have under British rule.[22] During this time of cultural reassurance, the Hausa-style gown, which had already been adopted by rulers in coastal regions in precolonial times, assumed a particular importance in Nigerian men's fashion. Its adoption by the presidents of independent Nigeria symbolically referred to precolonial greatness and to liberation from British rule. Public appearance in such glamorous garments was a powerful political statement with connotations pertaining to precolonial sovereigns. In the aftermath of the Biafra War (1967–1970), which had threatened to split the new state, politicians and businessmen throughout the country chose to wear these voluminous robes as a symbol of national pride in preference to the European three-piece suit (Bastian 1996: 105). The reinterpretation of the *agbada* or *babban riga,* now tailored in lighter imported cotton damask (called *brocade* in Nigeria) or industrial embroideries (lace), thus expressed a clear commitment to national unity (Bender 2007: 221). It was during this period that the first commercial contacts were established with producers of embroideries in Lustenau, Vorarlberg. They seemingly offered a product that was ideally suited to the newly interpreted clothing styles as it was much lighter and softer than hand-woven material, allowing freer movement.

This process of 'invention of tradition' (Hobsbawm and Ranger 2009), in which conventions are redefined, often by highly symbolic references to the past, is a potent instrument that frequently accompanies social changes. Clothing and uniforms in particular articulate strong messages that visually underpin these processes and several African leaders made use of them.

Kwame Nkrumah, head of state of Ghana, the first West African state to gain independence from colonial domination, appeared demonstratively in the *kente* fabric typical of the country's Akan population (Luttmann 2000: 130). Joseph-Desiré Sese Seko Mobutu also made a statement in Zaire by decreeing the use of the *abacost* (*à bas le costume*), a Congolese redefinition of the Western suit inspired by the Chinese 'Mao suit', worn without necktie but with a neck scarf.

Traditions are often erroneously considered as static, and their origins ascribed to a distant past. In fact they are subject to constant change and are continuously reinvented. Bastian (1996: 101) rightly emphasizes that, 'as several Africanist historians and ethnographers of clothing demonstrate, what seems most "traditional" about Nigerian traditional clothing practices is their constant creative experimentation and co-option of outside forms and objects'. The imported embroideries became an integral part of clothing traditions in Nigeria and their new definition after independence. Lace came to be perceived as an authentically Nigerian material, being at the same time traditional and contemporary, African and European. In reflecting upon the significance of imported fabrics for Nigerian fashion and identity, Toyin Odulate remarked:

> It appears Nigeria, and many parts of fashion-savvy Africa, have taken over other people's inventions (fabrics), improved on them and re-presented them to the world. ... My view on all this is that Nigerian fashion is not so much about being authentically Nigerian as about improving on other people's ideas and infusing an element of something unique, colourful and sometimes seemingly outrageous, and thereby transforming it into something PROUDLY NIGERIAN.[23]

Thus, the reluctance to wear European-style attire as a consequence of a nationalist attitude, developed in the course of liberation from colonial rule, induced a shift in dress culture. Ironically, a European industrial fabric became the material of choice for a newly introduced African/Nigerian style of clothing. While some Nigerians objected to this discrepancy, most saw no contradiction until lace became embroiled in nationalist politics.

In the late 1970s, a wave of nationalism within Nigeria impacted both economic and cultural spheres. The cultural aspect of the movement culminated in FESTAC, a major spectacle organized by the oil-rich state with the aim of celebrating Nigeria's emancipation from colonial influences and its self-determined, modern culture based on a return to their own roots. A policy of 'Nigerianization' was first initiated under the military regime of General Yakubu Gowon and continued by General Olusegun Obasanjo after 1976. Obasanjo's so-called Indigenization Decrees, limiting foreign ownership in local enterprises and industry, included a ban on the import of embroideries, a measure intended to strengthen local industry and preserve the country's foreign exchange reserves.[24] Aside from luxury fabrics, the import ban also covered champagne, certain car brands and wine qualities. Despite the import restrictions, the embroideries found their way into Nigeria, mainly via the neighbouring Benin Republic. During the early 1980s, Austrian embroidery exports even reached an all-time high. The ban remained in effect, on and off, until 2008 but never stopped the fabric from entering Nigeria. It was the creative ingenuity of the Austrian producers in finding ways to circumvent these barriers to their trade and their willingness to adapt to informal Nigerian market strategies that kept the business going.[25]

At the heart of public controversy, however, were the luxury embroidery articles then known as *wonyosi,* distinguished by hand-cut perforations, appliqué and set with Swarovski crystals. *Wonyosi* came to symbolize the extravagance and wastefulness of a class that had reaped the profits of the Oil Boom, scathingly portrayed by the Nobel laureate in literature, Wole Soyinka, in his *Opera Wonyosi* (1981: 38).

In the realm of fashion, the politics of 'Nigerianization' triggered a renewed interest in locally woven textiles counterpointing the popular lace fabrics, and *aso oke* production reached new heights. Politicians and others in the public eye increasingly appeared in hand-woven textiles. Fashion designers made a commitment to promote Nigeria's textile craft industry and developed contemporary styles using hand-woven strip cloth or resist-dye *adire* textiles (Thomas-Fahm 2004). Furthermore, the late 1970s saw a wave of innovations in the production of *aso oke* textiles, which were now available in a wider variety of colours and, with the introduction of imported lurex yarn, offered an attractive and modern alternative to the embroideries. This so-called *shain-shain* variant became a huge success, and *aso oke* textiles with decorative openwork (*eleya*) were in high demand. In the late 1970s, an *aso oke* style evolved evoking the aesthetics of industrial embroideries, copying them with machine chain-stitch motifs on hand-woven narrow strips. The process was later intensified by economic adversity, as purchasing power in Nigeria declined, but was equally advanced by patriotic ideals (Renne 1997: 774).

Over the last two decades, Asian copies of fine Austrian and Swiss products have flooded the Nigerian lace market and as a result have muddled categories and the status of materials, changing the context of their use. Embroideries are now increasingly also tailored into two-piece 'up and down' dresses or fanciful fashion creations with a brief lifespan. To counter the spread of cheap, so-called China lace, the rich and beautiful compete in using ever-newer pattern varieties and qualities of opulently embroidered fabrics to set themselves apart from the crowd. Made-to-order materials spark new fashions and must in turn continuously be replaced by new types. Generally, these appear at celebrations in the guise of the *aso ebi,* the uniform that proclaims group solidarity for the Yoruba (see fig. 1.5). Lace continues

Figure 1.5. Lace outfits paraded at a party of the elites in Lagos in 2010. In this case, the seventieth birthday celebration of Chief Alhaji Rasaq Okoya, a renowned business 'mogul' posing with the *Oloris* (Queens) of Lagos (*Ovation,* issue 118: 23).

to serve as a visible indication of class differences at the celebrations of the elite: 'Among the Yoruba, these include expensive *aso oke,* lace materials and costly items of food or drink. Among the Igbo, a Western-tailored suit shows class. With the Hausa-Fulani, the individual is expensively dressed in "Babbarriga" … there are subtle distinctions which mark status – for example, one type of lace material is cheaper than another' (Lawuyi 1991: 259).

Criticisms of such 'wasteful' displays of clothing continue to be raised. The Nigerian photographer and journalist Tam Fiofori situates lace in the arena of power dressing resulting in 'crimes of fashion' and criticizes the ostentatious presentation of wealth or social position by the Nigerian elite:

Vanity has become the hallmark of Nigerian traditional costumes. Flowing robes, sky-scraper headgears and caps, elaborate exquisite embroidery and trailing trains of fabric now distinguish the traditional outfits favoured by the rich and 'big' men and women. Clothes, it seems, now definitely 'maketh [market] the wearer' in Nigeria. Which explains why this gaudy display of traditional costumes, referred to as 'power dressing', is always guaranteed to open doors to high places and win social respect.

Fiofori also stresses the erotic and seductive component of lace, the perforations that may reveal rather than conceal, leading the fabric to acquire connotations of indecency or vulgarity, and its wearers to be derided as *nouveau riches*. In this sense, lace, according to Fiofori, is iconic for the kleptocratic elite in their flowing robes, the *agbadas*: 'These are people who are not serious about work and do not want to work. They just want to parade their presence in their workplaces.'[26]

The appropriation of lace into local culture, ambivalent as its position was and is, has been triggered by political and economic changes. Yet, political attempts to arrest the rise of lace through an import ban failed. Why, then, was the popularity of lace unbroken, and how, despite the critiques levelled at it, did it become widely perceived as 'traditional'.

When the Austrian producers entered the Lagos market, circumventing established import companies, the direct contact that gave them their competitive advantage based on market insights, also involved a larger risk. Until then, European producers had delivered exclusively to local trading houses that guaranteed payment. The Austrian manufacturers were willing to accept and to adapt to cultural differences and, at times, unusual business practices, in anticipation of large profits that promised to guarantee the survival of their industry. The connection further worked so well because two similar socioeconomic structures met in the interaction: on the Austrian side a multitude of small factories run as family businesses, on the Nigerian side a multitude of merchants that also operate on a family level. These structural contingencies made space for individual business networks, flexibility and personal interactions that would not have been possible if the production side had been a large industrial complex.

A decisive factor for the anchoring of lace in Nigerian society may have been the early involvement in the trade of wives or consorts of important politicians. Hannah Awolowo, the wife of Chief Obayemi Awolowo, and Faderera Akintola, wife of Chief Samuel Akintola, two famed Nigerian politicians of the First Republic in early Independence times, are both remembered as being among the early importers controlling the lace trade.[27]

Further, one of the largest importers of industrial embroideries in the 1970s was Chief Modupe A. Obebe, Iyaloja of Egbaland, a wealthy and highly influential woman and a cousin of Olusegun Obasanjo, the very president who introduced the import ban. The Austrian exporters had met the then up-and-coming politician-general at his cousin's home (see fig. 1.6). One of Obasanjo's girlfriends during the 1970s had also been engaged in the trade and he himself had accompanied her on a visit to Lustenau. In public, in accordance with his Nigerianizaton policy, President Obasanjo never donned lace. While he himself had no relations with the trade, some influential women in his personal environment seemingly profited from it. Then as today, political elites tried to get involved in businesses promising quick and high revenue that also were easy prey for corruption.[28] Yet, lace's association with the rich, beautiful and powerful has certainly added to its attraction in popular perception.

Finally, there seem to be other reasons for this industrial material's enormous popularity that tie aesthetic predilection and tastes to practical or societal considerations. In our interviews with lace merchants and producers, journalists and fashion designers, two chief reasons were repeatedly cited for the popularity of lace.[29] The fabric's lightness and airiness were frequently emphasized as its outstanding characteristics, setting it apart from hand-woven materials. A second aspect is the prestige value of the expensive, heavily embroidered fabrics signalling the high status of the wearer. Fur-

Figure 1.6. Austrian embroidery exporters dressed in lace together with Nigerian colleagues and friends at the title taking party for Chief Modupe Obebe (middle) in Abeokuta 1979. Second from right stands Olusegun Obasanjo, who like the other male guests wears a precious lace *agbada* outfit. Photo: Studio 22, Fritz Hagen; courtesy Oswald Brunner.

thermore, lace seems to correspond to a Nigerian preference for opulent, striking clothing. Dele Momodu, editor of the renowned society journal *Ovation,* summarizes this feature by describing it with a sound metaphor emphasizing its blatant visibility: 'Lace is very colourful, very loud. Nigerians love loud things.'[30] The attributes 'lightness' and 'airiness' refer to qualities of the light cotton voile as base material, which is more comfortable to wear than sturdier printed or hand-woven material. The holes and perforated motifs of the fabric are seen as permitting air to flow through the garment. Stiff double organza lace, so popular with ladies at the moment, accommodates the fondness for sculpting voluminous dress styles that amplify the personal presence.

From a historical point of view it can be shown that the industrial embroideries also correspond to certain long-existent aesthetic preferences. Elisha Renne (2010) investigated this phenomenon by attempting to deduce these from local textile traditions and the aesthetics of body decoration. As a distinctive trait of different Nigerian textile traditions, she identifies the interplay of figural, structured and empty spaces: something that also characterizes industrially embroidered fabrics with their relief-like structure. In addition, the presence of specific weaving techniques producing openwork patterns, otherwise unusual for West Africa, anticipate a number of aesthetic features of lace materials; the same holds true for the heavy Hausa embroideries of northern Nigeria. The elaborate weft float designs of some Yoruba narrow-strip weavings are also often erroneously perceived as embroideries, because they have a comparable colour structure establishing a contrast between base material and decorative yarn. There seems to be an identifiable continuity of such clothing features in the Nigerian economy of prestige.

Lace remains entangled in a clash of iconic values in Nigeria: on one hand, it may be seen as symbolizing tradition, wealth, achievement, taste, creative energy, cosmopolitan stature, modernity and contemporary style, flamboyance and Nigerian-ness. On the other, it can be seen as representing wasteful spending, corruption and disloyalty to the nation: as something outmoded, old-fashioned, associated with illegality, vulgarity, bad taste, ostentation and loose morals. Ultimately, African Lace appears to emerge from the interweaving of different value systems, sometimes opposed, sometimes complementary, that themselves form the threads from which the 'fabric' of postcolonial Nigeria, and the ongoing redefinition of its culture, is continually woven.

Circular Creative Inspiration

From a larger perspective, African Lace epitomizes in a special way the interlaced nature of global relationships: In west Austrian Vorarlberg, yarn and cloth from Asia are turned into luxury fabrics using machines invented and made in Switzerland, operated in Austria by skilled guest labourers from Turkey to become the 'national costume' of Nigeria. And again, the foundation of the embroidery industry in St Gallen and western Austria drew its first inspiration from Turkish hand embroideries in the eighteenth century.

The appropriation of the material into Nigerian clothing traditions was based on certain aesthetic predilections that may, again, have been triggered by foreign inspirations. On the one hand a taste for perforated airy textiles with a cooling effect and on the other a preference for richly embroidered fabrics enhancing status and prestige. In the area of what is now southern Nigeria we find a special kind of openwork weaving technique not known elsewhere in West Africa. We have no historical evidence that this style could have been inspired by Portuguese lace in the sixteenth century.[31] Perhaps significantly, however, we find crocheting work with a similar lace-like appearance crafted into capes for local elites in the coastal areas of the Congo, a region that also had close interaction with Portuguese merchants in the sixteenth century.[32] The art of embroidery in what is now northern Nigeria has other roots: the arrival of Islam from the first millennium and the Hausa states developing into centres of production of richly embroidered garments traded to local elites throughout West Africa (Kriger 2006: 67ff.). African Lace, then, a product born in transcultural interaction between Austrian manufacturers and Nigerian patrons, synthesizes all these historic strands into a single fabric. It exemplifies the dynamic nature and interconnectedness of creativity in the making of tradition.

Finally, the recent exhibition *African Lace* and its accompanying publication (Plankensteiner and Adediran 2010) may have played a role in inspiring a new wave of international fashion.[33] The summer 2012 trends of major brands such as Marni, Prada and Louis Vuitton all appear to imitate Nigerian lace styles of the 1970s. In line with the promotion of a trendy image of Africa in the fashion world, colourful eyelet or guipure embroideries in pastel tones dominated their collections. Although no documentary evidence for such connections is yet available, since our research and exhibition project had, for the first time, brought these Nigerian styles into larger popular awareness, the possibility that it inspired designers or their trend scouts cannot be discounted.[34] Certainly, such phenomena should lead us to question common assumptions regarding the nature of innovation and cultural transformation and reconsider how inspiration and agency may be multilaterally distributed. A unilinear movement of ideas or merchandise, as exports to Africa are often perceived, would be a far too simplified view of cultural appropriation and global interaction in the field of creativity. African Lace therefore offers a perfect material sample to trace the circular movements of creative ideas and their appropriation across continents. It shows how tradition depends on transregional networks in the sources of raw materials, the evolution of creative ideas, the technology and processes of production, the marketing and consumption of products. Each step in this chain involves creative acts that themselves depend upon personal, political and economic circumstances and interconnections that ultimately shape the richly textured fabric now known as African Lace.

Barbara Plankensteiner is the Frances and Benjamin Benenson Foundation curator for African Art, Yale University Art Gallery, New Haven, USA. Until August 2015 she served as deputy director, chief curator and curator of the Sub-Saharan Africa collection at the Weltmuseum Wien, Austria, and as lecturer at the Institute of Social and Cultural Anthropology, University Vienna. Her main research interests are African material culture and arts, collection history, museum anthropology and cultural policy. She was lead curator of the exhibition 'Benin. Kings and Rituals. Court Arts from Nigeria', shown at the Museum für Völkerkunde, Vienna, and the Musée du Quai Branly, Paris, in 2007, and at the Ethnological Museum in Berlin and the Art Institute of Chicago in 2008. She was also editor of the catalogue of the same name (Snoeck Publishers, 2007). She is author of *Benin: Art and History in the Benin Kingdom* (5 Continents Editions, 2010, French and English editions). In 2010 she was co-curator (with Mayo Adediran) of the exhibition, *African Lace: A History of Trade, Creativity and Fashion in Nigeria,* and co-editor (with Mayo Adediran) of the accompanying catalogue (Snoeck Publishers, 2010). For both projects she undertook field research in Nigeria, archival research in Europe and the United States and, for the African Lace project, additional field research in western Austria.

Notes

1. This chapter condenses research that led to the exhibition *African Lace* presented in Vienna, Austria, at the Museum für Völkerkunde in 2010/2011, the National Museum in Lagos in 2011 and the Vorarlberg Museum in Bregenz in 2013. The exhibition was a collaboration of the National Commission for Museums and Monuments, Nigeria, and the Vienna Museum für Völkerkunde, now known as Weltmuseum Wien. Some content from this chapter has already been published in the accompanying catalogue (Plankensteiner and Adediran 2010).
2. See Brumann (2011) for a discussion of the correlation of the invention of traditions with processes shaping nation-states.
3. The shuttle embroidery machine was invented by the Swiss Isaac Gröbli, who first presented it at the World Exhibition in Paris in 1867 (Längle 2004: 26). It allowed the embroidery of five to ten yards of fabric at once.
4. For a detailed insight into the ups and downs of the industry, see Fitz (1947: 100) and Längle (2004: 46).

5. The first country of interest was the Sudan (Oswald Brunner, personal communication, 3 June 2008.

6. When the British departed after nearly one hundred years of colonial rule, they left a country with the highest education rate in West Africa, one of the premier universities in Africa, Ibadan, a thriving export-trade in cocoa and agricultural production sufficient for local consumption. Nigeria had bright prospects, particularly after the discovery of oil in the Niger delta in the late 1950s. For further insight into postcolonial history, see Maier (2000: 7ff.) and Falola and Heaton (2008).

7. For a more comprehensive overview of this history of trade with Nigeria, see Plankensteiner (2010b: 113ff.)

8. The term *ankara* refers to all kind of industrially printed cotton materials including wax prints.

9. An excellent insight into Yoruba clothing styles around 1960 is given by Negri (1962a–b). However, many of the varieties described are no longer in use.

10. These fabrics are called *Atiku* in reference to the former vice president, Abubakar Atiku (1999–2007), who made them popular

11. This simple and easy-to-sew type of blouse was probably introduced by missionaries at the beginning of the twentieth century (Gerlich 2005; see also Wass and Broederick 1979). The ensemble is usually worn by married women or young mothers.

12. Portuguese seamen reached West Africa in the second half of the fifteenth century in their search for a sea passage to India. They landed on the coast of Senegal in 1444, reached the Benin Bight in 1472 and by 1482 they had established their most important base on the coast: Fort São Jorge da Mina in contemporary Ghana. For a more detailed overview of the textile trade with West Africa, see Plankensteiner (2010a).

13. Titilola Euba (1987) and Betty Wass (1979) describe their development in detail.

14. This reasoning was set forth by several merchants in Lagos whose shops set themselves apart at first glance by the distinctive atmosphere created by the pastel tones of the displayed fabric. The merchants considered these tones to be elegant and timeless, although they gave no reason for this perception (Plankensteiner 2010b).

15. The following information about the history of styles in African Lace is based on interviews with Helmut Ritter, Josef Blaser, Karl Hagspiel, Mobolaji Shittu and Oswald Brunner between 2008 and 2010, as well as on analysis of pattern books from the companies Oskar Hämmerle, HKG, Riedesser and Ernst Bösch.

16. Helmut Ritter has assembled an enormous collection of embroidery patterns over the years since he started as an apprentice, composed of clippings from fashion magazines, his own drawings, but also samples of fabrics that he used for inspiration.

17. *Aso ebi* in Yoruba refers to a uniform used to express group cohesion and worn for special occasions such as weddings or funerals by family members, friends or others aiming to show that they belong together.

18. In Lustenau, this time is remembered as a gold rush: the manufacturers could not produce enough to satisfy the market. The demand was so high that whatever was produced could be sold.

19. For an insightful analysis of the complex culture of corruption and its impact on Nigerian society, see Smith (2007).
20. I came across this idea through my participation at Peter Probst's panel at the ACASA Triennial in 2011 and through his suggestion. See also Probst (2012).
21. Wass drew her conclusions based on an analysis of the clothes of an extended family in Lagos using photographs taken between 1900 and 1974.
22. Tam Fiofori, 'Crimes of Fashion: Gaudy "Power" Dressing May Amount to Crimes of Fashion', in *Next on Sunday* (23 August 2009: 37).
23. 'Ankara, Damask, Lace and George – Nigerian or not?' in *Next* (14 February 2009, http://234next.com; accessed 22.2.2009).
24. In the course of these developments, embroidery factories had been founded in Nigeria itself, co-owned by Nigerian investors and Austrian producers. From approximately twenty companies that once existed, only one has survived to date.
25. Their openness in this regard might relate to the history of Lustenau's position right at the border with Switzerland. The involvement of its inhabitants in the cross-border trade throughout history has certainly contributed to a popular conception and derogatory view of them in the region as smugglers.
26. Tam Fiofori, 'Crimes of Fashion'.
27. I thank Joseph Nevadomsky for bringing this to my attention. I still have to further research the entanglements of both ladies in the early business, but in popular understanding it seems to be an acknowledged fact.
28. See Smith (2007) for the paradoxical nature of corruption in Nigeria and how average citizens are at once active participants, critics and principal victims of the system. He aptly describes how people climbing the social ladder profiting from the corrupt system are at the same time deprecated and admired.
29. Some of the interviews in Lustenau were conducted together with Mayo Adediran, some in Lagos together with Louisa Onuoha.
30. Personal communication, 3 April 2009.
31. Although not specifically mentioned on trading lists cited by historians of the textile trade so far (Vogt 1975; Alpern 1995; Reikat 1997), my impression is that Portuguese or possibly Flemish laces could have been included in the trade goods.
32. Such crocheted fibre mantles are part of the classical Congo regalia of chiefs and kings possibly since the sixteenth century (National Taiwan Museum 2004: 339).
33. The project, for the first time, addressed the sociocultural history and meaning of this industrial fabric in Nigeria. African Lace had never before been a subject of academic inquiry. The catalogue of the exhibition features numerous photographs of lace patterns and garments from the early 1970s on, which before could have been found only in fashion journals of the period. Only research in pattern archives of the embroidery industry could have brought them to the attention of designers and this would have been quite a remarkable coincidence.
34. A related research request in May 2012 to the influential trend agency Edelkoort remains so far unanswered. Claudio La Cioppa, general director of the company HOH Embroideries in Lustenau, however, has implied that such a connection could be possible, as Africa had been a guiding trend philosophy in the fashion industry in 2012 (personal communication, 11 July 2012). Franca Sozzani, influential editor of Italian *Vogue*, has, for instance, been nominated Goodwill Ambassador for Fashion4Development, aiming to use fashion-based initiatives

to support Africa's creative industry. See Suzy Mendes, 'Rebranding Africa', in the *New York Times* (14 May 2012). Unfortunately, the secrecy surrounding the high-end fashion business may inhibit the documentation of such movements of ideas.

References

Alpern, S. B. 1995. 'What Africans Got for their Slaves: a Master List of European Trade Goods', *History in Africa* 22: 5–43.

Bastian, M. L. 1996. 'Female *"Alhajis"* and Entrepreneurial Fashions: Flexible Identities in Southeastern Nigerian Clothing Practice', in H. Hendrickson (ed.), *Clothing and Difference: Embodied Identities in Colonial and Post-Colonial Africa*. Durham and London: Duke University Press, 97–132.

Bender, W. 2007. *Der nigerianische Highlife. Musik und Kunst in der populären Kultur der 50er und 60er Jahre*. Wuppertal: Peter Hammer Verlag.

Borgatti, J. 1983. *Cloth as Metaphor: Nigerian Textiles from the Museum of Cultural History*. Los Angeles: Museum of Cultural History, UCLA.

Brumann, C. 2011. 'Tradition', in F. Kreff, E-M. Knoll and A. Gingrich (eds), *Lexikon der Globalisierung*. Bielefeld: Transcript, 381–384.

Burton, R. F. C. 1863. *Abeokuta and the Cameroon Mountains: An Exploration*. London: Tinsley Brothers.

Eriksen, T. H. 2007. *Globalisation: The Key Concepts*. Oxford and New York: Berg.

Euba, T. 1987. 'Dress and Status in 19th Century Lagos', in A. Adefude, B. Agiri and J. Osuntokun (eds), *History of the People of Lagos State*. Lagos: Lantern Books, 139–159.

Falola, T, and M. M. Heaton. 2008. *A History of Nigeria*. Cambridge: Cambridge University Press.

Ferguson, J. 1999. *Expectations of Modernity: Myths and Meanings of Urban Life on the Zambian Copperbelt*. Berkeley, Los Angeles and London: University of California Press.

Fitz, U. 1947. *Die Vorarlberger Stickereiindustrie und ihr Export*. PhD dissertation, University of Vienna.

Frobenius, L. 1912. *Und Afrika sprach … Auf den Trümmern des klassischen Atlantis*. Berlin: Vita Deutsches Verlagshaus.

Hobsbawm, E., and T. Ranger. 2009. *The Invention of Tradition*, 17th edition. Cambridge: University Press.

Kriger, C. E. 2006. *Cloth in West African History*. Lanham and New York: Altamira Press.

Latour, B.. 2002. 'What is Iconoclash? Or is There a World beyond the Image Wars?' in B. Latour and P. Weibel (eds), *Iconoclash*. Cambridge, MA: MIT Press, 14–37.

Längle, E.. 2004. *Vorarlberg stickt für die Welt*. Vienna: Christian Brandstätter.

Lawuyi, O. B. 1991. 'The Social Marketing of Elites: The Advertised Self in Obituaries and Congratulations in Some Nigerian Dailies', *Africa: Journal of the International African Institute* 61(2): 247–263.

Luttmann, I. 2000. 'Globalisierung versus afrikanische Identitäten: Mode und Kleidungsverhalten in afrikanischen Städten', *Tribus* 49: 119–154.

Maier, K. 2000. *This House Has Fallen: Nigeria in Crisis*. London: Penguin Books.

National Taiwan Museum of Fine Arts. 2004. *Kongo Kingdom Art: From Ritual to Cutting Edge*. Taipeh.

Negri, E. de. 1962a. 'Yoruba Women's Costume', *Nigeria Magazine* 72: 5–12.

———. 1962b. 'Yoruba Men's Costume', *Nigeria Magazine* 73: 4–12.

Picton, J. 1995. 'Technology, Tradition and Lurex: The Art of Textiles in Africa', in John Picton (ed.), *The Art of African Textiles: Technology, Tradition and Lurex*. London: Lund Humphries Publishers, 9–30.

Plankensteiner, B. 2010a. 'Silesian Linens, English Woolens, Colourful Wax Prints: A Short History of the European Textile Trade with West Africa', in B. Plankensteiner and N. M. Adediran (eds), *African Lace: A History of Trade, Creativity and Fashion in Nigeria*. Vienna and Gent: Snoeck Publishers, 57–69.

———. 2010b. 'African Lace: Material of a Trans-Continental History of Relations', in B. Plankensteiner and N. M. Adediran (eds), *African Lace: A History of Trade, Creativity and Fashion in Nigeria*. Vienna and Gent: Snoeck Publishers, 113–151.

Plankensteiner, B., and N. M. Adediran (eds). 2010. *African Lace: A History of Trade, Creativity and Fashion in Nigeria*. Vienna and Gent: Snoeck Publishers.

Probst, P. 2012. 'Iconoclash in the Age of Heritage', *African Arts* 45(3): 10–11.

Reikat, A. 1997. *Handelsstoffe. Grundzüge des europäisch-westafrikanischen Handels vor der industriellen Revolution am Beispiel der Textilien*. Studien zur Kulturkunde 105. Cologne: Rüdiger Köppe Verlag.

Renne, E. P. 1997. '"Traditional Modernity" and the Economics of Handwoven Cloth Production in Southwestern Nigeria', *Economic Development and Cultural Change* 45(4): 773–792.

———. 2010. 'Figured, Textured, and Empty Spaces: An Aesthetics of Textiles and Dress in Nigeria', in B. Plankensteiner and N. M. Adediran (eds), *African Lace: A History of Trade, Creativity and Fashion in Nigeria*. Vienna and Gent: Snoeck Publishers, 71–89.

Sahlins, M. 2000[1988]. 'Cosmologies of Capitalism: The Trans-Pacific Sector of "the World System"', in M. Sahlins, *Culture in Practice: Selected Essays*. New York: Zone Books, 415–469.

Smith, D. J. 2007. *A Culture of Corruption: Everyday Deception and Popular Discontent in Nigeria*. Princeton and Oxford: Princeton University Press.

Soyinka, W. 1981. *Opera Wonyosi*. Bloomington: Indiana University Press.

Stengs, I. 2012. 'Sacred Singularities: Crafting Royal Images in Present-day Thailand', *The Journal of Modern Craft* 5(1): 51–68.

Thomas-Fahm, S. 2004. *Faces of She*. Lagos: Literamed Publications.

Ultzheimer, A. J. 1971. *Wahrhafte Beschreibung etlicher Reisen in Europa, Africa, Asien und America 1596–1610* (edited by S. Werg). Tübingen and Basel: Horst Erdmann Verlag.

Vogt, John. 1975. 'Notes on the Portuguese Cloth Trade in West Africa, 1480–1540', *The International Journal of African Historical Studies* 8(4): 623–651.

Wass, B. M. 1979. 'Yoruba Dress in Five Generations of a Lagos Family', in J. M. Cordwell and R. A. Schwarz (eds), *The Fabrics of Culture: The Anthropology of Clothing and Adornment*. Den Haag, Paris and New York: Mouton Publishers, 331–348.

2

HEADS AGAINST HANDS AND HIERARCHIES OF CREATIVITY
INDIAN LUXURY EMBROIDERY BETWEEN CRAFT, FASHION DESIGN AND ART

———◆•◆•◆———

Tereza Kuldova

'Darlings, follow me, no matter how much I am telling you, you are still being so unreceptive! You have to understand the essence of true style. You have to understand its soul, your soul! Let's go to the workshop!'[1] Rajinder[2] was getting frustrated with his clients: two sisters living and moving between their houses in Delhi, farm houses between Delhi and Dehradun, holiday homes in Goa and family houses in Jalandhar, while holidaying in Dubai, Thailand, Singapore and Hong Kong. The sisters, both in their late forties, were dressed head to toe in Western luxury brands, flaunting their Gucci sunglasses, D&G belts, Hermes scarves, Louis Vuitton handbags, diamond bangles and large sparkly diamond earrings. Their wealth had to show in the most blatant way. This provoked Rajinder, who no longer knew how to deal with these 'tasteless Punjabis', as he called them. To him these women, 'obsessed with bling and big brands', were second-rate customers, precisely because they were still buying into Western luxury brands. In contrast, Rajinder's first-rate customers, stemming from families of hereditary wealth, had ditched big-logo, Western luxury brands long ago. When it came to Western luxury, the old rich would devour only in unique customized pieces, always 'careful not to lose Indianness', as Rajinder repeatedly pointed out. Instead, they would impregnate Western luxury with Indian meanings. Customized automobiles for the maharajas (see fig. 2.1) became

Figure 2.1. Rolls-Royce Phantom II 'Star of India' (1934) built for the Maharaja of Rajkot, the only Rolls-Royce ever executed in saffron (*bhagwa*), the sacred colour of Hinduism, paradoxically also representing renunciation of material gains. Photo: www.vccci.com, 2012.

the example par excellence of this practice reiterated on numerous occasions. In these automobiles, Western expertise blended with distinctively Indian ornamentalism and aesthetics.

The old rich, according to Rajinder, truly understood style and appreciated quality and craftsmanship. The Punjabi sisters, to the contrary, had to be taught, instructed, advised and seduced. Paradoxically, no matter how much Rajinder praised his customers of hereditary wealth, he admitted that they were hard to deal with. They were careful with money, unwilling to splurge meaninglessly while always knowing exactly what they wanted; to them he could not be a style guru, to them he was a mere servant, eager to understand what they desired and why. Rajinder's income came largely from customers like these Punjabi sisters. People like them were keen to splurge in a big way, investing heavily in bridal wear and saris, but instead of appreciating the handicraft, Rajinder complained, they counted the number of Swarovski crystals. Eventually, however, most would recognize Rajinder's value as a cultural broker between the taste of the old rich and the new rich, indispensable to the staging of their prestige and to the aesthetic management of their eliteness.

Aesthetics, Hierarchy and the Confident India

The role of fashion designers in urban north India, and especially in New Delhi, has to be understood within the context of the city and its social pressures. Delhi is the *rajdhani,* the capital, the city of rulers. This status of the city has to be reinforced in its aesthetic and visual culture. Aesthetics often mirrors the ideologies of the given time (Panofsky 1976): Delhi's aesthetics are underpinned by hierarchical and feudal ideology, both in private and public (see fig. 2.2). The reinvention of the feudal logic of rulers and

Figure 2.2. The aesthetic return to feudalism is reflected in current popular visual culture, fashion and film that increasingly portray a clearly hierarchical feudal world of royals, their subjects and servants, pointing to the role of royal aesthetics in reflecting contemporary concerns. Backstage at India couture week 2014, collection by Rohit Bal. Photo: courtesy Nitin Patel Photography.

subjects becomes even more important in the context of democratization, seen as threatening by elites and, even more threatening, the rise of the Dalits (untouchables) and Other Backward Castes (OBCs) to political and social power. The rise of the lower classes to power threatens to destabilize the traditional hierarchies. This is where aesthetic distinction comes in. The designers are there to police the hierarchical boundaries through their aesthetic labour and to visually represent the regained confidence of India in the global economic space.

Manifesting power, prestige and wealth through aesthetics was important for all the elite customers of the fashion designers. Royal aesthetic extravaganzas were the easiest way to claim power and hierarchical distinction. 'Royal chic', a term I introduce here to describe this phenomenon, is characterized by remakes of attires of the maharajas and recreation of antique styles and cuts. Royal chic increased in popularity and intensity after the financial crisis of 2008. It replaced the previous 'Indo-western chic', a style defined by reduced layers and embroideries mixed with Western-inspired cuts. While the United States and Europe were hit hard by the 2008 crisis, India, relying on external trade for only about 20 per cent of its GDP (compared to China's 75 per cent) came out of the crisis largely unharmed by maintaining production for the internal market, a paradoxical remnant of the self-sufficiency policies and 'Hindu rate of growth' of the socialist era. Following the crisis, Shashi Tharoor (2009) proclaimed that 'instead of retreating from the world, India is advancing with more confidence than ever'.[3] This discourse of confidence, popular with economic analysts, also translates into current aesthetics of powerful Indianness that draw upon Indian royal pasts to aesthetically and ideologically recreate the new power of India and its ruling (now often business) elites.

Excavating and recreating royal pasts means rediscovering Indian heritage, especially the crafts that are perceived as the source of Indianness par excellence, since they embody nationalist sentiments, the rural as much as the royal. Craft connoisseurship in fashion has, in the past few years, transformed from a middle-class nationalist into an elitist pastime, a way of staging elite prestige and distinction (see fig. 2.3).

Crafts and Luxury Heritage

Recent concerns with Indianness relating to the new confidence of India in the economic field build on similar previous concerns traceable back to the early years after Independence. The post-Independence nationalistic idea of India drew on symbols from precolonial tribal and ethnic culture and celebrated the rural landscape as a repository of the autochthonous arts

Figure 2.3. Designer Samant Chauhan posing with a model in a village setting with the family of one of his weavers in the background. Photo: Vineet Modi, 2012.

and crafts, and therefore the 'authentic' past of the modern people (Kaviraj 1998). This idea became important again in the 1990s. The 90s saw the emergence of the Indian fashion industry, heritage discourse, tourist boom, economic liberalization, opening up of the Indian market, an upsurge of Hindu nationalism including the rise of the right wing *Bharatiya Janata Party* (BJP), the rise of the politics of recognition and concerns with cultural identity. Fashion designers suddenly assumed a new role alongside the already existing governmental schemes aimed at the protection and revitalization of national heritage embodied in India's crafts, be they pottery, weaving, painting or embroidery (Tarlo 1996). The crafts, idealized by the middle classes, the leaders of the nation, as much as by the fashion designers as the 'spirit that is India' (Singh 2009: 13) and as a resurrected symbol of 'self-reliance' that 'inspired freedom fighters to demand self-rule' (Poornalingam 2009: 15), suddenly faced the transnational capitalist marketplace and therefore needed to be reinvented, rediscovered and made contemporary and trendy. Imagined as static and traditional, their reinvention fell into the hands of the creative, innovative fashion designers, who saw it as their mission to help the disempowered craftsperson to face the new markets. Over the course of the years, however, the ethnic chic that emerged in the 90s and played on nationalist and democratic sentiments has reinforced nationalist *elitism* rather than democratic egalitarianism.

Royal chic enables north Indian urban elites to visually project themselves as ruling classes.

Today it is almost a cliché to say that the unique selling point of contemporary Indian fashion is the Indian 'heritage' – anything from hand-woven silk to exquisite embroideries. The word 'heritage' has slipped into popular usage, appearing in media, in advertising and marketing, in the rhetoric of designers and self-proclaimed 'ethical' consumers (Niranjan, Sudhir and Dhareshwar 1993). The idea of Indian heritage, wrapped up in exotic images of the flamboyance of royal courts and colourful and stylish Indian villagers has become an effective sales strategy. This strategy has today moved from the state-run craft emporiums and governmental schemes to high-end designer boutiques. Heritage, and even more so heritage luxury, is big business (Rowlands 2002). 'Heritage' in this context is an elitist concept. Those who produce the luxury heritage discourse and fuel the elitist politics of cultural recognition live at increasing distance from those who produce the material content of this heritage. Fashion designers often function as cultural brokers, both (re)producing heritage discourse and partaking in the material production of its content. This uneasy middle position means that they have to continually legitimize their own status within the hierarchy as superior to that of the craftspeople.

The Fashion Designer's Power Mystique

Rajinder had to convince his Punjabi customers of the value of connoisseurship of Indianness as embodied in the craft skills of India for the creation of what could be termed 'power mystique' (Cohen 1981): the quality these women desired to display on their bodies. Rajinder claimed that the essence of Indianness could be found in the skill, passion, simplicity and purity of the craftspeople and their products, and that the only way for elite bodies to incorporate Indianness was through a *transformation* not only of their surface but also of their substance, their selves. The idealized and abstract bodies of the craftspeople were paradoxically imagined to have a grounded connection to India, something that elite bodies lacked. However, the real bodies of the craftspeople in their physicality were considered impure, or even polluting, a social malaise that had to be dealt with. They had to be empowered, educated and sanitized. Many of the non-governmental organizations set up by the designers, in fact, reproduced further the divide between themselves and the craft-other, positioning themselves as patrons of the craft-clients. This also meant that every product had to go not only through rigorous physical washing, in order to remove every little stain and impurity, but also through imaginative sanitization, during which the material handmade product was turned into an abstract fragment of heritage luxury. In this process of sanitization and transformation of the craft product, the craftsperson was projected into the past, thus extending the already existing spatial and social distance into a temporal distance (Fabian 1983). This act of sanitization turned these products into objects of heritage luxury. Consequently, their value skyrocketed.

Creativity and Techniques of Mystification

While sanitizing the craft product and turning it into an object of heritage luxury, an element of the politics of elite belonging, Rajinder also had to claim his position within the system in order to legitimize his own value and the price tags of his garments. The notion of creativity played a crucial role in this process. Rajinder had to be acknowledged both as an *expert* claiming superior knowledge of taste and craft and as a *unique creative individual*. Otherwise, what would be the difference between him and a retailer or a tailor? Rajinder had to argue for his own individual creativity, which distinguished his garments and designs from those of his fellow designers, while at the same time arguing for the *collective* creativity of the craftspeople. Only an argument of superior individual creativity, as opposed to inferior collective creativity, could legitimize his endeavour as a designer to the elites. In order to do this, he had to navigate what appeared at first sight to be a contradictory terrain of what could be labelled *craftspeak, designspeak* and *artspeak*. Navigating this terrain was thus both a matter of deep belief for Rajinder, a result of socialization and conditioning at the design institute, and a matter partially utilitarian, in which he himself understood the importance of speaking in a particular way in order to claim his own value. This terrain was suffused with apparent, and yet complementary, contradiction. Where craftspeak played on notions of nationhood, tradition, collectivism, heritage, stasis, repetition and value, artspeak utilized the language of individualism, artistic vision and genius, inspiration, magic and creativity, and designspeak centred on notions such as innovation, progress, neoliberalism, branding, newness and change.

Let us now follow Rajinder from his studio office to his workshop and look at how he frames his own creativity against the creativity of the craftspeople as a creativity of mind (head) against a creativity of body (hands). Rajinder's studio is bright, well-lit, decorated with old miniatures and modern paintings by Indian artists, featuring a library, elaborate garments on clothes hangers, a stylish sofa in red velvet and a large carved wooden writing table with marble top matched by a throne-like yet comfortable chair. The workshop on the other hand, even though located in the same recently built box-like building of industrial design, is a dim-lit space with around fifty male *zardozi*[4] embroiderers sitting on the floor next to frames with stretched cloth, six tailors sitting at their *Usha* sewing machines and around thirty *chika*[5] women embroiderers working seated in the opposite corner of the room. Notice that the atmosphere of these two spaces reinforced and (re)produced the established hierarchical order.

Rajinder attributed the quality, execution and design of the embroidery to the 'hands of his workers'. When giving the Punjabi women and me a tour through the workshop, he described in detail the complex production process of the embroidery, from drawing, block-making and embroidering, to dyeing. While giving us this lecture, we stood above the 'workers' looking down at them, maintaining a safe distance. The artisans gazed at us briefly only to continue working. The Punjabi sisters, who touched and examined every single piece of the embroidery while in Rajinder's office, did not even contemplate touching the same embroidery in the making. Gazing at the workers attaching Swarovski crystals to the saris, and embroidering white flowers and golden and green peacocks, Rajinder emphasized the amount of 'traditional labour' that was put into each piece, framing it as national heritage that had to be kept alive. This performance established Rajinder, at least to the Punjabi women, as a patron, someone providing work and stability for the impoverished craftsperson, while keeping the national heritage alive. Towards the end of the visit he proclaimed: 'Without me, these people are nothing, they have to be told what to do, they do not understand the market and they cannot come up with any new idea: that is why they cannot survive on their own.' In addition to his expertise, knowledge of history, of elite tastes, and of the fashion market, he claimed a superior unique individual artistic creativity, clearly different from that of the craftsperson. Rajinder claimed that each single piece was dependent on his inspiration and innovativeness, and that craft development would not be possible without creative 'spirits' like him. While we could argue that what we are dealing with here is a simple case of casteism, or class hierarchy (since most of the workers were Muslims), and that it is Rajinder's schooling, capital and background that sets him apart, none of the discussions revolved around this theme. Instead, the ways in which Rajinder and other designers legitimized their position were formulated in accordance with the ideology of meritocracy.

Rajinder's power mystique was dependent on a combination of material and discursive techniques. From the atmosphere of his office, crafted to exude power and knowledge, via his claims to superior expertise, to his use of the romantic notion of the individual artist, all combined in order to increase the value of his products and turn them into artefacts akin to objects of art. He used the strategy of 'artification' (Shapiro 2004; Shapiro and

Heinich 2012), of turning non-art into art and he praised the craftsperson as someone whose work connected the elite to the essence of India. He would refer to himself as a style guru, someone who could teach his customers about their true nature, urging them to throw away the shackles of surface distractions such as Western brands. This particular positioning enabled Rajinder to navigate the terrain between particularistic hierarchical distinction and universal humanistic interest. At the same time, he was arguing a moral case around the impoverished craftspeople, turning them into a problem that had to be solved, thus creating added ethical value to his products, enabling his customers to purchase good conscience along with the garment (Žižek 2009).

Rajinder's power mystique can be likened to the 'charismatic ideology of "creation"', as understood by Pierre Bourdieu in his *Rules of Art* (1996: 167), an ideology that 'can be easily found in studies of art, literature and other cultural fields' and that presents an 'obstacle to a rigorous science of the production of the value of cultural goods'. This charismatic ideology directs the gaze towards the individual creator such as the designer, 'preventing us from asking who has created this "creator" and the magic power of transubstantiation with which the creator is endowed' (ibid.: 167). Not only does this ideology hide the ways in which the 'creator' is produced, but it also hides all the work, creativity and skill that went into the actual creation of what the creator claims to have created purely through his or her privileged unique creative abilities and imagination. Understanding and unravelling Rajinder's power mystique as a designer thus means uncovering the logic of valuation (Bourdieu 1977) within the Indian fashion industry as it is played out in the relationship between designers and craftspeople. David Graeber (2001) has argued that it is in people's imagination in the process of pursuing value that people create society, an imagination that draws both on *pasts* and desired *futures*. However, what is crucial is how different people position themselves in the social realm through imagination. It is also important to understand that when it comes to establishing and reaffirming the role of the fashion designer and the craftsperson, with their attached statuses (one privileged, the other underprivileged and yet both celebrated), the power of knowledge and discourse is immense. While it might be said that a 'successful trader transcends the relatively powerless role of object producer, becoming instead a producer of images' (Venkatesan 2009: 140), the Indian designer supersedes the Indian trader, realizing the power of narratives attached to these images. After all, any 'play with images remains incomplete if the affect that it generates cannot be captured and formalized within a discursive set of product narratives' (Mazzarella 2003: 46). Very often, the designers themselves are woven into those narratives and at times could even be perceived as the very products being sold, their own prestige

(as compared to traders) being transposed onto the garments that they produce and consequently worn as status enhancements on elite bodies.

Rajinder is known for his designs of chikan embroidery (see fig. 2.4) for
which he claims copyright, creative ownership and unique inspiration. Yet,
as he himself explained to the Punjabi women, ignoring any contradiction
in his statements, the production of chikan embroidery is a creative process that is multistaged, involving different people and demanding different
skills, knowledge, imaginations, techniques and intimate embodied knowledge at different stages of its production – from blockmakers and printers,
via embroiderers, dyers and finishers, to designers. Creativity involved in the
production of the luxury embroidered garments is thus clearly distributed in
different measures across these networks of production, involving multiple
creative players. This fact is, however, rather inconvenient for elite fashion
designers such as Rajinder who use the romantic notion of individual creative genius in order to legitimize the value of their garments and create
their fashion brands, which largely depend on their own unique persona.
This inconvenience is exacerbated by the fact that the unique selling point
of Indian fashion is India's handicrafts. While traditionally there was no
difference between art and craft in India and the craftsperson was the artist,
the romantic notion of creative artistic genius imported from the West has

Figure 2.4. Producing chikan embroidery, traditionally white-on-white embroidery
from Lucknow, the nostalgic capital of the precolonial opulent and mythologized
district of Awadh, known for the lavish lifestyles of its Nawab rulers. Photo: Tereza
Kuldova, 2011.

changed this, excluding craftspeople from the realm of art and associating them instead with manual labour.

Often, the idea of individual creativity as an *intellectual* endeavour on the part of the designer serves as a legitimization of existing hierarchical relations, in which craftspeople are represented as mere manual workers. The very possibility of *individual* creativity as much as imagination on the part of the craftsperson is effectively denied. At the same time, however, when talking about craftspeople and artisans in plural – as a collectivity – they are often labelled as the very source of Indian creativity.[6] Yet, this creativity is of a different nature, it is frozen by a static traditionalist framework within which the craftsperson is rendered incapable of innovation and therefore unworthy of being labelled 'creative', in the modern sense of the word. This idea of the idealized craftsperson as representative of the 'real' village and traditional India figures prominently in the narratives of the fashion designers, serving their desires for distinction by reproducing an image of an immovable craftsperson frozen in the past and thus incapable of change.

This logic manifests itself also in the double meaning of *authenticity* of the designer garment often employed on these occasions. The authenticity of the designer garment is perceived on one hand as stemming from the individuality, creativity and the very selfhood of the designer's persona, while on the other hand it seems to be derived from the perceived authenticity of Indian intricate craft heritage. Authenticity is thus inherently unstable, and could be better understood as subject to an ongoing politics of authentication, which may be seen in Rajinder's navigation through parallel notions of creativity, closely tied to parallel meanings of authenticity. Here, the authenticity of his designer piece as an art object subsumes the authenticity deriving from the traditional craft involved in its production.

Patronage, Craft and Art

As we have seen in the case of Rajinder, the trendiness of Indianness and revivalism also enables the fashion designer to position him or herself not only as an expert but also as a *patron* of the crafts and craftspeople. This is possibly best exemplified by Ritu Kumar, the famous revivalist designer, whose agenda is one of 'commercially inflected nationalism' (Bhachu 2004: 75).[7] Ritu Kumar follows a similar logic to the one of the Crafts Council of India, a logic of reconciling the 'demands of modernity', its tastes and aesthetics with the revival of crafts while aiming at recreating 'the quality and finesse of the originals by replicating … museum collections' (Crafts Council 2007). This has elevated designers like her into a position of cultural intermediaries (Bourdieu 1984), 'whose task is to build and serve the machinery of status' (Goffman 1951: 303) and prestige, while turning them into experts in creating visual representations of Indianness and selling 'idealized images of Indian culture to wealthy cosmopolitan elite' (Tarlo 1996: 315). In other words, it has turned them into 'people whose daily work requires them to become proficient in manipulating symbols which signify a position higher than the one they themselves possess' (Bourdieu 1984: 303). The commercial revival of crafts, using the logic of heritage preservation, has been transformed by designers such as Ritu Kumar and Rajinder into a specific segment of a luxury market serving the elite Indian customer's need for both cultural and class distinction, while providing visible belonging and identity in the global space (see also Kala Shreen, this volume).

Ritu Kumar is a connoisseur of craft, whose intention is to not only to showcase Indian craftsmanship but also to reconstruct the past glory of the artisan. Her intention is to enlighten the upper strata of Indian society about its own heritage; to this purpose she has published a coffee table book with encyclopaedic ambition entitled *Costumes and Textiles of Royal India* (Kumar and Muscat 2006), which features photographs of the contemporary descendants of royals from all over India in traditional attire no less lavish than that of their ancestors. Ritu Kumar also realized that competition has not only an economic but also a moral dimension and that appealing to both nationalistic sentiments and ethical consumption is critical in order to succeed. Ritu Kumar, much like Rajinder, exploits a variety of strategies in order to endow her products with extra value – she positions herself as a patron of the crafts (modelled upon the traditional royal systems of patronage of artisans), at the same time as she is the expert on the crafts (a part of the educated Anglophone elite, a valuable member of the knowledge society), and no less is she the individual creative designer and interpreter of the wealth of tradition that needs to be rendered meaningful to the elite consumer. She thus effectively plays on both traditional and modern sources of significance in order to legitimize her position within the hierarchy, simultaneously ensuring that the craftsperson remains in the position of a subordinate client incapable of interpreting his or her own work to the world.

The designer's urge to differentiate themself from the craftsperson and deny the material and manual dimension of fashion design is made explicit in the following dialogue between the author and Raghavendra, a revivalist fashion designer from Delhi:

> *Raghavendra*: According to Indian tradition, arts and crafts were one, the craftsman is the artist, there is no distinction between designer, artist and craftsman, we all do the same thing, fundamentally, we all are artists.
>
> *Tereza*: What is it that makes you different from the craftsman then?

Raghavendra: I guide the craftsmen; their creativity is of different nature, they repeat, they cannot innovate. That is where I step in. I create original pieces, they make my vision happen. And obviously, craft is great inspiration.[8]

Raghavendra referred, here, to the concept of *kala,* in which craftsperson and artist are subsumed into the same category, similarly to the Western concepts of *ars* and *tekhne,* which 'meant much the same thing, namely skill of the kind associated with craftsmanship' (Ingold 2001: 17). Troy Organ has pointed out that there is no real word for art in Sanskrit and that the closest one can get is the concept of *shilpa,* which is a 'word meaning "diverse" or "variegated". This term was used originally to mean "ornamentation", but later on was extended to denote skills in the broadest sense: painting, horsemanship, archery, cooking etc.' (Organ 1975: 11). Ananda K. Coomarswamy, the pioneering philosopher of Indian art, who promoted the idea of the Indian craftsperson as a metaphor of Hindu order and tradition, has even noted that the idea of an artist struggling to express him or herself and suffering lack of patronage is ridiculous to Indian thought, since Indian art always responded to the market demand (Coomarswamy 1966).

For Raghavendra, the craftsperson can be an artist solely in the traditional sense of the word. While the artistry of the craftsperson is recognized, it is recognized only as a part of collective creativity, effectively frozen in the remote past (Fabian 1983). The art of the artisan is imagined as qualitatively different, namely inferior, while the Western concept of the individual creative genius legitimizes the exorbitant amounts of money demanded by Raghavendra in exchange for his traditionally embroidered and crafted pieces endowed with the spark of his creative genius. The designers thus associate themselves with the intellectual and the creative, while disassociating from any reminder of the manual, material and bodily, which is reserved for the craftsperson. Separating intellectual and manual labour is one strategy, associating oneself with the Western notion of high art in order to enhance the divide and create a clear boundary between the work of the craftsperson and the designer, is another. 'Fashion is still attentive to the residual aura attached to what is revealingly termed "high art"' (Radford 1998: 153) and that is what certain designers aim to capitalize on. This is not surprising if we consider that 'fine art's symbolic value continually outstripped the cultural capital of craft and design, both of which have been conventionally invested with the use-value rather than conceptual distinction, based on the Western cultural primacy of the intellectual over the manual, content over form' (Lees-Maffei and Sandino 2004).

By seeking association with art, designers transpose the higher status of art onto their fashion creations, while at the same time distancing themselves from craft's association with manual labour. Rohit Bal, the *enfant terrible* of Indian fashion and one of the leading designers, portrays himself as an artist, a creative genius, whose 'brand is defined by Rohit Bal the man. It is almost as if the brand is merely an extension of the edgy (or at least perceived to be edgy) life of the man' (Sengupta 2009: 150). Buying Bal's designs is 'an investment, it is like buying art, it has value which only increases in time',[9] as a friend of mine and customer of Bal's pointed out to me.

The vocabulary of fashion has effectively adopted the language of art (Muller 2000) and the strategy of turning non-art into art is used by Indian designers in order to increase the value of their products. By linking their products to the magical aura of high art and its status, the designers reinstate their creative genius. Collaborations between artists and designers are also increasingly popular and seem 'to serve the purpose of endowing the garment with new meaning, and to elevate it to an art form' (Taylor 2005: 454). All these techniques of mystification effectively differentiate designer garments from often not very dissimilar garments found in the market, produced by the very same craftspeople. The charismatic ideology of creation not only increases the value of the designers' products, but also effectively hides the numbers of people who stand behind the production of these creations. This ideology also enables concomitant valuation and celebration of craftspeople and their devaluation.

The Rhetoric of Development and Innovation

The distinction between fine art and craft in the Western tradition followed Kant's privileging of 'interiority': denial of the body (Pinney 2002) and postulation of the autonomous subject, resulting in the idea of creative genius (Rampley 1998: 266), as a result of which, 'fine artists were thought to have God-given superior creative powers' (Svašek 2009: 64). The elevation of art went hand in hand with the debasement of craft to something merely technical, traditionalist and repetitive without any claim to imagination and innovation. The notion of a creative genius has, over time, moved from the realm of art to the realm of marketing and advertising, becoming the very language of media and branding. Creativity and innovation became blurred and self-help books on how to become a 'creative genius' are popping up everywhere (for instance, Fisk 2011) celebrating 'design visionaries' such as the recently deceased Apple 'mastermind', Steve Jobs. In creation of new commodities it is innovation that counts in the competitive neoliberal market (Liep 2001), where 'creativity has come to be seen as a major driver of economic prosperity and social well-being' (Hallam and Ingold 2007). In classical economic theory, innovation is often considered as the sole autonomous cause of economic development (Schumpeter 1934). The celebration of innovation also goes back to the split between art and craft and the emergence of the belief in progress and therefore innovation as something inherently good, which again feeds into the claims of the designers to help development of crafts. Thus: 'Forms of cultural production that did not aim for novelty were ridiculed for being outdated "stuck in the past". In the arts, "creativity" was equalized with "originality" and "innovation". In this view, traditions were either "authentic, unchanging practices" or "boring repetitions", and copying had to be regarded as ultimate form of non-creative conventionality' (Svašek 2009: 64).

While prior to the beginning of the nineteenth century, innovation was considered dangerous and suspicious, denoting a 'perverse and deranged mind' (Girard 1990: 9), after the turn of the century, 'innovation became the god that we are still worshipping today'. The new cult meant that a new scourge had descended upon the world – 'stagnation'. Before the eighteenth century, 'stagnation' was unknown; suddenly it spread its gloom far and wide (ibid.: 10). This same stagnation was discovered by colonial administrators everywhere in India and stasis became, in this context, 'akin to mortal sin' (Pollock 2001: 5). Craft, considered to be traditional, static, repetitive and imitative became an easy target, blamed for backwardness and inability to progress and develop. The 'European concept of the opposition of body and mind, savagery and civilization' (Howes 2003: 5) has gained a foothold in India, effectively separating the savage craftsperson from the civilized designer. It is this logic that lurks behind the perception of many designers that design intervention into contemporary craft is necessary. Some even advise craft to 'forge an alliance with design', suggesting that this would be 'the winning marriage, not the unhappy, fruitless stalking of the fine arts' (Clark 2010: 452). This approach is widely celebrated and promoted among those who teach and write about design, such as the established industrial designer and author, Singanapalli Balaram:

> One of the most pressing needs is helping people with design. This requires educating students to give design training to people who are illiterate.... Because most Indian traditions are living, what needs to follow the documentation is the application of traditional knowledge to contemporary or future design situations in new ways for new effects in creative fashion. It also means leaping from past traditions to future aspirations; connecting traditional materials, forms, techniques, and wisdom to the world's future materials, techniques, and needs. (2005: 20–21)

Similar attitudes were present among lecturers at the National Institute of Fashion Technology in Delhi, who believed that one of the most significant roles of current fashion designers is helping craftspeople in redesigning their products to suit the current market. The developmental discourse, in which the craftsperson is perceived as 'skilled but not knowledgeable' (Venkatesan 2009: 38) and incapable of creativity, imagination and change, is part of the education and socialization of the new generations of fashion designers. The same rhetoric can be found in UNESCO's advice on design intervention for the Indian crafts sector (UNESCO, Craft Revival Trust and Artesanias de Colombia S. A. 2005), a standard reference in the training of designers. The designer is thus turned into a 'development' helper. Since the idea of development rests on the notions of progress and innovation, who could be a more appropriate helper than a designer imagined as future visionary? The craftsperson is thus, time and again, positioned as someone who needs help and whose craft needs to be revived for him by someone from the outside, reducing the craftsperson to someone who is *dependent* and subordinate by default. And so, while the craftspeople are imagined as collectively looking backward, the designers are imagined as individually looking into the yet undiscovered future. This imaginative separation creates a distance and a gap between the work of the designer and the craftsperson. In reality, on the other hand, we can observe the designer digging into the archives, recreating attires of the past and interviewing craftspeople about their traditional designs. We can observe craftspeople continually developing new designs, following international fashion, creating new patterns and trying to adjust to the market. Yet the authoritative narratives produced by designers, fashion media, bloggers, international bodies such as UNESCO, non-governmental organizations and even lecturers at design institutes all perpetuate a narrative of a craftsperson as someone incapable of innovation, creativity and change, thus legitimizing their own position.

Let me provide one last example that illustrates the logic unpacked above and is representative of the attitudes of designers such as Rajinder, or even Ritu Kumar. This excerpt is from the press release supplied by veteran of the Indian fashion industry Tarun Tahiliani[10] for his bridal collection 'Artisanal: Bringing the Craft to the Fore':

> Real beauty, luxury and elegance require no tricks to seduce us. It is, rather, the timeless appeal of fine workmanship that truly pleases the style connoisseur. In India, the caress of luxury is the result of millions of artisan hands that pour their energy to define the ancient artisanal skill, exquisite taste and patience. *Only a fusion of soul and expert technique* will produce fine craft. Intricate workmanship, along with the return to organic textile celebrates and feeds Indian Couture, reinventing our historical traditions in the form of the *Modern Mughal*.[11]

The soul, the essence of Indianness, is thus delivered by the anonymous artisan, while the expert knowledge, innovation and originality are delivered by the designer. The artisan is effectively denied this modern form of creativity and is thus excluded from the expert knowledge society of middle- and upper-class India, while at the same time being incorporated into it by being recognized as valuable, even essential, but still inferior and backward at the same time.

Dependency Reversed: Mocking the Designers and the Heritage Discourse

Without us, they are nothing. – Jameela, a Muslim woman in her late twenties, while embroidering a chikan piece in a village near Lucknow

One day, I followed Arjun, a Delhi-based designer who notoriously labelled his embroiderers as mere manual workers, to a village near Lucknow, where he went in person to check on some of his special orders: saris for the wedding trousseau of one of Delhi's millionaire daughters about to tie the knot. Something rather typical happened that day. Arjun was unhappy with the quality of the embroidery, expecting something more delicate, and he became instantly frustrated, thinking of the problems ahead with the delivery. The embroidery takes time; a sari like this can take six embroiders up to three months to finish. He began shouting at the women, blaming them for being irresponsible and lazy, threatening to cut down the wage or give the work to someone else. The women sat still, staring at him, then one of them started laughing and, throwing the sari at his head, shouted:

> Then take it, we don't care for your money, we don't need people like you here shouting, get lost, and remember, we don't need to do this work, we do it because there is nothing else to do in the day; you come here and give us work and what you think you are? You designers come and go; one piece here, one piece there and think you are saving us. You are the irresponsible (*zimedaar nahi*) people here, not us. We don't care for your work, take it! You come here and you want embroidery, we don't run after your work. You are the one who is dependent on us. Without us you are nobody, you can't do anything (*hamaare binaa tumse kuch nahi hogaa*). Now stop shouting and making a fool of yourself and either get lost or let us continue working.[12]

> The other girls started nodding and laughing,

> She is right, we have seen those like you before, big people (*bare log*), you only keep thinking how big you are, in truth you are nothing without us, absolutely nothing (*sacchi mein aap log hamaare binaa kuch bhi nahi hai*).

Later the girls told me that designers like Arjun 'just think too much of themselves', and that you need to 'put them in their place, they think we are poor and we do anything for that little money they give us, they are wrong, even we have some respect/honour' (*izzat*). Arjun was angry and frustrated on the way back, complaining that these women are so hard to deal with;

then he alluded to the distinction between embroiderers based in the city and those in the village:

> Those who are in the city are much easier to handle, they do what you say and keep their mouth shut, they are dependent on the work you give them, and that makes them thankful and obedient; these women here think too much of themselves. They make my life hell. I have to establish a proper workshop in the city, or just drag some of the good ones to Delhi to work for me, but it is so hard to get good ones to move, they are all bound by tradition.

> The craftswomen in the villages, unlike those in the city, who were disciplined by the environment of the workshop into silence and submission (cf. De Neve 2012), were not afraid to mock the designers, laugh at their lifestyles, at the way they kept running after money, always appearing to be stressed and miserable. Positioning themselves as patrons and developmentalists, the designers often insisted that the village girls learn new stitches in order to earn more and thus have a better life, imposing their version of the 'good life' onto the village women. But this did not go down well with the women, who often refused to learn new stitches, saying that a hundred rupees extra made no difference to them and that they were not the ones who were crazy for money, they were not 'slaves of money' (*paise ke ghulaam*), as they called the designers. On one occasion, after such a designer's tirade, one of the girls said, 'We laugh at them, they have everything but still they are miserable (*dukhī*). They think that we are poor, that we don't have anything. But we have everything we need (*zaroorat*). Look at the village, everything is here, fresh air, water, fields, food, and look at the city, it is just dirt and people miserable and fighting, and they come to teach us how to live?'[13]

The value system of the designers was thus not only questioned, but directly mocked and laughed at (see fig. 2.5). Notions like heritage and nation faced the same treatment. The following conversation between Namrita, a trader-cum-designer from Lucknow, from whom I bought a piece for the collections of the Museum of Cultural History in Oslo, and village-based chikan embroiderers from one of her centres nicely portrays this widespread sentiment:

> *Namrita (addressing the 'girls'):* The sari you embroidered will be exhibited at the museum, very far away, in her country (*pointing at me*). She has bought it so that people over there will know about our craft traditions. You should be proud of yourself, now your work is in the museum. Through your work they will see India, our nation. You should be very proud, your work represents the Indian heritage and people come from so far away and truly appreciate it. They give you dignity and self-respect.

> (*The 'girls' are giggling while she is talking, watching her with suspicious smiles and a dose of scepticism, then Zehra speaks.*)

> *Zehra:* It is only words, nation and tradition, what does it mean, it means nothing (*laughs*). What difference does it make to us?

(*Other girls start nodding.*)

Jameela: Yeah, we are sitting here and ruining our eyes for nothing. Nation or no nation, tradition or no tradition … what kind of tradition is that anyway? You get your work done and money, she (*pointing at me*) gets her work done, what do we get?

(*Other girls keep on nodding, and then one after another start shouting.*)

All: What difference does it make to us?

(*Then Zehra makes her voice heard again.*)

Zehra: You people only talk, it is *only words*. But all you do is take credit for our work, I have TV, I see the designers on TV, we do the work and they just talk, as if they knew anything, they just live off us, like you do. You both do.

Namrita: You know, she (*pointing at me*) is doing a lot of hard work, she will write about you and so people will know; it will give you recognition. And me, I am trying my best to sell what you do, it is not easy, only few people are willing to pay for high-quality craft. You should understand, she will write and people become aware, even you will profit.

(*Mubinah, until now silent, suddenly raises her voice and states rather firmly.*)

Mubinah: Well, I don't care for any of that, the work is just useless, I hate the embroidery, I am just doing it while waiting to get married; there is nothing else to do over here. When I get married I will finally live *aaraam se* [easily or relaxed], sitting on my bed and watching soap operas on TV, I don't want to do this, it's a nonsense work. And what kind of pride? Everyone does it here. I do not care to learn new stitches or anything anymore. I just want to relax.[14]

The question then is: whose heritage are we talking? (Hall 1999). The conversation above reveals the elitist notion of heritage employed by the designers, which turns the craft product into tangible heritage while turning the craftspeople into an objectified living intangible heritage that needs to be protected and conserved. Within this discourse, development can happen only within the bounds of the craft, for instance, learning new stitches and producing higher-quality products, rather than learning new skills, such as marketing. Thus, the hierarchical status quo is reproduced. The luxury heritage segment with the designer experts and connoisseurs is, like the governmental heritage segment with its nation-building ambitions, related to governance and to an 'exercise of "power"' … the symbolic power to order knowledge, to rank, classify and arrange and thus to give meaning to objects and things through the imposition of interpretative schemas, scholarship and the authority of connoisseurship' (Hall 1999: 4). This exercise of power does not go unnoticed by the craftspeople. The fact that Indianness emerges only at a social and imaginative distance from those who are among its most significant abstracted symbols lends itself easily to irony in the craftswomen's interactions with designers.

Figure 2.5. Chikan embroiderers laughing while working, Lucknow, Uttar Pradesh. Photo: Arash Taheri, 2012.

Being treated as an idealization is directly offensive to real people and prompts the embroiderers' responses of irony and sarcasm. Turned into ghost-like creatures, existing only as a fantasy, a dream, a non-present present, the craftswomen reveal in their attitude, which can be understood in terms of Nietzsche's conception of irony, the hollow character of the authoritative craftspeak and of today's neoliberal ideals of progress, development, obsession with past, national identity and capital accumulation (Nietzsche et al. 2001). Their irony, which represents a clear conflict of perspectives, works to discredit this ideal and thus reveal it as a mere fantasy. Often, if repeated long enough, words acquire body and reality. Words such as 'nation' and 'heritage' have acquired flesh and blood in the minds of designers, indeed a fullness of meaning on which their own identities are built. The craftswomen challenge these words and their irony forces us, as much as the designers, to inspect these categories together with their contingent nature, while questioning their actual content.

Conclusion: Hierarchies of Creativity and Techniques of Mystification

We have focused on the ways in which creativity is used, in its multiple meanings, by fashion designers in order to legitimize and (re)produce, intentionally or unintentionally, both social hierarchies and hierarchies between fashion design and craft in India. Rather than inquiring into the nature of creativity per se, we have investigated the ways in which opposing notions of creativity, individual artistic creativity versus collectivist traditional creativity, are turned into techniques of mystification (Cohen 1981) employed by the designers in order to legitimize their position and differentiate themselves from the craft – on whom they are, at the same time, existentially dependent. The craftswomen have made this reverse dependence of the designers on the craftswomen very clear in their ironic subversive interpretations of the authoritative discourses of the designers, thus challenging their worldview, questioning their value system and threatening the sources of significance in their lives, while pointing out the contingent nature of the authoritative interpretations.

We have seen that the power of the designer garment lies ultimately in its semiotic value (Keane 2005). Its magic, its value and efficacy, resides in the added meaning. The designer garment, like art, opens up 'the possibility and the necessity of interpreting the work, of offering a theory as to what it is about, what its subject is' (Markowitz 1994: 60). It is the meaning, imagined as *transcending* the material, that is of consequence. In other words, it is in the level of connotation, symbolization and myth-making that significance lies (Barthes 1983). Trance, meditation, revelation, God-like genius, timelessness, eternity – all those words are employed, consciously or unconsciously, to create a supernatural world in which the designer is the 'creator' par excellence. It is no coincidence that the Hindi alphabet is called *Devanagari*, which literary translates as the abode of the gods (Tambiah 1968): gods both have power and they can 'create'. The language, which the designers employ, is, in this respect, no different and through this language, fashion becomes an adjunct to power (Simmel 1957; Wilson 2007).

By way of the power of language, the artisans and craftspeople are turned into relics of the past that need to be protected, educated and helped and whose crafts need to be continually revived *for* them. The modern orthodoxy that separates conception from execution, and in which skill is regarded as mere work, deprived of content and self-expression, lurks behind and legitimizes this hierarchy of creativity and knowledge. The modern educated elites, plugged into the global expert-knowledge society, have the power to decide who is to be traditional and who is to be modern (DeNicola 2004), no matter how much the reality defies this separation. These authoritative narratives powerfully underpin notions of 'us' and 'them', sustaining neat hierarchies and (re)producing social boundaries (Barth 1969). Valued as an abstraction and devalued as real living individuals, the craftspeople find themselves both celebrated and disdained, while the credit for their work is taken by a carefully staged image of a creative individual, legitimized by an ideology that sees creativity as separate from body and matter; no matter how many times the reality, overflowing with examples of the profound dependency of creativity on embodied skill and engagement with matter (Ingold 2000), proves such a view to be reductionist.

Tereza Kuldova is a social anthropologist, fashion curator and post-doctoral fellow at the Department of Archaeology, Conservation and History at the University of Oslo, Norway. She has been working extensively on the Indian and global fashion industry, socio-economic relations, structural violence, material and popular culture and ideology. She is the author of *Luxury Indian Fashion: A Social Critique* (2016) and editor of *Fashion India: Spectacular Capitalism* (2013).

Notes

1. The first draft of this chapter was presented at the CIM Project Final Conference, Utrecht, Netherlands (31 May–1 June 2012) under the title 'Hijacking Creativity, Denying Imagination: Unravelling the Mystery of Value Creation in Indian Fashion'. I would like to thank Maruška Svašek and Birgit Meyer for their invaluable comments on the draft. This chapter is based on my fieldwork in urban North India (2008, 2010–2011), when I followed luxury high-quality hand embroidery from its multistaged production process in Lucknow to high-end fashion boutiques and workshops of elite Indian fashion designers in New Delhi.
2. Rajinder is a Jat in his early thirties, a graduate from the National Institute of Fashion Technology in Ahmedabad, and comes from a middle-class family in Haryana, his father being a higher-ranking government official. Rajinder is openly homosexual, something that caused numerous problems with his family during his youth. At the beginning of his career he used to create garments inspired largely by Western cuts and free from any embellishment; during the last seven years he has completely changed his design aesthetics and perspective, becoming traditionalist, drawing upon India's past and the aesthetics of the courts.
3. The account is based on field notes, 21 October 2010.
4. Contemporary Indian heritage luxury has to be understood here in the context of global proliferation of heritage discourses largely stimulated by the agendas of transnational organizations such as UNESCO, which promote the value of conservation and revival of both tangible and intangible heritage on a global scale. The heritage discourse has been particularly influential in India, appropriated by the government, nationalist discourse and bodies such as the Crafts Council of India or INTACH (Indian National Trust for Art and Cultural Heritage).
5. Traditionally gold and silver embroidery from India, Pakistan and Persia, which prospered during the rule of the Mughal Emperor Akhbar and today is largely popular in northern India, especially produced in Lucknow, Delhi, Chandigarh, Farrukhabad and Chennai.

6. Indian copyright law protects the individual creativity of the fashion designers, who, after the case filed by Tarun Tahiliani in 2010, have been officially recognized as 'artists', thus liable to protection of their *intellectual* property. On the other hand, the only act that protects the craft producers is the Geographical Indications of Goods (GI) act indicating the origin of the product, assuring its quality and distinctiveness, defined by geographical locality, region or country.

7. Ritu Kumar (*1944) is a renowned Indian fashion designer and one of the first in the country, known for her work with craft communities and for designing attires for the Miss India competitors; she was awarded the Padma Shri award, the fourth highest civilian award by the Republic of India, in 2013.

8. Excerpt from an interview with a Delhi-based designer, 12 November 2010.

9. Statement by a nouveau riche businessman from New Delhi, 3 November 2011.

10. Famous Indian fashion designer, who in 1987 opened Ensemble, India's first fashion boutique.

11. Press release: Tarun Tahiliani Bridal Couture Exposition 2011, 'Artisanal: Bringing the Craft to the Fore' (my emphasis).

12. Reconstructed from field notes, 7 June 2011, translated from Hindi.

13. Reconstructed from field notes, 22 August 2011, translated from Hindi.

14. Conversation between myself, Namrita and her embroiderers, who are commonly referred to by her as 'my girls', 18 May 2011, translated from Hindi.

References

Balaram, S. 2005. 'Design Pedagogy in India: A Perspective', *Design Issues* 21(4): 11–22.

———. 2011. *Thinking Design*. New Delhi: SAGE.

Barth, F. 1969. *Ethnic Groups and Boundaries: The Social Organization of Cultural Difference*. Bergen: Universitetsforlaget.

Barthes, R. 1983. *The Fashion System*. New York: Hill.

Bhachu, P. 2004. *Dangerous Designs: Asian Women Fashion the Diaspora Economies*. New York: Routledge.

Bourdieu, P. 1977. *Outline of a Theory of Practice*. Cambridge: Cambridge University Press.

———. 1984. *Distinction: A Social Critique of the Judgement of Taste*. London: Routledge & Kegan Paul.

———. 1996. *The Rules of Art: Genesis and Structure of the Literary Field*. Stanford: Stanford University Press.

Clark, G. 2010. 'How Envy Killed the Crafts', in G. Adamson (ed.), *The Craft Reader*. Oxford: Berg.

Cohen, A. 1981. *The Politics of Elite Culture: Exploration in the Dramaturgy of Power in a Modern African Society*. Berkeley: University of California Press.

Coomarswamy, A. K. 1966. *Introduction to Indian Art*. Delhi: Munshiram Manoharlal.

Crafts Council, D. 2007. 'Reviving the embroidered art of Chamba Rumal', *Craft Revival Quarterly*, June.

De Neve, G. 2012. 'Fordism, flexible specialisation and CSR: How Indian garment workers critique neoliberal labour regimes', *Ethnography* (22 November): 1–24.

DeNicola, A. O. 2004. 'Creating Borders, Maintaining Boundaries: Traditional Work and Global Markets in Bagru's Handblock Textile Industry', PhD dissertation, Syracuse University.

Dhulia, T. 2011. 'Saheb, Biwi aur Gangster', 143 min. India.

Fabian, J. 1983. *Time and the Other: How Anthropology Makes its Object.* New York: Columbia University Press.

Fisk, P. 2011. *Creative Genius.* London: John Wiley & Sons.

Girard, R. 1990. 'Innovation and Repetition', *SubStance*, 19(2/3): 7–20.

Goffman, E. 1951. 'Symbols of Class Status', *The British Journal of Sociology* 2(4): 294–304.

Graeber, D. 2001. *Toward an Anthropological Theory of Value: The False Coin of our Own Dreams.* New York: Palgrave.

Hall, S. 1999. 'Whose Heritage? Un-settling "the heritage", re-imagining the post-nation', *Third Text* 13(49): 3–13.

Hallam, E., and T. Ingold (eds). 2007. *Creativity and Cultural Improvisation.* Oxford: Berg.

Howes, D. 2003. *Sensual Relations: Engaging the Senses in Culture and Social Theory.* Ann Arbor: University of Michigan Press.

Ingold, T. 2000. *The Perception of the Environment: Essays in Livelihood, Dwelling and Skills.* London: Routledge.

———. 2001. 'Beyond Art and Technology: The Anthropology of Skill', In M. B. Schiffer (ed.), *Anthropological Perspectives on Technology.* Albuquerque: University of New Mexico Press, 17–31.

Kaviraj, S. 1998. 'The Culture of Representative Democracy', in P. Chatterjee (ed.), *Wages of Freedom: Fifty Years of the Indian Nation State.* New Delhi: Oxford University Press, India, 147–179.

Keane, W. 2005. 'Signs are Not the Garb of Meaning: On the Social Analysis of Material Things', in D. Miller (ed.), *Materiality.* Durham: Duke University Press, 182–205.

Kumar, R., and C. Muscat. 2006. *Costumes and Textiles of Royal India.* New Delhi: Antique Collectors' Club.

Lees-Maffei, G., and L. Sandino. 2004. 'Dangerous Liasons: Relationships Between Design, Craft and Art', *Journal of Design History* 17(3): 207–219.

Liep, J. 2001. *Locating Cultural Creativity.* London: Pluto Press.

Markowitz, S. J. 1994. 'The Distinction Between Art and Craft', *Journal of Aesthetic Education* 28(1): 55–70.

Mazzarella, W. 2003. '"Very Bombay": Contending with the Global in an Indian Advertising Agency', *Cultural Anthropology* 18(1): 33–71.

Muller, F. 2000. *Art and Fashion.* London: Thames & Hudson.

Nietzsche, F., et al. 2001. *Nietzsche: The Gay Science: With a Prelude in German Rhymes and an Appendix of Songs.* Cambridge: Cambridge University Press.

Niranjan, T., P. Sudhir and V. Dhareshwar. 1993. *Interrogating Modernity: Culture and Colonialism in India.* Calcutta: Seagull Press.

Organ, T. 1975. 'Indian Aesthetics: Its Techniques and Assumptions', *Journal of Aesthetic Education* 9(1): 11–27.

Panofsky, E. 1976. *Gothic Architecture and Scholasticism*. New York: New American Library.

Pinney, C. 2002. 'Visual Culture', in V. Buchli (ed.), *The Material Culture Reader*. Oxford: Berg, 81–87.

Pollock, S. 2001. 'New Intellectuals in Seventeenth-century India', *The Indian Economic and Social History Review* 38(1): 3–31.

Poornalingam, S. R. 2009. 'Secretary (Textiles)', in A. Ranjan and M. P. Ranjan (eds), *Handmade in India: A Geographic Encyclopedia of Indian Handicrafts*. New York: Abbeville Press, 15.

Radford, R. 1998. 'Dangerous Liasons: Art, Fashion and Individualism', *Fashion Theory* 2(2): 151–164.

Rampley, M. 1998. 'Creativity', *British Journal of Aesthetics* 38(3): 265–278.

Rowlands, M. 2002. 'Heritage and Cultural Property', in V. Buchli (ed.), *The Material Culture Reader*. Oxford: Berg, 105–115.

Schumpeter, J. A. 1934. *The Theory of Economic Development: an Inquiry into Profits, Capital, Credit, Interest, and the Business Cycle*. Piscataway: Transaction Publishers.

Sengupta, H. 2009. *Ramp Up: The Business of Indian Fashion*. New Delhi: Dorling Kindersley (India) Pvt. Ltd.

Shapiro, R. 2004. 'The Aesthetic of Institutionalization: Breakdancing in France', *Journal of Arts, Managment, Law and Society* 33(4): 316–335.

Shapiro, R., and N. Heinich. 2012. 'When is Artification?' *Contemporary Aesthetics* 10: 1–20.

Simmel, G. 1957. 'Fashion', *American Journal of Sociology* 62(6): 541–558.

Singh, M. 2009. 'Prime Minister', in A. Ranjan and M. P. Ranjan (eds), *Handmade in India: A Geographic Encyclopedia of Indian Handicrafts*. New York: Abbeville Press, 13.

Svašek, M. 2009. 'Improvising in a World of Movement: Transit, Transition and Transformation', in H. K. Anheier and Y. R. Isar (eds), *Cultural Expression, Creativity and Innovation*. London: Sage.

Tambiah, S. J. 1968. 'The Magical Power of Words', *Man* 3(2): 175–208.

Tarlo, E. 1996. *Clothing Matters: Dress and Identity in India*. London: Hurst & Company.

Taylor, M. 2005. 'Culture Transition: Fashion's Cultural Dialogue between Commerce and Art', *Fashion Theory* 9(4): 445–460.

Tharoor, S. 2009. 'How India Avoided Turning Inward', *Newsweek Magazine, 29 December*.

UNESCO, Craft Revival Trust and Artesanias de Colombia S. A. 2005. 'Designers Meet Artisans'. New Delhi: UNESCO.

Venkatesan, S. 2009. *Craft Matters: Artisans, Development and the Indian Nation*. New Delhi: Orient Blackswan.

Wilson, E. 2007. 'A Note on Glamour', *Fashion Theory* 11(1): 95–108.

Žižek, S. 2009. *First as Tragedy, Then as Farce*. London: Verso.

3

THE SOCIAL LIFE OF *KOTTAN* BASKETS
CRAFT PRODUCTION, CONSUMPTION AND
CIRCULATION IN TAMIL NADU, INDIA

Kala Shreen

It was the afternoon of October 8, 2012. Clad in a magenta and yellow sari and surrounded by reproductions of naturally dyed palymra baskets which were winners of the 'UNESCO Seal of Excellence', Manimekalai, a kottan basket weaver from a village in central Tamil Nadu, India, was seated in a booth in a corridor at the ITC Grand Chola, a prestigious venue in Chennai. She was invited to participate in the event titled 'Living Legends'. This program was a confluence of eighteen master craftspeople from around the globe gathered to demonstrate their skill and display their masterpieces and signature crafts. This event was part of the World Crafts Summit organized by the World Crafts Council. Other expositions within the World Crafts Summit included a kottan exhibition in a gallery elsewhere in Chennai city where, again, Manimekalai provided a live demonstration of basket weaving. I was commissioned by Ms. Usha Krishna, President of the World Crafts Council to document the events at the World Crafts Summit, where I observed and interviewed Manimekalai. She shared with me stories about how kottan weaving had transformed her from a diffident yokel into a strong, confident woman. She proudly narrated her travels to many foreign countries for her weaving demonstrations. She spoke with excitement about the enthusiastic reception and successful sale of kottan baskets abroad. The kottan booth was thronged by visitors who were enthralled by the intricate weaving technique and I sensed Manimekalai's elation from her laughter in response to the compliments she constantly received. The stall was often visited and monitored by Ms. Visalakshi Ramaswamy, the founder of M Rm Rm Foundation, which was responsible for reviving kottan weaving. Ms. Ramaswamy opined that Ms. Usha

Krishna was keen and happy to include the kottan weaver in the 'Living Legends' program and had been a great supporter of kottan production with her generous patronage. The proof of her patronage was in the hands of every delegate at the summit in the form of kottan delegate kits which innovatively combined jute and kottan weaves.

That evening, on my way home, I had to run an errand for the celebration of the 80th birthday of my father-in-law, the following week. I was asked to purchase miniature silver kottan vermillion holders to be given as mementos to his cousins and nieces from the USA, Canada and the UK, who were expected to attend the ceremony. Therefore I went to Sukra, a silverware store where I could choose from the mass produced silver kottans stacked up in various sizes and weights.

The above passage provides a glimpse of cultural production in contemporary Tamil Nadu through one type of artefact, the *kottan,* a basket from Chettinad, a conglomeration of villages in central Tamil Nadu in South India. I seek to trace the trajectory of this craft by investigating the dynamic ways in which the baskets have been produced, consumed, appropriated and circulated. The chapter will demonstrate that the social life of *kottan* has been influenced by myriad factors. It will explore how the production and use of *kottan* has responded to the demands of a changing consumer base including urban elites, international buyers and Indian diasporic groups including Chettiars, and how *kottan* production has been made to fit the agenda of specific craft organizations. What was originally a basket has seen many different forms and uses.

I will draw on several approaches to material artefacts that have focused on the movement of objects and images through space and time, including the notions of 'social life' (Appadurai 1986), 'cultural biography' (Kopytoff 1986; Hoskins 1998) and 'life cycle' (Bijker 1992). Richard Davis (1997: 7), using a biographical approach, has referred to the recontextualizations and new meanings assigned to objects as 'shifts in mode of life' (see also Sharman 2004: 346). In Prasad Boradkar's perspective, 'meanings emerge and change continuously as people and things travel through their lives, constantly bumping into each other' (2010: 1).

John Liep (1988) and Elizabeth Hallam and Tim Ingold (2007) have taken different approaches to creativity that are helpful in understanding the social life of *kottans.* On the one hand, Liep (1988: 2) has defined creativity as 'activity that produces something new through the recombination and transformation of existing cultural practices and forms. The term innovation I regard as more or less synonymous with creativity.' By contrast, Ingold and Hallam (2007: 10) have emphasized that creativity is not just innovativeness of end results but the 'improvisations that went into the processes of producing them'. Attacking the idea that creativity would always lead to radical innovation, they have argued that 'there is creativity even and especially in the maintenance of an established tradition' (ibid.: 5). As social and cultural worlds, in other words, are always in the making – in process and never complete – they relate creativity to the ability to be responsive to changing conditions. Though Liep's (1988) notion of creativity overemphasizes innovation and novelty, I share his interest in the recombination and transformation of existing practices and forms to create innovative practices and products. And while I agree with Hallam and Ingold (2007) that innovation is not a condition of creativity, in this chapter I am mainly interested in understanding how and why innovative designs, products and uses come about.

To understand the mobility of the *kottan* across geographical boundaries and sociocultural contexts, their changing meanings and values and the correlated production of different subjectivities, I employ the terms, 'transit', 'transition' and 'transformation' (Svašek 2007, 2012). Svašek defines 'transit' as the movement of things and people across time and space, and 'transition' as transit-related changes in terms of artefacts' meanings, value and agency. This focus proves useful when analysing the social life of things. The concept of 'transformation', referring to changes in human subjects in terms of their social status, identity formation and emotional subjectivity, gives an additional perspective on the ways in which different producers and users of innovative *kottan* items have situated themselves in specific social and political settings.

Kottan Production and Appropriation

Kottan artifacts, traditionally made by weaving palm leaves, have seen many changes. *Kottan* was primarily used by the Chettiars for the gift-giving ritual during life cycle ceremonies and for storage purposes. Chettiars are a merchant-banking community native to the villages of Chettinad and have migrated to neighbouring cities such as Chennai as well as to other countries. During a period of increasing affluence among Chettiars between 1860 and 1930, the items were also produced in silver (Rudner 1994; Hardgrove 2002). As Chettiar women placed customized orders with the silversmiths of Madras (now Chennai), the Chettiar baskets appeared with a facelift: their woven patterns effectively reproduced in the shiny metal. The craftspeople appropriated the existing palm leaf weaving patterns, translating them through the use of a radically different technology. Given the prestige associated with pure silverware, these silver versions of *kottan* became a status symbol and reflection of wealth that attracted new customer groups. Made by urban silversmiths who displayed the silver baskets alongside other products in their retail showrooms, non-Chettiar consumers were also attracted by this novel item. A silverware retailer in central Chennai pointed out in 2012 that the aesthetic attributes of the basket that attracted these new customer groups were their intricate workmanship, the lustre of the pure polished silver and the durability of the material.

These silver baskets were replicated in various sizes to suit various ranges of affordability (fig. 3.1) and sold widely. While, among the Chettiars, they were used predominantly during gift-giving rituals in rites of passage, such as marriages and pre-puberty ceremonies, among non-Chettiars they were appropriated as flower baskets that were displayed on the welcoming table of weddings.

In its transit from the silver shop to Chettiar ritual spaces and non-Chettiar ceremonial contexts, the mass-produced commodities were individualized and gained new meanings and uses. In the Chettiar ritual context, the silver *kottan* became a ritual object of gift-giving that embodied kin relationships between givers and receivers. In non-Chettiar ceremonial contexts, the silver *kottan* was appropriated as a beautiful ornamental object with a visual appeal, not bearing the same kind of ritual significance as in the Chettiar rituals. Among some non-Chettiars and Chettiar migrants in Canada, the baskets have also been recontextualized as curio items displayed in people's living rooms. As an avid collector of ethnic objects in Canada explained: 'In my living room, I have a Nubian bow and arrow, a silver *kottan,* a musical instrument used during festivals in Kerala.... These objects become conversation pieces during parties, where my family and friends talk

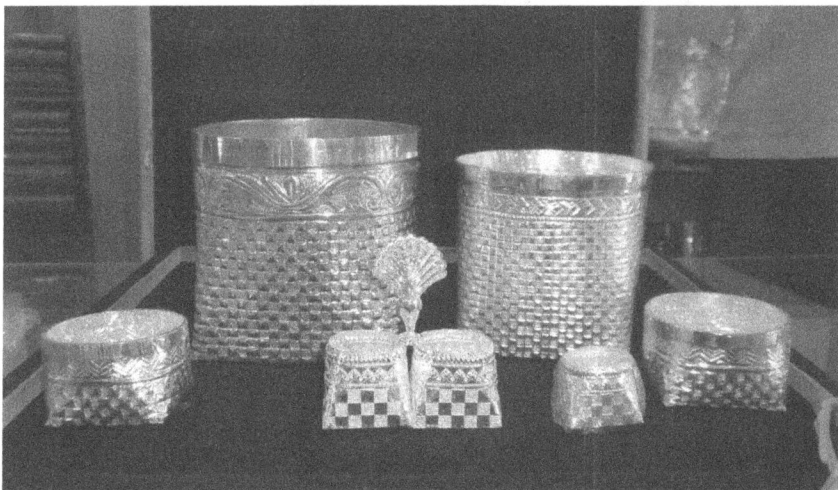

Figure. 3.1. *Kottan*s reproduced in silver in different sizes at the showroom of a silverware retailer in central Chennai. Photo: Kala Shreen.

about our cultural practices of the olden days, our travels.' A Chettiar lady in Canada, who displayed silver *kottan*s in her curio cabinet in the living room, alongside an antique painting by a renowned Indian artist, said: 'I would never display this in my house in India. It is very common there. Here people appreciate it because they would not have seen something like this. It is also one way for me to show them something about my country, my culture and where I come from.'

These words show that in its movement from India to diasporic settings outside the subcontinent, the Chettinad basket has been appropriated in new ways, gaining different functions. As curio objects they have been presented along with other 'ethnic' items on display, aiming to evoke stories about cultural difference and diversity. Chettiar migrants have also projected identities as diasporic 'Indians' and 'Chettiars' through *kottan* display.

The silver baskets also gained new meanings and functions when turned into the innovative product of turmeric and vermillion holders. The manufacturers incorporated new design elements, fusing two or more small-sized silver *kottan*s and embellishing them with a silver peacock motif (fig. 3.2). In India, this object is primarily used to offer turmeric and vermillion to visitors, particularly married Hindu women, on their departure. This practice is common among many South Indian Hindu women in India and abroad. In addition to this use, the item has become a collectible, a gift article and a

Figure 3.2. *Kottan*s reproduced as innovative turmeric and vermillion holders at a Chennai-based silverware retailer. Photo: Kala Shreen.

souvenir among Chettiars and non-Chettiars. As outlined at the start of this chapter, during eightieth-birthday celebrations in a Brahmin family, these silver turmeric and vermillion holders were given as mementos to relatives and friends from India and overseas who attended the ceremony. In this case, the mass-produced turmeric and vermillion holder became a memento that intended to carry with it the gratitude and blessings of the elderly host. It also functioned as a material reminder of participation in the family ceremony.

When these objects are given as presents or souvenirs to non-Indians, they also sometimes gain new pragmatic uses. A Chettiar woman in Canada said that she had 'gifted one such holder to my (Canadian) colleague at work. She has found a new use for it. She puts paper clips in one holder and board pins in another.' Silver *kottan*s, then, have traversed various geographical and social spaces. They have been moved across state boundaries, and have journeyed from the silver shops of Tamil Nadu to various sociocultural contexts, including Chettiar ritual spaces, living rooms of diasporic Chettiars, reception areas of non-Chettiar ceremonies and even to the office desks of foreigners. Thus, in its mobility across varied contexts, the *kottan* has made a transition from being a mass-produced object intended to generate profit for a retailer to becoming a ritual object, an ornamental object, an ethnic object, a curio item, a memento, a souvenir and even an everyday utilitarian item such as a stationery holder. In the next section, I will turn my attention to the appropriation of *kottan* by organizations that promote the production of indigenous craft.

Craft Organizations and Heritage Politics

As craft organizations in Tamil Nadu and key members of these organizations have spearheaded and propelled many initiatives with respect to palm leaf *kottan*s, a brief background on the propagation of crafts in Tamil Nadu is necessary. The Indian Crafts Movement began in conjunction with Mahatma Gandhi's glorification of Indian villages and his advocacy of handspun cotton cloth (see Kuldova, this volume). A key mover was Kamaladevi Chattopadhyay, a freedom fighter and social reformer. After India's independence, the new Government of India set up the All India Handicraft Board in 1952 under Kamaladevi Chattopadhyay, whose primary agenda was the identification and development of crafts. Subsequently, the Crafts Council of India was set up in Tamil Nadu under the aegis of Kamaladevi Chattopadhyay, one of its aims being to implement this governmental vision. The importance of crafts has also been stressed in many state and regional policy documents. The Eighth Five Year Plan 1992–1997 states, 'handicrafts are not only a part of the country's rich cultural heritage but have also been a unifying factor in the national life' (Greenough 1995).

Heritage, however, has to be made, constructed or framed. According to David Whisnant (1983), cultural institutions have shaped the image of the folklife of indigenous people in the southern Appalachians for public presentation. Marleen de Witte and Birgit Meyer (2012: 45) also argue that 'heritage is intrinsically mediated. It does not exist outside particular media forms (museums, monuments, written and illustrated canons, TV programmes, websites et cetera).' In the case of the *kottan,* local print media such as *The Hindu,* which in 2012 carried an article on the *kottan* titled 'Heritage Hues', and museums such as Dakshinachitra, have framed the artifact as heritage.

Dakshinachitra, a heritage museum, was created in 1998 by Madras Craft Foundation, and is a Chennai-based non-profit organization actively involved in the revival and perpetuation of lost traditions and vanishing crafts (see Desai, this volume). Dakshinachitra displays several South Indian crafts including those from Chettinad. It also projects the *kottan* as a hand-icraft, produced by traditional weaving skills that are now endangered. As Dakshinachitra works to promote South Indian arts, crafts and architecture; it has played an important role in positioning the *kottan* not only as representative of Chettiar heritage but also as part of Tamil Nadu's cultural heritage. Hence, *kottan*s are utilized to construct and present the image of contemporary Tamil Nadu. Thus, 'while it looks old, heritage is actually something new. Heritage is a mode of cultural production in the present that has recourse to the past' (Kirshenblatt-Gimblett 1998: 7).

Sowmhya Venkatesan (2009) argues that individuals hailing from elite business families play a crucial role in craft propagation and advocacy. Similarly, the (re)construction of *kottan* as a worthy craft is driven by influential members of society. Ms. Usha Krishna, a business entrepreneur, long-standing member of the Crafts Council of India and the first Indian president of the World Crafts Council (2008–2012), has played a leading role in devising the participation of the *kottan,* alongside other Indian and international crafts, in the international forum of the World Crafts Summit held in Chennai in October 2012. Ms. Visalakshi Ramaswamy, the proprietor of M.Rm. Rm. Foundation, which works to promote Chettinad crafts, architecture and textiles, is also an active member of the Madras Craft Foundation and Crafts Council of India. She plays an active role in the production of palm *kottan* baskets. She has also engaged with international cultural organizations such as UNESCO by participating in their competitions and with the World Crafts Council by curating a *kottan* exhibition and by accepting an invitation from Ms. Usha Krishna to have a skilled weaver from her foundation participate in the World Crafts Summit. Ms. Usha Krishna, Ms.

Visalakshi Ramaswamy and other key members of these craft organizations thus play a significant role in shaping *kottan* production and consumption. Taking Whisnant's (1983: 260) approach to cultural production, they can be called 'cultural intervenors' who 'by virtue of [their] status, power and established credibility, [are] frequently able to define what the culture is, to normalize and legitimize that definition in the larger society, and even to feed it back into the culture itself'.

Kottan and the UNESCO Award

A significant event that left a deep imprint in the *kottan*'s biography was when some products won UNESCO's Seal of Excellence award[1] in the years 2004 and 2006, as well as in select subsequent years. Ms. Ramaswamy, the producer of the *kottan* items, followed the prerequisite conditions and evaluation criteria[2] set by UNESCO in order to enter the competition and increase the probability of winning it. An example of such an award-winning *kottan* is discussed in the next section in connection with its consumption. Due to the positive evaluation by UNESCO, *kottan* products were propelled to a wider circulation through international exhibitions, fairs and markets and gained prestige and appeal both in India and abroad.

When I asked Ms. Ramasamy about what such international awards mean to her *kottan*-revival initiative, she claimed that this international recognition has helped them participate in international events and attracted wider visibility through local media publicity. As Indian products that win international awards evoke a keen interest with the media, several leading Chennai newspapers, including the *Times of India* and *The Hindu* have carried articles and photographs of the *kottan*s and details about the awards won by them.

Following the receipt of the UNESCO award, Manimekalai, one of the skilled weavers of the M.Rm.Rm Foundation, residing in a village in Chettinad, was selected to perform weaving demonstrations abroad and participate in national and international exhibitions. Consequently, she travelled to Scotland, Japan, New Mexico, the United States and New Delhi. Manimekalai said that the international travel greatly helped the *kottan*s in entering international markets. When I asked Manimekalai about what *kottan* weaving means to her, with excitement gleaming in her eyes, she said:

> *Kottan* has changed my life in so many ways. More than anything, I now possess a renewed social status and am respected in my village as I (*suyam*) am an economically independent woman. If I want to buy something that I like, I (*suyam*) can do it on my own. I am not dependent on my husband to buy it for me. I have heard people talking about women's freedom countless number of times. But now

I truly understand what that means and am able to experience and enjoy that feeling. I feel an enormous amount of self-respect (*suyam mariyathai*).... I come from a social background where as a woman I was never allowed to go out and experience the world. I was always cooped up at home doing household chores and always dependent on my husband. ... I had never gone outside my village before becoming a *kottan* weaver. The first time I stepped outside my village it was to go to Scotland; all because of *kottan*! Imagine that feeling.... I feel so proud that I was also involved in the making of an award-winning product. Today it has instilled in me the courage to go out into the world and face new experiences without inhibition.

Throughout our conversations, Manimekalai used the Tamil word *suyam* (meaning self), many times, indicating the development of a very strong sense of self. This relates to Janet Hoskin's (1998: 2) argument that an object can be 'used as a vehicle for a sense of selfhood'. It can also become a tool for autobiographical elaboration and a way of constructing oneself through things (ibid.). *Kottan* also became a powerful agent (Gell: 1998) in (re)constructing Manimekalai's social identity as a confident independent woman and evoking feelings of 'self-respect', 'pride', 'courage' and 'confidence'. This transformation of Manimekalai occured in tandem with the increased prestige of *kottan* and kottan producers across national and international forums.

Kottan Consumerism and Virtual Retailers

The receipt of the UNESCO award also widened the local consumer market of palm *kottan* products as they were now sold by boutiques and multinational retailers in Chennai. One such award-winning product showed an innovative use of different materials and design elements. The manufacturer combined the conventional material of palm leaves and the traditional weaving patterns with other materials such as a silk fabric, drawstring and beads to create a new type of bag. Non-Chettiars appropriated these items as gift and candy boxes for use in marriages and festivals such as *Deepavali*. Reproductions of the award-winning product, dyed with much cheaper brightly coloured chemical dyes, became a favourite choice among many consumers (fig. 3.3). In one of the exhibition events hosted by the M.Rm. Rm. Foundation in 2012, this colourful *kottan* was given as a return gift for guests. I attended the marriage ceremony of a Brahmin family in 2011 where this *kottan* was used as a *thamboola pai* (a bag containing fruits, betel leaves and nuts to be given for all the attendees according to ceremonial protocol). In a virtual shop called Moon River Store, the product is advertised as 'a candy pouch' ideal for carrying 'small goodies'. Thus, new uses

Figure 3.3. Reproduction of an award-winning *kottan* in brightly coloured chemical dyes. Photo: Kala Shreen.

and functions have been instigated, sometimes by the producer, sometimes by a consumer with a novel idea and sometimes by a retailer's advertising strategy intended to maximize the *kottan*'s utility potential.

To further elaborate on its wider circulation, an interesting turn in the journey of the *kottan* is its sale by Mahika, a virtual store run by a UK-based retailer. Mahika, 'a marketplace for unique designers' as it is called by its proprietors, has as its objective the search for new and unique talent in India and elsewhere. In their efforts to scout for interesting crafts in India, they visited the *kottan* production sites in Chettinad and subsequently its retail outlet in Chennai. Pleased with the products, M.Rm.Rm. Foundation has consequently become one of the virtual store's 'featured designers', and a range of *kottan* baskets can be bought through their website. As Mahika also presents its designers' products at exhibitions and market stalls across London, the *kottan*s have found a space in a stall in the London Hampstead Summer Festival and in Mahika's pop-up store in the O2 shopping mall in London.

The Mahika website markets the *kottan* with colourful, staged photographs. The salesperson in the *kottan* retail outlet in Chennai told me: 'They have taken such beautiful pictures of our baskets. It is interesting to see what they are calling our products. They are presenting some of them as picnic baskets, maybe, because picnics are more prevalent in the West; something we never thought of. I think that was a nice name for our product.' The photographs in the Summer 2012 collection presented the *kottan* as a functional object suitable for outdoor and indoor environments and for multiple purposes. One image shows a child storing her toys, games and books in this basket. In another image, a woman is shown pulling out a towel from the basket, suggesting that it could be used as a laundry basket. Yet another image shows the basket filled with bread, fruits and drinks, placed in lush green grass, indicating its suitability as a picnic basket.

Promotional materials utilized by Mahika (2012) and the Moon River Store (2012) highlight certain features of *kottan* production and thereby exoticize the product, as exemplified in the discourses below:

> Their range has come all the way from Chettinad, a town in south India, famous for its baskets or '*Koodais*'.
>
> *Kottan* baskets are traditional hand-woven baskets made in the south of India. The craft is extinct except for certain organizations working to preserve it.
>
> Palm leaves are dried and cut into thin strips. These are then dyed in brilliant colours and dried again. The strips are used to weave the base of the basket, and gradually worked upwards. They are woven with wet hands and the base is tightly gripped with the feet, even as the palm strips are frequently moistened to prevent them from breaking.
>
> *Kottan* products were awarded the UNESCO Seal of Excellence for Handicrafts in 2004.

Scholars have analysed the process of exoticization in various contexts and noted that it plays on a curiosity or fascination with things seen as strange and different, indigenous, from a remote place or a distant era (Santaolalla 2000; Nandan 2000). The *kottan* is projected as something from a remote village in the south of India and as something that utilizes a traditional skill, enabling it to be projected back in time, rendering it authentically exotic. Exoticization may be seen as closely linked to Orientalism. Edward Said (1978: 1) argues that the Orient seems to be a 'European invention and had been since antiquity a place of romance, exotic beings, haunting memories and landscapes, remarkable experiences'. The retailers also establish the 'indigeneity' of the product by incorporating the word *koodais*: a transliteration of the Tamil word used by natives of the production region.

The promotional materials draw attention to the fact that *kottan* weaving is labour intensive and requires technical excellence, while also projecting the *kottan* as a cultural product on the brink of extinction, implying a uniqueness and rarity value. Thus, the transition of the *kottan* into an exotic object is evident in its movement into the global retail market. The sale of languishing crafts produced by struggling artisans under strenuous working conditions in a developing nation also enhance the social image of the business house and transform them into socially responsible entrepreneurs who are not guided solely by a profit-making motive. The UNESCO award, a highly valued promotional tool outside the United States (Timothy and Boyd 2006), is also included in this promotion of *kottan*.

Recontextualisation of *Kottan*: Craft as Art

In the historical discourses relating to craft/artisan versus art/artist, craft is portrayed as a mindless material reproduction and the craftsperson as a skilled manual labourer, while art pieces are considered as unique products of creative ingenuity and the artist as a creative genius (Becker 1982; Svašek 2007). This perceived superiority of art over craft was reaffirmed by the statements of a well-established painter in Chennai, in response to my discussions with him about crafts. He said, 'Crafts are nothing like the artistic work of paintings. Every work of mine is a creation. Every work is original. Craft is just mere repetition. A craftsman is not creating anything. He is just repeating something again and again.'

The primary agenda of the organizing committee of the World Crafts Summit (also called *Kaivalam*) was to dispel this existing hierarchy of knowledge systems. Ms. Usha Krishna, president of the World Crafts Council (2008–2012), asserted:

> The aim of this event is to reinforce the importance of crafts in our society and culture. Why should crafts take a back seat to other forms of art such as paintings, sculptures, music, dance and films? Crafts are also works of art. Therefore at the summit I wanted to bring about a conglomeration of the best crafts from around the world. I also feel that craftspeople should be given the same kind of respect and social status that fine artists are given.

The effort of Ms. Usha Krishna and her team reinforces Judy Attfield's (2000) arguments regarding the work pursued by crafts organizations. She contends that organizations that work with crafts, such as governmental ministries or non-government organizations such as crafts councils, 'preserve ancient craft techniques while at the same time develop a contemporary aesthetic and a critical language with which to evaluate it on equal terms with fine art' (ibid.: 66). In the case of the World Crafts Summit, this struggle for an elevated status for crafts was apparent in the events such as those labelled by the coordinator, 'interdisciplinary art-craft exhibitions' and in the 'Living Legends' program in which the *kottan* and its weaver were revaluated in equal standing with 'art' and an 'artist'.

The organizers of the summit created an interface between art and craft in the art-craft exhibitions series, which was a synthesis of works of art and crafts at various art galleries in the city of Chennai. A range of crafts, including embroidered textiles, puppets, furniture and home accessories, moved into the art space in local art galleries. The concept of 'art by appropriation' was used by Shelley Errington (1998) in reference to objects that were produced for a different objective but was given the status of art. At the *kot-*

tan exhibition held in conjunction with this art-craft exhibition series, the curator appropriated the baskets into a visual display for public consumption. These baskets, which were made for ritual and storage purposes, were recontextualized into artistic objects. At this exhibition, the baskets were mounted on display pedestals and illuminated; *kottan* weaves were glass-framed and hung on the wall (fig. 3.4); the exhibits were neatly labelled with the *kottan* taxonomies and pertaining descriptions (fig. 3.5). The art-like display drew some interesting comments from visitors. A non-Chettiar said: 'I have seen many art exhibitions where paintings and sculptures are displayed. This is the first time I am seeing crafts displayed like works of art.' Another spectator remarked: 'I never thought that baskets could qualify to be displayed in the likes of an art exhibition.'

While Barbara Kirshenblatt-Gimblett (1998: 7) discusses how heritage production 'depends on display to give dying economies and dead sites a second life as exhibitions of themselves', the crafts exhibitions held in collaboration with art galleries have provided an additional life for crafts as 'art'. Thus, in its transition from craft to art, the languishing craft of *kottan* was made to downplay its mundane utility and ritual context and was perceived instead in an artistic context, as the above comments of spectators show.

Another instance of the recontextualizing of the *kottan* as a worthy craft was apparent in one of the events called 'Living Legends', which was a con-

Figure 3.4. *Kottan* weaves, glass-framed and hung on the wall at the *kottan* exhibition. Photo: Kala Shreen.

Figure 3.5. *Kottan* exhibits, neatly labelled with taxonomies and pertaining descriptions. Photo: Kala Shreen.

fluence of eighteen master craftspeople from around the globe. This event
was held at ITC Grand Chola, a prestigious venue in Chennai. It included
an exhibition of the participating artisans' masterpieces and signature crafts,
demonstrations of the pertaining craft-making and interactions with the
public through a discussion forum. Manimekalai, the *kottan* weaver from
Chettinad, was one of the artisans chosen to participate as a 'living legend'.
In the accompanying *kottan* exhibition, the *kottan*'s value was enhanced by
being displayed in the prestigious venue of the ITC Grand Chola, a hotel
that symbolizes luxury hospitality for the elites. The *kottan* exhibition was
held in conjunction with an important meeting in the World Crafts Council
calendar, namely the General Assembly, convened every four years. This assembly draws delegates from around the world and therefore the *kottan* had
the potential to impress a wide audience. It was also attributed an important
position in craft history as a work of high aesthetic quality.[3]

Alongside the display of the object at an important place and time, association with prominent individuals also plays a crucial role in assigning
an artefact an elevated aesthetic status. Several socialites of Chennai have
patronized the *kottan* products as recounted by Ms. Ramaswamy. For the
World Crafts Summit itself, Ms. Usha Krishna had ordered several hundred
kottan delegate kits (fig. 6.6) that innovatively combined jute and *kottan*
weaving. This kit is a bag containing details of the activities of the summit
and was therefore given to all delegates and registered participants. Thus as
Venkatesan (2009: 207) reiterates, 'large orders and invitations to exhibitions show the importance of elite patronage' in the identification of crafts
as 'fine crafts' in elite circles in Chennai.

The artisans also appropriated the values of art, applying them to their
crafts in many ways. For example, most of the artisans, during their many
conversations with me and in their public discussion forums at the summit, used the terms 'unique' and 'special' innumerable times in reference to
their crafts, reinforcing the perception of their craft as a work of art and
creative ingenuity rather than the mindless reproductions, as the aforementioned painter had characterized them. Every craftsperson had displayed a
piece designated 'a masterpiece', 'signature piece', 'unique piece', 'something
special' or 'a work of art' that individualized his or her craft and thereby
set them apart from similar crafts or commodities in the consumer market. These craftspeople, therefore, project themselves as 'artist-craftsmen'
(Becker 1982). Most of the artisans participating in the 'Living Legends'
program have individual studios and workshops. This correlates to Roberta
Shapiro and Nathalie Heinich's (2012) reference to individualization of labour while discussing the processes leading to the 'artification' of craft. The
artisans also often collaborated with designers or possessed some sort of a
design-based vocational training. The *kottan* weaver, for example, talked

Figure 3.6. *Kottan* delegate kit at the World Crafts Summit, which innovatively combined jute and *kottan* weaving. Photo: Kala Shreen.

about producing *kottan* jewellery in association with a designer from the National Institute of Design, a renowned design institution in India. Collaboration with noted designers thus renders the *kottan*s fashionable.

At the 'Living Legends' event, Manimekalai's neighbouring artisan was Joe Hogan, an Irish basket weaver who asserts that his baskets are 'art-like' and calls them 'sculpture baskets' or 'artistic baskets'. He opined, 'Because these baskets are done with natural wild materials and as no two pieces of willow or lichen can look the same, there is no way that I can produce two identical baskets. So each one is different and this makes the collectors happy about their purchase.' Manimekalai was seated next to Joe Hogan and the *kottan* products were displayed adjacent to the racks of 'sculpture baskets'. Close to the *kottan* objects was the booth of a *zardosi* master-craftsperson with his masterpieces and award-winning products.[4] The selection of Manimekalai to participate in the same forum as other master-craftspeople and the placement of the *kottan*s alongside the artistic/sculpture baskets and *zardosi* masterpieces assigned the *kottan*s a status akin to that of art.

Another facet in the *kottan* initiative of the M.Rm.Rm. Foundation is that every *kottan* product sold bears the name of its weaver, alongside the price tag and information about the NGO. The purpose of this tag seems to be multifold. The Chennai shop personnel said:

> This tag is for the purpose of quality control. If a product is not up to the mark then we will know exactly the person responsible and will help improve her skills. On the other hand when the product is good, due appreciation and credit also goes to her. Our proprietor will get very upset if she receives an item and does not see the name of the weaver on it. She would like people to know who actually made the product that one buys. It lends a personal touch to the purchase.

In this consumer market, where the artisan is often hidden behind a designer label or brand name, the *kottan* weaver is given equal visibility to the designer and the craft organization and shares the space with them on the product itself. The weaver name tag presents the *kottan* as a unique, individually crafted work of art, thus also presenting a new image of the craftsperson – as an 'individual artist'. This status of the craftsperson as artist clearly inflates the price of the works. Thus Shapiro and Heinich's (2012) reference to individualization of labour in the process of artification can also be extended to understanding the individualization of the *kottan* craft. A visitor's comment further reiterates the artifying of *kottan*. She remarked:

> I like this idea of having the weaver's name on the basket. It is like a painting that bears the artist's name. In fact, I am going to ask her to finish the piece that she is weaving for a demonstration and sell it to me with her name on it. This way I feel like I bought a customized piece that was made just for me.... Then, when I keep it in my house, I can tell people that it was done by a living legend and not just by *some* artisan.... I am very particular about having unique pieces. For example, I possess an original Ravi Varma painting that is very rare.... For special occasions I buy only designer saris because I want to wear something that is one of a kind.

The above statements clearly indicate the transformation of the weaver's identity from an unknown artisan to an individual artist. Manimekalai's participation in the 'Living Legends' event, along with international master-craftspeople claiming art status, has impacted her public image. She is thereby perceived as an esteemed artist who produces something of high aesthetic worth.

Concluding Remarks

In this chapter, I have tried to capture the dynamics of cultural production in Tamil Nadu by tracking the social life of the *kottan*. I have shown that the *kottan* does not have a fixed meaning, status or value in its transit across various geographical and sociocultural contexts. As a result, one can observe the shifting boundaries between various categories from ritual object to curio item, craft-artifact, heritage-piece and artwork. The traditional *kottan,* originally used among the Chettiars in their ritual spaces, storage areas and later in diasporic homes has transgressed the caste[5] boundary and has been commoditized and appropriated by non-Chettiars during different occasions as mementos, gifts and ornate objects. The *kottan* has crossed state borders to reach international consumers to whom it is marketed as an exotic object. The *kottan* has travelled from its production site in a south Indian village to art galleries in the metropolitan city of Chennai and to the international exposition at the summit. During this trajectory, the *kottan* has undergone a transition from craft to 'fine craft' to 'art'.

Another process connected to the transition of the *kottan* is the corresponding change in human subjects and the production of transformed social status and emotional subjectivities. For instance, by displaying *kottan*s in their homes, Chettiar immigrants enact their 'Chettiarness' and 'Indianness' in the transnational context, thereby being transformed into diasporic Chettiars and Indians. In the process of artification at the Crafts Summit, the *kottan* weaver is produced as an 'artist' and working members of the craft organizations are produced as protectors of the *kottan* craft. Retailers of the *kottan*s, sourced from struggling rural women weavers, are perceived as socially responsible business enterprises and their patrons are transformed into conscious consumers.

This chapter also highlights the political aspects in the production and consumption of the *kottan* with respect to their connection with craft organizations, heritage institutions and 'cultural intervenors', including powerful individuals and socialites. The intermingling of local craft producers and people working for local and transnational organizations has impacted the construction and valuation of the *kottan* as cultural heritage and art, rendering it worthy of preservation and perpetuation. Thus the life of the *kottan* reflects the interconnectedness of political and aesthetic dimensions in its production, consumption and circulation.

Kala Shreen is a sociocultural anthropologist and ethnographic filmmaker. She is the chairperson of the Centre for Creativity, Heritage and Development in Chennai, India (www.cchd.in). Her key areas of research are Indian material culture and visual arts such as material Hinduism, traditional artefacts, indigenous crafts, textiles and fashion. On these topics, she has delivered lectures, presented papers and screened her films in several international universities including Harvard University, University of Cambridge and University of Oxford. One of her recent publications is 'Dress and Textiles in Transition: The *Sungudi* Sari Revival of Tamil Nadu, India', in Charlotte Nicklas and Annebella Pollen (eds), *Dress History: New Directions in Theory and Practice,* London: Bloomsbury Academic, 195–208. Along with Maruška Svašek, she is also the director of Cultural Dynamics and Emotions Network (CDEN) at Queen's University Belfast (www.qub .ac.uk/cden/).

Notes

1. The UNESCO Seal of Excellence for Handicrafts was established in 2000 in order to establish quality standards and to enhance international awareness of handicrafts from the ten ASEAN countries. Due to the success of the Award of Excellence programme in Southeast Asia, UNESCO Bangkok was approached in 2003 by the Central Asia Crafts Support Association (CACSA) and the Crafts Council of India (CCI) requesting assistance in replicating the Award programme in West-Central and South Asia respectively. The first evaluation of the entries for South Asia was held in New Delhi in September 2004 with thirty-five products from Bangladesh, Bhutan, India, Maldives, Nepal, Pakistan and Sri Lanka being granted the award. The offices of UNESCO (New Delhi) and Crafts Council of India (CCI) are the coordinators of this award program in India.

2. The evaluation criteria listed in the UNESCO web portal are: (1) Eco-friendly – Respect for the environment in materials and production techniques: Exemplified through the sustainable use of natural dyes, natural fibers, recycled materials and the use of materials and production processes that are environmentally friendly. (2) Fair – Social responsibility: The producer must affirm that no labour law or copyright was violated and no individual or group exploited unfairly at any stage in the production of a handicraft submitted for the Award. (3) Selection Criteria – An international panel of experts, nominated by UNESCO, evaluates submissions and selects products meeting ALL of the following four criteria: (a) Excellent – Demonstrated excellence and standard-setting quality in craftsmanship: determined by the use of high-quality materials, a high standard of technique and the special attention to manufacturing and finishing details. (b) Authentic – Expression of cultural identity and traditional aesthetic values: demonstrated by a well-achieved application of aesthetic and cultural expression or traditional crafting techniques. (c) Innovative – Innovation in design and production: demonstrated by an effective and successful blend of traditional and contemporary, or inventive and creative use of material, design and production processes. (d) Marketable – Marketability of the craft products with potential for the world market: related to the functionality of the product, the safe use by potential buyers, a balanced price-quality relationship or the sustainability of production.

3. Svašek (2012) discusses the correlation between geographic and social mobility. She explains how a painting increases in value and impact when appearing in an important place and at an important time in an exhibition calendar. The

work of art increases in monetary value and is perceived as a work of superior aesthetic quality with an ability to impress particular audiences.

4. *Zardosi* is a traditional Indian art of embroidery.
5. Hindu caste system contains four groups, namely Brahmins, Kshatriyas, Vaishyas and Sudras. Each of these castes further comprises several communities such as the Chettiars who belong to the Vaishyas caste.

References

Appadurai, A. 1986. 'Introduction: Commodities and the Politics of Value', in A. Appadurai (ed.), *The Social Life of Things: Commodities in Cultural Perspective.* Cambridge: Cambridge University Press.

Attfield, J. 2000. *Wild Things: The Material Cultures of Everyday Life.* Oxford: Berg.

Becker, H. 1982. *Art Worlds.* Berkeley: University of California Press.

Bijker, W., and J. Law (eds). 1992. *Shaping Technology/Building Society: Studies in Sociotechnical Change.* Boston: Massachusetts Institute of Technology.

Boradkar, P. 2010. *Designing Things: A Critical Introduction to the Culture of Objects.* Oxford: Berg.

Davis, R. 1997. *Lives of Indian Images.* Princeton: Princeton University Press.

De Witte, M, and B. Meyer. 2012. 'African Heritage Design: Entertainment Media and Visual Aesthetics in Ghana', *Civilisations* 61(1): 43–64.

Errington, S. 1998. *The Death of Authentic Art and Other Tales of Progress.* Berkeley: University of California Press.

Gell, A. 1998. *Art and Agency: A New Anthropological Theory.* Oxford: Oxford University Press.

Greenhough, P. 1995. 'Nation, Economy and Tradition Displayed: The Indian Crafts Museum, New Delhi', in C. A. Breckenridge (ed.), *Consuming Modernity: Public Culture in a South Asian World.* Minneapolis: University of Minnesota Press.

Hallam, E., and T. Ingold. 2007. *Creativity and Cultural Improvisation.* Oxford: Berg.

Hardgrove, A. 2002. 'Merchant Houses as Spectacles of Modernity in Rajasthan and Tamilnadu', *Contributions to Indian Sociology* 36(1–2): 323–364.

Hoskins, J.. 1998. *Biographical Objects: How Things Tell the Stories of People's Lives.* New York and London: Routledge.

Ingold, T., and E. Hallam. 2007. 'Creativity and Cultural Improvisation: An Introduction', in E. Hallam and T. Ingold (eds), *Creativity and Cultural Improvisation.* Oxford: Berg, 1–24.

Kirshenblatt-Gimblett, B. 1998. *Destination Culture: Tourism, Museums and Heritage.* Berkeley: University of California Press.

Kopytoff, I. 1986. 'The Cultural Biography of Things: Commoditization as Process', in A. Appadurai (ed.), *The Social Life of Things: Commodities in Cultural Perspective.* Cambridge: Cambridge University Press.

Liep, J. (ed.). 2001. *Locating Cultural Creativity: London.* Sterling Virginia: Pluto Press.

Mahika 2012. Summer 2012 Collection. www.mahika.co.uk. Accessed May 1, 2013.

Moon River Store. 2012. Kottan Candy Pouch. www.moonriverstore.com. Accessed May 9, 2013.

Nandan, S. 2000. 'The Other Side of Paradise: from Erotica to Exotica to Exile', in I. Santaolalla (ed.), *"New" Exoticisms: Changing Patterns in the Construction of Otherness*. Amsterdam: Rodopi B.V.

Rudner, D. 1994. *Caste and Capitalism in Colonial India: The Nattukottai Chettiars*. New Delhi: Munshiram Manoharlal Publishers, Pvt Ltd.

Said, E. 1978. *Orientalism*. London: Penguin.

Santaolalla, I. (ed.). 2000. *"New" Exoticisms: Changing Patterns in the Construction of Otherness*. Amsterdam: Rodopi B.V.

Shapiro, R., and N. Heinich. 2012. 'When is Artification?' *Contemporary Aesthetics*, special vol. 4. www.contempaesthetics.org/newvolume/pages/journal.php.

Sharman, R. 2004. 'The Invention of Fine Art: Creating a Cultural Elite in a Marginal Community', *Visual Anthropology* 17: 345–367.

Svašek, M. 2007. *Anthropology, Art and Cultural Production*. London: Pluto Press.

———. 2012. 'Affective Moves: Transit, Transition and Transformation', in M. Svašek (ed.), *Moving Subjects, Moving Objects: Transnationalism, Cultural Production and Emotions*. New York and Oxford: Berghahn Books.

Timothy, D. J., and S. Boyd. 2006. 'World Heritage Sites in the Americas', in A. Leask and A. Fyall (eds), *Managing World Heritage Sites*. Oxford: Butterworth Heinemann, 239–249.

Veiteberg, J. 2010. 'Changing Craft', in L. Valentine and G. Follett (eds), *Past, Present and Future Craft Practice*. Somerset: National Museums Scotland and University of Dundee.

Venkatesan, S. 2009. *Craft Matters: Artisans, Development and the Indian Nation*. New Delhi: Orient Blackswan.

Whisnant, D. 1983. *All that is Native and Fine: The Politics of Culture in an American Region*. Chapel Hill and London: University of North Carolina Press.

4

ART AND THE MAKING OF THE CREATIVE CITY OF CHENNAI, INDIA

Amit Desai

In March 2012, strollers along Marina Beach in Chennai, South India, were greeted with the sight of a three-metre tall red pyramid, built on the sand not far from the shore. The sides of the pyramid were decorated with Japanese *torii* and placed underneath the structure was a collection of sandals. *Pyramid,* by Subodh Kerkar was one of four works on the beach and part of the second annual Art Chennai event. According to the artist, *Pyramid* was inspired by the devastation caused by the Indian Ocean tsunami of 2005.

> A day after the tsunami ... I went for a walk on Chapora Beach in Goa. I noticed hundreds of plastic and rubber slippers which were washed ashore by the waves. Though the tsunami did not affect the western coast of India, I could not help thinking that they belonged to the victims of the wave. I collected the slippers and arranged them in a composition on the beach. (Interview in *The Hindu,* 14 March 2012)

In the same interview, the artist discusses his deployment of the ancient Egyptian pyramid design and of the incorporation of the Japanese gateways commonly found at the entrances to Shinto shrines. Through a varied and composite articulation of the ways people and souls are said to leave the world, the installation commemorated not only those who lost their lives on the eastern Indian littoral, but those who died wherever the tsunami hit. It was a piece of art that spoke to local experience but was not identifiably 'national', much like the tsunami itself: it was a 'global' work about a 'global' event.

The brainchild of one of the city's leading industrialists and art collectors, Sanjay Tulsyan, Art Chennai 2012 was conceived in much broader terms than the inaugural festival held a year earlier.[1] In addition to a range of shows in city galleries and seminars by leading artists and critics from all over India and abroad, the organizers of Art Chennai 2012 also attempted to reach an audience that would not ordinarily visit galleries or engage with contemporary art, hence the art on the beach.

Elsewhere in the city, the central atrium of the glitzy Express Avenue Mall played host to several installations, including *Ghost: Transmemoir* by the Kerala-born, London-trained artist Bose Krishnamachari (2006). This work is comprised of two rows of *dabba*s, the steel lunchboxes delivered to office workers and others in Mumbai by the famous *dabbawallah*s.[2] Inside some of these *dabba*s are video interviews with a range of Bombay residents who are asked questions about their city. The films also show footage of everyday Bombay life. As the 'concept note' states,

> *Ghost: Transmemoir* documents the human condition in a city that has been catapulted into the process of modernization and has been catching up quickly with the forces of economic and cultural globalization, urbanization and con-sumerism. It is a picture of a rapidly changing city, one that is adapting to the best of its ability to meet the demands of the global world economy. (Art Chennai catalogue, 415)

The work therefore explores the transformations of the contemporary Indian city through the medium of art. In this chapter, I look at how art such as *Ghost: Transmemoir* is itself involved in changing the imagination of the city of Chennai. In addition to Art Chennai, there are other promi-nent artistic institutions in Chennai. Cholamandal Artists' Village lies about fifteen kilometres to the south of Marina Beach, further along the coast. It was for many years at the heart of the city's contemporary artistic life but has more recently been marginalized as a centre of artistic production. Ten kilometres south of Cholamandal is Dakshinachitra, a popular tourist attraction that showcases South Indian architectural history and art by way of reconstructed dwellings and artisanal workshops.

This chapter explores the ways in which creativity is framed at Art Chen-nai, Cholamandal and Dakshinachitra. It shows, in particular, how notions of creativity transform along with changing understandings of art, time and the politics of urban space, which together support the imagination of Chennai as a 'world-class' city, able to compete for capital with other global cities. Central to this imagination is the production of a 'creative city' able to nurture artists, entrepreneurs and others who make the city more attractive for inward investment. Thus, the chapter approaches 'creativity' as a political concept that is constantly in motion, defining and ordering places, people and the things people produce. As this volume shows, 'creativity' need not necessarily be understood in modernist terms as 'innovation', as privileging the apparent newness of end product over the transformations involved in production. The discussion of art in Chennai through the three sites mentioned above reveals how artistic people and institutions in the city negotiate and reconstitute the many meanings of 'creativity' and 'innovation' in their understandings of art and place.

Art Chennai offers a vision of creativity that aligns closely with that of 'global art', which itself is conducive to supporting the production of a 'creative city' through global connections and the remaking of urban space. This 'global art' seeks to break free from a defined position within conventional 'art history' and thus produces a temporality that is fully and always contemporaneous. Formal innovation in art practice or technique is valued less than the nature of the artist's ethical commitments.

By way of contrast, Cholamandal artists have been less able to participate in this 'global art' because of the importance they place on the mastery of skill and the elaboration of continuities with an Indian artistic past in their current work. As is the case with 'global art', creativity here is not defined solely by innovation. However, and unlike the sites of Art Chennai, Cholamandal is perceived as a place of pastness, marginalized in the production of the 'creative city' of Chennai. The chapter thus explores the ways in which the Cholamandal Artists' Village positions itself in the city and how it has recently begun to change in response to different, powerful ideas about what makes a place 'creative'.

Dakshinachitra is ostensibly a place that re-presents the past of South India. As such, one might expect it to be unable to play a role in presenting Chennai as a 'creative' place. Whereas the artistic production that goes on there articulates creativity in terms of improvisation rather than innovation, the unclear temporalities evoked by the objects presented at the site demonstrate the contemporary-making possibilities of the concept of 'heritage'.

By comparing these three artistic institutions in Chennai, we can better see how varied visions of creative action (which are not exclusive to any one site) work to produce an image of a 'new' city.

Chennai Art

The contemporary Indian art market has seen rapid growth since the turn of the twenty-first century.[3] Those years saw increasing international interest and the founding of the first Indian auction houses, Saffronart and Osian's.

This led to something of an art boom that finally imploded in 2008 as much of the world entered recession and the flow of capital dried up.

While always somewhat marginal to the centres of contemporary art in New Delhi and Mumbai, the Chennai art world was also greatly affected by this expansion of interest, the consequent boom, bust and recovery. New galleries opened to supplement the handful that had existed over the previous twenty years and established artists began selling work at vastly increased prices. The lore of that time has it that students graduating from the Madras Government College of Art with no history of sales would find ready buyers in this seller's market. While few of these buyers were involved in the rapidly expanding software industry, many were members of local and international elites who had been enriched by the liberalization of the Indian economy after 1991. Collectors included industrialists, property developers, construction magnates, architects and foreign senior executives at Renault and the many other global automobile companies located in and around the city. Another important category of collectors comprised visiting migrant South Indians now resident in Europe, North America and Southeast Asia, who could buy contemporary art at much lower prices than one would pay in the West. Indeed, following a series of visits to Chennai, a second-generation Sri Lankan Tamil from Britain established the Noble Sage Gallery in London in 2006, specializing in the work of South Indian artists. After the economic bust, many of the new galleries, especially the Chennai branches of Delhi and Mumbai art houses, shut their doors; and collectors who were left holding art that they could not liquidate were frightened off further developing their collections through new purchases. Since the crash, the situation has recovered somewhat: from 2010 to 2012, several new galleries have been established. Indeed, the inauguration of Art Chennai in 2011 can be read as a sign of renewed confidence among parts of the Chennai art world.

Despite over a decade of considerable activity in the Chennai contemporary art scene, it is fair to say that public understanding of contemporary fine art is minimal. Whereas, in much of the West, the publically funded museum is a central art-world institution, supporting and validating artistic endeavour, public art museums in India are few and far between. The Government Museum in Chennai holds a chaotic, inadequately curated collection of art that runs the gamut from Company paintings of the nineteenth century, to the romanticism of Raja Ravi Varma, to mid-twentieth-century Madras modernism. These are all displayed in one room and from a certain perspective represent 'European-Indian' art. The degraded state of this collection stands in stark contrast to the magnificently housed section devoted to the more solidly Indian medieval Chola and Pallava bronzes.

One long-standing Chennai contemporary art institution is the Cholamandal Artists' Village (see Fig 4.1). Conceived of as a cooperative venture

Figure 4.1. Main museum and gallery building, Cholamandal Artists' Village. Photo: Amit Desai.

and established in 1966, Cholamandal had close associations with the influential 'Madras Movement' of the 1940s and 50s in Indian modern art. Today, the Village consists of a central compound housing a museum of the Madras Movement that doubles as a gallery space for Cholamandal artists. While this building used to be rather modest with a corrugated iron roof, a new one on the same site was opened in 2008, funded in large part by the same Sanjay Tulsyan who organizes Art Chennai. Adjoining the main museum and gallery are now two new smaller galleries, Laburnum and Indigo, together with a sculpture park, residential accommodation for visiting artists and a newly established café. Surrounding the central compound, which is owned by the cooperative, are several lanes where the twenty-odd artists live and for the most part privately own the plots of land on which they have built houses.

The artists at Cholamandal do not produce conceptual or multimedia work such as *Pyramid* or *Ghosts: Transmemoir*. Rather, they work as painters or sculptors (in stone or metal), and the salient distinction they generally use when discussing art is that of abstraction as against figuration. A New York art student who stayed and worked at Cholamandal for several weeks while I was conducting fieldwork told me that she was surprised that the Cholamandal artists introduced themselves to her as 'painters' or 'sculptors' rather than 'artists'. It was their mastery of a medium that marked out their artistic status. From the American student's perspective, this was an unfamiliar way of 'being an artist'. She thus found it very difficult and uncomfortable to answer the questions posed to her in return, regarding the material in which she worked. Such enquiries made little sense to her self-understanding and she felt unable to give a satisfactory answer. As she said to me, 'I don't even feel comfortable saying I'm an artist!' Cholamandal 'artists' never expressed such doubts.

Whereas Mumbai, Delhi and other Indian cities have well-regarded art schools that operate international networks of association in the realm of the new 'global art' (discussed in more detail below), artists in Chennai lack such an institutional focus: the city's Government College of Art is widely dismissed by Chennai artists as a poor shadow of its former prestige; and Cholamandal has hitherto been unable to fill the gap because of its association with 'pastness'. Art Chennai, on the other hand, provides an arena for the production and circulation of 'global art'. In doing so, it projects an alternative vision of 'newness' as an aspect of creativity to that historically produced at Cholamandal. This vision of newness is intimately tied up with the presentation of Chennai as a 'global city' in competition with other cities in the global arena.

Imagining the Indian City

The imagination of the Indian city and the village within the narrative of the nation has been the subject of considerable debate over the past seventy years (see Nandy 2001 for an overview). For the Gandhians, the city was an 'un-Indian' place: real India lay in its villages and it was there that moral order could be properly maintained. By way of contrast, Nehruvian socialists saw rural India as the source of caste and religious divisions, wedded to outdated modes of production, all of which prevented the nation from fully embracing modernity. India's future, they argued, lay in the towns and cities and in massive programmes of industrialization. These tensions existed throughout the post-Independence period and the city embodied all that was wrong with modernity: dirty, decadent and individualistic, disrespectful of tradition and culture. In her study of India's middle class, Christiane Brosius argues that this conversation has fundamentally changed since economic liberalization: now, Indian cities like Delhi, Mumbai and Chennai are regarded as 'bridgeheads of globalisation', attracting global capital that can then be used, in theory, to develop the hinterland (2010: 62–64). This transformation of the place of the city in the nation is inextricably linked with the imagination of the Indian city as 'world-class' (ibid.: 40).

Brosius's exploration of the visual representation of 'world-class', a key buzzword for policymakers and urban planners in the new Indian economy and the means by which Indian cities are seen to achieve global status (ibid.: 47), is instructive for our examination of various materializations in Chennai. Brosius shows how shopping malls and advertisements for new 'luxury' housing developments link pleasure and consumption in innovative ways that produce an 'out-of-this-world' India. Together with gleaming new infrastructure projects such as highways, airports and metro systems, they build an image of Indian city life that elevates it for members of the Indian middle class from that of the 'Third World' to 'World-Class'. The emphasis here is on 'new urban sensations' of order, cleanliness and culture that are presented as spectacle and stage and to which citizens learn to respond appropriately. As she writes: 'New identities in the process of being imagined and shaped require new spaces in (and stages on) which they can be manifested, visualised, converted from imagination into actuality and vice versa' (ibid.: 342).

Art Chennai, Cholamandal Artists' Village and Dakshinachitra contribute to the image of a 'world-class' city for their audiences and participants in Chennai. They do so, however, in ways that offer different configurations of 'creativity', 'newness' and 'time'. These notions of creativity are inflected with particular understandings of political economy. The Nehruvian imagination depended on state investment under centralized Five Year Plans to produce 'newness' and 'creativity' in the city manifested in a 'new India', creative social relations transcending caste or religious affiliation, and transformed patterns of work and production. By way of contrast, innovation and creativity since economic liberalization are imagined by the urban middle class as proper to activity in the private sector, witnessed by the adulation visited on entrepreneurial software gurus and billionaire businessmen.

Art Chennai and the Promotion of the 'World-Class' City

Marina Beach was one of the main public venues for contemporary art display during Art Chennai 2012; the installation *Pyramid* that I described at the start of this chapter was erected and exhibited here. The beach itself is 3.5 kilometres long and abuts the eastern side of Chennai. It is a place where young couples conduct (often secret) romantic assignations, families eat picnics and where middle-aged matrons, concerned about their health, march along the promenade that skirts the beach in doctor-mandated morning and evening walks. The second longest urban beach in the world (after the one at Rio de Janeiro), Marina Beach has in recent years been subject to attempts at 'bourgeoizification' by the state government and middle-class civic organizations.

In her work on the transformations of Marina Beach, Pushpa Arabindoo (2011) shows how the beach, as an aspect of the Chennai urban landscape, has oscillated between and combined in the imagination, a 'public' space, denoting values of cleanliness, order and rationality, and a 'common' space associated with the 'crowd': a site for large gatherings such as processions, bazaars and political rallies. As such, the articulation of what kind of city space the Beach constitutes has never been clear. Since the turn of this century, however, the state government, together with civic organizations, has sought to 'purify' the space in order to enact beautification schemes. The most ambitious proposal was launched in 2003 when the Government of Tamil Nadu signed a Memorandum of Understanding with the Construction Industrial Development Board (CIDB) of Malaysia. With a budget of Rs 1,000 crores (US$250 million), the project proposed 'complexes of international standards to provide office accommodation for multinationals and embassies, and world-class facilities for international tourists'[4] (cited in Arabindoo 2011: 390). This was a clear indication of creating the visual stage for a 'world-class' city in the terms discussed by Brosius. As Arabindoo writes, 'the strength of the "we are going global" signal was obvious, as the state talked confidently about global collaborations, targeting a global community, and the need to create a global architecture' (ibid.). Several prominent civic groups campaigned for the proposals and were met by objections from other groups comprising middle-class environmentalists and fisher-folk that lived on the beach. Resistance to this large redevelopment succeeded in halting it, but Arabindoo suggests that this has caused bourgeois civic organizations and the state to commit themselves even more firmly to the idea of urban space as 'ordered', where pleasure and consumption can be carried out in security and have hardened their stance against what they see as the intransigent 'crowd' preventing the emergence of Chennai as a global city.

The site at which Art Chennai held its installations is therefore contested space; and, appropriately, the art on the beach, and the motivations for placing it there are similarly complex. The strikingly contemporary, even 'global' nature of *Pyramid* and the other pieces of *Catastrophe* temporarily made the space of Marina Beach into a site of order in accordance with the imaginary of a 'world-class' city. But Marina Beach was attractive precisely because it is still a place open to all sorts of citizens, for all sorts of purposes. Thus, Art Chennai's organizers were seeking to *train* the eyes of the 'crowd' into appreciating contemporary art, thus enabling them to 'see' the global city that Chennai aspires to be while at the same time providing *evidence* to those already 'living the dream' that Chennai had indeed arrived as 'world-class'.

The other main spaces of 'outreach' – the atria of upscale malls and luxury hotels – contrast with Marina Beach in that they are already part of the 'urban spectacular', offering proof of Chennai's move to global status for the city's middle and upper classes. The ritziest new shopping and entertainment centre in Chennai – the Express Avenue Mall – hosted three installations, including Bose Krishnamachari's *Ghost: Transmemoir* (2006), described at the beginning of the chapter. The mall contains high-end shops, global clothing and food chains, expensive restaurants serving international cuisine and a state-of-the-art multiscreen cinema with eight theatres each individually themed and showing a range of the latest Indian and American blockbusters. Thus, the contribution of the art object to this space was to offer a further enhancement of the definition of 'world-class'. Indeed, it was to suggest to high-income Chennai residents that the consumption and appreciation of contemporary art could be desirable and pleasurable. Given the pervasive invisibility of contemporary art in India as noted earlier in the chapter, this exhibitionary purpose also sought to cultivate new possible collectors in an otherwise limited art market. As Sanjay Tulsyan said in an interview with *The Hindu* newspaper: 'We thought, why not take art to more people this year? … The idea is to introduce art into different atmospheres so that more people connect with it, and art doesn't seem as intimidating anymore' (Kumar 2012).[5]

What materialized in Art Chennai was the promotion of a particular vision of the city and its possibilities to citizens and to art-world actors. The art conclave was less about promoting the work of Chennai contemporary artists to the rest of the world; few galleries focused on local art production and the most widely seen pieces – those on the beach and at malls – were by Indians from other, perhaps more 'world-class', parts of the country, and from foreign artists. Some local artists found this somewhat surprising: they thought that the organizers and gallery owners had missed a crucial marketing opportunity.[6] In fact, their very response to this situation demonstrates that Art Chennai's central effect was rather different. From the local artists' perspective, the event seemed to take place at one remove and they attended, for the most part, as spectators and consumers rather than participants. But they were also excited at the opportunities the event offered for them to view art they might not otherwise see and to meet prominent contemporary artists who might otherwise be inaccessible to them. Even for some city artists critical of aspects of the fair's organization, therefore, Art Chennai was nevertheless a spectacle, simultaneously making a claim for the 'global' (i.e. non-'local') possibilities of Chennai and providing evidence that such a status had already been achieved.

Art Chennai confirms and enhances the value of 'newness' to the imagination of the city. Existing spaces need to be remade in order for the city to become truly 'world-class' in the eyes of citizens who, from the perspective of Art Chennai's organizers, both wittingly and unwittingly desire it. In terms of the art world, Art Chennai places the city within a network of 'global art' that also makes possible the imagination of the 'global city'. However, and ironically, the rise of 'global art' through the networks of global cities dispenses with the notion of innovation and newness to define artistic creativity. Thus, while the art fair promotes and supports the idea of the 'new city', the art that is exhibited is ostensibly less concerned with 'being new'.

The Place of 'Global Art' in the 'Creative Economy'

Scholars have traced the emergence of 'global art' to the years following the political and economic upheavals of 1989. Harnessed to global processes of intensified forms of capital accumulation and flow, the unprecedented expansion of 'art' across the world has had the effect of decoupling its production, consumption and criticism from a modernist Eurocentric narrative of art history (e.g. Belting 2009: 39). As Hans Belting explains, art as global art is not defined by the dominance of any particular style, such as abstraction. Rather it is distinguished by 'contemporary subject matter and a contemporary performance' (ibid.: 53). Thus, a modernist understanding of creativity as innovation is dispensed with and one participates in the art world by virtue of offering a critical perspective on the most contentious issues of the day (ibid.). The 'globality' of a piece such as *Ghost: Transmemoir* was explicitly remarked on by the 'concept note' in the Art Chennai catalogue, which lauded Krishnamachari's approach for using a 'global art vernacular' that makes the content of the work accessible for a global art audience (Art Chennai catalogue, 415–416).

Artistic practice in global art becomes a matter of correct and properly cultivated ethical disposition rather than formal aesthetic innovation. In this way, argues Belting, global art is truly contemporary (2009: 39). This ethic is reflected in *Pyramid* and other major Art Chennai pieces. Referring to another installation at the mall, *White Builder and Red Carpet*, Krishnamachari suggested that the work offered a way for people to supply their own responses to questions posed by the artist: 'This piece is a critique of our times. But I don't give answers, because that's not what people want. We're not satisfied with answers unless we come up with them and the work speaks for itself' (quoted in Parthasarathy 2012).

Belting also draws attention to the ways in which global art has come to be associated with the creation of appropriate stages for its performance. At the same time, cities are being remade throughout the world in order to emphasize and cultivate their 'creative' qualities. Sharon Zukin suggests that 'culture' is increasingly the business of cities and the industries of art, fashion, food and music produce what she calls a 'symbolic economy'. This 'economy' complements those consisting of manufacturing, government or finance and at the same time is more able to provide a sense of uniqueness to the city, thus enhancing its ability to compete effectively in those other economic fields (1995: 1–2). Artists and art play a crucial role in this symbolic economy: '[they] have become a cultural means of framing space.... They confirm the city's claim of continued cultural hegemony' (ibid.: 23). Key to this framing of space is the emphasis on how creativity is cultivated through the imagination of the city as a spectacular space (ibid.: 16; Edensor et al. 2009: 2).

In addition to some of the exhibited art objects themselves constituting 'global art', the type of 'art world' that was present for Art Chennai made apposite the label of 'global city': a city able to sustain a 'creative economy'. The fair gathered contemporary artists and gallery representatives from all over India, and art critics and collectors from across the globe. The promotion of a 'creative economy' for Chennai is inextricably linked to the reimagining of the city that Art Chennai effects; but this reimagining needs to reach as much of the populace as possible. Goutham, an advisory board member of Art Chennai 2012, explained the placing of installations on Marina Beach, rail stations and malls by linking it to the broader desire to develop a 'creative economy': 'Besides, the creative economy – art, culture and tourism – will have a larger economic impact only if it achieves the trickle-down effect' (Srinivasan 2012).

In relation to the contemporary art world, the reshaping of cities in pursuit of the spectacular is linked to two broad moves. Firstly, one witnesses the recent extraordinary programme of building new museums and gallery spaces in cities in China and other 'emerging economies' as part of 'cultural zones' that include shopping, entertainment and other forms of leisure (see e.g. Hing-Kay 2009). Secondly, and slightly predating the first, is the growth of the 'biennial industry' (Fillitz 2009: 117) since the mid-1980s. The proliferation of biennials has been noted by many commentators (Stallabrass 2004; Fillitz 2009). Some twenty to thirty biennials are held every year, and of the eighty cities around the world that regularly host them, forty are outside the traditional centres of contemporary art in Europe and North America (Fillitz 2009: 117). According to Julian Stallabrass, the response of the global art world to the expansion of the biennial concept has been overwhelmingly positive: it is seen as a further step away from a Eurocentric modernist vision of art and towards one which is diverse and multiple (2004: 34). Moreover, the biennial has come to constitute a key part of the symbolic economy of the cities that host them, indicating an aspiration to 'global city' status. By demonstrating their openness to the 'creative industries', such cities also enhance their capacity to compete effectively with other cities for global capital flows (Edensor et al. 2010: 2–3). Taken together, these two (interconnected) moves provide the means by which city space is being transformed in order to cultivate an economically valued and productive 'creativity'. As Tim Edensor et al. state: 'The centrality of creativity – and by extension, arts and culture – to economic competitiveness is not only extended to marketable outputs; it has also become enmeshed in recent efforts at place making. Here, the emphasis is one the construction of spectacular spaces of culture and consumption' (2010: 2).

Central to this notion of the 'creative economy' is the 'creative class' (Florida 2005), a group of artistic and technological entrepreneurs who make the city 'creative'. In this understanding, the 'global art' actors that are identified with biennials (artists, critics) are part of a transnational 'creative class', as are the artists and others taking part in Art Chennai and the contemporary art world in the city more broadly.

Edensor et al. (2010) offer a critique of the notions of 'creative class' and by extension 'creative city' and 'creative economy'. They suggest that the concept of 'creative city' advocated in urban and arts policy has valorized particular forms of creativity, 'including a proclivity to promote only those cultural activities whose products are easily commodifiable in terms of intellectual property rights and copyright material' (ibid.: 4). Moreover, the artist has been redefined as an entrepreneur and risk-taker, who in assuming total responsibility for his or her own success, comes very close to the type of subject promoted by neoliberal political economy (see also Martin 2009). Drawing on Ingold and Hallam's (2007) reconsideration of creativity as relational, non-individualistic improvisation throws this entrepreneurial conception into relief: 'The creative city script thus presents an idealised image of an entrepreneurial creative subject, neglecting the power relations, discipline and risks that confront members of the so-called creative class. Such a conception of creativity also neglects less commodified, alternative and often more subversive forms of creativity in the city' (Edensor et al. 2010: 5).

While at first sight this neoliberal understanding of 'creative, innovative artists' making the 'creative city' seems at odds with Belting's discussion of a 'global art' that denies the importance of formal aesthetic innovation and instead privileges artistic ethical positions, they are in fact part of the same narrative. The emphasis on ethical practice allows individual artists to distinguish themselves from other artists who may cultivate different, though not necessarily opposing, ethical practices: it is in this way that 'creativity' is defined as individualizing activity, and it is this aspect of the artistic person, rather than the art object itself, that is being commodified.

Making a Creative Place at Cholamandal

The ways in which a place is made creative are also a central concern at Cholamandal Artists' Village. Artists described the area on which they established the Village in the 1960s as 'empty land'. The views to the ocean were unobstructed by buildings, and save for a few fisher-folk families, 'there was nothing here'. The water and the beach were very much part of the Village, and artists would often walk singly or together down to the sand, spending much time there. Today, the Village is cut off from the sea by lanes of large houses, some of them the second homes of wealthy people who otherwise live in central Chennai, built when the small hamlet of Injambakkam in which the Village is located felt more removed from the clamour of the city than it does now. And artists seldom go down to the shore these days, complaining of the large buildings, construction sites and the workers and others who use the beach as an open-air latrine.

Few artists lived at Cholamandal in the early years of the Village. The vast majority continued to live in the city, travelling to the Village every day to work and meet the other cooperative members. From the late 1970s, nearly fifteen years after the Village was founded, the first artists began to live there permanently with their families. One artist, however, a man called Gopinath, took up regular residence quite early on and it is striking that he was regarded then as a sort of 'wild man', a person who was at ease wandering the Village, carrying small mammals in his pockets, and who did nothing to chase away the animals, some of them dangerous, who came to share his home. From one perspective, the lack of human cultivation in the area and the emptiness of the land meant that even a human being would eventually become wild by living there. The area in which the Village was located was regarded as a dangerous place, far from the civilization provided by Madras. Artists tell of the hazards of travelling from Injambakkam to Chennai and back, of being waylaid by thieves. Gopinath was said to have become 'wild' in a wild place; as more 'civilized' people came to live there, the place itself became 'civilized' through processes of artistic cultivation and engagement. The fact that artists live long-term at the Village is central to the way in which Cholamandal is imagined as an artistic and 'creative' place.[7]

As I have explored in another essay (Desai forthcoming), Chennai artists articulate these relations in slightly different ways. One Cholamandal artist, P. S. Nandhan, understands the sources of his creativity as located in his relationship to the environment of the Village. Plants, birds and gardens of Cholamandal provide the lines that then make their way through the consciousness of the artist into the art object. Creativity also flows between artistic people who live in the same space; thus, members of the Village who together have transformed empty, uncivilized land into a productive and creative place make kinship with one another through these flows, which the land then further enables.

Such creative flows are exemplified in the sculpture park that sits at the heart of the Village, which contains pieces by Madras Movement artists as well as foreign artists who stayed at Cholamandal for a number of months, either at the guesthouse or at the homes of Village artists, whilst working on-site. From one perspective, this sculpture park could indeed be seen as enhancing the imaginary of Cholamandal (and thus Chennai) as an appropriate spectacle that demonstrates the Village as 'world-class', in the terms discussed above. But from the perspective of artists and residents, the sculpture park is a constitutive part of the Village and it is recruited into sustaining the 'art' that Cholamandal has cultivated. Every Sunday morning, for instance, some of the artists gather with their children and visitors to hold a drawing session. This takes place among the sculptures and they often choose as their subject one of the pieces of art. By being subject to skilled observation by artists and others, the park becomes an active coproducer of artistic affect in the Village. Thus, through their permanence, the sculptures in the park become enmeshed in a series of relations between residents, in ways that are different from the Art Chennai installations at Marina Beach or at the Express Avenue Mall.

This issue of permanence is intriguing and one that I raised with Cholamandal artists. As they entered old age, how did they view the future of the Village? Some were pessimistic, suggesting that Cholamandal would hollow out. Indeed, according to them, this process had already begun, as artists and their families disposed of property on the site either following retirement or death and sold it to non-artists. Among wealthy non-artists, Cholamandal is seen as an attractive place to live because it constitutes a quiet, ordered site of large plots and a substantial upper-middle-class population. They come also because of its reputation as a 'creative centre', which is seen as more 'civilized' and 'cultured' than some of the other upmarket housing colonies south of Chennai. Marketing executives, journalists, academics and retired businesspeople are among some of the non-artists who have moved into the Village in recent years. Thus, while some artists see the presence of increasing numbers of 'others' as impinging on the 'creative' abilities of the Village as a collective, those same 'others' are attracted to Cholamandal precisely because it is 'creative'. This latter creativity is very much in the mould associated with the new 'creative economy' and its conceptions of being 'world-class': these new residents see in the Village an imaginary that is present too in other middle-class sites of consumption in the city.

Take, for example, the new café located at the centre of the Village compound. The Shiraz Café was established five years ago by an Iranian couple who studied in India in the 1970s and stayed on after they graduated. It consists of a main building in which there are a few tables, chairs and sofas, and a large shady garden dotted with sculpture and containing seating for about eighty people. People come here throughout the week for mint tea, juice or cake but the place really fills up at the weekend when the owners serve Iranian buffet lunches. The café has become central to forms of artistic sociality in the Village: artists and their families hang out there and they also use it as a place to entertain collectors and other people from the Chennai art world. While people who visit the museum and galleries also tend to visit the café, it is becoming a 'destination' in itself, competing with the other leisure attractions of the East Coast Road (ECR) area of southern Chennai. The attraction of Shiraz for upper-middle-class and elite people is that it is an orderly and tranquil space located away from crowded and noisy commercial centres, serving exotic and unfamiliar food.

Compare Shiraz with Stella's Canteen, which is the other place in Cholamandal that serves refreshment and meals. It is located on the edge of the Village and is built across the compound wall that separates Cholamandal from the busy ECR beyond. The canteen is thus accessed from the roadside and from within the Village. Run by Augustine and Stella, a Tamil Christian couple, it was for many years the only place in Cholamandal where one could obtain food and drink. It caters to a working-class clientele who gather at the main counter of the canteen facing the road and who do not come into the Village, as well as to residents and visitors to Cholamandal who access the shack from the rear, behind the counter.

The differences between the canteen and the café are striking. Whereas the café has ample seating in a lush garden cooled with the aid of fans and where patrons can linger in comfort for several hours over mint tea and cake, the canteen is small and cramped with little space to sit; few hang around once they've finished eating, and it is situated on a dusty, polluted highway. And while Shiraz Café brings the 'global' to Cholamandal and thus makes it a more desirable place to visit for the urban middle class, the canteen is very much a 'local' place, serving familiar food such as steamed riceflour cakes (*idli*) or *kurma* curry.

The original conception of the Village was oriented around the principle that there was no distinction between the space of work and home: ideally, artists lived where they worked and worked where they lived. This ideal only gradually came to be realized as artists who were part of the cooperative started making their homes at Cholamandal rather than simply commuting to their studios from the city. Thus, the spaces at which they gathered – Injambakkam beach, the sculpture garden or the atrium of the museum – were seen and experienced in non-dualistic terms. In many ways, the Village was conceived in the image of the Gandhian village: a cooperative community held apart from the distractions and tumult of the city. That Cholamandal is now a 'destination' for various reasons has altered the understanding of the relationship between artistic activity and place that was present at its inception. Cholamandal has also become a stage for the presentation of 'world-class' qualities that are in alignment with cosmopolitan imaginings of the 'creative city'.

Time and Newness in the 'Creative City'

We have so far considered the politics of space and how different spaces of contemporary art enable particular imaginings of the city. The constitution of Cholamandal as a 'creative place', for instance, is undergoing transformation: the space of the Artists' Village now also incorporates elements that make Chennai people see the 'global' in the imagination of their city.

Obstacles to participation in this global imagination remain, however, when we turn to consider the art objects produced by the Cholamandal artists at the Village. Whereas the 'global art' of Art Chennai is properly 'contemporary', breaking from a conventional art history and innovative in terms of artistic ethic rather than formal technique (Belting 2009), the contemporary art and artists of Cholamandal are aspects of 'pastness' for many in the Chennai contemporary art world. In this, they jar with the 'world-class' image promoted by Art Chennai.

Cholamandal artists are regarded as closer to 'Indian tradition' than many other Indian or Chennai artists. Nandagopal, a prominent Cholamandal sculptor, is fond of asking, 'If we cannot draw on five thousand years of history, then what kind of artists are we?' The explicit engagement and dialogue by many Cholamandal artists with Indian or Hindu myth and forms of representation makes Cholamandal itself part of tradition: the long-term tradition of Indian art and Cholamandal's close association with the mid-twentieth-century Madras Movement was itself a reaction against the European-inspired modernism of the Bombay Progressive Artists. The significance of tradition in Cholamandal is also reinforced by the emphasis these artists place on the mastery of particular techniques, rather than on the cultivation of a recognizably contemporary artistic ethic (see Fig 4.2). So while there is 'creativity' at Cholamandal, the kind of work produced there by people also regarded as 'past' ensures that the place is not fully cotemporal with that of other spaces and artistic actions in other parts of the city, or indeed of the 'global art' scene that has emerged in the last thirty years and which is represented in the work shown at Art Chennai.

From the point of view of Cholamandal artists themselves, however, the Village is not a space of pastness. This is because the artists do not recognize the split between past and present posited by powerful players in the Chen-

Figure 4.2. A sculpture by Cholamandal artist Nandagopal in the home of a Chennai collector who has presented it surrounded by 'traditional' representations of the god Ganesh. Photo: Amit Desai.

nai art world. Just as creativity is held to flow between artist and place, so creativity is held to flow through time without the rupture separating past from present that modernity requires. The art objects they make do not perform the work of rupture but of continuity. The dilemma for many Cholamandal artists is that their work is therefore not valued as truly 'creative' under the new regimes of 'global art' that do not concern themselves with contributing to art history. Thus, the work produced by most artists at Cholamandal has, through the attribution of 'pastness', served to marginalize this once important artistic centre.

Yet, if we examine the articulation of temporality in the 'creative city' in India – which must be able to feed the imagination of its 'world-class' status – we see that 'pastness' of a kind in artistic activity is in fact valued by middle-class Chennai people (see also chapters by Kuldova and Shreen, this volume). This valorization of pastness is made clear by the high profile of Dakshinachitra, a heritage complex located several miles south of Cholamandal. Dakshinachitra was founded with the purpose of reviving interest in 'traditional' ways of living and producing in rural South India. The site comprises reconstructed houses from the different states of South

India (Tamil Nadu, Kerala, Andhra Pradesh and Karnataka), which demonstrate the differences within and between the four regions. 'Tamil Nadu', for instance, contains houses from different castes and occupational groups (Brahmin priests, Chettiyars, potters, weavers and so on). There are also conventional museum spaces displaying everyday household and ritual objects. While the original intention was to create a thriving live-in community of 'traditional' artisans, this has largely failed and only one family of potters actually resides there (Hancock 2008: 169). Nevertheless, there are daily demonstrations of production by artisans who commute to the site and the complex contains both an outdoor 'bazaar' and a museum gift shop in which the objects made on-site and others from around South India are sold. In recent years, the museum has also hosted academic conferences on art, craft and visual culture and opened a gallery space for exhibiting contemporary art. Dakshinachitra has become an enormously popular destination, both as a day trip for Chennai people and for tourists to the region. As such, 'Dakshinachitra is framed to be understandable to an English-speaking global audience familiar with transcultural discourses of "heritage" and with Eurowestern conventions of historiography and museology' (Hancock 2002: 696).

Like Cholamandal, Dakshinachitra has to deal with the issue of 'pastness' in a 'creative city'. Dakshinachitra offers supposedly deracinated middle-class city dwellers a vision of their rural pasts and suggests that these pasts are not actually all that distant. This is demonstrated by the way in which the exhibits in Dakshinachitra play with time. The past is not historicized in the display boards and is presented as somewhat eternal and unchanging; very few dates are given, and social, political and economic change is seldom mentioned. Thus, as viewers, we are never quite sure how distant a past Dakshinachitra shows us. This slippery notion of time enables visitors to access the objects depicted and displayed at Dakshinachitra and make them proximate. In her analysis of Dakshinachitra, for instance, Mary Hancock discusses a film shown on-site (2002: 699) that proposes the existence of these continuities across time. She describes how scenes shot at the museum are put side by side with scenes shot on Chennai's streets and homes; the same actors are used in both types of scene, dissolving to some extent the differences between them (ibid.). As she writes, 'the video thus intimates that there can be fluidity between past and present, village and city' (ibid.).

As we have seen, the growth of Chennai and the new role given to cities under Indian economic liberalization has transformed the imagination of the 'village' and of the 'city' and of the relationship between them. Dakshinachitra offers an image of a closed, self-sufficient village economy in accordance with Gandhian nationalist visions of a post-Independence India. But this vision of the 'village' is very different to that which was enacted at the Cholamandal Artists' Village. The difference lies in the altered economic context in which they operate: the Artists' Village valorized the co-operative social arrangements idealized in the 1960s and 70s in reaction to the perceived 'modernity' of the cities; Dakshinachitra, on the other hand, represents the mourning that follows the transition to a neoliberal political economy through which new nostalgic formations emerge (2008: 12). Thus, while at first sight 'heritage' of the kind promoted at Dakshinachitra seems alien to the moves associated with a symbolic economy centred on 'creativity', it is in fact part of the process of making Chennai 'world-class'.

The particular politics of the materialization of space means that as an artistic site, Dakshinachitra is more 'contemporary'-making in relation to Chennai than Cholamandal, despite the latter's undisputed place in the history of South Indian contemporary art. Key to this is Dakshinachitra's ability to offer a 'specular order'[8] oriented around the centrality of the commodification of 'culture'. This process is linked to the promotion of tourism, leisure and consumption as paths to city and national development that prompted the reimagination of Marina Beach and which Art Chennai encourages. As Hancock notes, '[Dakshinachitra] … is premised unabashedly on consumerist hopes, sharing with pro-liberalization businesspersons and analysts the expectation that by enhancing economic growth, a free market economy will revitalise local cultural production and conservation' (ibid.: 151).

Dakshinachitra offers a vision of being 'world-class' as well as providing a reassuring 'Indianness' to middle-class and elite Chennai citizens, intimating that the loss of the past is not the price that has to be paid to create a different sort of city. Like Art Chennai, Dakshinachitra speaks a global language of art and display, but one that emphasizes 'heritage' rather than 'contemporary art'. And within its sphere of 'heritage', Dakshinachitra offers an understanding of craft that challenges the notion that it is repetitive activity. The artisans who work on-site, for instance, encounter mechanized tools of production such as electric potters' wheels that are unaffordable in their rural workshops (ibid.: 172). This offers them the chance for experimentation. Indeed, this is something emphasized by the founder of the museum, Deborah Thiagarajan, who, Hancock notes, argues that 'craft is not rote reproduction but a body of knowledge and practice based on continuous adaption and innovation' (ibid.: 159). The focus here, then, is on the ability of practices labelled 'craft' to be 'innovative' because they are about improvisation rather than complete new-ness. By yoking together craft, consumption and tourism, involving them in a vague temporality, Dakshinachitra manages to make the concept of heritage a key component in the 'creative city' of contemporary Chennai.

These dual understandings of 'innovation' – the innovative artistic ethic of 'global art' as represented by Art Chennai on the one hand and the improvisational emphasis on 'heritage' as articulated by Dakshinachitra on the other – which encode aspects of differentiation and competition between artists and cities, leave little temporal space for Cholamandal artists as 'contemporary'. This perhaps explains why Dakshinachitra is able to host contemporary art exhibitions and international academic conferences: the image of the place as fully 'world-class' contrasts with that of Cholamandal, which has belatedly begun to contribute to this particular imaginary of Chennai.

Cholamandal has in recent years taken up the competitive challenge posed by other artistic centres in Chennai such as Dakshinachitra and attempted to become visible in the 'creative' infrastructure of the city. In addition to the new café and museum building, a major plan is underway to build conference and accommodation facilities in the Village, funded with financial support from Sanjay Tulsyan. In this way, Cholamandal is responding to the powerful combination of leisure and consumption as key economic generators and linking them to its already existing but somewhat 'past' reputation of cultural activity.

The Village has also instituted a series called 'Artist of the Month', in which a local Chennai artist is invited to exhibit their work at the gallery at no cost and make a presentation on their work. The three talks I attended followed a similar pattern: the artists spoke about their influences and their commitments, and then traced the evolution of their ideas through their work, which was shown on PowerPoint slides. They then answered questions from the floor. The artists, critics, enthusiasts and others who attended these talks differed in their views on the success or failure of presentations. To some, particularly the younger artists from the city, the talks that were the most appealing offered a compelling narrative of personal transformation and exploration of ethical issues such as religious faith, political activism and the obligations to kin and society. They focused less on the art objects as products of skilled composition. Conversely, many older Cholamandal artists tended to privilege the latter in their evaluations of the artist's work. While these differences reflect the many understandings of 'contemporary art', the presentation format of the event itself favours both the new understandings of artistic creativity as ethical commitment that have emerged through the category of 'global art', and the idea of artist as entrepreneur. In this way, the Village can begin to take part in conversations about 'creativity' with those parties that are interested in the 'truly contemporary', a category to which it now seeks readmittance.

Conclusion

An examination of these three artistic sites in the city reveals the transformations of place and creativity involved in creating and sustaining a symbolic economy in Chennai. The process is by no means uniform and the history of Cholamandal, in particular, offers alternative understandings of how places are made creative through the practice of art. And we have seen that what constitutes 'art' is itself in movement. These changes are generated by and perceived through the lens of the economic liberalization policies enacted in India and elsewhere in the world from the late 1980s onwards. Tellingly, what the three sites have in common is that they are arenas of activity from which the state government has been largely absent.

Explaining the lack of state involvement in these art institutions solely by reference to liberalization is not, however, sufficient. The 'global' orientation of much of this art bypasses the powerful and long-standing Dravidian political ideology of consecutive Tamil Nadu state governments. Dravidian ideology emphasizes Tamil chauvinism, populism, atheism and the memorialization of a history of conflict against upper-caste hegemony. That the Tamil Nadu state government lavishes money on the display of South Indian bronzes at the Madras Museum but fails to provide funds for the proper curation of the 'elitist' modern art collection is indicative of this politics.

Cholamandal has never sought nor received direct state government assistance. This is because they do not want 'politics' to enter the Village; they are apprehensive of the ways in which Cholamandal could become involved in the propagation of Dravidian ideology. The cooperative relies, therefore, on the philanthropy of wealthy patrons such as Sanjay Tulsyan to make the Village 'world-class'. But the ways in which Cholamandal has articulated how artistic endeavour makes a place creative, based on a cooperative artistic production reflecting a vision of the village economy in retreat from the city, is also at odds with a Dravidian ideology that emphasizes the 'village' as a site of conflict and oppression of the common people by Brahmins and other upper castes. Cholamandal has not only been marginalized by the emergence of 'global art' but also by the Tamil chauvinist reshaping of the city: public funds are spent on public sculpture and memorials of key Tamil poets and politicians produced in a 'traditional' idiom. The 'urban spectacular' gains a different meaning in this context: the city is remade as a stage on which to play out the glories of Tamil culture to a largely Tamil audience. Likewise, the 'global' orientation of Dakshinachitra's articulation of 'heritage' is produced in opposition to a parochial Tamil politics of pride with which it cannot converse, as Hancock has shown (2002, 2008). From the perspective of many of the dominant figures in the local art world, the way in which contemporary art becomes entangled in the making of the creative city of Chennai is therefore by necessity both 'global' and 'non-state'. One of the consequences is that the 'world-class' city is ever more estranged from the realm of democratic politics.

Amit Desai was a research fellow at the School of History and Anthropology, The Queen's University of Belfast, and is a member of the HERA-funded project, 'Creativity and Innovation in a World of Movement'. He has conducted fieldwork in central and southern India and his interests include devotional Hinduism, religious transformation, personhood and creativity. His work has appeared in several journals and collections and he is coeditor with Evan Killick of *The Ways of Friendship: Anthropological Perspectives* (Berghahn Books, 2010).

Notes

Fieldwork was conducted in Chennai, India, from October 2010 to February 2011 and again in April 2012. An early version of the chapter was presented at the CIM Project Final Conference at the University of Utrecht in May 2012. My thanks to the participants at that conference and to Christiane Brosius in particular for her insightful comments as discussant. My thanks also to Birgit Meyer, Maruška Svašek and Chris Fuller for helping me develop and improve the ideas presented here.

 1. Art Chennai was organized by Sanjay Tulsyan and other major gallery owners and collectors in the city. It was sponsored by Tulsyan's steel company (Tulsyan NEC Steel), *Good Homes* magazine and various other large manufacturing, transport and retail businesses. The hospitality partner was the Taj Coromandel Hotel, Chennai, owned by the Taj Group, the international luxury hotel company.
 2. *Dabbawallah*s are lunchbox couriers who collect freshly cooked food from the homes of workers or restaurants and deliver it to their offices, and then organize the return of the empty lunchboxes back to where they originated. It is an intricate and complex network that covers the entire city of Mumbai. A *dabba* is the term for lunchbox.
 3. Accurate data is difficult to access, but Poulsen offers a total value estimate of US$2 million in 2001 rising to US$400 million in 2008 (2010: 188).
 4. One crore in the Indian numerical system equals 10 million in Western terminology.
 5. In another article published in the same newspaper a few days earlier, Tulsyan is quoted as saying, 'The first edition remained high-networked and we showed only at gallery spaces. This year, we want to make the festival inclusive; involve the public; help them learn about art and promote awareness, which in turn will promote appreciation of art' (Srinivasan 2012).
 6. Of the twenty-one local galleries involved, eight included work by Chennai-based artists. None of the public spaces or seven visiting galleries displayed work by Chennai-based artists; nor were they represented in any at the 'Video Lounge' installations.

7. Although Cholamandal artists did not refer to the Village as their *ur* (home, village), and indeed regarded their *ur*s as existing elsewhere in Tamil Nadu or in the neighbouring states of Kerala or Andhra Pradesh, the Tamil concept can be used to highlight some of the ways in which Cholamandal was said to become a 'creative' place. In his study of exchange and personhood in a Tamil village, Daniel (1984) explores the reciprocal relationship between the 'qualities' (*kunam*) of people who regard a place as their *ur* and the qualities of the local soil, which affects the 'intellect' (*putti*) of the inhabitants. Thus, village, soil and person come to be composed of similar substances through ongoing processes of exchange between them.

8. This is Hancock's (2008: 154) formulation.

References

Arabindoo, P. 2011. '"City of Sand": Stately Re-Imagination of Marina Beach, Chennai', *International Journal of Urban and Regional Research* 35(2): 379–401.

Belting, H. 2009. 'Contemporary Art as Global Art: A Critical Estimate', in H. Belting and A. Buddensieg (eds), *The Global Art World: Audiences, Markets, Museums*. Hatje Cantz: Ostfildern, 38–78.

Brosius, C. 2010. *India's Middle Class: New Forms of Urban Leisure, Consumption and Prosperity*. London: Routledge.

Daniel, E. V. 1984. *Fluid Signs: Being a Person the Tamil Way*. Berkeley: University of California Press.

Desai, A. (Forthcoming). 'Images of Society among Chennai Artists', *Anthropology and Humanism*.

Edensor, T. J., et al. 2009. 'Introduction: Rethinking Creativity: Critiquing the Creative Class Thesis', in T. J. Edensor et al. (eds), *Spaces of Vernacular Creativity: Rethinking the Cultural Economy*. London: Routledge, 1–16.

Fillitz, T. 2009. 'Contemporary Art of Africa: Coevalness in the Global World', in H. Belting and A. Buddensieg (eds), *The Global Art World: Audiences, Markets, Museums*. Hatje Cantz: Ostfildern, 116–134.

Florida, R. L. 2005. *Cities and the Creative Class*. London: Routledge.

Hancock, M. 2002. 'Subjects of Heritage in Urban South India', *Environment and Planning D Society and Space* 20: 693–717.

———. 2008. *The Politics of Heritage from Madras to Chennai*. Bloomington: Indiana University Press.

Hing-Kay, O. H. 2009. 'Government, Business, and People: Museum Development in Asia', in H. Belting and A. Buddensieg (eds), *The Global Art World: Audiences, Markets, Museums*. Hatje Cantz: Ostfildern, 266–277.

Ingold, T., and E. Hallam. 2007. 'Creativity and Cultural Improvisation: An Introduction', in E. Hallam and T. Ingold (eds), *Creativity and Cultural Improvisation*. Oxford: Berg, 1–24.

Kumar, D. 2012. 'The City is the Canvas', *The Hindu*, 7 March.

Martin, E. 2009. *Bipolar Expeditions: Mania and Depression in American Culture*. Princeton: Princeton University Press.

Nandy, A. 2001. *An Ambiguous Journey to the City: The Village and the Other Odd Ruins of the Self in Indian Imagination*. New Delhi: Oxford University Press India.

Parthasarathy, A. 2012. 'Of Wit and Wisdom', *The Hindu,* 14 March.

Poulsen, N. 2010. 'Creative Tensions: Contemporary Fine Art in the "New India"', in A. P. D'Costa (ed.), *A New India? Critical Reflections in the Long Twentieth Century*. London: Anthem Press, 179–193.

Srinivasan, M. 2012. 'Art Takes to the Streets', *The Hindu,* 3 March.

Stallabrass, J. 2004. *Art Incorporated*. Oxford: Oxford University Press.

Zukin, S. 2005. *The Cultures of Cities*. Oxford: Blackwell.

Art Chennai 2012 Event Catalogue.

5

APPROXIMATION AS INTERPRETATIVE APPROPRIATION
GUARANÍ-INSPIRED CERAMICS IN MISIONES, ARGENTINA

———◆•◆•◆———

Arnd Schneider

The aim of this chapter is to investigate and critically theorize practices of appropriation from indigenous cultures among urban-based potters in Posadas, the capital of Misiones province in northeast Argentina, and Santa Ana, a small nearby town and former Jesuit Mission.[1] Its principal argument is that hermeneutic appropriation, understood by the research subjects as 'approximation', is at the root of their practices. The chapter extends some arguments I have made previously on the topic, specifically in a theory article, 'On Appropriation' (Schneider 2003; see also 2006b), and a monograph, 'Appropriation as Practice' (2006a). In these publications, I had argued that appropriation is best understood as an interpretive hermeneutic practice, which goes beyond a simple taking out of context and transplanting into a new one, but entails a learning process for the appropriating agents. Ultimately, this creative experimentation with past cultural artefacts brings about a creative construction of culture in the present. I shall also address some of the ethical implications in the appropriating process as they emerge from my ethnographic field.

Appropriation, Hermeneutics, Ethics: A Short Introduction

Before I address how appropriation is contextualized as approximation in my ethnographic material, some brief remarks on the concepts used are necessary. It is worthwhile to remind ourselves first of how appropriation has been defined in an art-historical context that is as: 'the direct duplication, copying or incorporation of an image (painting, photograph, etc.) by another artist who represents it in a different context, thus completely altering its meaning and questioning notions of originality and authenticity' (Stangos 1994: 19).

The concept of appropriation is not without controversy in art and anthropology, and in a very simplified fashion its connotations can be positive, negative or both. Among those who define themselves as belonging to indigenous communities, there is often resistance to outside appropriation of images, stories, material and immaterial cultural items that are seen as intangible. Not only is appropriation resisted, but appropriation can also come at a price for those appropriating, as the appropriated 'things' can also 'overwhelm the appropriator', in the words of art historian Robert Nelson (2003: 165)

Appropriation, obviously, means different things to different people and is an inherently unequal business, depending on one's position, especially in postcolonial contexts in which it is tied inextricably to power differences. Therefore, practices of appropriation also carry with them an ethical burden, which is often unequally distributed among the parties involved. The solution to ethical problems for artists is not to abandon appropriating practices, but to be reflexively self-aware and make visible ethically complex encounters with cultural Others. It is clear that one cannot think of cultural practice *without* appropriation. In this sense, I side with Canadian philosopher James O. Young, who writes in his book *Cultural Appropriation and the Arts,* 'arguably, the world needs more content appropriation, not less' (2008: 157). Young is clear about the fact that not all types of appropriation are equally desirable: that object appropriation can become theft, while certain types of content appropriation may be profoundly offensive.[2] So, appropriation is often, but not always, negatively connoted, by both theorists and the subjects of our research. In fact, as I shall explain further on, my research subjects preferred the term 'approximation' to appropriation, precisely because of the latter's inherent negative associations.

As I shall demonstrate in this essay, however, 'appropriation' can only be fully understood when seen as part of hermeneutic interpretive practice. In this, I follow philosopher Paul Ricoeur, one of the eminent theoreticians of appropriation, who writes: 'An interpretation is not authentic unless it culminates in some form of appropriation (*Aneignung*) if by that term we understand the process by which one makes one's own (*eigen*) what was initially other or alien (*fremd*)' (1981: 178; German terms in original).

Ricoeur also emphasized that interpretive appropriation, contrary to both its popular use, and more narrow legal understandings, does not imply 'taking possession' of the other. To the contrary, it entails a process of transformation for the appropriating agent, as 'relinquishment is a fundamental moment of appropriation and distinguishes it from any form of "taking possession"' (ibid.: 191; see also Schneider 2003: 221). Approximation, as we shall see throughout this essay, entails precisely this interpretive, hermeneutic practice, which includes transformative aspects for the appropriating agents (for instance, in terms of their identities), and ultimately brings about creativity and innovation.

Museums as Institutional and Public Arenas for Appropriation and Identity Constructions

The ethnographic field for this study is constituted by a number of institutions and their activities in the wider ambit of the promotion of cultural heritage. In particular, the chapter focuses on pottery classes, and on notions of creativity and innovation, and the relation to indigenous communities, past and present, who are seen by the potters as the sources of inspiration for their practices. Intricately linked to pottery practices is their insertion into the context of museums, and municipal agencies that promote traditional crafts. The Museo Regional Aníbal Cambas and the Museo Provincial Andrés Guacurarí are the two principal museums in Posadas dedicated to archaeological, and to a lesser degree, contemporary, manifestations of indigenous cultures.[3] As part of their programme to revalorize indigenous heritage, especially that of the historical Guaraní cultures of Misiones province, both the Museo Aníbal Cambas and the Museo Andrés Guacurarí in Posadas hosted ceramics classes. The nearby municipality of Santa Ana, about 20 kilometres from Posadas, organized the Taller Municipal de Artes Brasanelli, which focused primarily on ceramics. In the recent past, the Museo Aníbal Cambas has also offered Guaraní basketry classes, and the Museo Andrés Guacurarí regional cooking classes, using also vessels made in the ceramics classes.

These heritage politics and the specific agents operating within them (museum personnel and workshop leaders) are targeting the European-descended majority population of Misiones, and focus almost entirely on the *past* archaeological Guaraní culture, not on the *present* situation of the Guaraní and their political struggles. These institutions and the people connected to them are structurally placed as white state or non-state agencies or institutions, in a more or less hegemonic position, and are perceived as such by contemporary Guaraní groups in the province who engage state and non-state actors over a wide range of conflictive issues including land rights, agro-industrial development and 'eco'-tourism, with further repercussion in terms of cultural property rights such as the knowledge of medicinal plants (cf. Seymore and Roberg 2012; also Salamanca 2012).

In contradistinction to the Buenos Aires potters whom I studied previously (Schneider 2006: 63–90), and who appropriated from a wide array of different pre-Columbian cultures in northwest Argentina, as well as more generally in Latin America, the Misiones pottery initiatives investigated here are directly related to the Guaraní culture of the area, including the neighbouring province of Corrientes, as well as adjacent areas of Paraguay and Brazil. Despite their singular focus on what they perceived as a homogenous Guaraní cultural area, the Misiones workshops shared certain characteristics with the Buenos Aires workshop, in that the techniques of appropriation were similar, derived both from secondary sources, such as books and manuals (e.g. Chiti 1997), directly from archaeological pieces and occasionally through visits to indigenous communities. In contrast to the Buenos Aires pottery workshop, the two workshops in Posadas, due to their location within the museums, benefited from an unrivalled proximity to the archaeological pieces embedded in a context of public culture that emphasized and promoted practices of appropriation and identity construction by relating to the historical Guaraní cultures of the area. The archaeological artefacts were seen and used as direct sources of inspiration for the recreations, and the newly created pieces exhibited alongside. Some of the members of the workshop in the Museo Andrés Guacurarí had also visited indigenous communities, although not with the primary intention of learning about pottery techniques. While this was not explicitly stated to me, one generic reason for not engaging with the contemporary Guaraní might have been an intention to stay away from current conflicts within the wider society, such as those over land rights, or avoiding taking sides in these conflicts – none of which the workshop participants, as city dwellers, were personally involved in. The specific reason given for seeking inspiration from archaeological pieces, however, stemmed also from the assertion, repeated to me on many occasions, that the contemporary Guaraní no longer practice ceramic production, with the exception of small pipes (fig. 5.1).[4]

This opinion seems to be mirrored by some observers who write about the relative simplicity, if not poverty, of Guaraní material culture, in contrast with the richness and artfulness of their poetic and mythological production (Melia 1988). Indeed, one project by Carmen de los Santos from the Taller Municipal de Artes Brasanelli from Santa Ana aimed to reintroduce pottery techniques to a nearby Mbya Guaraní community, through running

Figure 5.1. Guaraní pipe, partly restored, Museo Provincial Andrés Guacurarí, Posadas, Misiones, Argentina. Photo: Arnd Schneider.

a ceramics workshop in their settlement. While this represented a certain novelty, it also revealed the ethical complexity of this enterprise, in terms of appropriation, and reimportation of indigenous techniques, as I will show in the final part of this essay.

The Multiple Meanings of Guaraní

I should clarify that I use 'Guaraní', unless otherwise specified, as used by my largely European-descended, urban Argentine interview partners and research subjects to designate indigenous people past and present that lived and continue to live in Misiones province of Argentina, and in neighbouring areas of Paraguay and Brazil. However, as suggested above, they mostly use the term to refer to the Guaraní communities in Misiones, which are the ones they are mostly familiar with and which represent the immediate indigenous 'other' to them. Thus I do not in the present essay address the more generalized notion of creole Guaraní or *yopará*, which constitutes a wider notion of Guaraní culture, shared by Paraguayans of European as well as mixed European and indigenous descent, and which includes Guaraní as Paraguay's second official language. The historical migrations both before and after the Spanish and Portuguese colonization of these areas, including the Jesuit Missions of 1609–1756 (cf. Wilde 2009), have been widely explored, and given rise to changing and conflicting definitions of Guaraní in the literature, as well as changing definitions of different subgroups of Guaraní. The most commonly accepted subdivisions in the present are Mbya Guaraní, AváGuaraní and PaiTaviterã, as well as the Guaraní of Eastern Bolivia, often called Chiriguanos in the literature and by outsiders, but who call themselves Guaraní (cf. Gustafson 2009). Sometimes the Aché-Guayakí are also included, representing somehow archaic Guaranies, having, according to some sources, descended from ancient Guaraní, and their languages being related (cf. Bartolomé 2009: 66; Münzel 1983; Melia 1991; Clastres 1998[1972]: 29; Mayntzhusen 2009[1948]). It is estimated that in 2008, approximately 5,500 Mbya Guaraní and 1,000 Avá Guaraní lived in Misiones (Bartolomé 2009: 66; Wilde 2007). The majority of Mbya Guaraní and Avá Guaraní live in villages (*teko'a* in Guaraní; variably *aldeas, pueblos* or *comunidades* for Spanish speakers), some of them in close proximity to towns such as San Ignacio Miní, a UNESCO world heritage site famous for its Jesuit mission ruins. Given the great mobility of the Guaraní and recent legislation that requires communities to legalize their titles, estimates of the number of communities also vary considerably.[5] The Mbya Guaraní used to practice a mixed economy, consisting of subsistence horticulture, fishing, hunting and gathering (e.g. Crivos, Martínez and Pocchetino 2004), as well as complementary craft production for sale on roadside stalls, and occasional salaried work by the men in the maté, tea, tobacco and tung tree plantations. More recently, large-scale deforestation resulted in the Mbya Guaraní becoming dependent upon government food handouts, as well as low-salaried occupations including auxiliary teachers, sanitary agents or health aides (Wilde 2007; vom Hau and Wilde 2010: 1292). Compared to the white, creole-majority society, most Mbya Guaraní live in a very marginal situation of precarious nutrition and living conditions, often characterized by extreme poverty (e.g. Wilde 2007; vom Hau and Wilde 2010: 1284; Zonta, Oyhenart and Navone 2011).

Furthermore, 'Guaraní' can mean different things to different people in northeast Argentina. For instance, Chela Liuzzi, who taught Guaraní language in Corrientes, the provincial capital of the homonymous Argentine province, was highly critical of what she saw as a general attitude in neighbouring Misiones province, whose people and especially politicians do not appreciate its Guaraní heritage, despite having contemporary Guaraní populations, whereas the province of Corrientes, with no indigenous Guaraní population, but a number of Guaraní speakers in the villages and towns of the interior, is proud to have promoted and approved a provincial law on the Guaraní language.[6] Guaraní can obviously be dissociated from its perceived or constructed ethnic base, and be recreated as a new cultural construction according to the position and interest of the speaker, or interest groups and institutions, including provincial governments, parties and politicians (cf. Gandulfo 2007 for Corrientes; and Gustafson 2009 for the Bolivian Guaraní).

Hence, the activities of the potters have as their point of reference a past archaeological culture, whose presumed present-day descendants, the Mbya Guaraní in Misiones, live, in terms of political and economic power, in a peripheral position to the majority society. The knowledge and appropriation of the archeological artefacts that inspire the potters is, then, mediated through the historical collections and present-day exhibitions of museum institutions representing the majority society, rather than in direct contact or dialogue with the contemporary Mbya Guaraní. In this sense, these pottery practices are indicative of a wider politics of difference, where past cultural producers are more highly valued than the contemporary Guaraní, with whom only sporadic attempts to engage have been made by the museums. Notwithstanding the structural hegemony of the museums vis-à-vis present-day indigenous communities, they are still able to formulate and express a specific agenda and ideology of preservation, recuperation and recreation. Within the long-dominant European identity model of the Argentine nation-state, and the particular identity formation of Misiones province, which is largely populated by people of European descent, this can be read as a practice of resistance. It is this wider ideological context that also motivated the teachers, and participants of the ceramics classes.

The Ceramics Classes

At both museums, the vast majority of participants in the courses were women, in groups ranging from five to fifteen people, aged from approximately 25 to 60 years, overwhelmingly from middle-class backgrounds, living in the central neighbourhoods of Posadas.

At the Museo Andrés Guacurarí, the classes were taught three days a week by Karina Gabriela Benítez, who graduated from the Arts Faculty of the National University of Misiones at Oberá[7] in central Misiones, an important centre for the diffusion and teaching of ceramic techniques. At the Museo Aníbal Cambas, the courses were usually run over five Saturday sessions. The courses were led by specialized teachers Stella Maris Muñoz de Cribb, a medical doctor responsible for municipal health programmes in disadvantaged neighbourhoods, and Liliana Rojas, a historian and the museum director, who offered theoretical classes. Rojas also taught history at the province's foremost teachers' college, the Instituto Superior Antonio Ruiz de Montoya in Posadas, where she is part of the history research centre (Centro de Investigaciones Históricas 'Guillermo Furlong'). Javier

Gastaldo,[8] a member of the Arts Faculty at the National University of Misiones, whom I also interviewed, has been a constant promoter of Guaraní ceramics and since 2006 has offered courses at the Museo Aníbal Cambas, in which also Elba González, the curator of the Museo Andrés Guacuraí, also participated. The objectives of the course, as described by Liliana Rojas (2006: 19), were:

> (1) to recuperate ceramic techniques of Guaraní culture, (2) to make replicas of the material existing in the museum (i.e. the funerary urns), which could serve didactic purposes and disseminate the history of Misiones ... , (3) to acquire basic theoretical knowledge of the techniques and working processes of artisanal pottery, [and] (4) to train oneself in techniques of reproduction of specific ceramic forms and decorative ceramic designs of the culture of the Mbya Guaraní. (my translation)

The archaeological artefacts exhibited in both museums – tellingly, in the Museo Aníbal Cambas alongside the re-creations (fig. 5.2.) – became the cultural materials that were reinterpreted for new creative efforts, directly linked to the construction of new identities.

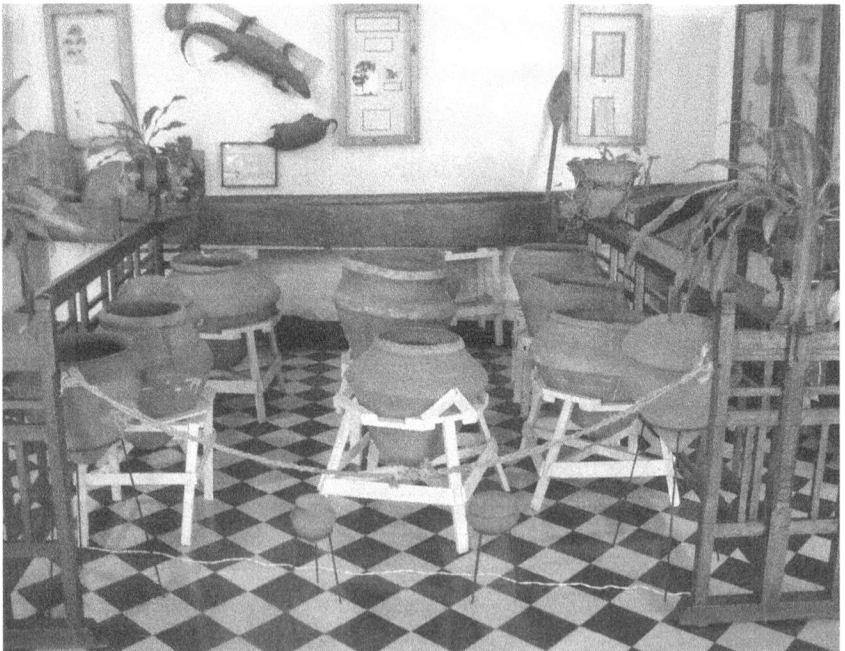

Figure 5.2. Historic Guaraní funerary urns (*yapepó*) on view at the Museo Regional Aníbal Cambas, Posadas, Misiones, Argentina; two small re-creations in the foreground. Photo: Arnd Schneider.

In the first classes theory and practice were taught, and in the final class replicas of the museum artefacts manufactured. At the end of the course, the pieces were heated in an open pit fire (*fogata*). As teachers and students pointed out, this was the same technique used by the Guaraní. Pit-firing is, indeed, a very ancient method of firing and attested in several myths throughout the Americas (cf. Lévi-Strauss 1988: 54). The *fogata* was followed by a *fejoada* (the traditional Brazilian beans-and-pork stew), and a critical evaluation by the professors and everybody in the group. This format was repeated on several more occasions, and I also had a chance to witness the *fogata* in 2010.

In contrast to the Buenos Aires workshop with which I had previously worked (Schneider 2006a), the workshops in Posadas did not use potters' wheels, the justification being that the Guaraní would not have possessed these. Nevertheless, they both use the same techniques of building the ground structure of the vessels – that is, by using clay sausages to build up the wall of the vessel from a base. The main sources of inspiration are the large Guaraní funerary urns (*yapepó*) as well as smaller vessels from the archaeological collections. To fire the pieces, both electric kilns, as well as open fires with wood burnt down to charcoal around an open mould in the ground (*fogata*), are used – the latter inspired by traditional Guaraní techniques.

The pieces made in the workshops are used for a variety of purposes. The pieces are for sale at the Museo Aníbal Cambas and the Taller Brasanelli, as well as for private, largely ornamental use by the makers. As Liliana Rojas explained to me, the pieces could serve three purposes: (1) private use, mainly for adornment of the home, (2) for sale at the museum and (3) as gifts in homage to people who are honoured on specific public occasions in Posadas, such as the award of literary prizes, or other outstanding contributions to the culture of the province of Misiones. In addition, at the Museo Andrés Guacurarí and the Museo Aníbal Cambas, the 're-created' pieces have also been used in cooking classes, and one member also used her vessel for cooking at home.

Motivations for Participation: Recuperation, Preservation, Re-creation

From the conversations I overheard during pottery classes, and in direct answers to my questions, it became clear that most people participated in the two courses because they wanted to learn about, and recreate Guaraní culture, in this case through ceramic artefacts. For them, pottery is a particularly suitable vehicle for achieving this aim, first because it is a craft that, at this amateur level at least, requires no prior specialist knowledge, and with relatively little effort, satisfactory results can be readily obtained. Second, in contrast to basketry, which has been appropriated by design companies (Schneider 2012), ceramics is seen by workshop leaders as *the* Guaraní craft that is most in need of recuperation, preservation and renewal inspired by archaeological sources (*recreacíon*). As I observed when attending classes and speaking to people, to recuperate meant, for them, to retrieve the 'ancient' Guaraní pottery and make it applicable to the present, since these are the only surviving material artefacts really appreciated from what otherwise is regarded to have been a 'poor' material culture. Preservation was more narrowly understood, as the preservation or conservation of found archaeological pieces (also to be achieved through 'recuperation' techniques), whereas re-creation applied to the newly created pieces inspired by the old ones. That the production of new pieces was, indeed, a re-creation of the tradition, was emphasized by the unanimous statements from members of all workshops, that ceramic production, with the exception of the small pipes described above, is no longer practiced in contemporary indigenous Guaraní communities in Misiones

This assertion, however, should be interpreted more as a justification for the activities of the members of these ceramics classes rather than as a factual statement about *all* contemporary Guaraní communities. In fact, it might only apply to the situation in Misiones, and even there, only partially. For instance, Liliana Rojas told me she had heard of older Guaraní in Santa Rita still practicing some limited ceramic activity, making small vessels but not large funerary urns, although neither she nor I had any opportunity to corroborate this information. Certainly, pottery is practiced among contemporary Guaraní groups in Paraguay, as the collections of the Museo del Barro in Asunción attest (Museo del Barro 1998; also Escobar 1986, 2004: 57, 2007), as well as among Brazilian Guaraní in the southern states of Rio Grande do Sul, Santa Catarina and Paraná (cf. Dutra 2005). Furthermore, some more distant Guaraní groups in eastern Bolivia, for example, in the town of Cocota, in the Department of Santa Cruz, are actively involved in producing commercial pottery for the tourist market.

Creativity and Innovation through Hermeneutic Appropriation

In conversation, both Stella Maris Muñoz de Cribb, the ceramics teacher at the Museo Aníbal Cambas, and her husband, Guillermo Cribb, expressed explicitly, 'that they will not be, or become Guaraní' through their art practices. Yet they want to retrieve and recuperate cultural practices (see figs. 5.3. and 5.4).

Figure 5.3. Guillermo Cribb showing a recreation of a funerary urn (*yapepó*) with lid. Photo: Arnd Schneider.

Figure 5.4. A variety of re-creations of Guaraní ceramics, by Stella Maris Muñoz de Cribb and Guillermo Cribb, Posadas. Photo: Arnd Schneider.

The concept Guillermo Cribb used was experimental archaeology,[9] and it is worth reporting his thoughts on this in some length:

> Our work is part of what we call 'experimental archaeology' [see note 10], to try to experiment and find out about things which have not reached to us through time, because nothing has been written or recorded about them. And at this point in time, we do not have Guaraní ceramic sculptors who could tell us how they made the pieces. So we need to find out how they did it.... Our idea is not to become craftsmen, but experimental archaeologists, trying to recuperate what we haven't got any longer, and even imagine how it would be if they [the ancient Guaraní] would have done the pieces. (Cribb in conversation with Arnd Schneider, Stella Maris Muñoz de Cribb and Liliana Rojas, 9 August 2010)

At the same time, Guillermo was very clear about how they were different from the ancient Guaraní:

> Because we are not making these ceramics for an immediate purpose, for instance, to use the vessel to feed our children. We are not making the *yapepó* [originally large funerary urns, or other vessels of similar form and manufacture, see below] to brew *chicha* in them. Our intention behind the replicas of Guaraní art is artistic, whereas for them it was utilitarian.... So the change of paradigm is interesting. One has to directly dissociate oneself from the 'white', western thinking, and start to think like a Guaraní, in order to see if one achieves an interpretation of how they made the pieces; and what they would have thought when they were working on the pieces. (Cribb in conversation with Arnd Schneider, Stella Maris Muñoz de Cribb and Liliana Rojas, 9 August 2010)[10]

Their approach, trying to balance faithfulness to the original sources, and the inherent, inevitable and also intended creativity, which is part of 'experimental archaeology', was well expressed by Liliana Rojas in our conversation: 'Not one piece of Guaraní ceramics is like another; all are different. As they did not work with moulds ... every piece is a creation. We will never make an exact copy. There will always be a small difference. ... We are doing experimental archaeology, we are always experimenting' (Rojas in conversation with Arnd Schneider, Estela Maria Muñoz de Cribb and Guillermo Cribb, 9 August 2010).

In some instances this creative experimentation implied significant changes in the form, dependent also on the requirements of the workshop and the students' abilities. For instance, the large funerary urns (*yapepó*) were reproduced in smaller sizes that are more manageable for the students. This was done by taking photos of the originals, and then making drawn plans for the smaller ones, 'but always looking at the large original ones for the details', as Liliana Rojas explained. There was an eminently practical and material side involved in this as well, because, as Liliana outlined, 'one has to work the clay with the hands and to know how one achieves the final form, and this is not easy. And the Guaraní had so much perfection because the large pieces are perfect. But this technique is lost – they don't do it any longer.'

Originally, the *yapepó* were large funerary urns. In the workshops, smaller replicas and vessels of the same form were also designated with this term. According to Branislava Susnik (1986: 36; also Brochado 1973; Torres 1987), there were four styles of Guaraní ceramics: corrugated-incised, brushed, simply painted or with motifs and interwoven. Corrugated-incised and painted are the most common in the archaeological record. In the corrugated-incised style, often adopted by the ceramics classes and in the project of Brazilian arts teacher Eduardo Dutra (2005), the incision was achieved directly with the fingernail or a small spatula; the technique always applied in spiral form following the building up of the vessel wall in 'sausages', or clay rolls. The *yapepó* also had lids but, as Liliana Rojas explained to me, these often get destroyed by the plough when farmers find them. Typical sizes range from 45 to 80 centimetres, and the same measurements apply to the diameter, and when the pieces were ornamented with the same patterns as in Guaraní basketry (Susnik 1986).

The Hermeneutics of 'Small Differences'

In our conversations, Guillermo Cribb expressed the thought that one has to 'start thinking like a Guaraní' without becoming a Guaraní. This is perhaps one of the most significant statements in this process of appropriation, which does not seek full congruence, taking possession of ancient (and by extension contemporary indigenous) Guaraní culture, but rather, an approximation following the tenets of experimental archaeology. Although the ceramicists see themselves as experimental archaeologists, their approach in fact resembles or mirrors much of the *Verstehen* approach in the social sciences and humanities: the hermeneutic tradition inspired by philosopher Wilhelm Dilthey and sociologist Max Weber. Weber's famous dictum 'You don't have to be Caesar to understand Caesar' (1978: 5) rejects any simple congruence with the other in the process of understanding and so does Guillermo Cribb's statement that one can start thinking like a Guaraní without becoming one.[11] In the same vein, Liliana Rojas spoke of the 'small difference', which they are trying to achieve in each recreation of a ceramic piece. For want of a better term, one could perhaps call this process a product of *Nachempfindung* rather than a copy of a presumed stable original. *Nachempfindung* is usually translated from the German, as 'feeling' and 'adaptation', but literally is a 'feeling *after* something', 'after-empathy' or 'sympathetic intuition'. In more abstract terms, this process almost implies a longing from the past projected to the future that is received in the present and, of course, changed on the way – which resonates with the ideas workshop members have of reinterpreting ancient Guaraní ceramics. The foreshadowing of the past into the future, current in the present, is also captured by the concept of 'anticipatory imagination' (Crapanzano 2004: 19), although in the ceramicists' case under review here, such imagination is directed towards the past. The physical and imaginary engagement with past practices of skilled vision (Grasseni 2007) gives the ceramicists some kind of access to the perspective of the past creators – perhaps a kind of 'transvision', as Maruška Svašek and Amit Desai have recently suggested (in this volume, and Desai and Svašek 2015; cf. also Svašek 2012a, b). One can also think here of 'dialogical anthropology' that puts emphasis on full acknowledgement of the other as interlocutor in anthropological fieldwork and texts (Tedlock 1983), and is further developed in the hermeneutic strands of anthropology (Maranhão 1986, 1990, 1998; Maranhão and Streck 2003; Crapanzano 1990; Verde 2003). The important difference here being, that the interlocutors, as living persons, for the ceramicists are located largely in the past, while their agency through archaeological objects is newly interpreted and made meaningful by the ceramicists in the present (cf. Svašek 2012). Furthermore, the art historian George Kubler (1962) suggested that stylistic variation in the archaeological record is expressed in so-called series, consisting of open and closed 'sequences' (1962: 35). However, as Kubler himself acknowledged, no sequence is really ever 'closed', as it is 'capable of reactivation under new conditions' (ibid.: 35, cf. also 106). Arguably the historical sequence of the *yapepó* manufacture has been concluded, but it is now being revived and recreated through the ceramic workshops.

The process of creativity, then, lies in these 'small differences', in trying to empathically capture the ceramic 'thinking' of the Guaraní in the production of new forms, and thereby providing also a fresh interpretation of the 'originals'. A variety of concepts were used by my interlocutors, such as appropriation, approximation, fusion and re-creation. Power differences – such as those between the majority society and present-day indigenous communities, remain unresolved in this process, but can at least be acknowledged. In fact, some academically trained Native American critics of hermeneutics in the United States suggest developing research agendas with communities and feeding results back, rather than positioning oneself as representative of an outside-led, cognitive interest (Ranco 2006). One further way of theorizing in this context is to think through Trinh T Minh Ha's (1994: 443) concept of 'Speaking Nearby', which implies that we cannot take the voice of the 'other' but at best can speak 'close' to another person, community or ethnic group.

Consequently, Guillermo, Estela and Liliana consider the ancient Guaraní pottery as an art, despite their acknowledgement of the utilitarian uses of the original items, and through their pottery practices, they seek to retrieve and re-create the ancient beauty of this art, now lost among the Guaraní. At the same time, they distance themselves from more artistic, or abstract approaches to Guaraní pottery (represented for them by the Taller Brasanelli), which through the members of the Arts Faculty of Oberá teaches a range of artistic techniques relating to ceramics.

One of the most radical approaches to reference Guaraní archaeological artefacts in a contemporary arts idiom, and use them for both for contemporary identity construction, and for critical questioning of such constructions, was made in the early 2000s by arts teacher Eduardo Dutra (2005) at the Universidade Comunitária Regional de Chapecó (Santa Catarina State, southern Brazil).[12] Dutra's work has important implications for thinking through issues of appropriation, hermeneutics and identity construction, as well as artistic creativity. The principal objective of Dutra's project, after a careful investigation of the material practices involved (for instance, in recreating *yapepó,* or funerary urns), was to analyse the practices and representations expressed in the ceramic production of past Guaraní groups in the western part of the State of Santa Catarina, in order to interrogate a changing regional identity and develop new educational practices among future art teachers (Dutra 2005: 97). Dutra reflexively acknowledged and incorporated the constructed nature of identity for his project, and then interestingly linked these objectives to the idea of multiculturalism, basing himself on Stuart Hall's notion that one can only develop an identity when confronted by others, in a hybrid and random process of exchange (Dutra 2003: 101–102). Therefore, at the beginning of the project, students were asked, in an auto-analytic process, to describe their own identities. In this exercise, the majority identified with the cultures of descendants of European, mainly German, Italian and 'gauchos', including their food, folkloric dances and music, which characterize this part of southern Brazil, and have now even become tourist attractions.

Most noteworthy, in relation to this essay, was an installation for the exhibition *In Memórium* (2002) by a participating group, which specifically addressed the topic of multicultural identity. The work was simply called *Identidade* (Identity) (Dutra 2005: 183–189). As one student expressed it, 'Thus we perceive that our proper identity is constantly on the move, turning into a multicultural medium as multicultural individuals in constant modification. And here indigenous identity is also included, as yesterday's "Indian" is not any longer the same today within a system constantly on the move.' (Dutra 2007: 186)

The installation *Identidade* then demonstrated this notion of the mutability, variability and changeability of identity in interconnected social and historical relations, by arranging the ceramic egg forms (loosely inspired by Guaraní ceramics), individually decorated, on sisal ropes on a large rectangular web in the exhibition room (fig. 5.5).

Appropriation, Approximation, Fusion, Re-creation

We can now start to rethink the concept of appropriation. Repeatedly and polemically, I confronted my interlocutors with this concept in our conversations. They largely rejected the notion of appropriation, however, aware of the negative connotations in the context of arts and crafts and in relation to indigenous cultures. On one occasion Liliana Rojas put forward the idea that, in the case of the pottery classes, it was more appropriate to speak of *approximation* rather than appropriation, as they were not directly copying but *re-creating*. Participants in the pottery classes also emphasized that their practices were inspired by respect for indigenous cultures. Daniela

Figure 5.5. Partial View of Installation *Identidade* (Group C), Universidade Comunitária Regional de Chapecó (Santa Catarina State), Brazil (from Dutra 2005: 185; also Nunes and Dutra 2015). Photo: courtesy of Eduardo Dutra.

Oliveira, a designer and promoter of the private design company Misiones Creativa, also rejected the term 'appropriation', and in contrast spoke of fusion and re-creation (cf. Schneider 2012 for a more detailed review of this project). When I put to the members of the ceramics workshop at the Museo Andrés Guacurarí the question of whether the Guaraní themselves would perceive their practices as appropriation, one woman answered that this was not certain, and that one could not generalize about 'the' Guaraní as they have very individual opinions. It could be asked whether this was merely a specious argument aimed at avoiding the question. There was a story that the other workshop of the Aníbal Cambas had, in the past, included a Mbya Guaraní man, who was dissatisfied with his vessel, as it broke during the *fogata*. His explanation of this event was that (his) 'God did not want it [to turn out well]'.[13] The few indigenous people I spoke to, for example, at the Office of Indigenous Affairs (*Oficina de Asuntos Guaranies*) of the province of Misiones, did not directly comment on the ceramics workshop, but thought that the collaboration with the design company Misiones Creativa was a good thing, as it provided rural communities with some work. Since the Guaraní decided on the design patterns, appropriation was not seen as a problematic issue (cf. Schneider 2012 for more details of this collaboration).

When I met the group of women from the Museo Aníbal Cambas ceramics class in a shopping mall, we had a round-table discussion on their activities. They commented on particular features, such as handles, brims and length of pipes, and emphasized the beauty of some pieces. The women were clearly proud of their work and enthusiastic about it, taking pictures of each others' artefacts with their mobile phones and digital cameras. One woman, whose parents had emigrated from Italy, lamented the economic decline of the middle class in Posadas, and in Argentina more generally, and found in her activity a new motivation for identity-creation, no longer wanting to identify with a European ancestry but seeking to create new 'roots' from the historic Guaraní culture (cf. Schneider 2006a for similar processes among Argentine contemporary artists). Another woman, of Ukrainian descent, said that her parents had been actually very 'racist' (*racistas*), and depreciative towards anything indigenous. She suggested that this had been a general feature of European immigrant society in Misiones. In this case, Guaraní had been constructed as the proverbial 'other', directly opposed to the industrious European immigrants. To some degree, such ethnic stereotyping is still prevalent in the parts of society that are descended from immigrants in Misiones. For example, the Museum of Immigration in Oberá, which organizes the yearly festival of immigrant communities *Fiesta del Inmigrante* with high national exposure, only as late as 2010 included Guaraní artefacts, and invited a Guaraní community to build a house for the festival. On the other hand, for the Ukrainian-descended woman at the ceramics class, to work with Guaraní pottery was a new way of connecting to the history and identity of Misiones.

Can There Be Restitution and on Whose Terms?

Much discussion in recent decades has focused around the politics and ethics of 'returning' artefacts from museums to indigenous communities, and collaborations of museums with so-called source communities (e.g. Peers and Brown 2003). In this final section, I shall focus on the 'return' of a technique – or in a larger sense, cultural practice to the Guaraní – that is, pottery, by way of running a ceramics workshop within the indigenous community as an extension of the Taller Municipal de Artes Brasanelli (see also Magowan and Øien, this volume).

In an abstract, theoretical sense, there can, of course, be no 'return' if this is to mean a restitution of equivalents, of giving back what has been taken. For this would mean, in the strictest sense, that what is given back is equivalent to what has been taken, a false equivalence that cannot be fulfilled. Due to the time that has passed in this delayed action, what is given back is always different to what has been taken, which makes the wishful identification of like with like a logical impossibility. Both in involuntary taking (stealing, robbing) and in voluntary, agreed gift-giving, objects, practices and other phenomena always attain a new social history through time. In such transactions (sometimes exchanges) they change their meaning, and even their material appearances, if not their substances. Hence in any theorization, and, in fact, in empirical investigations of restitution practices, one would have to look for what things are restituted for, or with what, and how; in other words what becomes of an artefact, or other objects and cultural practices more generally, during and as a result of a restitution process.[14]

The project by Carmen dos Santos to run a ceramics workshop once a week at the indigenous community of Santa Ana[15] (in close proximity to the village of Santa Ana en Jesuit Mission ruins; cf. Poujade 2009; Halberstadt 2010), then, has to be seen in the larger context of a long process of marginal, and marginalized, indigenous communities in Misiones as a result of colonial and postcolonial history. This marginalization of indigenous lifeways was only counteracted, under doctrinal premises, through a revitalization of craft activities during the Jesuit Missions period. The Guarani, then, have lost, recreated and then partly abandoned their ceramic knowledge.[16] Carmen got a degree as *técnica ceramista* through the extramural course the Arts Faculty of Oberá had been running in Santa Ana. Though Carmen de los Santos was not theorizing her activity, and made genuine efforts to bring ceramics and its working techniques 'back' to the community, her rationalization, when reflecting on the process, revealed the attitudes of the majority creole 'white' society of Misiones towards indigenous communities. She asserted that it was very difficult to 'work' with the Guaraní, and that they would not finish pieces independently when she was not present, as they did not have the same sense of continuity in working practices. The *cacique* of the community, Paulito Villalba, however, welcomed the project when we spoke to him.[17] Beyond the remit of this chapter, which focuses on issues of creativity between appropriation and approximation, this project – as others in the tourism sector (cf. Seymore and Roberg 2012) – also begs the question of how Mbya Guaraní themselves will ultimately benefit from this. The finished pieces, already glazed, were kept in a small cardboard box by Ana, a Mbya Guaraní woman who participated in the workshop, and ranged from small, oblong, rectangular vessels to round vessels, and one ashtray in the form of a *yacaré*, the native caiman (fig. 5.6).

On the shelves, in the workshop building, there were more pieces, yet unfinished, awaiting their final firing in a small kiln built outside. The pieces included the same types as those in the box, but there were also others, such

Figure 5.6. Pottery from the ceramics workshop in Santa Ana, Misiones. Photo: Arnd Schneider.

as birds, snakes, turtles, and a number of round vessels of various shapes and forms with various types of ornamentation. The animals resembled the small wooden figurines that the Guaraní produce for sale, and which provide an important complementary income for the communities (Crivos et al. 2012: 52–54; also Schneider 2012). Some were drying and awaiting their first firing; others were already painted with ceramic pigments and awaited their final firing. Ana also showed us a yet unfinished front piece for a pipe, which had the same form as those traditionally manufactured by the Guaraní. Some pieces have simple geometric ornaments that are engraved or painted, similar to those used in Guaraní basketry.[18]

Carmen de los Santos also showed me the mould, which was used for slip casting simple round forms, emphasizing 'we provide the mould' (*nosotros proveemos el molde*), reflecting somehow the philosophy behind the project. This is both the case in a literal, material sense, where the Guaraní make vessels from the mould, but also for other pieces, where the teacher might suggest the particular form, execution or even the subject (e.g. the kind of animal) for a piece. The Taller Brasanelli provided all the materials for the community workshop.

Conclusions

The different projects reviewed in this chapter allow us to recalibrate ideas about where creativity is located, and how it is worked through in social and material practices. In the ceramic workshops of the two museums in Posadas (Museo Aníbal Cambas and Museo Andrés Guacurarí), creativity is expressed through the elaboration and interpretation of 'small differences' (an expression of Liliana Rojas), that is, the recreation of archaeological pieces from the ancient Guaraní inhabiting the area. While this activity is incorporated into the construction of a new identity for people who are principally descended from European immigrants, at the same time there is clear acknowledgement that one cannot become Guaraní, but at best can start thinking like a Guaraní. Thinking vs. becoming – the approaches and techniques used in these endeavours, then, can only be approximate, never exactly matching what one wants to retrieve. It is for this very reason that participants and leaders of the group, such as Liliana Rojas, favoured the concept of approximation over appropriation. In this sense, as I have shown, their approach can be likened to that of a dialogical and hermeneutic anthropology, aimed at a process of 'understanding', but not full congruence with the Other – which, however, is located in the past. With the project of Eduardo Dutra in southern Brazil, paradigmatic of approaches in the contemporary arts, the interpretation of archaeological Guaraní ceramics was explicitly used to create a new visual discourse about identity construction. Dutra incorporated notions of multiculturalism and regional belonging to develop new forms of identity creation together with his students.

A different kind of appropriation, as a directed or controlled restitution, is most clearly at work, not in a direct visual practice of taking indigenous symbols and techniques, but as a (delayed) reverse practice, bringing ceramics 'back' to the communities that have to stand in for those 'ancestors' who once possessed this technique. This is the case in the project run by Carmen de los Santos from the ceramic workshop, Taller Brasanelli, of Santa Ana. Here, creole 'white' society literally provides the mould for the Mbya Guaraní to work with and also the material (i.e. the clay), as well as setting the working hours, and the workshop. As well intentioned as this project may be in communities marginalized from the mainstream of Misiones society, it still has an underlying flavour of a patronizing approach from white society that, in the wider political realm, was also commented upon by leaders of the Mbya Guarani, such as the *cacique* Aurelio Duarte from the Oficina de Asuntos Guaranies in Posadas. Against this background it is perhaps understandable that workshop leaders do not want to describe their practice as through the negative connotations of appropriation, but rather as 'approximation'. Yet, it might be perceived by the Guaraní themselves as appropriation, and more research is needed to explore this uneven cultural traffic. The ceramicists at the Museo Aníbal Cambas and Museo Andrés Guacurarí on the one hand, and the Taller Brasanelli in Santa Ana on the other, complement each other. While the former seek to retrieve and recreate ancient Guarani pottery, largely through a hermeneutic practice, Carmen dos Santos 'returns' pottery as a technique literally moulded by white society, based on the very same principles of creatively understanding difference, between approximation and appropriation.

Notes

1. I am grateful to Øivind Fuglerud for comments on an earlier draft of this essay, as well as to participants of the international conferences 'Materiality, Movement, Museum' at the Museum of Cultural History, Oslo, 19–20 September 2011, and 'Creativity in Transition: Politics and Aesthetics of Circulating Images', at the University of Utrecht, 31 May–1 June 2012. Fieldwork was carried out in August and September 2010 in Misiones province (especially the provincial capital, Posadas) and the city of Corrientes, Argentina. In Argentina, I am grateful to the following institutions for access to premises, collections and archives: Museo Regional Aníbal Cambas, Museo Provincial Andrés Guacarí, Instituto Superior Antonio Ruiz Montoya, Faculty of Education, University of Misiones, Museo de Ciencias Naturales e Históricas, Oficina de Asuntos Guaraníes, German Consulate (all in Posadas), Taller Muncipal de Artes

Brasanelli, Santa Ana, Faculty of Arts, University of Misiones (Oberá). I thank everybody who has made themselves available to me during my research, in particular Karina Gabriela Benítez, Guillermo Cribb, Daniel Costa, Aurelio Duarte, Elba González, Rolando Kegler, Stella Maris Muñoz de Cribb, Ruth A. Poujade, Liliana Mirta Rojas (all Posadas), Carmen de los Santos (Santa Ana), Javier Gastaldo (Oberá), Chela Luizzi (Corrientes) and Gabriel Romero (Corrientes). A special thanks also to Eduardo Dutra, Chapecó (Santa Caterina, Brazil) for his copyright permission regarding figure 5.5. I am grateful to the European Science Foundation for support of fieldwork and research time for writing up, as part of the Foundation's HERA project, 'Creativity and Innovation in a World of Movement (CIM)' on which this volume is based. I am also grateful to the Department of Social Anthropology, University of Oslo, for providing financial support for transcriptions of interviews, and to my research assistant, Jonathan Delgado, for meticulously carrying out this task.

2. Young (2008: 5–9) distinguishes between object, content, style, motif and subject appropriation.

3. In addition to the two principal museums in the city centre, at the outskirts of Posadas, on the campus of the Faculty of Education of the University of Misiones, there is the small, relatively recent Museo de Ciencias Naturales e Históricas (part of the Instituto Superior Antonio Ruiz de Montoya), formerly housed in a building in the city centre. It has a number of artefacts from different precontact and Jesuit periods, as well as small wooden statues made by indigenous artisans for the dioramas in the former museum. In a small museum depot opposite the museum, a number of funerary urns (*yapepó*) are kept. In 2010, the museum had one part-time curator, Daniel Costa, who looked after the archaeological artefacts. No ceramic classes, or other extracurricular activities were offered. However, at the Instituto Superior Antonio Ruiz de Montoya in downtown Posadas, classes were offered on Guaraní history and culture.

4. An assertion already made by Ambrosetti (1894: 714). The pipes are also sometimes described as *ñaú*, however this term is more often used to describe a particular kind of grey clay from Misiones, whereas the pipes are more specifically named *petynguá*. Susnik (1986) also confirms that the contemporary Mbya Guaraní continue to make angular-shaped clay pipes, where bowl, chamber and draught hole are made of clay, whereas the rest (roughly corresponding to tenon, stem and mouthpiece in a modern pipe) is made of organic material, usually *tacuara* reed. Susnik does not indicate the material of the tubed piece to be inserted. However, this can be discerned from the description of a pipe in the collection of the Weltmuseum, Vienna, donated by the German explorer Wanda Hanke in 1935, inventory no. 124.804 "Tabakspfeife" (i.e. tobacco pipe), with the description: 'brown reed'; I am grateful to Dr. Claudia Augustat for having made the collections and inventory books available to me. The website of the Museo Etnográfico Andrés Barbero in Asunción, Paraguay, also indicated *tacuara* reed as the material used; see 'La manaufactura indígena a través algunos objetos de las colecciones del museo', http://www.museobarbero.org.py/visita _guiada.htm.

5. For instance, a map reproduced by Bartolomé lists ninety-three communities (2009: 373; the number also confirmed by vom Hau and Wilde 2010: 1301), while Remorini (2009: 108), and an undated map given to me in the Dirección de Asuntos Guaraníes in the provincial capital Posadas (Direccíon de Asuntos Guaraníes: no date), indicate fifty-four communities. More recently, Salamanca (2012: 192–193) provides a map based also on data from the Direccíon de Asuntos Guaraníes, which lists ninety-four communities.

6. Law no. 5598, 28 September 2004. The Law was promoted by Provincial Deputy Dr. Walter Insaurralde, to whom I am also grateful for the full text (consisting of seven articles, the first two of which demand specifically the introduction of Guaraní as an alternative language at all levels in state schools).

7. Oberá is a provincial town two hours away by bus from Posadas, and known primarily for its yearly immigrant festival, the 'Fiesta Nacional del Inmigrante'.

8. Javier Gastaldo is the son of sculptor Arturo Gastaldo, a deceased founding member of the Arts Faculty.

9. Cf. http://jorge-msb.blogspot.com/2007/04/15-de-abril-da-de-la-alfarera.html.

10. 'Experimental Archeology' was a term first coined by Robert Ascher (1961) to signify the practices of interpreting archaeological data through practical, 'imitative' and 'replicative' experiments.

11. Weber's dictum was notably followed in anthropology by Clifford Geertz (1973: 5, 1983: 56–58).

12. Cf. Dutra's thesis in art education at the University of Santa Maria (Rio Grande do Sul State, Southern Brazil) (Dutra 2005).

13. *Ñamandú*, or *Ñanderú*, 'our ancestral father, a superior deity, for variations; see Bartolomé (2009: 177f.) and Melia (1991).

14. For recent examples, see Tythacott and Arvanitis (2014).

15. Carmen dos Santos called it the community of the *cerro de Santa Ana*, but in fact it is community of *Santa Ana Poty*.

16. For the broader historical-ideological configuration, see also Fausto (2007) and Fausto and Heckenberger (2007); and for the specific archeology of the colonial Jesuit reduction of Santa Ana, Poujade (2009) and Halberstadt (2010).

17. Paulito Villalba is a renowned *cacique* and he appears on images used by the Guaraní and their official organisms in Misiones to promote their cause. The *Oficina de Asuntos Guaranies,* which includes the *Consejo de Caciques de la Nación Mbya Guaraní*, Council of the *Caciques* of the Mbya Guaraní Nation and *Consejo de Ancianos y Guías Espirituales de la Nacón Guaraní,* Council of Elders and Spiritual Guides of the Guaraní Nation.

18. I did not establish whether basketry was practiced among this group.

References

Ambrosetti, J. B. 1894. 'Los Indios Cainguá del Alto Paraná (Misiones)', *Boletín del Instituto Geográfico Argentino* 15: 661–744.

Ascher, R. 1961. 'Experimental Archaeology', *American Anthropologist* 63(4): 793–816.

Bartolomé, M. A. 2009. *Parientes de la Selva: Los Guaraníes Mbya de la Argentina.* Asunción: CEADUC.

Brochado, J. P.. 1973. Migraciones que difundieron la Tradicion Alfarera Tupi Guaraní. *Relaciones*; Tomo VII Nueva Serie. Buenos Aires: Sociedad Argentina de Antropología.

Chiti, J. F. 1997. *Cerámica Indígena Archeológica Argentina: Las Técnicas. Los Orígenes. El Diseño.* Buenos Aires: Condorhuasi.

Clastres, P. 1998[1972]. *Chronicle o the Guyaki Indians.* London: Faber and Faber.

Crapanzano, V. 1990. 'On Dialogue', *The Interpretation of Dialogue* (edited by Tullio Maranhão). Chicago: University of Chicago Press.

———. 2004. *Imaginative Horizons: An Essay in Literary-Philosophical Anthropology.* Chicago: University of Chicago Press.

Crivos, M., et al. 2004. 'Nature and domestic life in the Valle del Cuñapirú (Misiones, Argentina): Reflections on Mbyá-Guaraní ethnoecology', *Agriculture and Human Values* 21: 111–125.

———. 2012. 'Changing Life Strategies: Mbya People and Their Relationship with Tourism', in P. Seymore and J. L. Roberg (eds), *Tourism in Northeast Argentina: The Intersection of Human and Indigenous Rights with the Environment.* Lanham: Lexington Books.

Desai, A., and M. Svasek. 2015. 'Transvisionay Imaginations: Artistic Subjectivity and Creativity in Tamil Nadu', in Ø. Fuglerud and L. Wainwright (eds), *Art, Objects and Value: Perspectives on Creativity and Materialization.* Oxford: Berghahn Books.

Dutra, E. 2005. Da Cerâmica Arqueológica Indígina à Cerâmica Artística Contemporânea: Uma Questão de Identidade Cultural na Formação e Ação de Professores.Dissertação de Mestrado. Universidade Federal de Santa Maria – UFSM, Brazil. Available at http://cascavel.cpd.ufsm.br/tede/tde_arquivos/18/TDE-2007-04-20T170557Z-514/Publico/EDUARDODUTRA.pdf

Escobar, T. 1986. *El mito del arte y el mito del pueblo: cuestiones sobre arte popular.* Asunción: Peroni Ediciones & Museo del Barro.

———. 2004. *El arte fuera de sí.* Asunción: CAV/Museo del Barro.

———. 2007. *Interpretación de las Artes Visuales en el Paraguay.* Asunción: Servi-Libro.

Fausto, C. 2007. 'If God were a Jaguar: Cannibalism and Christianity among the Guarani (16th–20th Centuries)', in C. Fausto and M. Heckenberger (eds), *Time and Memory in Indigenous Amazonia: Anthropological Perspectives.* Gainesville: University Press of Florida.

Fausto, C., and M. Heckenberger. 2007. 'Introduction: Indigenous History and the History of the "Indians"', in C. Fausto and M. Heckenberger (eds), *Time and Memory in Indigenous Amazonia: Anthropological Perspectives.* Gainesville: University Press of Florida.

Gandulfo, C. 2007. *Entiendo pero no hablo: el Guaraní 'accorentinado' en una escuela rural: usos y significaciones.* Buenos Aires: Editorial Antropofagia.

Geertz, C. 1973. 'Thick Description: Toward an Interpretive Theory of Culture', *The Interpretation of Cultures.* New York: Basic Books.

————. 1983. "'From the Native's Point of View'": On the Nature of Anthropological Understanding', *Local Knowledge*. New York: Basic Books.

Goulart, M. 1997. *Projeto Salvamento Arqueológico Uruguai*. Volume IV Cerâmica Universidade do Vale do Itajaí – Univali, Centrais Elétricas do Sul do Brasil S/A – Eletrosul.Itajaí: Impressão COPITEC – Florianópolis.

Grasseni, C. (ed.). 2007. *Skilled Visions: Between Apprenticeship and Standards*. Oxford: Berghahn Books.

Gustafson, B. 2009. *New Languages of the State: Indigenous Resurgence and the Politics of Knowledge in Bolivia*. Durham: Duke University Press.

Halberstadt, L. 2010. 'Puesta en valor de fragmentos cerámicos recuperados en intervenciones arqueológicas concretadas en la reducción jesuita de Santa Ana', MA thesis, Universidad Nacional de Misiones, Facultad de Artes, Maestría en Culturas Guaraní Jesuítica, Posadas.

Inventarbuch (Post VII – 1935, Sammlung: Frau Dr. Wanda Hanke), Weltmuseum, Vienna.

Kubler, G. 1962. *The Shape of Time: Remarks on the History of Things*. New Haven: Yale University Press.

Lévi-Strauss, C. 1988. *The Jealous Potter*. Chicago: University of Chicago Press.

Ley 5598, Honorable Legislatura, Provincia de Corrientes, 28 September 2004.

Maranhão, T. 1986. *Therapeutic Discourse and Socratic Dialogue*. Madison: University of Wisconsin Press.

———— (ed.). 1990. *The Interpretation of Dialogue*. Chicago: University of Chicago Press.

———— (ed.). 1998. 'Anthropology and the Question of the Other', *Paideuma* 44 (themed issue)

Maranhão, T, and B. Streck (eds). 2003. *Translation and Ethnography: The Anthropological Challenge of Intercultural Understanding*. Tucson: University of Arizona Press.

Martin, M. 2000. *Verstehen: The Uses of Understanding in Social Science*. New Brunswick: Transaction Publishers.

Mayntzhusen, F. 2009[1948]. *Los Aché-Guayakí*. Posadas: Junta de Estudios Históricos.

Melia, B. 1988. ‚Die schönen Ur-Worte: Die Kunst des Wortes bei den Guaraní', in M. Münzel (ed.), *Die Mythen sehen: Bilder und Zeichen vom Amazonas*. Frankfurt: Museum für Völkerkunde.

————. 1991. *El guaraní: Experiencia Religiosa*. Asunción: CEADUC.

Museo del Barro. 1998. *Catálogo*. Asunción: Museo del Barro.

Münzel, M. 1983. *Die Aché Ostparaguays*. Frankfurt: Museum für Völkerkunde.

Nelson, R. S. 2003. 'Appropriation', in R. S. Nelson and R. Shiff (eds), *Critical Terms for Art History*. Chicago: University of Chicago Press.

Nunes, A. L. Ruschel, and E. Dutra. 2015. *Da cerâmica arqueológica indígena à cerâmica artística contemporânea: identidade(s), cultura(s), educação e arte visual na formação de professores*. Educação em arte na contemporaneidade. Eds. Moema Martins Rebouças / Maria GoreteDadalto Gonçalves. Vitoria, ES: Editorial UFES.

Peers, L., and A. K Brown (eds). 2003. *Museums and Source Communities: A Routledge Reader.* London: Routledge.

Poujade, R. A. (y equipo). 2009. *Aproximaciones a la reducción de Santa Ana y su
contexto –ARSA – Misiones – Argentina.* Posadas: Editorial Universitaria / Universidad Nacional de Misiones.

Ranco, D. J. 2006. 'Toward a Native Anthropology: Hermeneutics, Hunting Stories,
and Theorizing from Within', *Wicazo Sa Review* 21(2, Fall): 61–78.

Remorini, C. 2009. *Aporte a la Caracterización Etnográfica de los Procesos de
Salud-Enfermedad en las Primeras Etapas del Ciclo Vital, en Comunidades
Mbya-Guaraní de Misiones, República Argentina,* PhD thesis. La Plata: Edito-
rial de la Universidad Nacional de la Plata.

Ricoeur, P. 1981. *Hermeneutics and the Human Sciences.* Cambridge: Cambridge
University Press.

Rojas, L. 2006. 'Curso Taller "Introducción a las técnicas y formas de la cerámica
guaraní"', *Boletín Junta de Estudios Históricos de Misiones,* October, 19.

Salamanca, C. 2012. *Alecrín: Cartografías para territorios en emergencia.* Rosario:
Editorial Universidad Nacional de Rosario.

Schneider, A. 2003. 'On "Appropriation": A Critical Reappraisal of the Concept and
its Application in Global Art Practices', *Social Anthropology* 11(2): 215–229.

———. 2006a. *Appropriation as Practice: Art and Identity in Argentina.* New York:
Palgrave.

———. 2006b. 'Appropriations', in Arnd Schneider and Chris Wright (eds), *Contemporary Art and Anthropology.* Oxford: Berg.

———. 2012. 'Beyond Appropriation: Significant Overlays in Guaraní-inspired Designs', *Journal of Material Culture* 17(4): 345–367.

Seymore, P., and J.L. Roberg, (eds). 2012. *Tourism in Northeast Argentina: The
Intersection of Human and Indigenous Rights with the Environment.* Lanham:
Lexington Books.

Stangos, N. 1994. *The Thames and Hudson Dictionary of Art and Artists.* London:
Thames and Hudson.

Susnik, B. 1986. *Artesanía Indígena. Ensayo Analítico.* Asunción: Asociación Indi-
genista del Paraguay.

Svašek, M. 2012a. 'Introduction: Affective Moves: Transit, Transition and Transformation', in *Moving Subjects, Moving Objects: Transnationalism, Cultural
Production and Emotions,* ed. M. Svašek. Oxford: Berghahn Books.

———. 2012b. 'Improvising in a World of Movement: Transit, Transition and Transformation', in H. Anheier and Y. Raj (eds), *Cultural Expression, Creativity and
Innovation.* Isar. London: Sage.

Tedlock, D. 1983. *The Spoken Word and the Word of Interpretation.* Philadelphia:
University of Pennsylvania Press.

Tythacott, L., and K. Arvanitis (eds). 2014. *Museums and Restitution: New Practices,
New Approaches.* Farnham: Ashgate.

Torres, D. G. 2007. *Cultura Guaraní,* 2nd edition. Asunción: Servilibro.

Trinh, T. M., and N. N. Chen. 1994. 'Speaking Nearby', in L. Taylor (ed.), *Visualizing
Anthropology.* New York and London: Routledge.

Verde, F. 2003. 'Astrónomos e Astrólogos, nativos e Antropólogos – as virtudes epistemológicos do etnocentrismo', *Etnográfica* 7(2): 305–319 (also available in English as 'Truth as the Critical Edge: Gadamer's Hermeneutics and Anthropological Knowledge', available at http://iscte.academia.edu/FilipeVerde/Papers).

Vom Hau, M., and G. Wilde. 2010. '"We have Always Lived Here": Indigenous Movements, Citizenship and Poverty in Argentina', *Journal of Development Studies* 46(7): 1283–1303.

Weber, M. 1978. *Economy and Society.* Berkeley: University of California Press.

Wilde, G. 2007. 'De la depredación a la conversacón. Génesis y evolución del dicurso hegemónico sobre la selva misionera y sus habitantes', *Ambiente & Sociedade* 10(1): 87–106.

Young, J. O. 2008. *Cultural Appropriation and the Arts.* Oxford: Blackwell.

Zonta, M. L., E. E. Oyhenart and G. T. Navone. 2011. 'Nutritional vulnerability in Mbyá-Guaraní adolescents and adults from Misiones, Argentina', *American Journal of Human Biology.* doi: 10.1002/ajhb.21175

6

POSITIONED CREATIVITY
MUSEUMS, POLITICS AND INDIGENOUS ART
IN BRITISH COLUMBIA AND NORWAY

Øivind Fuglerud

In her book *Primitive Art in Civilized Places,* Sally Price (1989) tells the story of a man in Suriname setting up a stall next to the road leading to the airport to sell carved objects to passing tourists. Responding to repeated questions from his customers about the symbolic meaning of his work, the artist used to explain – truthfully – that they were decorative objects only. Perceiving the buyers' dissatisfaction, he finally gave up and bought a dictionary of local iconographic motifs. Although not able to understand it since he was illiterate, he started using the illustrations in the book as models for his own carving. When selling his works, he simply showed the book to his customers so they could look up the meaning of their purchases themselves. Price drily notes that, through this technique, 'the man's life became more tranquil, his profits picked up considerably, the tourists boarded their planes in better spirits, and the myth of a pervasive iconography in the arts of the Maroons circumvented a potentially troubling setback' (1989: 118).

The case presented by Price illustrates two points. Firstly, in the present-day world what may be perceived as 'traditional' cultural expression is often – most often – a response to external influences; secondly, in the case of indigenous art, such responses may reflect demands for the natural, the authentic, the handmade – the primitive (cf. Miller 1991). As pointed out so clearly by Nelson H. H. Graburn in the introduction to his pioneering book *Ethnic and Tourist Arts: Cultural Expressions from the Fourth World* (1976:

1), artistic expressions of the 'Fourth World' are today rarely produced for internal consumption or according to unmodified tastes. Instead, they reflect the difference from, and accommodation to, the realities of the majority societies surrounding them. The study of Fourth World art is different from the study of 'primitive art' of early anthropology; it is the study of changing arts – 'of emerging ethnicities, modifying identities, and commercial and colonial stimuli and repressive actions' (ibid.: 2).

In his book, Graburn suggests a classification of the different directions taken by processes of change in Fourth World art. While a detailed discussion of his categories is not needed in this chapter – partly because I find the categories of First, Second and so on World a bit outdated – his general point that changes in indigenous art may take different directions came to occupy my mind during a stay in British Columbia in 2010. Coming from Norway, a country where indigenous politics, including cultural politics, has been as high on the political agenda as in British Columbia, I was struck by the difference in artistic practices in the two regions. The present chapter starts from the observation that First Nations art is identifiable and visible in a very different way to that of Sami art in the Norwegian capital Oslo, or indeed in Norway as a whole. One aspect of this difference is the appearance in British Columbia of standardized, indigenous shapes and forms, such as stylized thunderbirds, killer whales and salmon, on mass-produced items and nick-nacks. As observed by Charlotte Townsend-Gault (2004: 184), on anything you buy, be it to eat or drink, or to protect yourself from sun, wind or rain, you may find a First Nations crest or a motif derived from a crest, an insignia marking status in First Nations communities.[1] This kind of circulation of images is unknown in Norway. Another aspect is the presence of easily identifiable First Nations art in Vancouver museums, galleries and public spaces, and the contrasting lack of easily identifiable Sami art in Oslo (see fig. 6.1). First Nations art in general, and art of this kind produced by a small group of recognized and well-promoted artists in particular, today serves as a trademark for the Canadian Northwest Coast. In Vancouver itself, one finds, within walking distance, an impressive number of private and public galleries promoting indigenous art centred on standardized

Figure 6.1. Robert Davidson, *Sgaan Sgaanwee*. Photo: courtesy Robert Davidson.

shapes and forms. In Norway, Sami art is not easily distinguishable from mainstream Norwegian art, and the only place in the capital, Oslo, where you can be certain to find Sami culture exhibited in some form would be the Norsk Folkemuseum, a museum of cultural history displaying local variants of Norwegian material culture.

Against this backdrop, the question I wish to pose concerns the interaction and interchange between museums and what happens outside museum walls – more specifically, between museums and artistic practices. In the last decade or so, within the field of museum research, there has been an interest in museums as not only reflecting a particular state of the world but as contributing to forming this world in a more systematic sense, acting as historical agents. Sharon Macdonald, for example, argues that museums 'have acted not simply as the embodiment of theoretical debates, but also as part of the visualizing technology through which such ideas were formed' (1996: 7). Christopher Whitehead (2009) argues that the development and clarification of different roles by museums in the United Kingdom in the nineteenth century were crucial to the formation of academic disciplines in Britain and thereby to the ways in which material worlds were conceptualized within these disciplines. The question posed in this chapter is: in what ways have museums in British Columbia and Norway stimulated and reinforced the production of particular discourses and practices of indigenous art? To shed light on this issue I discuss the work of two academic institution-builders and two artists, one of each kind from both countries.

The reasons for taking this approach are several. As a point of departure I take it that art is produced by people; if one wishes to understand artistic practices, one needs to look at what artists are doing. This activity, however, does not play out in a void; more than many other forms of activity, practicing art is intertwined with institutional support and economic patronage. What I hope to show is that institutions relevant to artistic practices are not carved in stone, but are susceptible to political shifts and the influence of strong-minded leaders. Analysing the interplay of institution-building and individual artistic practices, this chapter seeks to throw light on the social production of creativity. In the two cases explored below, institutional changes were crucial to the establishment of local 'art worlds' – loosely defined as the routine interaction between producers, critics, distributors, consumers and others involved in bringing forth an artwork (cf. Becker 1982). As will become clear, institutional intervention allowed the two forms of indigenous art to take different directions. If we are to get a better grasp on how processes of cultural change develop and take shape, we need to be more specific with respect to both the characteristics of the wider world-in-formation to which individuals adjust and contribute, and to the conceptual and cultural tools they use in this process.

Historical Legacies in British Columbia and Norway

The starting point, and possibility, for a comparison of indigenous art in British Columbia and Norway lies in the fact that in both areas there have been and still are artists identifying themselves as 'indigenous artists', and/or institutions defining artworks in this particular way. Nevertheless, one may ask to what extent social conditions in the countries are at all comparable. Certainly, there are important differences, not least in scale. According to the 2006 Census, a total of 1,172,790 people in Canada identified themselves as Aboriginal persons, that is, as First Nations, Métis or Inuit. Compared to Norway's total population of around 5 million and approximate Sami population of 50–60,000, Canada's size and the magnitude of the country's Aboriginal population are of course both formidable. However, if we limit the study to the province of British Columbia, the situations are more comparable. This province has a total population of approximately 4.5 million, out of which 4.8 per cent reported an Aboriginal identity in the 2006 Census.[2] The larger First Nations communities include the Haida, Tsimshian, Nuxalk (Bella Coola), Northern Wakashan, Kwakwakw'wakw (Kwakiutl), Nuu-chah-nulth (Nootka) and the Coast Salish. Among these large groups, however, are a number of distinct languages and countless dialects. Every group has their own unique elements, but in general they share a similar social and cultural structure. Both in British Columbia and Norway the First Nations / Sami population is divided between the traditional homelands of the groups in question and urban areas. In the city ('census metropolitan area') of Vancouver, the largest city on the Canadian West Coast, 1.9 per cent of the population in 2006 had Aboriginal backgrounds (Environics Institute 2010). In Norway, the traditional Sami homeland is primarily in the northernmost part of the country, in the sparsely populated county of Finnmark, while the urban area of most importance is the capital, Oslo, located in the south. According to a rough estimate, which is the only kind possible, the Sami constitute around 5 per cent of Oslo's population (Sami Instituhtta 2006), making Oslo today the part of Norway with the largest Sami population.

Before continuing, a brief note on terminology may be in order. The label 'Aboriginal' is the official term referring to the first inhabitants of Canada, and includes First Nations, Inuit and Métis peoples. This term came into popular usage in Canadian contexts after 1982, when Section 35 of the Canadian Constitution defined the term as such. However, when not referring to official registration, I here prefer 'indigenous', as this is a more common term used by the Sami population in Norway to refer to themselves and other first inhabitants in English and is also uncontroversial in Canada. In Canada, 'First Nations' is a term used to describe Aboriginal peoples of

Canada who are ethnically neither Métis nor Inuit. This term came into common usage in the 1970s and 80s and generally replaced the term 'Indian', although unlike 'Indian', the term 'First Nations' does not have a legal definition. In day-to-day use, the term 'Indian' is in Canada outdated, and is sometimes perceived as derogatory and offensive, somewhat in the same way as the older term for Sami, 'Lapp', is perceived as offensive in Norway. However, 'Indian' refers to the legal identity of a First Nations person who is registered under the Indian Act, and as such still has a legal content. The term 'Northwest Coast Art' is a commonly used term for First Nations art from the west coast of Canada.[3]

Both in Canada and Norway, the general situation of the indigenous populations and their rights to land, resources and economic compensation have been sensitive political issues, in large part because of the assimilation policies and discriminatory practices to which the indigenous populations have been subjected. In Norway, language policy – 'Norwegianization' of the Sami – was a focal point of the state's politics for more than one hundred years. This first took shape with the establishment of the Lapp-foundation ('Finnefondet') in 1851, involving an annual allocation of substantial resources over the national budget to eradicate Sami language and culture. This policy of assimilation culminated in the decades before and after World War II, when the Sami issue became part of a perceived threat to Norwegian security from its eastern borders with Finland and the Soviet empire. While the interior of the Sami areas populated by nomadic reindeer-herders to some extent escaped this practice, the coastal areas, where sedentary Sami made a living from fishing and farming, felt the consequences of this cultural onslaught. In the municipality of Kvænangen, for example, the rate of the population identifying as Sami in the period 1930–1950 went down from 44 per cent to zero (Bjørklund 1985). As will become apparent in what follows, this national policy slowly started changing from the 1950s onwards when the Sami population increasingly gained recognition as a separate First Nation ('Urbefolkning') with specific rights within the territory of Norway.

As in Norway, Canadian schools in general and residential schools in particular were used consciously as a tool for suppressing indigenous identities. This residential school system has left in its wake a tragic legacy. In addition to the ethnic oppression practiced, many former students have reported experiences such as forcible confinement and physical and sexual abuse. In June 2008, the government of Canada formally apologized to former Aboriginal students of residential schools. The apology recognized that the policy of assimilation implemented through these schools 'was wrong, has caused great harm, and has no place in [this] country' (in Environics Institute 2011: 29). Eight out of ten Aboriginal people in Vancouver say they have been affected by the residential school system, either personally or through family members. This may be one explanation why only 52 per cent of Aboriginal people in Vancouver say that they are proud to be Canadian (Environics Institute 2011).

Today, relationships between First Nations and the federal government of British Columbia remain tense and entangled in legal complexities. While the Canadian Constitution Act of 1982 recognized Aboriginal rights without defining them, the principle position of the authorities of British Columbia was, until recently, that First Nations' land rights were extinguished by the colonial government before British Columbia became part of Canada in 1871. In one important case in the late 1980s, the chief justice ruled that as a result of this preconfederation legal history, Aboriginal rights in general existed 'at the pleasure of the crown'.[4] Although this position has now changed, British Columbia has been slower in establishing treaties with its First Nations than most other provinces in Canada and there have been recurrent conflicts between First Nations and the provincial government over logging, fishing rights and other natural resources over decades. Incidentally, one of the ongoing conflicts concerns the permission given to Norwegian companies to establish fish farms in waters claimed by British Columbian First Nations.

The Hawthorns at MoA

Moving on to the role of museums, the most influential institution in British Columbia in shaping perceptions of indigenous people and their art is the University of British Columbia (UBC). In 1947, the university appointed anthropologists Harry and Audrey Hawthorn to establish an anthropology program and to expand a collection of ethnographic material. Harry Hawthorn became the first professor of anthropology at UBC. In 1949, he took up the position of director of the Museum of Anthropology (MoA), a position he still held when the new museum building was completed in 1976. Audrey Hawthorn worked as curator in the museum. Under the Hawthorns, MoA developed a long-lasting interest in British Columbian First Nations art. Their involvement provides a fascinating case with considerable historical depth for discussing the relationship between art and anthropology, including the role of ethnographic museums. Central to MoA's engagement was the museum's active role in projecting a particular image of the First Nations communities in British Columbia as being on the brink of social and cultural extinction. Over time, this discursive framing opened up the possibility for the Canadian government to appropriate 'primitive' motifs in forging symbols of a modern cultural identity different from that of the country's former colonial masters.

Harry Hawthorn's first engagement with First Nations issues was to write a report on Native Indian Affairs issued in 1948 (Dawn 2004). In this report, which also dealt with questions of First Nations health, welfare and education, art was given priority. The Hawthorn report was subsequently integrated into the *Report of the Royal Commission on National Development in the Arts, Letters and Sciences 1949–51,* which became instrumental in reformulating the concept of Canadian national identity as expressed in the arts. As a result of Hawthorn's interests and ideas, the University of British Columbia in 1949 initiated a totem pole project through which a number of woodcarvers of First Nations background restored old poles and carved new ones on-site at the university. In 1954, Hawthorn and the Indian Affairs Branch initiated a totem pole salvage program where totem poles were brought from abandoned villages for conservation and display. Many of the poles recovered through this program are now found in the Great Hall of MoA, the museum's main exhibition hall (see fig. 6.2). This recovery project was part of a conscious effort on the part of UBC, Hawthorn and the museum to salvage the remains of a tradition regarded as dead (Duffek 2009: 18). It should be said that at the time when the Hawthorns arrived, this understanding was already well established – their particular role became to try to do something about it. For example, in the catalogue of the

Figure 6.2. MoA's Great Hall. Photo: Øivind Fuglerud.

first exhibition in Canada to display First Nations artefacts in an art gallery context, the 1927 *Exhibition of Canadian West Coast Art: Native and Modern,* shown in Ottawa, Toronto and Montreal, the director of the National Gallery, Eric Brown, lamented: 'The disappearance of these [Indian] arts under the penetration of trade and civilization is more regrettable than can be imagined' (1927). 'Native art' in the exhibition was only represented by old museum pieces, while 'modern' works of art were borrowed from non-indigenous living artists. The exhibition thus presented indigenous art as belonging to the past, a tradition absorbed and replaced by modern landscape painting (Nemiroff 1996; Dawn 2004). Through this appropriation it evaded the issue of oppression, and projected the Canadian state into the past. As ethnologist Marius Barbeau, who was involved in organizing the exhibition expressed it: '[a] commendable feature of this aboriginal art for us is that it is truly Canadian in its inspiration. It has sprung up wholly from the soil and the sea within our national boundaries' (1927: 4). Not only can this paradigm of cultural decay be said to have made invisible the complex processes of continued resistance and accommodation of First Nations communities to white society, Marcia Crosby has pointed out that it also served as a construct for defining and knowing what she terms the 'Imaginary Indian' (1991) – that is, white society's construction of 'Indian-ness' for their own purposes.

The understanding that the golden age of indigenous cultural and artistic tradition was over was, until recently, shared by anthropologists and art historians alike. The anthropologist Joan Vastokas, as late as 1975, dated the total death of all indigenous culture on the West Coast as occurring between the potlatch ban of 1885 and the 1920s (Vastokas 1975). This paradigm has been promoted also by certain First Nations interests. In a eulogy from 1982 to Mungo Martin, a First Nations artist central to MoA in its early years, the B.C. Indian Arts Society holds: 'The dying of Kwakiutl society was a close and terrible reality. The vanishing of a proud culture meant … desertion of villages and ebbing in interest in ways of the old…. It was Mungo Martin who brought back the Native's historic heritage after the Native arts had almost dropped out of existence, … restoring his arts and traditions to survive in the new age' (in Glass 2006: 28, 32).

Aron Glass (ibid.: 33) notes that the Kwakwaka'wakw – that is, the current proper name for the Kwakiutl – in general have been amenable to participating in projects of ethnographic salvage and cultural objectification, something that 'has contributed directly to the maintenance of their global recognition and centrality in the Native art world'. In other words, rather than a sign of deprivation, promoting a need for salvage anthropology may be seen as the Kwakwaka'wakw exercising agency in the form of what Mary Louise Pratt (1992: 7) has termed 'autoethnography', the self-representation of colonized subjects in ways that engage with the colonizers' own terms. Paradoxically, the perspective of cultural disintegration may be directly related to a growing appreciation of native aesthetics in British Columbia. Glass (2006) suggests that the paradigm of salvation was instrumental in establishing a British Columbia art world, in the sense that the redefinition of artefacts as art requires the removal of objects' use value. This was accomplished in British Columbia through embracing the inevitability of cultural decay and the non-functionality of objects in the present (ibid.: 36). This perception of 'fatal impact' brought by the colonial powers (cf. Thomas 1994) was perpetuated after World War II when 'renaissance' – the rebirth of something already deceased – established itself as a paradigm for judging and positioning contemporary, native artistic production.

Guttorm Gjessing and the Ethnographic Museum in Oslo

Like MoA, the Ethnographic Museum in Oslo has had its influential personalities. One of the most important was Guttorm Gjessing, who served as director of the museum from 1947 until his retirement in 1973 and was as significant in shaping popular perceptions of indigenous people in Norway as the Hawthorns were in British Columbia. Gjessing, born in 1906, was educated as an archaeologist and spent the first part of his career working on one of the main questions in Nordic archaeology at the time, the origin of Sami culture and its relationship to the more recent Germanic migration to the North. From 1929 to 1936, Gjessing researched rock carvings within the area covered by Tromsø Museum in the northernmost part of the country. From 1936 to 1940, he worked as a conservator at this museum, and after settling in Oslo he continued to work on the same question. During these years, before and after the Second World War, he published six dissertations. With the exception of one on Sami costumes published with his wife, all dealt with archaeological material from northern Norway. With the 500-page publication *The Younger Stone-age in Northern Norway* ('Yngre steinalder i Nord-Norge'), he established himself as the most important archaeological expert in this field.

Gjessing's central argument was that archaeological findings from northern Norway, including the rock carvings, belonged to a stone age culture having its origin in a particular Arctic way of life. He dismissed earlier theories that had stipulated that artefacts and rock-carving techniques found in northern Norway had been brought there by migrants from the south or the east. Instead he argued the existence of a Palaeolithic 'proto-Lappish' (Sami) population in Norway. To explain the emergence of this population, he coined the idea of a separate 'circumpolar' cultural area that had resulted from the particularly harsh living conditions close to the North Pole. This concept is still used widely by specialists in the field. Gjessing's academic career is an example of the ways that research may have far-reaching impacts on state policy. From 1956, Gjessing became an important member of the government-appointed Sami committee ('Samekomiteen'), whose recommendations are regarded by historians as a turning point in Norwegian–Sami relations. Among the suggestions put forward by the committee was to consolidate a separate Sami territorial area around the municipal areas of Karasjok, Kautokeino and Polmak – all in the northernmost county of Finnmark – where Sami cultural and political institutions could be developed and particular regulations for the use of Sami language could be implemented. This was the beginning of the contemporary two-nation policy of the Norwegian government, which recognizes that the Norwegian state is established on the territory of two nations, the Norwegian and the Sami, and that the Sami population, consequently, has special rights to land and resources. However, five years before this committee was established, Gjessing more or less singlehandedly made another decision of great importance when, as director of the Ethnographic Museum, he transferred the Sami collections to the Norsk Folkemuseum. This should be seen as an act of institutional innovation. In assessing the radicalism of this decision, it should be noted that the Sami collection was the very origin of the Ethnographic Museum. In a letter to the Board of the University of Oslo ('Akademiske Kollegium') seeking permission for the transfer, Gjessing writes:

> One of the problems that the Sami have always faced is the understanding, in the general opinion, of not being equal to other Norwegian citizens. In our museum Sami culture is treated in a way comparable with cultures outside Europe, it is by necessity classified as an 'alien culture' in Scandinavia. Both in terms of science and in terms of 'cultural politics' this is, in my opinion, most questionable.

By removing Sami material culture from the ethnographic realm, Gjessing helped to open the door for a conceptualization of Sami culture and aesthetics as dynamic and contemporary, rather than as a relic of the past.

My argument here is that Gjessing's understanding of Sami culture as indigenous to northern Norway from prehistoric times until the present has influenced the perception – and therefore also the practice – of Sami art. In one of the first thorough reviews of Sami art, written by art historian Harry Fett (1940), we find Gjessing's concept of a circumpolar cultural region reflected in the linking of Sami art to contemporary tribal art in Siberia, North America and Greenland. This is not to say that this assessment was unbiased or free from derogatory evaluations. Seeing Sami art as the cultural expression of a 'living Paleolithicum', the review lacks nothing in racial orientalism. Fett's text is teeming with observations like the following: 'It is in the world of the animals that the Paleolithic art includes us, the magical adventures of primitive boredom. Animals are what these people know, the animals they kindle to their minds.'

Nevertheless, where Fett's conceptualization differs from ideas in contemporary British Columbia is that, according to Fett, the primitive and their Palaeolithic art are still alive among us. Even in his discussion of John Andreas Savio (1902–1938), the first artist of Sami background to enter the contemporary Norwegian art world, a man who was educated at the Norwegian Academy of Art and exhibited his paintings in Paris in 1937, Fett has no qualms in tracing the historical line back ten thousand years, describing the technique used in Savio's later works as an 'impressionistic Paleolithic style'. Savio's art, according to Fett, describes 'a people that in our own time live their pre-historic life with animals and great nature'; Savio has portrayed a part of Norway 'not through the eyes of the tourist or the stranger, but with the eyes of the race itself' (1940: 246). This interpretation was part of Fett's somewhat peculiar 'psycho-archeological' understanding of human history, where he identified four basic human dispositions existing throughout history, one of them being the nomadic. While such ideas may now seem dated, Harry Fett was not just any art historian. In addition to being a wealthy industrialist, he was the first ever director general for the protection of cultural heritage in Norway ('Riksantikvar') and a very influential person in upper-class conservative circles in early-twentieth-century Norway. He was also centrally involved in the establishment of the Norsk Folkemuseum, the museum receiving the Sami collection from the Ethnographic Museum, and as such part of Norwegian museum history (Aavitsland 2014).

Creativity and Innovation

In the second part of this chapter, I look briefly at two artists, Bill Reid and Iver Jåks, the former Canadian, the latter Norwegian, working in approximately the same period, who through their importance to the indigenous art worlds emerging in the two countries became positioned as pathfinders and gatekeepers to contemporary indigenous art in Canada and Norway respectively. Born in a period when indigenous culture in both countries was severely repressed, they personally contributed in significant ways to change this situation by giving legitimacy to indigenous aesthetics. The two must both be characterized as 'modern' artists in the sense that their artistic journeys were highly individual and their works came to transcend the respective categories of craft seen as the proper artistic expressions within the two cultures at the time. What interests me is that, in spite of these similarities, their works are very different and their transition from craft to art was accomplished in different ways. I suggest that by examining these differences in relation to their different positions with respect to their societies and cultures, one may gain insights into how artistic creativity is socially produced.

The framing of the two artists as 'modern' and as important to the contemporary justifies a brief theoretical detour. The comparative study of art is fraught with challenges that are not easily overcome. One difficulty is that 'art' is a category of cultural production that emerged in a particular historical era as the result of particular social circumstances, those of European modernity (Miller 1991; Svašek 2007, 2010). Being a product of individualism, social fragmentation and a compensating faith in human progress developing from the fifteenth century onwards, the figure of 'the artist' came to be seen as able to re-create the authentic through the innovative capacity of his or her own genius. The European notion of art is closely connected with the understanding – as formulated for example by Georg Simmel in his *Philosophy of Money* from the year 1900 – that art is the one area where the fragmentation and alienation involved in capitalist production can be overcome. According to Simmel, the autonomy of the work of art signifies that it expresses a subjective, spiritual unity. The work of art requires only one single person, but it requires him totally, right down to his innermost core (Lloyd 1991: 96). Art, as understood in modern society is, therefore, fundamentally concerned with transcending the fragmented nature of contemporary life. Driven by an assumption that there may exist, at least in potential, a form of humanity that is integral and cohesive, art, in its quest for this state critically opposed to the present, tends to focus on the innovative, the spiritual and/or on the primitive other (cf. Miller 1991).

This historic specificity of the phenomenon – or at least of the label of 'art' – does, of course, complicate comparison. The debate surrounding the New York Museum of Modern Art's controversial 1984 exhibition *'Primitivism' in Twentieth Century Art: the Affinity of the Tribal and the Modern*, in which 'primitive' objects and objects of modern art were exhibited side by side, showed that presenting diverse cultural productions as equally 'artistic', whether or not a conception of art exists in the producing cultures, is not unproblematic (cf. McEvilley 1984; Foster 1985; Clifford 1988; Price 1989). As noted by Fred Myers (2006: 271): 'By finding similarities where there should be differences … MOMA's "primitivism" operated, it was argued, to universalize the aesthetic doctrine of Western Modernism – emphasizing the formal, material dimensions of art objects as their central quality and indirectly supporting a separable or autonomous dimension of human life that was "art".' This debate, on what Sally Price has called 'the universality principle', articulated in the proposition that 'art is a universal language' (1989: 32), has resurfaced on a number of subsequent occasions, for example, in relation to the new ethnographic museum in Paris, Musée du

Quai Branly, which tends to underline the aesthetic qualities of the objects it exhibits (cf. Ruiz-Gómez 2006; Price 2007; Dias 2008; Thomas 2008).

In the introduction to the present volume, the editors draw on Ingold and Hallam's (2007) discussion of innovation and improvisation as an alternative comparative tool to the 'universality principle' in relation to cultural creativity. According to Ingold and Hallam, reading creativity as innovation is to read it 'backwards' in terms of results, a reading said to be symptomatic of modernity, rather than 'forwards' in terms of the movements that gave rise to particular forms of creativity – that is, as improvisation. There is much to be said for this as an approach to exploring the maintenance of established cultural traditions, the authors' point that carrying on requires active regeneration being particularly apt (ibid.: 5–6). This perspective is, however, inadequate for my present purpose, since systematic differences in artistic results are precisely what I seek to elucidate in this chapter. Furthermore, there are deeper objections to Ingold and Hallam's approach, which can be illustrated by using one of their own examples: that of a new building designed by a famous modern architect (ibid.: 3). Why, the authors ask, do we not celebrate the creativity of the builders equally to that of the architect, given that materializing the design requires constant, creative improvisation? The answer, they argue, is that 'we are inclined to say that something is created only when it is *new*, meaning not that it has been newly produced, but that it is the manifest outcome of a newly concocted plan, formula, programme or recipe' (ibid.: 5). This 'modernistic' emphasis on *design*, in all dimensions of this word, goes against the authors' view that 'because it is the way we work, the creativity of our imaginative reflections is inseparable from our performative engagements with the materials that surround us' (ibid.: 3). This last sentence provides Ingold and Hallam's solution to the comparative challenge: that of focusing on concrete human-material interaction without regard to art or innovation.

To this I have two objections, both relevant to the subject of this chapter. The first is that in most cases the building being improvised on by the builders that Ingold and Hallam want to celebrate would not have been built was it not for the architect. To stay with their use of the example as a general allegory, their own case, therefore, may be said to refute the opening sentence and the most basic claim in their book, namely that 'there is no script for social and cultural life'. This is simply wrong, I argue, not because life is scripted by God, Culture or Society, but because people in fact script-write as part of their own intentional action. As argued so well in Kirsten Hastrup's contribution to Hallam and Ingold's own volume: 'Without a sense of plot, meaningful action would be precluded. The sense of plot is what integrates individual actions into a larger vision of the world, filled out imaginatively and acted upon. In that sense any social action is a creation, contributing to a history that outlasts (and outwits) our imagination' (2007: 199). This, we will see below, is also the case with artists, who do not simply engage with the material, but incorporate visions of time, space and social surroundings in their artworks.

My second objection is that while builders are no doubt important to make a building rise from the ground, their improvisation with materials is not necessarily what is most interesting about a construction project. A particular architectural design and the way it ties in with surroundings in terms of space and price reveal many things about the way human life is conceptualized in a particular time and place. The approval or not for a particular project design, whether this process of approval is institution-alized or informal, may have much to tell about social networks, political authority, economic influence and so on. To some of us, this may be as interesting as watching bricklayers build a wall. The general point, trans-ferable but not limited to art, is that what is accepted or not, and accorded value or not, is decided in social settings where market forces and power are at play – that is, not by the human-material exchange itself, but by what goes on *around* this interaction. This brings us back to MOMA's exhibition discussed above. As so perceptively noted by James Clifford (1988: 198), the exhibition more than anything documented 'a *taxonomic* moment', a redefinition of the status of non-Western objects and 'high art'. I would like to add that this taxonomic moment was in part also *constituted* by MOMA through the institutional power wielded by the museum in organizing the exhibition. The art from British Columbia and Norway I discuss below underwent parallel taxonomic reclassifications, but in different ways. While Jåks opened the existing art world to new forms of Sami artistic practices, Reid was instrumental in having traditional forms of craft reclassified as fine art.

Reid: Becoming Haida through Artistic Production

Bill Reid (1920–1998) is without doubt the most important artist in the so-called revival of Northwest Coast art developing from the late 1940s. Reid was born in Victoria and was of mixed white Canadian and Haida origin. He was brought up by a single mother in white Canadian society, and only became conscious of his mother's Haida ancestry in his teens. Reid told his biographer, Doris Shadbolt (1986), of remembering visits from his mother's relatives and the bracelets they wore with native designs on them without reflecting on the fact that the relatives were of First Nations background. Later, when he began to take an interest in the Haida side of his heritage, his mother was, in his own words, less than enchanted when he 'began digging up those old bones which she had spent her life trying to bury' (Shadbolt 2004: 28). It was only at the age of twenty-three that Reid, on a voyage of self-discovery, travelled to Queen Charlotte Islands, as the Haida Gwaii were then still called, and met his grandfather Charles Gladstone in Skidegate. As a young man, Gladstone had been adopted by his uncle, Charles Edenshaw (1839–1920), one of the great nineteenth-century carvers on the Northwest Coast. The experience led Reid to complete a course in jewellery-making while working as an announcer for the Canadian Broadcasting Corporation in Toronto, and to start exploring native aesthetics (see fig. 6.3). When attending his grandfather's funeral in 1954 he was, for the first time, exposed to carvings by Edenshaw, later characterized by him as being 'really deeply carved' (in Shadbolt 1986: 84). In his own words, after seeing the bracelets 'the world was not really the same' (in ibid.). Edenshaw's 'deep carving' set the direction of his artistic activity for many years to come.

What I find interesting in these life-story fragments is Bill Reid's position as outsider to Haida culture and art at the start of his artistic career. Reading his biography and his own lengthy writings on art and Haida culture, it is obvious that Reid made a conscious choice to become Haida, and that this transformation involved great personal efforts as well as a focused process of enskilment and interpretation (see also Schneider, this volume). It seems quite clear that a large part of what art meant to him was that it offered a way to recover something that was missing in his personal life. To Shadbolt's question of why, when approaching a fork in the road, he had chosen to follow the 'native path' rather than the mainstream route, he responded that Western culture lacked the mythical world that could affirm life for him and

Figure 6.3. Bill Reid, Raven design in gold, carving 1971. Photo: courtesy MoA.

give him the sense of inner conviction, knowledge and community he longed for (Shadbolt 2004: 30). The native path was made all the more difficult as it was a lonely journey and, in a sense, an imaginary one. The title of the anthology of his writings, *Solitary Raven,* is in this sense most appropriate. Throughout most of his career, Reid based his artistic activity on the firm belief that Haida culture was long dead (Duffek 2004: 71) and that the nineteenth-century art that he appreciated could not have been produced by contemporary Haida. Writing in 1956, he saw himself and his fellow carver Mungo Martin, both involved in activities organized by British Columbian museums, as 'atavists groping behind us toward the great days of the pasts, out of touch with the impulse and social pattern that produced the art' (Reid 2009). Referring to his carving of a new totem pole for the Haida Band Office in Skidegate in 1978, he stated that he had carved this pole 'as a memorial to the Haida of the past, not an attempt to turn the clock back' (in Duffek 2004: 88).

What is significant in terms of art history is that rather than using his artistic talent to explore new expressive possibilities, this position drove him into researching the formal dimensions of Haida art, a project conducted over the years in partnership with the ethnologist and Northwest Coast art expert Bill Holm (Holm and Reid 1978; also Holm 1965). As he saw social inclusion as no longer possible, since there was no longer anything in which to be included, the only way to locate 'Haida-ness' was through the essence of their cultural products. In a panel discussion on art organized by MoA in 1984, Reid was clear on this:

> I suppose the whole magic secret of art is that it does express the personality or the essence of not only the culture but of the individual who creates it and the people of his own generation and, if it's a long, containing culture, the whole background that led to that stage of its development. It is the wonderful thing about Northwest Coast art particularly that it has these many layers of meaning on a nonverbal level, where you can identify with and empathize with somebody so far removed from you culturally, geographically, in time. (In Duffek 2004: 80)

Interestingly, this statement was made at a time when Reid's position was starting to change. Through the 1980s, Reid became increasingly involved in the ongoing political struggle of the Haida community and came to see the struggle for cultural survival not as a lost cause of the past but as a continued concern. One important milestone in this development was the Haida protest against logging on Lyell Island, where Haida protesters came together in unity and for forty days stood up against the authorities. Reid supported the struggle economically through the sale of lithographic prints, and in a statement before the provincial Wilderness Advisory Committee in 1986 acknowledged: 'Recently ... I've finally had to face up to what it really

Figure 6.4. Bill Reid, *The Spirit of Haida Gwaii,* carved bracelets 1997. Photo: courtesy MoA.

means to be Haida in the latter part of the twentieth century and at last, in fact, may have to become a Haida' (in Shadbolt 1986: 177).

Significantly, it is in the 1980s and 90s, after bridging this distance in time and cultural identity, that Bill Reid produces his most personalized interpretations of Haida cosmology, in sculptural works like *Killer Whale* (1984) for the Vancouver Public Aquarium and *The Spirit of Haida Gwaii* (1991), releasing his favourite mythological creatures from the two-dimensional stylized form of Northwest Coast art (see fig. 6.4). The latter, which became his last work, was made in two versions for the Canadian Embassy in Washington and the international airport in Vancouver.

Jåks: Making Sami Art Contemporary

Moving to Norway, Iver Jåks (1932–2007) was born the second-youngest of eleven children of reindeer-nomads in Karasjok, northern Norway; six of his siblings died young. Although, like Bill Reid, he came to be positioned as an outsider to the social life of his community in some ways, he was in his childhood very differently positioned in terms of cultural background. As a child, he spoke only Sami and travelled with his family and their animals between the winter pastures in Karasjok and their summer land on the coast. At the age of eight, an accident put a stop to this. As a result, he spent eight years, including the time of German occupation, first in hospital and later at a home for the disabled run by the Sami mission, growing up away from his nomadic family. Jåks has described his childhood drawings as a way of overcoming his isolation and as a means of communicating with those around him who did not speak Sami. He never fully recovered from the accident, and struggled with a painful disability for the rest of his life (Aarseth 2002: 21).

After receiving basic training in *duodji* (Sami traditional crafts) at the Sami Community College ('Samisk Folkehøgskole') in Karasjok, Jåks was educated at the Academy of Art, before returning to the college as a *duodji* teacher. Then, in 1958, he was accepted to the Copenhagen Academy of Art, where he received training in graphic arts. He worked as an illustrator, painter, wood engraver and sculptor. Characteristic of his art is the subtle use of references to Sami cosmology, including Christian images, while avoiding stylized iconography. In his sculptures he incorporated materials from Sami daily life in the *duodji* tradition, especially wood, reindeer-horn and leather. He consciously avoided the use of standardized symbols associated by many in Norway with Sami culture. Several of his works, like the series of wood engravings *Homo Sapiens* from the 1970s, brought out the tension between strict Protestantism and pre Christian cosmology in contemporary Sami culture. In many of his works, he plays with the shapes of the shaman drum and drumstick, associated in Sami culture with the female and male sex, to express his understanding of eroticism as an integral part of the human condition. In this play with images he aims to re-create tradition, liberating it from its handicraft conventions and transforming it into art (see fig. 6.5 and fig. 6.6). In this respect, Jåks was a true pathfinder, laying the ground for the

Figure 6.5. Iver Jåks: *Gudenes Dans* (Dance of the Gods), relief, wood and concrete, 1972. Photo: courtesy RidduDuottar Museat.

Figure 6.6. Iver Jåks, *Kvinnene* (The Women). Photo: courtesy RidduDuottar Museat.

next generation of Sami artists. It seems reasonable to argue that what made this pathfinding possible in the highly politicized period of the 1970s and 80s discussed below, was his internalization and embodiment of cultural references and his confidence in articulating their coherence and tensions.

Codifying Northwest Coast Art

The artist and art critic Rashid Araeen (2000) argues that Western modernism in general, and Western modernist art in particular, has depended on excluding non-European and non-white artists from subject-positions. Their art is defined not by their artistic qualities but by their geographical, cultural and/or racial positions vis-à-vis the modern and modernist centre. Historically, modernism was a hegemonic project, initially forced upon the colonized world. After independence, former colonies made these ideas their own. Independence did not, therefore, result in a reversion to precolonial structures and practices, but in efforts to redefine modernity to include themselves: to free modernity from its Eurocentric foundation. These efforts were met with rejection by the power embedded in the international art world. Instead, Araeen argues, artists from subjugated groups were offered the option of being included as 'different', to enter carrying an ethnic identity card – to have their work accepted as 'ethnic art'.

I suggest that this ongoing form of subjugation is relevant to the different ways in which institutional settings in British Columbia and Norway have helped assign indigenous art to different niches. This is the paradox I find interesting: While highly formalized indigenous art, conceptualized as 'ethnic art', has become a provincial – if not national – trademark in Canada, the more open and playful art by Sami artists has in Norway become defined as national Sami art, located in the geographical and political periphery of Norway. Let us look at how this came about.

In British Columbia, the Museum of Anthropology (MoA) in Vancouver played a significant role in the development of indigenous art motifs into provincial or national symbols. From the late 1950s until today, British Columbia First Nations art has been promoted and defined through a number of exhibitions: *People of the Potlatch* (1956), *One Hundred Years of B.C. Art* (1958), *Arts of the Raven* (1967), *The Legacy* (1971) were some of the early events. While some of these were organized by private art galleries, some by MoA, central to all of them were a small group of anthropologists and art historians – and Bill Reid. This group, and Reid himself, shared the understanding of a fundamental discontinuity between the living tradition that existed before the fatal impact of colonialism and Reid's own work already discussed. Through this discontinuity, as it were, Northwest Coast material culture was redefined from primitive curio to fine art. *Arts of the Raven* – significantly exhibited at Vancouver Art Gallery and not in the ethnological museum – was curated by Doris Shadbolt, Bill Reid's later biographer. In her catalogue for the exhibition, Shadbolt refers to the 'shift in focus from ethnology to art' that the exhibit represents. While the choice of venue marked this shift, it is most likely that the University of British Columbia salvage programs helped this upgrading while at the same time consolidating the conception of classical forms as superior to contemporary developments. The words of Harry Hawthorn, the first director of MoA, confirm that museum patronage contributed to formal conservationism in Northwest Coast art. In a 1961 paper, Hawthorn notes: 'It would seem that committees and museums which carry out programs of manufacture and marketing of tribal arts generally follow a somewhat similar policy, conservative where standards are judged to have been maintained at a high level to the present, and returning to the past where an earlier style is rated more highly than the existing one' (70). What took place over two or three decades was a *codification* of the principles of Northwest Coast art, a standardization of design and technique (Ames 1992: 49–69). As Helen Codere remarked in her introduction to Boas's *Kwakiutl Ethnography* (1966: xx–xxi): 'even rather superficial knowledge of the elements of this art and its symbolic and operational conventions ... makes it simple to specify what is wrong with anything that is not, but purports to be Northwest Coast art.' This 'code' became the means through which scholars and collectors engaged with Northwest Coast art, objects and histories (Glass 2001); it became the form modern indigenous art took in British Columbia. Maria Crosby notes: 'In the post-1967 revival discourse and modernist paradigm that positioned "uncontaminated" traditional work as modern art, all the contemporary work that preceded it was relegated to the past.'[5]

Political Struggle and Modernist Art in Norway

In Norway, development took another course. Through his personal capacity as role model for the next generation of Sami artists, Iver Jåk's modernist version of Sami art became important (see fig. 6.7). In the mid-1970s, when acting as consultant for the artistic decoration of the Sami school in Lahpoluoppal, a small Sami community outside Kautokeino, he brought together what later became known as the 'Máze-group', the most important group of Sami artists in Norway towards the end of the twentieth century. Among the central artists were Aage Gaup and Synnøve Persen. As in Jåk's own art, one sees in their works few signs of ethnic stylization. Instead of seeking inclusion into the established art world under an ethnic label, Sami artists physically and mentally withdrew to the north in order to establish their own centre and their own institutions. The group established itself as a collective in the small community of Máze, where the first demonstrations

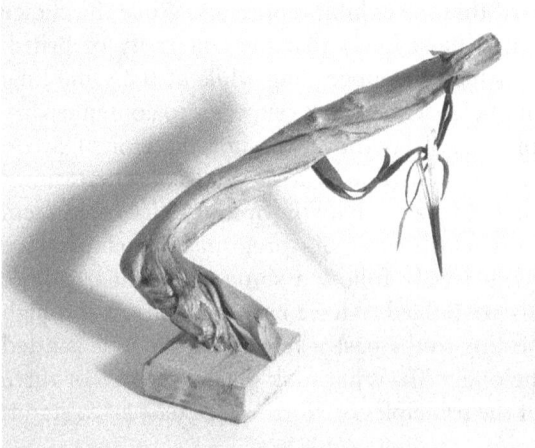

Figure 6.7. Iver Jåks, *Oppadstrebende samekultur* (Sami culture striving upwards), perishable sculpture 1994–1996. Photo: courtesy RidduDuottar Museat.

against the building of the Alta dam and power station were held. More than any other question, the Alta issue brought Sami rights to land and water to the top of the political agenda in Norway in the late 1970s and early 1980s. During the many long-drawn-out protests against the ongoing construction of the Alta dam, involving repeated police action against protesters, tabloid headlines and large-scale political mobilization not only in the North, but also at universities and workplaces in the southern part of the country, the art studios in Máze became political workshops as well. The artists belonged to the first Sami generation to have passed through the common school system in Norway. Intimately familiar with Norwegian society, some of them no longer speaking the Sami language, and now radicalized by the political struggle over resources in Finnmark, their aim was to establish a Sami nation – Sápmi – but also to construct a new way of being Sami. Their Sami identity lay less in locality and traditional knowledge, more in the global struggle for native rights. As they saw it, Sami-ness is not identifiable from the outside – a Sami can be anyone, but not everyone can be a Sami. As noted by Hanna Hansen (2010), the Máze artists were not objects or victims of modernization, they implemented modernity (see fig. 6.8 and fig 6.9). In this

Figure 6.8. Eirik Wuohti, *Spor* (Traces). Photo: courtesy RidduDuottar Museat.

Figure 6.9. Synnøve Persen, *Labyrint II*. Photo: courtesy RidduDuottar Museat.

project they moved beyond what defined them as different. One example of the way this translates into art can be seen in Geir Tore Holm's *Parabol* ('dish antenna') from 1993 (see fig. 6.10). Glued together from a cheap, disposable plastic cup and paper plate of a kind used by many Sami when

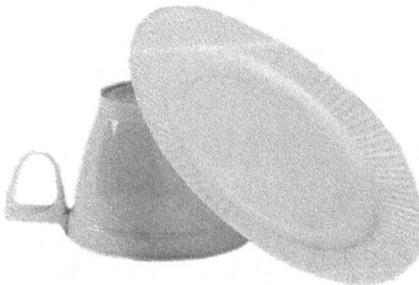

Figure 6.10. Geir Tore Holm: *Parabol* ('dish antenna'), assemblage 1993. Photo: courtesy RidduDuottar Museat.

travelling with their reindeer, the work communicates an understanding of the fragility of the Sami world in their open relationship to the outside, established through the domestication of external elements and 'tuned in' on world events.

Positioned Creativity

Native artists in British Columbia and Norway today are positioned differently by the respective art discourses in the two countries. In British Columbia, indigenous art, seen as 'ethnic art' in Araeen's sense, has become accepted as part of the regional and/or national art world, providing a niche for aspiring artists of First Nations background. Consequently, we find a proliferation of 'ethnic' images circulating inside and outside galleries and museums, ranging from those produced by acclaimed artists like Robert Davidson (great grandson of Charles Edenshaw) and Tony Hunt (grandson of Mungo Martin), to the most sketchy tourist art. It should be remembered, however, that as discussed in the first part of this chapter this acceptance of First Nations artists into an ethnic niche in the Canadian art world does not necessarily signify an absence of political controversy – rather the opposite. As pointed out by Townsend-Gault (2004: 189): 'Spectacle deflects attention from, or masks, the conflicts of the present.'

The relationship between art and ethnic identity is also ambivalent in Norway, but in a somewhat different way. As we saw in an earlier part of this chapter, the political struggle in which a number of Sami artists were involved in the 1970s and 1980s has to a large extent been successful. The Sami parliament was established in 1989, and has gradually taken over responsibility for the Sami cultural sector, including Sami museums in the North. These museums hold many of the works produced by the younger generation of Sami artists. Since 2012, a process has been ongoing to repatriate the old ethnological collection originally assembled by the Ethnographic Museum in Oslo to the same Sami museums. There is a saying that one should be careful what one wishes for, however, as it may come true. There are indications that today, with their cultural identity no longer under threat, the embrace of their works by Sami political interests and regional Sami museums is experienced by many Sami artists as a caging in – or out – of their artistic activity. Unsurprisingly, artists differ in their responses to their current situations. To some the Sami label today is unrelated to their artistic work and is seen mainly as marker of marginalization; to others being Sami seems to be a way to express something universal about the human condition. None of them, however, see themselves – or can be characterized – as 'ethnic artists'.

Notes

1. Crests are markers of status, insignia displaying characteristics of animals or other non-humans, often in combination with humans.
2. http://www.bcstats.gov.bc.ca/StatisticsBySubject/Census/2006Census.aspx
3. For a further discussion of terms in the Canadian context, see http://indigenous foundations.arts.ubc.ca/?id=7400.
4. http://www.gov.bc.ca/arr/treaty/landmark_cases.html#aboriginal_rights, accessed 4 May 2012.
5. www.vancouverartinthesixties.com/essays/making-indian-art-modern.

References

Aavitsland, K. B. 2014. *Harry Fett. Historien er lengst*. Oslo: Pax forlag.
Aarseth, B.. 2002. 'Iver Jåks – fra samisk tradisjon til universell modernisme' ['Iver Jåks – from Sami tradition to universal modernism'], in B. Eilertsen et al. (eds), *Ofelas – Iver Jåks veiviseren*. Tromsø: Ravnetrykk.
Araeen, R.. 2000. 'A New Beginning: Beyond Postcolonial Cultural Theory and Identity Politics', *Third Text* 50(6).
Becker, H. S. 1982. *Art Worlds*. Berkeley: University of California Press.
Bjørklund, I. 1985. *Fjordfolket i Kvænangen [The coastal people of Kvænangen]*. Oslo: Universitetsforlaget.
Boas, F. 1967. *Kwakiutl Ethnography*. Edited and abridged, with an introduction, by H. Codere. Chicago: University of Chicago Press
Brown, E. 1927. 'Introduction', in *Exhibition of Canadian West Coast Art: Native and Modern*. Ottawa: National Gallery of Canada, 2.
Clifford, J. 1988. *The Predicament of Culture. Twentieth-Century Ethnography, Literature, and Art*. Cambridge, Mass.: Harvard University Press.
Dawn, L. 2004. 'RE: Reading Reid and the "revival"', in K. Duffek and C. Townsend-Gault (eds), *Bill Reid and Beyond: Expanding on Modern Native Art*. Seattle: University of Washington Press.
Dias, N. 2008. 'Double Erasures: Rewriting the Past at the Muse´e du quai Branly'. *Social Anthropology* 16(3): 300–311.
Duffek, K. 2009. 'The British Columbia Aboriginal Collection', in C. E. Mayer and A. Shelton (eds), *The Museum of Anthropology at the University of British Columbia*. Seattle: University of Washington Press.
———. 2004. 'On Shifting Ground: Bill Reid at the Museum of Anthropology', in K. Duffek and C. Townsend-Gault (eds), *Bill Reid and Beyond; Expanding on Modern Native Art*. Seattle: University of Washington Press.
Environics Institute. 2010. *Urban Aboriginal Peoples Study. Main Report*.
———. 2011. *Urban Aboriginal Peoples Study. Vancouver Report*.
Foster, H. 1985. 'The "Primitive" Unconscious of Modern Art'. *October* 34(Autumn): 45–70.
Glass, A. 2001. 'Sun Dogs and Eagle Down: The Indian Painting of Bill Holm', *BC Studies* 130.

Graburn, N. H.H. 1976. *Ethnic and Tourist Arts: Cultural Expressions from the Fourth World.* Berkeley: University of California Press

Hansen, H. H.. 2010. *Fluktlinjer: Forståelser av samisk samtidskunst.* Avhandling levert for graden, Philosophiae Doctor, Universitetet i Tromsø. (*Lines of flight: Understandings of Sami contemporary art.* PhD thesis, University of Tromsø)

Hawthorn, H. 1961. 'The Artist in Tribal Society: The Northwest Coast', in M. W. Smith (ed.), *The Artist in Tribal Society: Proceedings of a Symposium held at the Royal Anthropological Institute.* London: Routledge and Kegan Paul.

Hastrup, K. 2007. 'Performing the World: Agency, Anticipation and Creativity'. In E. Hallam and T. Ingold (eds.), *Creativity and Cultural Improvisation.* Oxford: Berg.

Holm, B. 1965. *Northwest Coast Indian Art: An Analysis of Form.* Seattle: University of Washington Press.

Holm, B., and B. Reid. 1976. *Indian art of the Northwest Coast: A Dialogue on Craftmanship and Aesthetics.* Seattle: University of Washington Press.

Ingold, T., and E. Hallam. 2007. 'Creativity and Cultural Improvisation: An Introduction', in E. Hallam and T. Ingold (eds), *Creativity and Cultural Improvisation.* Oxford: Berg.

Lloyd, J. 1991. 'Emil Nolde's Ethnographic Still Lifes: Primitivism, Tradition, and Modernity', in S. Hiller (ed.), *The Myth of Primitivism: Perspectives on Art.* London: Routledge, 90–112.

Macdonald, S. 1996. 'Theorizing museums: an introduction', in G. F. and S. Macdonald (eds), *Theorizing Museums: Respresenting Identity and Diversity in a Changing World.* Oxford: Blackwells, 1–18.

McEvilley, T. 1984. 'Doctor, lawyer, Indian chief', *Artforum* 23(3): 54–60.

Miller, D. 1991. 'Primitive Art and the Necessity of Primitivism to Art', in S. Hiller (ed.), *The Myth of Primitivism.* London: Routledge, 50–71.

Myers, F. 2006. 'Primitivism, Anthropology, and the Category of "Primitive Art"', in C. Tilley et al. (eds), *Handbook of Material Culture.* London: Sage Publications, 267–284.

Nemiroff, D. 1996. 'Modernism, Nationalism and Beyond: A Critical History of Exhibitions of First Nation Art', in R. Greenberg, B. W. Ferguson and S. Nairne (eds), *Thinking About Exhibitions.* London and New York: Routledge.

Pratt, M. L. 1991. 'The Arts of the Contact Zone', *Profession* 91: 33–40.

———. 1992. *Imperial Eyes: Travel Writing and Transculturation.* London: Routledge.

Price, S. 1989. *Primitive Art in Civilized Places.* Chicago: University of Chicago Press.

———. 2007. *Paris Primitive: Jacques Chirac's Museum on the Quai Branly.* Chicago: University of Chicago Press.

———. 2010. 'Return to the Quai Branly', *Museum Anthropology* 33(1): 11–21.

Reid, B. 2009. *Solitary Raven: The Essential Writings of Bill Reid,* 2nd edition. Vancouver, BC, and Toronto: Douglas & McIntyre.

Ruiz-Gómez, N. 2006. 'The (Jean) Nouvel Other: Primitivism and the Musée du Quai Branly', *Modern and Contemporary France* 14(4): 417–432.

Sami Instituhtta. 2006. 'Bor det flest samer I Oslo?' ['Are most Sami living in Oslo?'], www.sami-statistics.info, accessed 15 April 2012.

Shadbolt, D. 1986. *Bill Reid*. Vancouver, BC, and Toronto: Douglas & McIntyre.

———. 2004. 'The Will to be Haida', in K. Duffek and C. Townsend-Gault (eds), *Bill Reid and Beyond: Expanding on Modern Native Art*. Seattle: University of Washington Press, 26–36.

Svašek, M. 2010. 'Improvising in a World of Movement: Transit, Transition and Transformation', in H. K. Anheier and Y. Isar (eds), *Cultures and Globalization: Cultural Expression, Creativity and Innovation*. London: Sage Publications, 62–77.

Thomas, D. 2008. 'The Quai Branly Museum: Political Transition, Memory and Globalisation in Contemporary France', *French Cultural Studies* 19(2): 141–157.

Townsend-Gault, C. 2004. 'Circulating Aboriginality', *Journal of Material Culture* 9(2): 183–202.

Whitehead, C. 2009. *Museums and the Constructions of Disciplines: Art and Archaeology in Nineteenth-Century Britain*. London: Duckworth.

7

'WE PAINT OUR WAY AND THE CHRISTIAN WAY TOGETHER'

TRANSFORMING YOLNGU AND NGAN'GI ART THROUGH CREATIVE ANCESTRAL-CHRISTIAN PRACTICE

———◆•◆•◆———

Fiona Magowan and Maria Øien

Christian Aboriginal art is a relatively understudied phenomenon in Australia and there is a paucity of comparative material on the relationship between Aboriginal art and theology.[1] While much has been written about the impact of missions upon Aboriginal livelihoods (McKnight 2002; Harris 1990), discussions of Aboriginal Christianity seldom problematize religious politics in relation to denominational differences that have shaped Aboriginal Christian faith, beliefs and aesthetics. In this chapter, we compare and contrast some doctrinal influences upon the artworks of Yolngu and Ngan'gi[2] artists who live in two remote mission-based communities in the Northern Territory, Galiwin'ku and Nauiyu,[3] which were established by Methodist and Catholic missionaries, respectively.[4] As Christian Aboriginal art and belief are processual in nature and therefore always in a state of becoming (Morphy 2008), they have the potential to mediate faith, doctrine and lived experience by reflecting degrees of religious interpretation, as well as sensuous engagements with the divine (cf. Meyer 2010). Thus, we ask, to what extent are artistic representations of composite senses of Christian-Ancestral personhood consistent with Ancestral beliefs; and in what ways are Ancestral design templates modified in the depiction of Christian ideas?

Contextualizing Yolngu and Ngan'gi Art Practices

An aestheticized Aboriginal art market has emerged from the sensorial responses and perceptions of largely Western critics who have shaped the
conditions in which art values are interpreted and negotiated.[5] While such
aesthetic judgements arise from cultural responses informed by the social
contexts in which they take place, they cannot always account for different
interpretations of the same work. The conditions for shared sensuality de-
rive, in part, from the background that individuals have acquired in relation
to a particular aesthetic form and the extent to which they hold common
understandings of its aesthetic effects.

Yolngu and Ngan'gi artists have been involved in the production of commercial and saleable art intended for public domains for many years, circulated through two governmentally funded non-profit centres: Elcho Island
Arts in Galiwin'ku and Merrepen Arts in Nauiyu, each owned and managed
cooperatively by local artists as their formal art distribution outlets.[6] While
artists regularly provide the art market with works depicting public Ancestral designs, more rarely do they sell paintings that speak to both Christian
and Aboriginal identities.[7] Customers' personal judgements of style and
value, as well as shared standards of taste, have aestheticized the Australian
Aboriginal art market. Their purchases are subject to aesthetic judgements
that have the power to transform the art's value and the status of the artist.
Thus, customers' desires for particular kinds of designs have affected the
choices that Yolngu and Ngan'gi artists make when developing their art
visually. The aestheticization of the art market entails an ongoing negotiation of aesthetic desire and effect. Consequently, we consider how Ancestral
painting practices have allowed for a particular form of artistic creativity to
emerge, wherein some images may be altered for Christian purposes, while
others may not. We explore what constitutes creativity in the production of
Christian Aboriginal art as artists work with their distinctive experiences of
Christian and Ancestral pasts and presents. Finally, we argue that Christian
Aboriginal art is expressed in the nexus between Christian aesthetics and
the politics of Ancestral painting conventions. We explore tensions in the
flux and flow of revelation through art, as Aboriginal Christian artists seek
to express identities that are intimately connected to the politics of land, kin
and Ancestors.

Controlling Aesthetics through Cosmology

The Ancestral stories and designs of Yolngu and Ngan'gi art comprise separate bodies of law pertaining to each region.[8] Regionally specific narratives

describe the epic deeds of supernatural Ancestors who travelled through an unshaped world, creating and naming geographical features, as well as plants, animals and humans at the beginning of the universe, in turn, generating a body of judicial and moral rules (Morphy 1991; Munn 1973).[9] The Ancestors then left the ownership of various sacred sites in each region to kin groups to be inherited through patrilineal descent.

Art is also an essential aspect of ritual display in both communities, as elsewhere in Aboriginal Australia and, as such, it encodes authorial claims over place and kin, permitting some kin to paint particular designs, others to hold knowledge about them and, yet others, merely to be able to view the works (cf. McCulloch 1999).[10] These differentiated ritual rights are spoken of as forms of inherited and shared artistic knowledge (cf. Morphy 1991)[11] and they delineate the grounds for learning to paint. Artists from both regions interpret and value their art as *manifestations* of spiritual and kinship based identity, providing re-embodiments of Ancestral acts, thereby linking the past to the present (Morphy 1991; Taylor 2007). Luke Taylor (2007: 71–72) defines Aboriginal art training as embodied in an 'apprenticeship network', that is, Yolngu and Ngan'gi artists acquire painting skills and the knowledge of painting conventions by listening to the stories and by observing and imitating the painting techniques and design templates of senior members of their immediate kinship group. The main stories and designs used in commercial art are part of an 'outside', public sphere known by all community members, while certain designs are restricted in an 'inside' sphere of understanding according to age, gender and kinship rights in clan knowledge.

Our ethnographic material will illustrate that, although Yolngu and Ngan'gi art production is 'conventional' in the sense that it is rooted in this visual practice of depicting shared knowledge of Ancestral stories, this does not exclude the possibility of using innovative techniques, as well as artistic creativity, when producing saleable artworks. For Yolngu, creativity is expected to operate within the limits of Ancestral design. Innovation is spoken of as something that is new (*yuta*) or has been changed (*djambi*) and this has very clear implications of transformation in painting practice. Creative elements that extend beyond, adapt or reinterpret existing aesthetic templates require clan authorization before the new style or genre can be used. Artists are thus constrained by painting obligations to uphold the tenets of the Ancestral Law, and introducing changes to images requires negotiation with appropriate kin and clan elders. Other design innovation includes the use of new formats such as screen and block printing, batik designs and the development of commercial artefacts, such as mats, lampshades and purses woven from *pandanus*. Ngan'gi creativity manoeuvres within the agreement of painting Ancestral designs that are publicly known by all in the production of commercial art. Ngan'gi artists are nevertheless bound to respect kinship-based authority as certain designs can be reproduced solely by the owning kinship group. Regardless of these painting conventions, Ngan'gi artists embrace a form of artistic creativity that allows for much individual variation and innovation in design composition, styles and use of colours. Ngan'gi artists are also innovative in their techniques as their art production includes acrylic painting on canvas, silk painting, etchings and serigraphy on paper and fabric, looping of sand palm string bags, coiling of *pandanus* basket and batik.

It should also be noted that for Aboriginal artists, the significance of Christian artwork is primarily understood as residing in the ability of designs to encapsulate the interconnectedness of religious, moral and emotional values with the politics of Aboriginal identity. Creating Christian Aboriginal art thus contains within it a politics of hierarchy that is intimately productive of social relationships. Any realignment of Ancestral artworks within a Christian domain is constrained by 'a grammar of social intercourse' (Scott 1990: 47), which corresponds to a hierarchical aesthetics of religious knowledge. This hierarchy contrasts with a broad evangelical Christian worldview, which propounds free access to religious knowledge. The power and politics of artistic representation thus raise questions about continuities and discontinuities of personhood, religiosity, denominational practice and collective rights. The aestheticization of Aboriginal art is further subject to the dynamics of sociality in the communities and regions in which the art is produced. We contextualize the ways in which aestheticization has been under constant renegotiation with an overview of the denominational agendas and mission histories that have led to the development of Yolngu and Ngan'gi artistic forms in the Northern Territory.[12] We analyse how the subject matter[13] of acrylic paintings, made by one Yolngu artist and two Ngan'gi artists, conveys both Christian and Ancestral significance as part of a broader system of transferable religious meanings and practices.

The Development of Galiwin'ku Mission

Missionaries have played a major role in shaping the ethos of contemporary Christianity, providing leadership and direction in the development of mission stations across the continent. In some regions, missionaries also helped set up local arts and crafts centres to assist Aboriginal artists in their endeavours. The Methodist Overseas Mission Board (MOM) established three missions in the early 1900s: at Goulburn Island in 1916,[14] Milingimbi in 1923 and Yirrkala in 1934.[15] The last of the Methodist missions, Galiwin'ku, established in 1942, became part of the Uniting Church in 1976.

Previously known as Elcho Island, Galiwin'ku is located in the Arafura Sea, three kilometres off the Napier Peninsula. It is one of the largest Arnhem Land communities with an estimated population of 1,856 Yolngu[16] and about 500 non-Aboriginal people. Galiwin'ku is a designated 'growth town' in the Australian government's current legislation, and is now part of the East Arnhem Shire, comprising nine communities.[17] The pioneering missionary, Rev. Harold Urquhart Shepherdson (b. Bunbury W. A., 1903; d. Adelaide S. A., 2000) is renowned today for his tireless efforts over fifty years of service to the community. He established the town on the southwestern tip of the island, arriving in 1942 as a missionary engineer and leaving in 1977, the year after Methodist missions were taken over by the Uniting Church of Australia.[18] As a result, the religious ethos of Galiwin'ku changed from Methodist teachings to a more charismatic evangelical Christianity that has informed Yolngu Christian-Ancestral artistic and musical practices (cf. Gordon and Magowan 2000; Magowan 2003). A Christian Revival on Galiwin'ku in 1979 led to new music and forms of worship being introduced by Yolngu. Yolngu were supported by visiting evangelists from Australia and overseas who also brought new American gospel and contemporary Christian music. Visual materials for worship became more prominent with the rise of technology: the ability to project videos and DVDs in the 1980s and 90s and the increasing accessibility of Christian materials through the post and online.

In its formative mission days, questions about Ancestral beliefs were not at the forefront of the missionary agenda; rather their remit was to instigate a Protestant work ethic, order and discipline through the institutions of the church, hospital and school as well as the farm, sawmill and fishing industry (see Clarke 2010: 81). Most missionaries in this region did not directly challenge Yolngu religion or ritual as they either selectively avoided or simply did not engage with Aboriginal practices. Thus, missionaries had limited understandings of Yolngu Ancestral meanings and it would have been difficult for most missionaries to appreciate how Christian doctrine spoke to Yolngu religious forms. These missionaries did not try to alter Yolngu artistic practices by asking them to adapt their Ancestral painting conventions to Christian images and symbols. However, Yolngu themselves sought to understand the synergies and tensions between the two religious domains in reinterpretations of ritual meanings of song, dance and art. Yolngu were especially wary of missionaries who felt it their duty to persuade Yolngu to leave their culture behind, since such demands forced an unacceptable choice between faith in Ancestral Law, upon which all things rested, and Christian spiritual tenets (see Clarke 2010: 85–86).

Instead, Methodist missionaries were primarily concerned with communicating the Gospels in word and song. Yolngu became familiar with Christian stories through sermons and in children's biblical teaching at school but they were not taught to paint these stories. Yolngu were quick to adapt text-based scripture messages into their artistic designs, incorporating them into rituals and transforming their meaning in the process (see Wearing 2007: 161–165; Magowan 2013). For example, they understood the symbol of the Christian cross to be akin to a slightly modified shape at the ends of the cross used in some Ancestral designs. Such parallelisms of form facilitated a recontextualization of Ancestral meanings within a Christian framework. The missionary-linguist Beulah Lowe was acutely aware of how doctrinal concepts could be misinterpreted. In her work of Gospel and hymn translation, she had learned first-hand how misreading of scripture could occur through the ambiguities of language (see Wearing 2007; Magowan 2013). It was not until the late 1960s that Yolngu at Galiwin'ku were encouraged to participate in producing artworks for sale on acrylics and canvas by a missionary teacher, John Rudder, who established an arts and crafts outlet.

The work of Methodist missionaries laid the foundations for Yolngu to explore the meaning of Christianity on missionaries' terms as a Western paradigm, as well as through Yolngu creative processes arising from ritual song, dance and art. Yolngu, who had accepted Christianity, meanwhile, derived their own Christian interpretations from what they perceived to be parallels of meaning between Christian teachings and the Ancestral Law. As we shall see, Methodist approaches diverged, to some extent, from those of Catholic missionaries who had populated the northwest of the continent many years earlier, where, at Nauiyu, they influenced new forms of local art production and the adaptation of such forms to suit Christian contexts.

The Development of Nauiyu Nambiyu Mission

Nauiyu Nambiyu is a small Aboriginal community located 220 kilometres southwest of Darwin, in Fitzmaurice region on the border of Arnhem Land, in the Northern Territory. In the mid-1880s, a short-lived Jesuit mission was established on the banks of the Daly River around a sugar plantation and the Daly River Cattle Station (Pye 1976).[19] The presence of settlers attracted members of all the surrounding clans who chose to leave their traditional Homelands eager to obtain 'white fella' material goods. The MalakMalak, who were the Traditional Owners of the geographical area where the community was established, were forced to accept that they and their land had been subject to colonization and the migration of other Aboriginal clans (Stanley 1985; Stanner 1933a, 1933b).[20] The Daly River settlement grew as the number of locals working for goods in the plantations and farms increased, leading to an mounting concern with the lack of educational facilities for the expanding numbers of children. In 1952, a group of locals approached Bishop O'Loughlin of the Darwin diocese asking for a school (Patricia Marrfurra in interview with Øien, 25 October 2007). With government funds, an Aboriginal Apostolate Mission was established in 1955 as Bishop O'Loughlin created a block of Freehold land by purchasing several farms in Daly River, employing priests of a Catholic order, 'The Missionaries of the Sacred Heart' (Derrington 2000; Stanley 1985).[21]

For Catholics, as for the Methodists in Arnhem Land after them, the mission policy, as stated by Bishop O'Loughlin, was that of 'providing schooling, medical care for the sick, and spiritual values' (Pye 1976: 18). Thus, the missionaries and locals built a boarding school, a clinic, a Church, a convent, accommodation, work sheds and an air strip. Unlike Yolngu, who lived in family camps with children congregating daily at the school, local Nauiyu children were enrolled in dormitories at the boarding school and Ngan'gi children consequently experienced a more pervasive exposure to Christianity than did Yolngu children. Children of both communities were given a rudimentary European-style education. By 1975, as many as fifty-two people were working for Nauiyu Mission, a majority of whom were locals.

The Politics of Christian Practice

In pursuit of a Christian way of life, both Catholic and Methodist missionaries taught that 'what is bad is to be gradually eliminated and what is good is to be encouraged' (Stanley 1985). Thus, Owen Stanley (1985) claims that certain customs such as polygyny, arranged marriages and ritual punishment were strongly discouraged and seen to be in conflict with Christian values. In the late 1950s, the Catholic missionaries in Nauiyu explicitly encouraged painting and dancing, which they considered a positive form of cultural production.[22] A particular form of artistic production was initiated at this time as part of the Catholic boarding school curriculum, introducing the Ngan'gi to new art media. As explained to Øien by several Senior Ngan'gi artists, they were encouraged by the nuns to paint biblical stories and landscapes in a figurative and naturalistic Western style, using acrylic on canvas. This Christian-inspired painting practice was significantly different to the abstract style of senior artists at that time, who painted landscapes in which birds, rivers, paths and waterholes were depicted through a birds-eye view using symbolic elements such as dots, lines and circles.[23] This difference indicates that the production of Christian-inspired artwork, on the one hand, and of publicly restricted ceremonial art design, regulated according to Ancestral painting conventions, on the other, took place separately in different contexts. More recently, emerging localized Christian designs differ from both the naturalistic style taught by the nuns and from the abstract Ancestral style, while drawing upon both. Using figurative styles, Ngan'gi artists express in Christian designs what, for them, unites Ancestral and Christian religiosity, as they perceive similarities or parallels between Christian Catholic bible stories and their own local contextualization of Ancestral stories and visual symbolism. Some of these paintings are analysed below.

Nauiyu ceased to operate as a Catholic Mission in 1988, nevertheless Nauiyu's history, particularly its Catholic boarding school, has given Catholic doctrine a lasting influence in the lives and art practices of the Ngan'gi today. This influence explains why most Ngan'gi view their religiosity, as well as painting practices, as simultaneously Roman Catholic Christian and rooted in a pre-Christian or Ancestral past, neither one excluding the other (Toren 1988; Duelke 2005). Thus, Christian practices have continued, and many Ngan'gi still participate weekly in Christian rituals at the local St. Frances Xavier Catholic Church. A Catholic priest and nun, residing in Nauiyu, perform regular services twice every Sunday and a midnight mass is held on Christmas night. Since 1988, to encourage local participation, the Catholic Church has changed its liturgy to include forms of worship that might be more relevant to Aborigines. For instance, two local Ngan'gi artists, Patricia Marrfurra and Miriam-Rose Ungunmerr Bauman, whose artworks are introduced below, have translated selected Christian hymns to Ngan'gi, often leading the congregation in singing. In reminiscing about their mission past, some locals explained that the former priest, Father John Leary, who gave lifelong service to Nauiyu, placed great emphasis on trying to affect a unity between Christian and Aboriginal spirituality. In his sermons, he even compared Christ with an Ancestral Dreamtime Being. The Ngan'gi have since continued this focus on unity and are resolving certain teleological dissimilarities by uniting their Ancestral beliefs and Christianity, stating that they believe in both an omnipresent God and Ancestral presence. This is particularly evident in the creative practices of painting, in which Ngan'gi artists create contemporary Christian art designs that visualize this united Christian and Aboriginal identity, as will be illustrated by the analysis of paintings presented below.

Unlike Father Leary, Rev. Shepherdson did not combine Christian and Ancestral teachings in his sermons on Galiwin'ku or develop a visual culture in relation to Christianity. However, as Yolngu became increasingly well-versed in Christianity, they sought to resolve eschatological incongruities between Ancestral and Christian ideologies. As a result, three major politico-religious expressions emerged in Yolngu art, each with its own set of motivations. The first, the so-called 'adjustment movement', took place on Galiwin'ku in 1957 when Yolngu sought to engage Shepherdson and other resident Elcho Island missionaries concerning the relationship between Aboriginal Law and Christianity in a memorial of Ancestral designs adorned with a cross. Created by consensus between clan leaders, this memorial nevertheless contravened Ancestral practices by making restricted Ancestral paintings visible to everyone (cf. Berndt 1962; Morphy 1983). This Yolngu-led initiative paved the way for debates between missionary and Yolngu views of authority as to the ways in which Ancestral Law could coexist with Christianity (see Keen 1994). It has been argued that Christian Yolngu on Galiwin'ku wished to demonstrate to missionaries that their Ancestral Law was on an equal footing with Christianity in terms of its social and moral tenets (cf. Berndt 1962), as well as offering a forum for dialogues about Yolngu and Western spirituality.

Political discourses of art were later to become powerful tools and weapons in the preservation of Yolngu identity when Yolngu at Yirrkala employed a politics of art in order to negotiate with the Australian government over land-rights issues (Morphy 2005). Although Yirrkala Yolngu had refused to engage with the 'adjustment movement' as it revealed restricted objects, five years after the 'adjustment movement' they created two large masonite church panels depicting the major Ancestral journeys of the Dhuwa and Yirritja moieties respectively. Just as the Galiwin'ku 'adjustment movement' had brought out key Ancestral designs from resident clans in a memorial sculpture, so these two panels displayed the political identities of Yolngu clans at Yirrkala and their Ancestral connections to kin and country.[24] Positioned on either side of the New Yirrkala Church altar (Morphy 2005), this installation inspired the creation of two bark petitions that were sent to Canberra in 1963 in response to mining on Ancestral land. The petitions sought Indigenous recognition and constitutional change regarding land rights through the Commonwealth Parliament. The medium of bark was intended to convey the potency and authority of Aboriginal designs to the state. Rather than being sent as a telegram, a typed paper was attached to a 'bark painting bordered with designs belonging to the clans whose lands were most immediately threatened by the mining' (Morphy 1991: 18). Sending Ancestral designs on bark embodied a specific political sociality of rights in land through those who had participated in collecting and preparing the bark, as well as those who had painted it. Such a system of rights could not easily have been imprinted in a telegram with the same complexity and depth. This was the first time that a petition had been created using a combination of Indigenous and Western graphic and textual styles. Each petition comprised a central body of text in English and Gumatj languages surrounded by moiety-specific designs continuing the practice begun in the church panels. Frustrated by a lack of consultation over government agreements with the mining company, Nabalco, and with the support of the superintendent of the Yirrkala Methodist church mission, Rev. Edgar Wells, Yolngu had sent the petitions to the Australian House of Representatives in 1963 to voice their dissent.[25] Wells understood that if Yolngu were to engage effectively with Australian politics, they needed to appeal to a new kind of governmental recognition of the politico-religious dynamics of art as the foundation of Ancestral law.

While the barks were subject to Yolngu processes of aestheticization,[26] we would suggest that they were framed in a differential legal aesthetic across two contexts of production and reception that rendered them ambiguous as both 'art' and as 'not art'. As Yolngu artworks are statements of legal rights, the artists felt that their painted barks would convey a key political message to effect legal outcomes and not simply be appreciated as pieces of art.[28] However, the House of Representatives did not accept the significance of the artwork, instead relegating the designs to the status of colourful edging. They reappropriated the political aesthetic of the borders as an aesthetic frame, undermining the sociopolitical import of the work. Indeed, analysts frequently refer to the petitions as historic documents rather than as art, raising questions about the politics of the term 'art' and its usages. The Yolngu have continued to challenge this discourse and fight for acceptance of the combined artistic and legal status of their petitions.

The bark petitions eventually went on to form part of a court case that resulted in an amendment to the Australian Constitution in 1967 that recognized Aboriginal people in the nation. Their appeal for land rights, subsequently heard and turned down in the Gove land-rights case in 1968, was eventually upheld in 1971 with the recognition that Yolngu rights were intricately related to the land. This ruling marked a shift in relations between the Yolngu and the Australian state, and a growing recognition of the inseparability of Yolngu artistic identity and political practice. Although Yolngu missionaries and anthropologists were at the forefront of land-rights developments, and Yolngu art was deployed as a unique and successful bargaining tool with government, this political strategy was not replicated by other Aboriginal communities. Cultural difference and geographical isolation, as well as denominational differences such as those reflected through the aesthetic practices at Nauiyu, were all factors that mitigated against Yolngu joining with artists from other regions.

The examples given above show how creative artistic interpretations may innovatively extend aesthetic practices of the past and present, enabling expressions of personal religiosity, the negotiation of faith and the role of Christianity in the life of Yolngu and Ngan'gi artists. It is only in more recent years that the practice of painting has provided an opportunity for Yolngu and Ngan'gi artists to communicate religious sentiments nationally and internationally through art-market circulation, as part of a broader identity politics of Aboriginal Christianity, providing a way into Aboriginal religiosity, knowledge-systems and kinship practices for those customers interested in appreciating the design stories as expressions of identity.

Making Christian Aboriginal Art

The denominational backgrounds of Yolngu and Ngan'gi artists are compared here to illustrate how their religious designs encode Ancestral-Christian meanings. We are concerned with how Protestant and Catholic teachings have impacted upon artists' perceptions of their creative processes and their interpretations of their works. We seek to show how these denominational differences influence the selection and representation of Christian elements, such as the dove, the cross and sacraments of Baptism and Eucharist, in relation to the events of the Nativity, the Passion and resurrection of Christ when they are combined with Ancestral visual symbolism.

In order to outline the dilemmas of painting practices, we examine how a religious aesthetic is expressed in different ways within the Christian frames of reference of one Yolngu and two Ngan'gi artists. Yolngu artist Gali Gurruwiwi expresses his faith through the reinterpretation of Yolngu Ancestral images, while the Ngan'gi artists, Patricia Marrfurra and Miriam Rose Ungunmerr Bauman, evoke the Ancestral basis of their Christian beliefs by painting elements of biblical stories in locally contextualized imagery. As we shall see, their creativity demonstrates how Christianity does not replace Indigenous cosmological concepts, but rather, is reconstructed and absorbed according to personal and cultural interpretation through artists' active negotiations around competing world views (Kabo 2001; Shaw and Steward 1994). The following case studies offer a comparative analysis of Yolngu and Ngan'gi expressions of Indigenous art styles and aesthetics from these respective artists and areas.

Yolngu Christian Art: Gali Yalkarriwuy Gurruwiwi

Renowned international Yolngu artist, Gali Yalkarriwuy Gurruwiwi (b. 1942) is a senior ritual specialist, a Gälpu clan leader and prominent member of the Galiwin'ku Uniting Church. His authority in Yolngu social and ritual structures affords him particular status in holding and teaching sections of his Ancestral Law of the Morning Star to his relatives. He is a prolific artist who makes, sells and exhibits Morning Star poles on a regular basis,[27] having learned the design and meaning of his clan's Morning Star complex from his father, Gakupa.[28] Through songs, the spirits who dance for the Morning Star call the names of the countries connecting the clans who hold and control the knowledge of the Morning Star (see Congreve

2002: 11).[29] While there are many complex layers of meaning around the Ancestral narratives and spirits associated with this journey, the basic story of the Morning Star is that it is kept in a basket by an old woman who lets it out on a long string before dawn when it flies over Arnhem Land encouraging people with the news that a new day has arrived (Rudder 2002: 23). Just as the Morning Star travels back and forth across the sky on its diurnal and nocturnal journey, so Gali has taken his artwork around the world for international exhibitions in London and the United States. Gali commented, '[It] tells about the land itself. It tells the season. Morning Star … different different star … [it] changes – another and another and another but the special part does not change and that's the top part [the feathers] because that's the Morning Star itself. We always put it like that' (Gali in Interview with Magowan, November 2010; see figs 7.1 and 7.2).

In Yolngu cosmology, the pole is the transformation of the male line in the clan it represents, while its branches are a metamorphosis of the related clans' children. These inheritance rights provide the rationale for the ongoing transmission of Ancestral knowledge through an intergenerational network that includes reinterpretation for Christian contexts. Gali's father, Gakupa, first sought to reposition his identity as simultaneously Christian

Figure 7.1. Gali Gurruwiwi exhibition at the Rebecca Hossack Gallery, 15 July–10 September 2010. Two large Morning Star poles (centre). Photo: Fiona Magowan.

Figure 7.2. Gali Gurruwiwi's completed Banumbirr poles at the Rebecca Hossack Gallery, 15 July 2010. Photo: Fiona Magowan.

and Yolngu, a perspective of which his son was aware but which he would also come to discover for himself through the significant Yolngu medium of dreams. Gali told of how God spoke to him in dreams of light and the Star. As Gakupa was involved with the early establishment of the art industry on

Galiwin'ku in the 1960s, he was aware that the art curator was a Christian.
Rather than seeking to meet market demands that were not well-established
at that time, he produced art as part of the curatorial relationship with his
mentor. The adjustment movement and bark petitions had gained considerable influence by this stage, a development that may have fuelled his desire
to engage in a cultural exchange of meaning. Gali recounted how his father:

> decided that his law had to change and that he should share the Banumbirr Pole
> with the *balanda* [white people]. So he made a beautiful Banumbirr pole but
> without the human bone or hair. This rendered it incomplete and so not sacred.
> He then presented this pole to Dr John Rudder[30] and Mr Fletcher ... on Elcho
> Island as a gift to help the *balanda* understand and respect his culture. (Gurru-
> wiwi 2008)

One of the issues for Yolngu who seek to reorient their understanding
of the spiritual power of Ancestors through Christian expressions of faith
is how to account for the significance of Ancestral power that is commonly
understood to reside within Ancestral designs. While the Morning Star pole
was never intended to be shown beyond those directly related to this law,
Gakupa believed that there was no division between Ancestral and Christian
stories and that the two belonged together, just as other Yolngu families did
at Yirrkala (see Clarke 2010: 86). This correspondence between image and
spiritual effect does not render their forms synonymous with one another.
While the forms remain separate, their effects may be interchangeable, creating a synchronicity of religious efficacy in plural modes of representation.
While Gakupa was teaching Gali the inside meanings of the Ancestral Law,
his son was also attending church and had heard how the prophets foretold
of the coming of Jesus as the bright Morning Star. Gali sketched for me how
he conceptualized the relationship between God, Jesus and his Ancestral
image of the Morning Star, with the backbone of the star pointing to God
and its feathers synonymous with the Star of David (see fig. 7.3). The top
of the star indicates its Trinitarian relationship with the God the Father, the
Son and Dhuyu Birrimbirr, the Holy Spirit.

Gali's wife then revealed how his encounter with God transformed him
and in turn his artistic practice:

> There are many Morning Stars and through this artwork God spoke to him. 'Gali,
> Gali I am the bright morning star....' God would use him in his own special way,
> he has a plan to use for his ministry. He came back, walking from house to house,
> visiting Yolngu all the clans to tell stories of *djalkiri* [the Ancestral foundation]
> inside – he didn't know what was inside – God knows. God said [to him]
>
> 'Heaven is my throne and earth is my footstool.' 'What does this mean', he asked
> God. 'People don't understand this is your footstool what does this mean?' [It

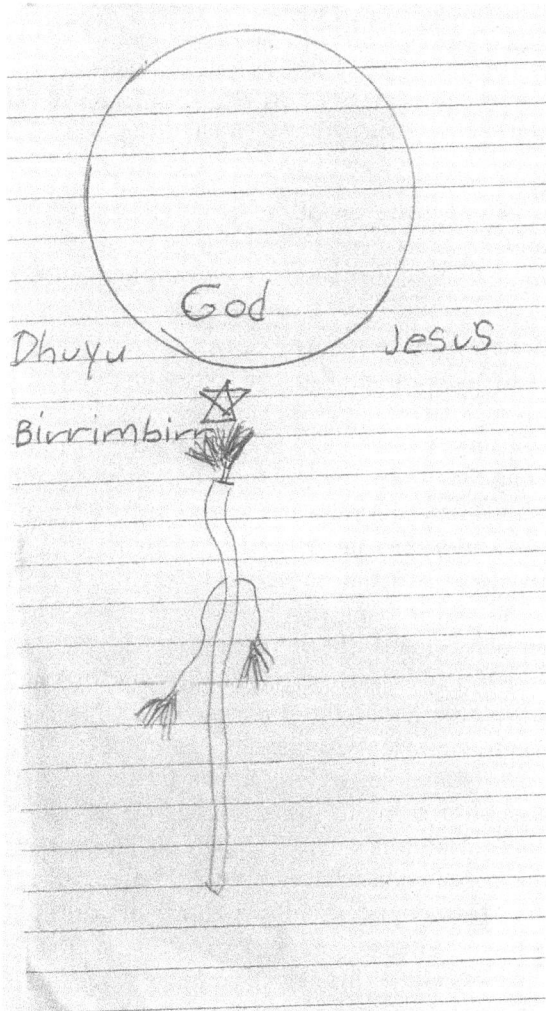

Figure 7.3. Sketch by Gali Gurruwiwi of the interrelationship between the Morning Star and Christian theology. Photo: Fiona Magowan, Galiwin'ku, 22 November 2010.

meant] I am Gali, Gälpu, God is speaking through my *madayin* (Ancestral Law / ritual objects). That was his translation to every *bäpurru* (clan) no matter but Yolngu think it was their *wangarr* (Ancestral being). *Yaka* (No), it is God speaking through their *madayin* (Ancestral Law / ritual objects). (Garrutju in interview with Magowan, November 2011).

Whether he is performing for a ritual in Arnhem Land, dancing at exhibition openings or painting on gallery windows, the Christian significance of Gali's work is an integral element of the performance of the Morning Star, which he sees as uniting Indigenous people around the world. He commented:

Much later in my life I received the opportunity to travel to Israel. I went to see the birthplace of Jesus. There I saw the Star of David. It was exactly like the Banumbirr. I knew it must be true. ... The Inuit people of Canada, the native Indians of America and the indigenous people of Japan all shared the same story of the celebration of the lifecycle and its connection to this bright star in the night's sky. (Gurruwiwi 2008)

In this reflection, Gali adopts an inclusive use of the term 'Indigenous', referring to Christians and non-Christians alike. In so doing, he is identifying spiritual power as the mediating force of Indigenous belief, which underpins both perspectives.

As Gali's art speaks both ways to Ancestral and Christian precedents, it may be interpreted as both Christian art and ritual art depending upon the viewer's understanding and perspective. Gali evokes and presents Ancestral expressions of Christianity intimately embodied in creating, dancing and singing the Ancestral Morning Star pole. The pole not only indexes and is an extension of his patrilineal and matrilineal connections over many generations, but its sentience exudes a contemporary and living expression of his synchronous Ancestral-Christian identity. He noted: 'When I work on *banumbirr* pole painting, I feel spiritual feeling inside me. When I work on it, [I feel] the spiritual being or the spiritual presence of Djewarrpuy Yolngu, that's Jesus. I feel *bili* (because) He is the Morning Star. So, when I work I feel that because Jesus said "I am the bright Morning Star"' (Gali Gurruwiwi in interview with Magowan, November 2010). This synchronicity of Ancestral-Christian feeling allows Gali to recompose the meanings of his Ancestral rights to the Morning Star as both a 'public' and 'hidden transcript' of performativity through his identities as a respected clan leader and Christian elder. James Scott (1990: 45) argues that the performance of 'public transcripts' (usually by elites) gives 'the impression of unanimity', thereby denying any autonomy of social action by subordinates. This kind of public code of behaviour conceals other forms of action, thereby creating hidden and unofficial transcripts that are not always openly declared or displayed. By performing for elite art audiences, Gali is able to display *Banumbirr* as a 'public transcript' in conventional Ancestral song and dance. While his performance may confirm the assumptions of some elite critics about the historical conventions of Arnhem Land art practices, Gali's personal Christian faith remains an invisible aspect of the artwork and the performance. Unless he chooses to elaborate on his Christian interpretations of the pole, the audience will be unaware of the 'hidden transcript' of his life journey. These multiple interpretations of the pole allow him to obfuscate certain dominant or normative expectations of Western art audiences concerning Yolngu Ancestral art which differ in substance and interpretation when compared with those of Ngan'gi artists.

Two Ngan'gi Artists: Patricia Marrfurra McTaggart and Miriam-Rose Ungunmerr Bauman

While the genesis of the Yolngu art market was initiated by men, the creative origin of Ngan'gi commercial art practices grew out of the efforts of female artists based at Magellan House Women's Centre in Nauiyu, which later developed into the thriving art centre Merrepen Arts. A group of local Ngan'gi women negotiated with the male elders of the community, who feared that the restricted Ancestral designs under their authority would be publicly revealed if these images were used for commercialized art production. Thus, they agreed that Ngan'gi women artists could paint the designs that are known and allowed to be seen publicly by all in the community. Commercial painting practices are nevertheless constrained by the restriction that certain Homeland and Dreaming designs can be painted solely by the kinship group that owns them. Though their art is founded on Ancestral stories taught by senior artists, their artworks are not direct imitations, as each individual artist complements their paintings with their own creative elements when interpreting the stories visually. Ngan'gi artists recognize the development and improvisation of individual artistic styles that use and play with particular Ngan'gi stylistic elements, figures, patterns and local contextualizations to express spiritual communality with Christianity. For example, a crossed placement of Aboriginal fire sticks in a design becomes a symbolic element that makes a visual reference both to the cross of Jesus's crucifixion and the Aboriginal way of making fire. Further, Ngan'gi creatively interpret the Nativity as part of a bush scene to visualize relevant parts of their life-world. They also paint biblical events in their own seasonal calendar: Easter is illustrated by painting the Lotus lily nuts, *miwulngini,* gathered at that time of year according to Ngan'gi bush-tucker knowledge. When illustrating the Christian Eucharist, Ngan'gi depict the chalice as a paper-bark tray *coolamon*, while Jesus's body is designated by the yam, *mimuy,* the Ngan'gi equivalent for bread symbolizing Holy Communion.

All Ngan'gi artworks are produced as a visual interpretation of a story. This story is conveyed to the customers not only visually, in paintings, but also as a narrated story, written in the words of the artist, and given with each painting on a certificate of authenticity.[31] The meanings of the artworks of Patricia Marrfurra McTaggart and Miriam-Rose Ungunmerr Bauman and their design stories show how painting has become a performative practice through which the Ngan'gi artists communicate their understanding of a combined Christian religiosity and Ancestral connectivity cross-culturally.

Patricia Marrfurra McTaggart

Patricia Marrfurra is of the Ngen'giwumirri language group and owner of Rak Malfiyin Homeland. She is president of Merrepen Arts and one of the most prolific and recognized artists in Nauiyu.[32] Her painting *Welcome to Country* visualizes a parallel between Christian baptism and a Ngan'gi ceremony of welcoming new arrivals to the Ancestors in the land; both of which use water. A particular relationship with the land is the foundation of the performance of this Ngan'gi ceremony. Before settling in the Daly River region, the Ngan'gi lived in temporary settlements in and around the areas of their Homelands; today these areas are visited regularly to maintain certain obligations, one of them being to carry out the Welcome to Country ceremony. Performed by senior members of the family, who are also Traditional Owners of this land, newborn and young children are introduced according to the law, so the Ancestors residing in the land will know them, and therefore protect them rather than threaten their presence in this sacred place. Marrfurra recalls how her father performed this ceremony in what she describes as the 'proper' way, introducing her and her sisters to the land and to the Ancestors: 'We speak to the Ancestors that live in this country. When my father took me and my three sisters to that country, he called out really loud talking to the Ancestors "hey we have visitors. I been bringing my kids here" and then he called us out by name.... This place is very sacred to us.' Marrfurra's painting offers a symbolic and visual manifestation not only of the ritualistic events in this Welcome to Country ceremony, but also of her conception of a visualized parallel between the Ngan'gi way and the Catholic way.

The design story of this painting explains this parallel; in the words of the artist:

> When a stranger is coming to our land for the first time a special ceremony must take place. An elder takes the person to the edge of the water and calls out to the Ancestors. When this happens, the pigeons are heard calling – they represent the Ancestors. The elder takes a hand full of water and puts it in his mouth. The water is then spat on the head and navel of the person visiting the land. They have been accepted and will always be welcome to come again. John the Baptist also welcomed Jesus when he baptized him and the Holy Spirit spoke. When we are baptized we become children of God. When our elders put water on our head our sweat is carried by the water and we become a child again with the Ancestors. (Information on Certificate of Authenticity, September 1991)

There are many layers of meaning in the subject matter of this painting. Taking a closer look at the design, a large yellow pigeon is positioned in

Figure 7.4. Patricia Marrfurra, *Welcome to Country*, 1991. Photo: courtesy Eileen Farrelly.

the upper half of the composition, spreading its wings over the event. This is Marrfurra's representation of the Ancestors. Marrfurra has painted the senior elder performing the ceremony with black and brown concentric circles located behind the pigeon. Finally, the person who is to be welcomed to the country in the Ngan'gi ritual, or baptized in the Christian ritual, is painted with a yellow dotted circle centrally placed in the painting, at the river's edge, which is depicted with light blue, wavy lines and brown, round pebbles at the lower end of the composition. When the senior elder leading the ceremony calls out to the Ancestors present in the sacred Homeland, the Ancestors answer through the call of the pigeon, *owollulu*, as described in the design story. It is commonly believed that birds such as the crow, the kookaburra, the white cockatoo and pigeons are Ancestors in bird shape that can communicate messages to people, explaining why Marrfurra chose to paint the Ancestor in the shape of a pigeon.[33]

The Welcome to Country ceremony takes place when someone visits a Homeland for the first time, ensuring that the Ancestors will accept their presence on the land. Thus, this event instantly creates a lifelong connectivity with the Ancestors in their Homeland. Through the ceremony, one becomes one with the Ancestors from whom one comes and to whom one returns after death. There is yet another level of meaning to Marrfurra's depiction of a pigeon, however. In addition to expressing this Ancestral connectivity, the bird has a visual similarity to a dove, a universal Christian symbol. The conflation of the pigeon and the dove visually manifests Marrfurra's parallel between traditional aboriginal belief and Christianity.

It is in the symbolism surrounding water, however, that the parallel becomes most explicit. Marrfurra explained to Øien how water for the Ngan'gi manifests rebirth, healing, initiation and inclusion, and creates a tangible connection between land, Ancestors and humans when used in rituals. This makes water, as Nancy Munn (1973: 220) describes, a 'multivocal symbol'. In Christian doctrine, water is also a multivocal symbol for incorporation, purification, renunciation and transformation. The circle representing the ritual participant in the painting is covered in white dots, which symbolizes how the water is being sprayed on the participant. The radiating white and orange lines represent the air around the welcoming site as it becomes filled with the presence of this person after the ceremony. Marrfurra parallels visually, and in her story, the Welcome to Country ceremony with Christian baptism, in which water is used similarly to welcome people as children of God, incorporating them into the body and Church of Christ.[34] Marrfurra also equates the unity created between Traditional Owners and Ancestors in a Welcome to Country ceremony, with the unity created between humans and God in a baptism, as both are mediated by water. Finally, the pigeon's embrace of the event with its spread wings is also a visual manifestation of how the Ngan'gi conceive both the Ancestors and God as omnipresent in the world, seeing the event, but also being the event, as the Ancestors and God are present in the land and in the water.

Cross-cultural communication is central to Marrfurra's art. The painting *Welcome to Country* in particular expresses her artistic creative vision of a parallel she identifies between the Ngan'gi traditional practice of Welcome to Country ceremony and the Christian ritual of baptism. Simultaneously, the design illustrating this ceremonial parallel is critical to mediate her particular and personal form of Christian faith; this design is focused on the unity of being both Christian and Ngan'gi.

Miriam-Rose Ungunmerr Bauman

Miriam-Rose Ungunmerr Bauman is a member of the Ngen'giwumirri language group and owner of Rak Malfiyin Homeland, and she was one of the founders of the Merrepen Arts and the Ngan'gi art movement.[35] Ungunmerr describes herself as a devout Christian and states that her goal is to express 'our religious story for all the Christians of the world to hear' though her art. (Ungunmerr in interview with Øien, 25 October 2007). She notes, 'I long for the day when our deep ceremonial instincts can find genuine expression in our Christian celebrations. When this happens the Christian celebrations will no longer be foreign but truly ours' (Ungunmerr 2000: 166). Ungunmerr described how she was asked by the local priest in 1974 to illustrate the Catholic 'Stations of the Cross' in her own manner, giving a personal account of her combined religious beliefs. Her aim was to interpret the biblical event of the crucifixion by creating a version of the Stations of the Cross that was more accessible and relevant to Aboriginal people. Thus, her paintings and stories held many references to Ngan'gi customs, spirituality and traditional visual practices, illustrating communality and comparability in Aboriginal and Christian spirituality.[36]

The painting, *Both Ways to Heal the Spirit*,[37] illustrates her own suggested comparison between Ngan'gi healing practices and Christian absolution. Ungunmerr explained that the Ngan'gi believe nothing happens coincidentally. Sickness, accidents or deaths could be the result of 'bone pointing', a ritual performed by a person angered by conflict, casting sickness or death on another.

Her design story outlines, in Ungunmerr's own words, the healing powers for the victim of such ill deeds, suffering from pains and fever, both in the rituals of an Aboriginal 'faith healer' and in the prayers of a Christian:

> Healing takes place in many ways. In my painting I have expressed the duality that many Aboriginal people experience. In the Western form of prayer (rosary beads) people recognize that God is the greatest healer of all. This is true for many Aboriginal people, but they also have their own traditional customs. They know that certain tribal members have a special power. This can be transmitted through the laying of hands. Branches of the ironwood tree, warmed over a fire, release an essence that has a healing effect, particularly for those who are emotionally depressed. It can help to break the spell for those who believe themselves to be 'sung' and can will themselves to die. I have painted the central figure in such a

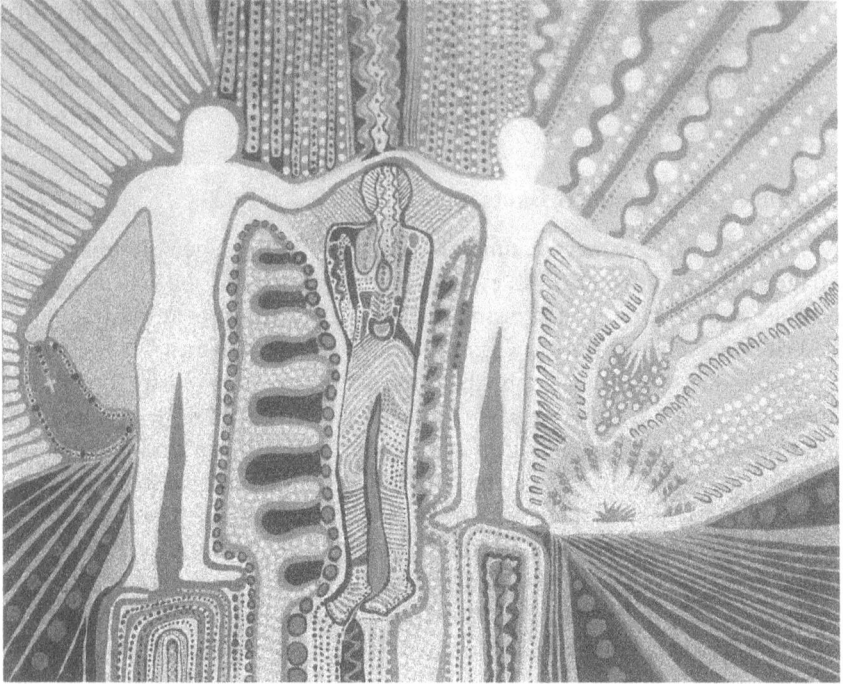

Figure 7.5. Miriam-Rose Ungunmerr Bauman, *Both Ways to Heal the Spirit,* 1987. Photo: courtesy Eileen Farrelly.

way to indicate that the whole body is involved when healing takes place. In the lower part of the painting I have used mainly browns, illustrating sadness, depression or pain, while the brighter colours at the top indicate spiritual and temporal release as a result of the healing. (Information on Certificate of Authenticity, January 1987)

In Ungunmerr's painting, the person in the centre is depressed, sick or in fear of death due to bone pointing. The sick have two possibilities for redemption, represented by two figures clutching their healing regalia: the smoke of burning ironwood branches and the Rosary beads. The Rosary holds important prayers for Catholics, and when praying, the fingers grip each bead while contemplating the five mysteries in Christ's life. This form of worship is, according to Patricia Derrington (2000: 72), similar to meditation due to its repetitive nature. As Yolngu, like other Protestants, do not use the Rosary, this imagery may not resonate with them in the way it does with the Ngan'gi, as their concepts of healing differ due to the segregated mission histories outlined earlier. Ungunmerr has painted the body of the sick person heavily decorated, and the sick person appears defeated by his suffering – his heart and stomach are revealed in the style of an 'x-ray', representing the fears and sorrow he holds there. This represents a stark visual contrast with the blank, white bodies of the healers. Around the figures at the bottom of the painting, Ungunmerr notes how downwards-sloping, diagonal lines are illustrations of the pain of the sufferer. Colours change from dark to light at the top of the canvas, filled with diagonal lines, radiating from the sick, and manifesting the continuing healing process. The victim's suffering flows from the top of his head in a wavy line as he is experiencing spiritual release; this is Ungunmerr's painted manifestation of how he is being 'healed both ways'.[38]

Although the painting of Christian designs was introduced under the guidance and authority of missionaries in boarding schools during the days of the Catholic mission, these artists have made the production of acrylic painting a practice of their own, creating art that acts as a marker of their own contemporary cultural and religious identity. As we have seen, particular theological and artistic conventions result in complex visual expressions that are peculiar to Yolngu and Ngan'gi art (Nichols 2002). These two paintings are examples of how Ngan'gi artists are innovatively extending past aesthetic practices united with their own understandings of Christianity.

Circulation of Christian Aboriginal Art in the Art Worlds

The form of artistic creativity illustrated by the Christian Aboriginal art designs analysed above poses certain dilemmas for the Aboriginal art market. When artists encounter art curators and customers together in the shared spaces of the art world, the status and value of their art is affected by the preferences of authoritative art-world representatives. Certain non-Aboriginal customers and critics may have a limited appreciation for, or understanding of, Christian Aboriginal art, interpreted by them as 'inauthentic', syncretic, Christian mergers rather than contemporary art. Refuting this ethnocentrism, Galiwin'ku artists who use the same design templates for Ancestral and Christian meanings argue that interpretation rather than form is critical and, therefore, do not accept that their Christian artwork is of lower value than Ancestral works. They do, however, recognize that customers may have preferences for certain genres of their work over others. Paintings with explicit Christian imagery are not directly sought by the art gallery on Galiwin'ku, and thus, they are mostly created for particular Christian events or as gifts for relatives or commissioned pieces. As a result, a separation in systems of valuation between Ancestral and Christian art as a commercial enterprise seldom arises.

Concerning Ngan'gi art, however, the segregation between Ancestral and Christian genres has led to the recognition among the customers at Merrepen Arts that Christian art is of lower economic value in the marketplace. Customers preferred paintings with Ancestral designs, being more interested in so-called traditional pieces. As a consequence of low saleability, the production of paintings with Christian designs is currently declining at Merrepen Arts. Nonetheless, Christian designs are still produced for sale on commission from churches or individuals. As we have seen, in both cases, Aboriginal Christian art is a means of externalizing religious knowledge and affirming believers' relationships with their united Christian and Ancestral senses of self and relational personhood.

Conclusion

Art is always in a state of 'becoming', emerging from many creative discourses. In the analysis of these artists' works, we have shown how processual diversity encapsulates and juxtaposes art-making, creative thinking, artistic communication and art-market judgements. Indeed, Aboriginal Christian art, as evidenced through the paintings presented in this chapter, has developed as much from entangled worldviews of Christianity and Ancestral cosmology as from Catholic or Protestant doctrine. These entanglements have facilitated a wider range of cross-cultural exchange in differentiated art-world settings. As Christian Aboriginal art production continues to emerge from the circumstances of local painting traditions, so we have shown how it embodies continuities of Aboriginal identity, as well as encapsulating and reflecting the histories of particular mission backgrounds and aesthetic practices.

Contemporary Aboriginal Christian art production simultaneously incorporates the continuity of well-established practices with the creation of new forms and ideas. This chapter has shown that the transformations of meaning arising from the interrelationship of art production, circulation and representations of identity make the production of Christian designs both beneficial and problematic in terms of cross-cultural communication. The presence of Christian Aboriginal art in the art market has increased acknowledgement of artistic diversity within the Aboriginal art movement, and acceptance of these artists in transforming and extending their aesthetic practices. Nevertheless, Christian Aboriginal art is still not as well appreciated as Ancestral genres due to the prevalence of aesthetic regimes that restrict its definition in certain art-world contexts.

We have shown how artists have sought to engage missionaries in dialogue on their own terms as Aboriginal communities have actively appropriated and influenced Catholic and Protestant doctrine for their own use and understanding through art. Christian Aboriginal art production in each region illustrates processes of contemporaneity through which artistic practices simultaneously incorporate the continuation of old practices with the creation of new design elements, media and aesthetic forms. Nevertheless, the foundations of the Ancestral Law still provide stability through a social and religious order, which demands that innovations in thought or practice be brought into articulation with it. We have shown how commonalities between Catholic and Protestant artists are not dependent upon predetermined mergers between disparate denominational approaches to Christian theology; rather both cases reflect their own creative dynamics and politics of representation. The proliferation of diverse approaches to Christian Aboriginal art may be attributed to the fact that some Christian Aboriginal artists have realized the commonalities that exist between Ancestral structures, templates and regulations available to them and have been able to adapt them for broader Christian purposes. In so doing, they have also transformed ontological connections of relationship between land, Ancestors and kinship in order to extend their Christian beliefs to others in their communities and, through consumers, to the nation.

Fiona Magowan is professor of anthropology in the School of History and Anthropology at Queen's University, Belfast. Her publications focus on Australian Aboriginal performance and Christianity, cultural tourism, religion and ritual, and sex and gender. She has conducted fieldwork in Arnhem Land, Northern Territory, Queensland and South Australia. Her books include *Melodies of Mourning: Music and Emotion in Northern Australia* (Oxford, 2007); *The Anthropology of Sex* (Berg, 2010, co-authored with H. Donnan); and the co-edited volumes *Performing Gender, Place and Emotion* (University of Rochester Press, 2013, with L. Wrazen); *Landscapes of Performance* (Aboriginal Studies Press, 2005, with K. Neuenfeldt); and *Telling Stories* (Allen and Unwin, 2001, with B. Attwood).

Maria Øien is a visiting research fellow in the Department of Ethnography and at the Museum of Cultural History at the University of Oslo. Her PhD thesis (2015) is entitled 'Our Art Comes from Our Dreaming: Exploring Change and Continuity in the Transforming Merrepen Art from Nauiyu, Australia'. Her main research interests are Indigenous art production, artistic creativity and market circulation of Aboriginal art. She has conducted fieldwork in Nauiyu, Tiwi and Arnhem Land, Northern Territory, Australia. She was the head curator of an Aboriginal art exhibition, *We Paint the Stories of our Culture,* at the Museum of Cultural History in February 2011.

Notes

1. Although Aboriginal is a contested term (see Attwood 1989; Broun 1995), it is used to describe Indigenous Australians in general. The title is taken as a response that Øien received from Patricia Marrfurra when asking about her Christian designs.
2. Yolngu is the name that Aboriginal people of the northeast Arnhem Land region use to refer to themselves. The Yolngu are divided into seven language groups and sixty dialects. In Nauiyu there are members of twelve language groups present, yet a great majority of the community inhabitants are Ngan'gikurung-gurr and Ngen'giwumirri speakers. The abbreviation Ngan'gi will therefore be applied when describing the people of Nauiyu specifically.
3. Nauiyu community was first called Daly River and was renamed Nauiyu Nambiyu in 1970. It means 'one place, one people', 'meeting point' or 'coming together in one place', referring to the different language groups living there (Lindsay et al. 2001). Today the name is often shortened to Nauiyu.
4. Fiona Magowan has worked with Yolngu on Galiwin'ku at different times since 1990 and published on ritual, missions and Christianity (see, for example, Gordon and Magowan 2000; Magowan 2007). This fieldwork on Yolngu art was carried out in 2010 and 2011 as part of the HERA-funded project, Creativity and Innovation in a World of Movement (09-HERA-JRP-CI-FP-005). Maria Øien undertook fieldwork with Ngan'gi artists for six months in 2003 and from August 2007 to July 2008. She completed her PhD in 2014.
5. Svašek (2007: 9–11, 26, 40, 59–60) uses the term 'aestheticization' to conceptualize how people's sensorial or aesthetic experiences, perceptions and interpretations are processual in nature, grounded in changing social contexts and practices, and used to reinforce abstract ideas about the meaning and value in objects.
6. The Australian State, from as early as 1975, took the role as a powerful patron of Aboriginal art (Lattas 1991). The development of an Aboriginal art and craft industry, though initiated on a local level, became a national endeavour as governmental funding provided support to non-profit art centres, owned cooperatively by local artists (Altman 2007), such as Elcho Island Arts and Merrepen Arts. This state support was part of the government's wider aim of respecting Aboriginal wishes and supporting the development and maintenance of a living cultural heritage embodied in the art *and* improving the social and economic well-being of the artists and their families by providing local employment and income (Altman and Hunter 2005; Taylor 2005).
7. It should be noted that Aboriginal Christian art is not the major form of artistic practice in this region as it has emerged sporadically and by particular individuals at different points of mission and post-mission history.
8. The Ancestral Law is popularly known as 'the Dreaming' in English and in some Aboriginal contexts and regions. The potential for misunderstanding its connotations have been widely debated (see Wolfe 1991; Hume 2002). The terms Dreaming and Ancestral Law are used here interchangeably, as they are by the Ngan'gi.

9. The body of judicial and moral rules is known as *Maḏayin* by Yolngu and *Deme* by Ngan'gi.

10. Ancestral painting designs are specific to Ancestral activity within Homeland areas, but there are some differences: for Yolngu the same design may be shared by several clans who are joined by the same Ancestral Law, such as Shark (*maṉa*), King Brown Snake (*ḏarrpa*) and Honey Ancestral Being (*wuyal*). Such clan groupings are known as *rringgitj*. Clans distinguish themselves by slight variations in the ways the same ancestor is depicted. In contrast, Ngan'gi artists' Homeland is called *Dede Putymemme*. They paint the ancestral stories of their Homeland sites with stylistic patterns known as *durrmu*. Ngan'gi designs are known by the kinship group to which they belong. For example, paintings of the *Rak Malfiyin* kin group include creational stories of King Brown Snake *Anganisyi*, Sand Frog *Niyen*, Chicken Hawk *Angan'pipi*, Pelican *Burro*, Black Brim *Awoin* and Bittern *Agiminy*.

11. Morphy (1991: 96) analyses the Yolngu terms 'inside' (*djinaga*) and 'outside' (*warrangul*) as they pertain to degrees of gendered knowledge restriction along a continuum. Rights to ritual knowledge and designs are further determined by a close relationship between inheritance and shared knowledge, the latter acquired through teaching, exchange and watching paintings being produced in ceremony (ibid.: 58). The painting of these 'Dreamtime stories' for sale illustrates how visual reproduction practices simultaneously reorganize and build on this conventional distinction between 'outside' and 'inside' knowledge (ibid.).

12. Yolngu art comprises both geometric and figurative elements (see Morphy 1991). Ngan'gi art is regionally and culturally distinct from Yolngu in Arnhem Land with a differentiated artistic practice of colourful and figurative designs with geometric elements that do not include the Arnhem Land style of cross-hatching infill.

13. The subject matter of a painting refers to the total content of a design, including the imagery, style, story and meaning.

14. Methodists came to the Northern Territory twenty years after the first Jesuit contact with Aboriginal communities.

15. Anglicans established their first mission at Roper River in Arnhem Land in 1908 and then set up another two Western Arnhem Land missions at Groote Eylandt in 1921 and Oenpelli in 1925.

16. These statistics are taken from the Australian Bureau of Statistics 2011 Census Community Profiles, http://www.censusdata.abs.gov.au/census_services/get product/census/2011/communityprofile/ILOC70600401?opendocument&nav pos=230, accessed 23 September 2012. As these figures do not include non-Aboriginal people, the total of five hundred is an estimate.

17. The island of Galiwin'ku is forty-eight kilometres long from the town of Galiwin'ku to the furthest homeland, Gäwa and eleven kilometres wide.

18. The Uniting Church of Australia was established as an amalgamation of the Methodist, Presbyterian and Congregationalist churches.

19. An early Jesuit Mission was established in Uniya at Daly River in 1886 and ended three years later in 1889. By 1914, the government had divided the Northern Territory into different church regions in order to prevent conflict

between denominations (see also Riseman 2008: 246). Catholic missionaries continued to expand to the northwest, setting up missions at Bathurst (1911), Port Keats (1935) and Arltunga (1943). The second Catholic mission came to Daly River at Nauiyu in 1955.

20. The MalakMalak people are a declining linguistic minority in Nauiyu today. Instead, Ngan'gikurunggurr and Ngen'giwumirri are spoken by the majority (Reid and McTaggart 2008).

21. The Missionaries of the Sacred Heart is a Catholic Order founded in France in 1874 by Father Jules Chevalier, with the motto 'May the Sacred Heart of Jesus be everywhere loved'. The community came under the superintendence of Father Leary, assisted by nuns from the MSH's Sister Congregation 'The Daughters of Our Lady of the Sacred Heart' for the next thirty years (Hearn 2003; Pye 1976). There has been a long-standing mystical devotional tradition and particular pictorial practices around the Sacred Heart of Jesus see (Meyer 2011; King 2010). Ngan'gi artists have occasionally painted their own particular depictions of 'Our Lady of the Sacred Heart of Jesus' in colourful, figurative designs with a central female figure, with the light of the world emanating from her head as a halo, holding the baby Jesus in her arms, and her finger pointing to the exposed heart of the baby Jesus, which is encircled by thorns and surmounted by flames and a cross.

22. Notably, this approach was adopted prior to the Second Vatican Council (1962–1965), which reassessed Catholic traditions in response to social change, taking into account indigenous practices. (Stet 'I').

23. These historic designs have been described to me orally by Senior Ngan'gi artists. Because of a devastating flood in 1997, all the archives and older artworks of Merrepen Arts were destroyed, so I cannot provide photographs. However, this manner of painting indicates ceremonial links to Wadeye art (a neighbouring community) or further south along the Victoria River through to the 'Desert' culture. Thus, a visual parallel can be found in Desert regions where the artists still paint abstract country maps in this manner, using circles and lines to represent specific geographical places and features.

24. Dhuwa and Yirritja are the names of the two patrilineal halves or moieties of the world from which every animate and inanimate object, person and substance takes its identity.

25. This petition resulted in the commencement of land rights when the case moved to the Supreme High Court of the Northern Territory in 1968 in what became known historically as 'Gove Land Rights case'.

26. Errington (1994: 203) distinguishes between art as intention and art as appropriation. The former comprises works that were intended to be seen 'as art' for art contexts. Art as appropriation 'becomes art by being *framed*' when it is taken out of its normative context (ibid.: 207; see Svašek 2007 for further discussion of aestheticization).

27. As Yolngu bark paintings encode rights to land, their designs are handed down over generations.

28. Since 1989, he has created works for twenty-five exhibitions, six internationally in Canada, the United States and Europe, and has been twice finalist of the

TELSTRA art award as well as winner of the Kate Challis RAKA Award for Contemporary Visual Arts.

29. The Morning Star complex refers to the material and spiritual dimensions of the object, its ritual songs, dances and artistic components. As an object, the Morning Star pole comprises a wooden central pole made of red kurrajong with strings and feather tassles along its length. At the top of the pole, cockatoo feathers symbolize the Morning Star. Morning Star poles are made in several areas with different designs that are connected by the associated song cycles that describe the journey of the soul of the deceased to the island of the dead called Burralku (Robinson 1956; Rudder 1993).

30. John Rudder was a missionary to Galiwin'ku and the community's first art adviser (1969–1972) before completing a PhD on Yolngu cosmological principles, which included a study of Banumbirr (1990, 2002).

31. The certificate contains the documentation of the artist's name, date of birth, language, size of painting, date of completion, medium, catalogue number, title and design story in the words of the artist, along with the Merrepen Arts logo and details. These certificates not only communicate the artists' design stories, they also act as proof of authenticity by ensuring the necessary authorization of design ownership and financial return to the artists.

32. Patricia Marrfurra was born on the 9 March 1959. Marrfurra's inherited Dreamings are the King Brown Snake (*Anganisyi*), Water or Rain (*Kuri*), Sand Frog (*Niyen*), Chicken Hawk (*Angan'pipi*), Pelican (*Burro*), Black Brim (*Awoin*) and Bittern (*Agiminy*). She has an advanced diploma in linguistics and arts and in her work as a linguist she has contributed to several publications (Reid and McTaggart 2008; Lindsay et al. 2001; Marfurra et al. 1995). Marrfurra is also a board member on the local Nauiyu Nambiyu Council and Nauiyu Nambiyu Inc. From 1987 until today, she has participated in numerous painting and print exhibitions in Darwin, Katherine, Perth, Sydney and Melbourne. Her artworks have been acquired by the Robert Holmes á Court Collection, Perth, the Museum of Arts & Science, Darwin, Berndt Museum, Perth, Art Gallery of Western Australia, Perth, Christ Church Anglican Cathedral, Darwin, and the Museum of Cultural History, Oslo, Norway.

33. See Magowan 2007 for a musical analysis of how Yolngu birds communicate spiritually.

34. A baptism also includes the purification of sin, the renunciation of and separation from the past, spiritual transformation and rebirth to a new life (Dillistone 1985, 1986).

35. Miriam-Rose Ungunmerr Bauman was born on 1 July 1950 on the banks of Daly River at Wunbal. Her Dreamings are King Brown Snake (*Anganisyi*), Sand Frog (*Niyen*), Chicken Hawk (*Angan'pipi*), Pelican (*Burro*), Black Brim (*Awoin*) and Bittern (*Agiminy*). She has a master's degree in education, a bachelor's degree in art and an honorary doctorate in writing. She began teaching at St Francis Xavier School at an early age, where she later became principal. As a teacher, she has taught many of the current artists in local painting practices. As one of the instigators of Merrepen Arts and the previous president of the board, her influence on the style and subject matter of Ngan'gi art has been substantial.

She was a CEO of the local Nauiyu Nambiyu Council for years, and is currently a board member. From 1987 until today, Ungunmerr has participated in numerous painting and print exhibitions in Darwin, Katherine, Adelaide, Perth, Sydney and Melbourne. Her artworks have been acquired by the Robert Holmes á Court Collection, Perth, the Museum of Arts & Science, Darwin, National Gallery of Victoria, Northern Territory University, Darwin, and the Museum of Cultural History, Oslo, Norway.

36. These paintings are currently exhibited in the St Frances Xavier Church in Nauiyu. The *Stations* were temporarily moved to be exhibited at the High Court of Australia, for the Aboriginal Art and Spirituality Exhibition at the World Councils of Churches Assembly (Derrington 2000: 13). They were also reproduced in a Dove Communications publication in 1988 titled *Stations of the Cross* (Ungunmerr-Bauman 1984).

37. Ungunmerr was chosen by the Northern Territory government to meet with Prince Charles of the British Royal Family when he visited Darwin in 1988. She presented this painting to him as a commissioned gift representing all the Aboriginal people living in and around the Darwin area (Derrington 2000). At that time, the painting was titled *The Healing Ceremony,* a title also used in Derrington's (2000) volume. However, in Øien's conversation with the artist, when receiving oral permission to reprint it, the artist spoke about the work using the title *Both Ways to Heal the Spirit.* Furthermore, upon locating the original Certificate of Authenticity for this work in the Merrepen Arts archives, the work was titled *Both Ways to Heal the Spirit,* which is the title Øien has chosen to use here.

38. See Derrington (2000) for her analysis of this and other works by Ungunmerr.

References

Attwood, B. 1989. *The Making of the Aborigines.* Sydney: Allen and Unwin.

Altman, J. C. 2007. 'The Howard Government's Northern Territory Intervention: Are Neo-Paternalism and Indigenous Development Compatible?' *Centre for Aboriginal Economic Policy Research* Topical Issue (16): 1–19.

Altman, J., and B. Hunter. 2005. 'Economic Life' in B. Arthur and F. Morphy (eds), *The Macquarie Atlas of Indigenous Australia: Culture and Society through Space and Time.* New South Wales: The Macquarie Library Pty Ltd, 182–193.

Berndt, R. 1962. *An Adjustment Movement in Arnhem Land.* Paris: Mouton.

Broun, M. 1995. 'Aboriginal Women's Craft: Creation and Re-Creation', in L. Kaino (ed.), *The Necessity of Craft: Development and Women's Craft in the Asian-Pacific Region.* Nedlands: University of Western Australia Press, 1–10.

Clarke, B. 2010. *Larrpan ga Buduyurr: The Spear and the Cloud.* South Australia: Bernard Clarke (self-published).

Congreve, S. 2002. 'The Morning Star in north-east Arnhem Land', in *Banumbirr* (n.a.). Sydney: Elcho Island Art and Craft and Bandigan Aboriginal Art and Craft, 10–13.

Derrington, P. R. 2000. *The Serpent of Good and Evil: A Reconciliation in the Life and Art of Miriam-Rose Ungunmerr Baumann.* Flemington, Victoria: Hyland House.

Dillistone, F.W. 1985. *Christianity and Symbolism*. London: SCM Press.
———. 1986. *The power of symbols in religion and culture*. New York: Crossroad.
Duelke, B. 2005. '"No Matter That Modern World": An Aboriginal Approach to a Polychronic Past. A Case Study from Northern Australia', in T. Otto and P. Pedersen (eds), *Tradition and Agency: Tracing Cultural Continuity and Invention*. Aarhus: Aarhus University Press, 267–90.
Errington, S. 1994. 'What Became Authentic Primitive Art?' *Cultural Anthropology* 9(2): 201–226.
Glaskin, K. 2010. 'On dreams, innovation and the emerging genre of the individual artist', *Anthropological Forum*, Creations: Imagination and Innovation Special Issue 20(3): 251–267.
Gordon, J, and F. Magowan (eds). 2000. 'Beyond Syncretism: Indigenous expressions of world religions', *The Australian Journal of Anthropology* special edition 13(2), 253–58.
Gurruwiwi, G. Y. 2008. 'Gali Yalkarriwuy Gurruwiwi', 29 February. http://www.rg.co.uk/artists/bio/artist_statement_gali_yalkarriwuy_gurruwiwi/150,0,0.html, accessed 12 May 2012.
Harris, J. 1990. *One Blood: 200 Years of Aboriginal Encounter with Christianity: A Story of Hope*. Sydney: Albatross Books.
Hearn, P. 2003. *A Theology of Mission: Diocese of Darwin 1949–1985*. New South Wales: Nelen Yubu Missiological Unit.
Hume, L. 2002. *Ancestral Power: The Dreaming, Consciousness and Aboriginal Australians*. Melbourne: Carlton University Press.
Kabo, V. 2001. 'Australian Aboriginal Art and Russian Icon Painting', in A. Anderson, I. Lilley and S. O'connor (eds), *Histories of Old Ages: Essays in Honour of Rhys Jones*. Canberra: Pandanus Books, 267–275.
Keen, I. 1994. *Knowledge and Secrecy in an Aboriginal Religion*. Oxford: Clarendon Press.
King, E. F. 2010. *Material Religion and Popular Culture*. New York: Routledge.
Lattas, A. 1991. 'Nationalism, Aesthetic Redemption and Aboriginality', *The Australian Journal of Anthropology* 2(3): 307–324.
Lindsay, B. Y., et al. 2001. *MalakMalak and Matngala Plants and Animals*. Northern Territory: Parks and Wildlife Commission of Darwin.
Magowan, F. 2003. '"It is God who Speaks in the Thunder …": Mediating Ontologies of Faith and Fear in Aboriginal Christianity', *Journal of Religious History* 27(3): 293–310.
———. 2007. *Melodies of Mourning: Music and Emotion in Northern Australia*. Oxford, Washington and Perth: James Currey Press, SAR and University of Western Australia.
———. 2016. 'The Intercultural Dynamics of Missions and Music in Yolngu Spiritual Experience', in J. Dueck and S. Reily (eds), *The Oxford Handbook of Music and Missions*. Oxford: Oxford University Press, 55–77.
Marrfurra, P, et al. 1995. *Ngan'gikurungurr and Ngan'giwumirri Ethnobotany Aboriginal Plant Use from the Daly River Area Northern Australia*. Darwin: Northern Territory Botanical Bulletin No. 22, Conservation Comission of the Northern Territory.

Mcculloch, S. 1999. *Contemporary Aboriginal Art: A Guide to the Rebirth of an Ancient Culture*, 2nd edition. New South Wales: Allen and Unwin.

McKnight, D. 2002. *From Hunting to Drinking: The Devastating Effects of Alcohol on an Australian Aborginal Community*. London: Routledge.

Meyer, B. 2010. 'Aesthetics of Persuasion: Global Christianity and Pentecostalism's Sensational Forms', *South Atlantic Quarterly* 109(4): 741–763.

———. 2011. 'Mediating Absence – Effecting Spiritual Presence: Pictures and the Christian Imagination', *Social Research* 78(4): 1029–1056.

Morphy, H. 1983. 'Now You Understand: An Analysis of the Way Yolngu Have Used Sacred Knowledge to Maintain Their Autonomy', in N. Peterson and M. Langton (eds), *Aborigines, Land and Landrights*. Canberra: Australian Institute of Aboriginal Studies, 110–133.

———. 1991. *Ancestral Connections: Art and an Aboriginal System of Knowledge*. Chicago: University of Chicago Press.

———. 1998. *Aboriginal Art*. London: Phaidon.

———. 2005. 'Mutual Conversion? The Methodist Church and the Yolŋu, With Particular Reference to Yirrkala', *Humanities Research* vol. XII, no. 1, Bigotry and Religion in Australia 1865–1950. ANU epress, http://epress.anu.edu.au/hrj/2005_01/mobile_devices/index.html, accessed 12 May 2012.

———. 2008. *Becoming Art: Exploring Cross-Cultural Categories*. Sydney: University of New South Wales.

Munn, N. D. 1973. *Walbiri Iconography: Graphic Representation and Cultural Symbolism in a Central Australian Society*. Chicago: Chicago University Press.

Nichols, C. 2002. 'God and Country: An Analysis of Gali Yalkirriwuy's Three Wise Men', *A Forum for Theology in the World Beyond Idols and Icon* 5(1).

Pye, R. J. 1976. *The Daly River Story: A River Unconquered*. Darwin: J. R. Coleman.

Reid, N., and P. M. Mctaggart. 2008. *Ngan'gi Dictionary*. Armidale: Australian Linguistic Press.

Riseman, Noah. 2008. 'Disrupting Assimilation: Soldiers, Missionaries and Aboriginal People in Arnhem Land during World War II', In A. Barry et al. (eds), *Evangelists of Empire?: Missionaries in Colonial History*. Melbourne: University of Melbourne eScholarship Research Centre. http://msp.esrc.unimelb.edu.au/shs/missions, accessed 12 May 2012.

Robinson, R. 1956. *The Feathered Serpent*. Sydney: Edwards and Shaw.

Rudder, J. 1993. 'Yolngu Cosmology: An Unchanging Cosmos Incorporating a Rapidly Changing World?' Unpublished PhD thesis, Australian National University.

———. 2002. 'The Ceremonial Complex Banumbirr the Morning Star', in *Banumbirr* (n.a.). Sydney: Elcho Island Art and Craft and Bandigan Aboriginal Art and Craft, 21–29.

Saussure, F. de. 1959. *Course in General Linguistics*. New York: McGraw Hill.

Scott, J. 1990. *Domination and the Arts of Resistance: Hidden Transcripts*. New Haven: Yale University Press.

Shaw, R, and C. Steward. 1994. 'Introduction: Problematizing Syncretism', in C. Steward and R. Shaw (eds), *Syncretism/Anti-Syncretism: The Politics of Religious Synthesis*. London: Routledge, 1–26.

Stanley, O. 1985. *The Mission and Peppimenarti: An Economic Study of Two Daly River Aboriginal Communities*. Darwin: Australian National University, North Australia Research Unit.

Stanner, W. E. H. 1933a. 'The Daly River Tribes: A Report of Field Work in Northern Australia', *Oceania* III(4): 377–405.

———. 1933b. 'The Daly River Tribes: A Report of Field Work in Northern Australia', *Oceania* IV(1): 10–29.

Svašek, M. 2007. *Anthropology, Art and Cultural Production*. London: Pluto Press.

Taylor, L. 2005. 'The Visual Arts', in B. Arthur and F. Morphy (eds), *The Macquarie Atlas of Indigenous Australia: Culture and Society Through Space and Time*. New South Wales: The Macquarie Library Pty Ltd, 114–125.

———. 2007. *Seeing the Inside. Bark Painting in Western Arnhem Land*. Oxford: Clarendon Press.

Toren, C. 1988. 'Making the Present, Revealing the Past: The Mutability and Continuity of Tradition as Process', *Man* 23(4): 696–717.

Ungunmerr Bauman, M-R. 1984. *Australian Stations of the Cross*. Blackburn, Victoria: Dove Communications.

———. 2000. 'Indigenous Pedagogy', in M. A. Bin-Sallik (ed.), *Aboriginal Women by Degrees: Their Stories of the Journey Towards Academic Achievement*. St Lucia: University of Queensland Press, 164–176.

Wearing, B. 2007. *Beulah Lowe and the Yolngu People*. New South Wales: Coast Biographers.

Wolfe, P. 1991. 'On Being Woken Up: The Dreamtime in Anthropology and Australian Settler Culture', *Comparative Studies in Society and History* 33(2): 197–224.

8

Undoing Absence through Things
Creative Appropriation and Affective Engagement in an Indian Transnational Setting

———◆•◆•◆———

Maruška Svašek

In 2010, I visited Manika, a 53-year-old migrant from the Punjab who had settled in Northern Ireland with her family when she was a child in the 1960s. Sitting on the sofa in the lounge, we discussed the omnipresence of Hindu god images in public spaces in India. To demonstrate her own urge to be surrounded by such imagery, she showed me a digital copy of Lord Ganesh on her mobile phone. 'Whenever I turn my phone on in the morning and see him', she explained, 'I acknowledge his presence and pray to him in my mind. That's how he comes in my mind.' Laughing, she added, 'I carry my phone with me, so he is with me all day.' Ten minutes later, after a cup of tea, we walked up the stairs to a room that in most Northern Irish households would be used as a small bedroom or office.

When she opened the door, a dazzling sight of colourful pictures and statues depicting Hindu gods (*murtis*) confronted me. This was the family's *puja* room, the place where she performed acts of worship (*puja*), demonstrating feelings of love and respect for the divine. The divine (*Brahman*) is perceived by most Hindus as an abstract, timeless force that pervades everything and becomes manifest in various forms, for example through depictions of Hindu gods (Huyler 1999: 27–28). This seeming contradiction – the divine being omnipresent *and* manifesting itself through specific material forms – is rooted in developments in Hindu thought that can be traced back to written sources from the seventh and eighth centuries. As Richard H. Davis (1997: 27) explained, according to the *Vaisnava samhitas* and the *Saiva agamas*, 'the nature of the Supreme' has 'two primary modes of being', namely 'undifferentiated and differentiated, formless and corporeal, unmanifest and manifest, without attributes and with attributes, supreme and accessible, and so on'. Following Davis (ibid.), I use the term 'transcendence' to refer to unmanifested supreme divinity and 'immanence' to manifested divine power.

The wooden temple structure in the centre of the room contained small bronze figures dressed in red silk garments, representing Ganesh, Vishnu, Lakshmi and other deities. Manika explained that performances of worship for these gods helped her to gain inner harmony. Worship also meant to increase auspiciousness and secure divine protection for the whole family. Placed around the temple structure were numerous artefacts depicting various gods, manufactured out of different materials in various shapes and sizes (see fig. 8.1). Looking at the deities, I wondered what Manika's repeated engagement with them could reveal about her experiences as Hindu living outside India. What was her drive, and how did she position herself, drawing on different dynamic traditions? To what extent was her engagement influenced by specific regimes of religious practice?

Figure 8.1. The *puja* room in Manika's house. Photo: Maruška Svašek.

Transition-Transformation

To answer these questions, this chapter looks more closely at Manika's use of artefacts and digital imagery in religious spheres of action, and pays specific attention to the creative and emotional dimensions of her activities. The analysis further develops the perspective of 'transition and transformation' (Svašek 2001, 2012), conceptualized as a dynamic process whereby artefacts and images in transition are transformative as they come to be interpreted and experienced by individuals and groups of people in specific ways (see also the introduction to this volume). This dual process of person-thing causality (Gell 1998) relies on thinking and feeling human beings, who, through the production, handling and appropriation of artefacts, situate themselves in their surroundings, in some situations consciously using them to claim particular (shared) identities (Hall 1997; Spyer and Steedly 2013). The perspective also acknowledges that people cannot fully control the impact of material things, agreeing with Webb Keane that 'things always contain properties in excess of those which have been interpreted and made use of under any given circumstance' and therefore 'do not only express past acts, intentions and representations', but also 'invite unexpected responses' (2006: 201).

The perspective of transition-transformation refers to the embeddedness of mobile humans in material, multisensorial and affective environments, and draws attention to the ways in which subjectivities are constituted through appropriated material things. In the act of being used, the objects participate 'in a process of social self-creation in which they are directly constitutive of our understanding of ourselves and others' (Miller 1987: 215). The analysis that follows shows that the material presence of the god images in Manika's home shrine propelled her to reproduce herself as someone following Hindu traditions by showing specific emotions in particular ways. Together with the sounds of her prayer and chanting, and the smells of incense, the sight and handling of the objects performed feelings of love, respect and care that bound her to her homeland.

Mediation and the Immediate

Seeing the variety of artefacts in Manika's *puja* room, I wondered about the different ways in which the various objects afforded specific, bodily felt transformations. As Ulf Hannerz (1992: 9) has pointed out, 'not all ideas can be stated equally well in every mode of externalization; new external modes allow new modes of experiencing and new modes of thinking'. Through which kinds of interactions did each artefact or picture in the room mediate religious experiences, and did these experiences differ in any way? Was there any difference, for example, between the workings of a three-dimensional Ganesh *murti*, a Ganesh picture printed on a wedding card, and a digital Ganesh image on a mobile phone?

In an increasingly technologically advanced and interconnected world, in the past decades a growing number of academics have explored the effect of innovative media technologies on human interaction (Baym 2010; Miller and Slater 2000). According to Christiane Brosius and Melissa Butcher (1999: 11), '[o]bserving the journey of images within a media landscape provides a creative platform from which the complexity of cultural change can be approached and contextualized'.

Numerous anthropologists have explored how different types of technologies, from written texts to sculptural pieces through poster prints to digital imagery, mediate and remediate religious experiences (Jain 2007; Meyer 2009; Morgan 1998, 2009; Pinney 2004; Prakash Upadhyay and Robinson 2011; Weibel 2011). Birgit Meyer (2013: 5) has convincingly argued that the assumptions of 'an originally unmediated state into which media enter with their alienating logic' must be rejected. Instead, mediation should be understood as 'a process that produces a shared world to be in-hibited, taken for "real" and experienced as "immediate"'. This chapter contributes to the debate by showing that technologies of mediation can be conceptualized as manipulated and manipulating technologies that provide experiences of immediacy to bodies searching to overcome perceived distances.

Overcoming Distance through Creative Appropriation and Affective Engagement

Focusing on diasporic Hindu places of worship, this analysis is specifically interested in the interrelated creative and affective dimensions of practices of 'overcoming distance'. The theme of creative appropriation, a central focus in this volume, emphasizes that religious traditions, whether repetitive, imitative or altering, are never static but always in the making (see also this volume's introduction). Drawing on Elizabeth Hallam and Tim Ingold (2007) and Rob Pope (2005), I understand creativity as a process of cultural improvisation in which people actively produce and respond to specific opportunities and limitations in unfolding and mediating environments. It is a process that involves quotation and configuration, and produces both expected and unexpected outcomes (see also introduction).

It must be emphasized that acts of improvisation can only be understood when analysed in tandem with the larger structural processes that shape the conditions in which they take place (Anheier and Isar 2010; Fuglerud and

Wainwright 2014). As will become clear, in the case analysed in this chapter, the establishment of global networks of Hindu temples and ashrams is an important structuring factor.

The second focus of affective engagement highlights the emotional dimensions of improvisation. The case explored in this chapter shows that Hindu worship can be strongly motivated by intensely felt needs and responsibilities, and that diasporic tradition-making practices take place in affective fields that stretch across the globe (see also Bruland, this volume). As will become clear, to Manika the *puja* room was most of all a space in which she could create and experience what may be called affective immanence, a direct embodied sensation of emotional connection.

Making God Immanent through Emotional Interaction

For the purpose of this research (2010–2012), I visited the homes of eight Hindu families in Northern Ireland, and spoke with around twenty-five Northern Irish–based Hindus about their religious practices. Manika's home shrine was the largest of all. In most other homes, the shrines were placed in corners of kitchens or corridors, and contained fewer god images, in one case only three.[1] The decision to transform a whole room into a home shrine was partially a matter of having enough space. For Manika, having the separate *puja* room also meant that she could withdraw from family life, having some 'peace and quiet'.

When I asked Manika in 2010 to describe her experience of worship, she explained, with a glow in her eyes:

> I think you feel like a, how would you say, like a shiver as you feel something close to you sometimes even when you're reciting something you can feel tears going, coming down because of emotions, what you're feeling. You feel maybe your soul is connected to someone being up there that is looking after you. We all know there's somebody up there looking after us but it's connecting with that [what is essential].

The transformative emotional process was directly stimulated, and thus mediated, by the physical presence of the god images. As Stephen Huyler (1999: 28) noted, 'Most Hindus … believe in an Absolute that manifests itself and its powers through the Gods and Goddesses. By selecting one or more of these deities to worship, and by conducting rituals designed to facilitate contact with them, a Hindu devotee is striving to recognize his or her unity with the Absolute.'

Several authors have pointed out that *puja* has strong emotional dimensions. As performances of respect and honour to the gods, the ritual reinforces a status difference between Hindu worshippers and the supernatural.

At the same time, the ritual provides space for expressions of love for the divine and can trigger an experience of complete merging. This combination of 'subordination and intimacy' is typical of Hindu worship (Appadurai 1990: 94). In the words of Chris Fuller, '*Puja,* at its heart, is the worshippers' reception and entertainment of a distinguished and adored guest. It is a ritual to honor powerful gods and goddesses, and often to express personal affection for them as well; it can also create a unity between deity and worshipper that dissolves the difference between them' (1992: 57).

As material manifestations and mediators of *Brahman,* the wooden, bronze and paper deities in Manika's home shrine provided an important visual and tactile focus of affective ritual attention and interaction. As Cynthia Packert (2010: 20) pointed out, in devotional Hindu practices, 'it is through material things that the devotee connects with the divine and the divine connects with the devotee'. Manika explained that dressing the gods, making offerings to them, praying and chanting in their presence, made her realize herself as a happy and confident person. The artefacts, aestheticized as manifested gods, worthy of beautification and affective attention, stimulated her desire to perform repeated acts of care.[2] The causal dialectics of transition-transformation also produced the *murti*s as active agents who expected regular attention (see fig. 8.2). Manika imagined her interaction with the gods as a two-way process of communication, realized through acts of exchange. Her gift of loving devotion resulted in protection and harmony, and led occasionally to the experience of divinity within the self, described by her as 'vibrations'. This word was frequently used by people during my fieldwork among Hindus in India and Northern Ireland. Some used it to refer to the importance of sound vibrations in Hindu ritual practices and theories of creation, the sound '*om*' being the source of all creation (see also Dyczkowski 1987, 1992).

The sacred was also accessible through the gift of *prasad,* a material substance of food, which was infused with the deity's blessing during *puja.* Its consumption by worshippers mediated a sense of bonding through tradition, linking individual Hindus to an 'imagined whole' or 'social body' (Morgan 2009: 141) of devotional Hindus around the world. In Manika's view, performances of *puja* and *prasad* could not be replaced by a glance at Ganesh on her mobile phone. The performative complexity of these rituals, the emotional investment needed and the knowledge that they had been performed for centuries in quite similar ways, set them apart. So did the intentional function of the shrine environment, purposely created to produce a care relationship with the manifested divine. By contrast, mobile phones were not bought with the aim to produce a religious experience, but rather provided a technology that could be used to upload a deity's image. Consequentially, *darshan* (visual engagement with Hindu deities; see below) through digital means did not replace conventional *darshan,* but presented an additional opportunity to feel divine presence, in this case mediated by a battery-powered device (see also Rickli, this volume).

In various ways, however, digital *darshan* was in line with older devotional traditions. Mobile phone technology, reproducing god images on screens, evoked brief moments of imagination in which inner divine presence could be sensed, a process that was strengthened by memories of previous religious experiences. In their brevity and place-independency, these moments of visual focus were comparable to the short recitations of *mantras* that Manika often did when driving to town. 'I would do "*aum bhur bhuwah svaha*"', she said, 'that's the Gayatri mantra.'[3] The complete text of the mantra shows clearly how God is constructed as imminent co-presence and source of motivation through recitation[4]:

> Aum bhur bhuvah svaha,
> Tatsavitur varenyam
> Bhargo devasya dhimahi
> Dhiyo yo nah prachodayāt.

> Oh God (Parabrahma) the bestower of life,
> Creator of the universe,
> Who removes our suffering,
> Who bestows happiness upon everyone,
> We meditate on You,
> May you inspire and guide our intellect.

The example shows how written and recited texts, as well as visual externalizations, can mediate and thereby shape the experience of divine presence.[5]

Interestingly, mobile phone technology, allowing control over the visual presence of Ganesh (by pushing a button), resonates with the Hindu notion of fluctuating manifested and unmanifested forms of divine presence. More importantly in practical terms, the medium also allows its users to respond to the time pressures of contemporary life. As Manika explained, she experienced occasional feelings of guilt when, because of her busy lifestyle, she had less time to worship in her home shrine. Her more playful engagement with the re-appearing Ganesh on her phone must therefore be understood not only as a creative act of religious commitment, but also as an additional form of remediation that both continued and transformed traditions of *darshan*.[6]

Devotion: Repeated Acts of Care

Manika had arrived in Belfast in the 1960s at the age of seven.[7] She belonged to a group of Indians from the Jullundur district in Northern India (particularly from the villages of Talwan and Phillaur) who had settled in Northern Ireland from the 1920s onwards and who formed a tight community. By 2011, the number of people of Indian descent had risen to 6,200, also including Indians from many other parts of India and East Africa.[8] During the second half of the twentieth century, Manika's father and grandfather had taken an important position in the Indian community in Northern Ireland. Even though they had not been trained as priests, she explained, being educated Brahmins they had often been approached to conduct certain Hindu rituals: 'My grandfather when he came over in the 50s, if anybody wanted any of the rituals done – when a new baby was born or during weddings, my grandfather performed the first weddings here in Northern Ireland, [he performed them]. He did all the rituals and then of course my father came, he would have joined then the two of them done them together.'

Her father had also been one of the main driving forces behind the establishment of the Indian Community Centre and Hindu temple in Belfast.[9] He co-organized the commissioning and ritual installation of *murti*s in the temple, an important event for which numerous priests had come over from England and India. In the light of all this, Manika felt personally responsible for the transmission of Hindu values to the next generation. Socialized in Hindu devotional practices, and maintaining active connections to other Hindus of similar persuasion in India and the United Kingdom (see below), she accepted that the presence of the sacred in material form brought with it certain responsibilities. Her religious activities in the temple in Belfast and her own *puja* room at home were partly driven by a moral and affective regime that had been passed on by her parents.

When I asked her about the daily rituals, she presented an image of worship as intimate family affair, portraying the gods as parents who wanted their children, the worshippers, to be close to them. Again, she indicated that the inner urge to worship brought with it potential feelings of guilt:

> It was lovely that somebody said, he says 'when we read our daily prayer we said "you're [i.e. God is] the father, you're the mother"'. They said 'every mother wants to see their child happy and they want to see them everyday'. So going to the *mandir*, to the temple or to the little shrine if you have some, you're kind of visiting, feeling near to your parents. So when you go and do *namaskar* and do *puja*, or whatever you're saying 'thank you for another day', and you feel you get their blessing when you've done your little bit. The day you don't go in, 'oh God I meant to go in', you're feeling guilty maybe. You haven't done it or you haven't been to the temple or vice versa so it's, you're not as, you're kind of, what's the word I'm looking for, you're, you're not contented. You feel, 'oh God I haven't done my *puja* this morning'.

Temporarily, she said, it was acceptable to do the minimal, to conjure up the image of a deity through 'visualization' and by 'say[ing] a prayer in

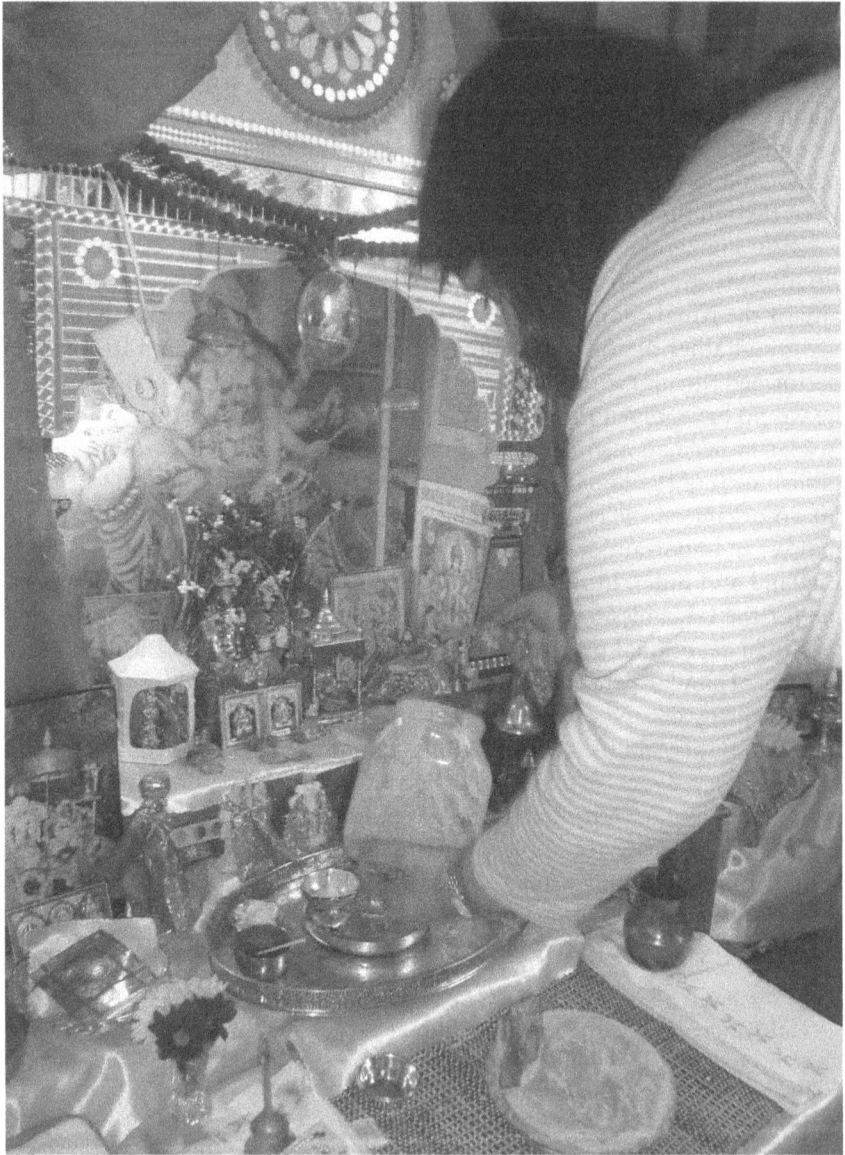

Figure 8.2. Manika fills a lamp with ghee. Photo: Maruška Svašek.

your head'. Her use of the word 'visualization' indicated that interactions with visible, materially manifested Gods made it easier for her to imagine and concentrate on the divine.[10] The appropriated artefacts thus had a clear transformative purpose. Manika found exposure to remediated televised imagery also effective, saying, 'My husband and I are reading Durga's treaty at the minute; a lot of it is in Sanskrit and then they have the description in Hindi. I'd watched the whole serial of that on TV so when he's reading that to me I could actually visualise it because I've already watched it. Once you watch it I find you get that picture in your mind.' She added that the televised epic stories were tools of instruction that appealed to the younger generation. Yet over a longer time span, Manika insisted, she felt the need to worship God in temples and her home shrine. Repetitive performance of love and respect was necessary not only to please the gods, but also to revitalize her sense of inner harmony, experiencing herself as a caring and cared-for being. Doing *puja* engaged her in a way that was more intense and intimate than watching a television series as it produced the god images as objects of active devotion. She hoped that by setting the right example of repetitive ritual behaviour, she had taught her now adult children the value of commitment, and had made them aware of 'Indian' traditions. Her ritual actions were therefore also an attempt to 'create, revitalise and affirm cultural heritage' (Brosius and Hüsken 2010b: 8; see also Shreen, Desai and Kuldova, this volume)

Home Shrines as Sites of Creative Appropriation

Devotional Hindus do not aim to directly copy existing shrines when creating their own; their knowledge of diverse ritual traditions and their preference for certain deities inform their incorporation and treatment of specific artefacts. Individual devotees generally worship their own *ishtadevata*, 'the deity or deities chosen by the devotee for personal reasons' and their choice is 'an intimate decision based on one's own spiritual experience' (Huyler 1999: 79). They may of course decide to follow their parents' preferences, having gained benefit from *puja*s for these gods during their childhood.[11] Placing items in and around the shrine frames them as religiously significant objects that are strongly valued, having specific sensorial and affective appeal and spiritual potential. This process is situational and may entail shifts in valuation and appeal. A photograph, for example, originally taken as a family snapshot and pasted in a photo album, is differently sensed when placed in a shrine, becoming an object of religiously motivated attention and affection.

As noted earlier, one of the central practices in devotional Hinduism is *darshan,* a visual absorption of the idols and a gaze into their eyes (see also Bruland, this volume). The practice is grounded in the perception of direct communication between the worshipping devotee and the blessing god, a 'merging of consciousness' (Gell 1998: 117; Eck 1998; Pinney 2001: 61; Packert 2010: 12). Dressing the gods in colourful, sparkly outfits is also taken as an essential part of religious practice, since 'adornment and aesthetic elaboration' increase the chance to sense *bhakti-rasa,* the uplifting spiritual-emotional experience aimed for in loving devotionalism (Packert 2010: 11). *Darshan* and ornamentation thus allude to transition-transformation dialectics; people who learn to attend to *murti*s necessarily attune the senses, learning to see, hear, smell, taste and touch them in specific ways. As Packert found in her research on the ornamentation of Lord Krishna imagery, in the sensorial dynamics of devotion, aesthetic and affective dimensions are closely interlinked, and can become a catalyst for spiritual transformation:

> Beautiful ornamentation is considered critical to the cultivation of an emotional state of happiness, enjoyment, or bliss – both for the deity and the devotees. If a visual presentation is successful, devotees speak of it as 'having *bhav*', as constituting a meaningful aesthetic experience. The same terminology is used for poetry, music, and dance, indeed for any occasion in which the emotions are stimulated by aesthetics. (2010: 16)

As Manika's case shows, ornamentational practices can also be understood as acts of creative improvisation. Manika's family shrine included numerous bronze *murti*s, and during my second visit to her house, she commented on the colour of their garments. Pointing at one of them, she explained that she normally takes the freedom to dress them in colours of her own preference:

> He is now in turquoise, I changed it from red. I use whatever colour I like. I do as I please, I do not follow the *Pandit* [the Hindu priest in the temple in Belfast]. As long as it pleases your eyes, it is good. Your eyes, not anyone's eyes. How would you like to see yourself dressed? I will treat the gods in my *puja* room accordingly. Nobody has seen god, so you don't go for a realistic depiction. It's like having your own child; you want to show it at its best.

In this statement, she described her dressing of the deities as an act of motherly love and pride, which could only be actualized by claiming parental responsibility and taking creative authority to make the right selection. Proper devotional tradition-making, in other words, assumed a level of choice. Manika alluded to her ability to move items around, as long as the activity was informed by a caring attitude and an eye for uplifting beauty. This attitude could be playful and performative, demonstrating a sense for colour and composition and an interest in visual narrative. Her symmetrical placement of two depictions of Ganesh above a decorated plywood panel, against the background of yellow, red and pink wall hangings that coordinated harmoniously with the colours of the other artefacts, exemplifies this (fig. 8.3). The compositional choice was not random, but informed by

Figure 8.3. Curatorial play: placement of two Ganesha figures. Photo: Maruška Svašek.

internalized knowledge and experience of worship in different settings, and by the material qualities of the actual artefacts.

Manika explained that she frequently rearranged objects in the shrine, at least every couple of months when she cleaned it. Some had recently been moved into the *puja* room. The painted Ganesh (in fig. 8.3), for example, had hung for years in the living room as a decoration above the fire place. While in the lounge, exhibited against an empty wall, it had most of all been effective as an 'appealing work of Hindu art', though its presence had also caused occasional religious engagement. Every morning when first entering the room, Manika had shown her respect to the deity by the performance of *prnam,* putting her hands together in greeting and bow.

Talking about what could be called her 'curatorship' of the *puja* room, Manika said that she wanted all godly images 'to been seen, not to be hidden'. When I asked her whether she wanted all of them to be seen at all times, she laughed. It was impossible to show them all, she had so many idols! Placing them behind each other was not a sign of disrespect. And since *brahman* was everywhere anyway, it did not really matter. Yet keeping idols out of sight for a long time was not good, she said. The double-understanding of the divine as transcendental/unmanifested force *and* materially mediated immanent/manifested power framed the improvisational space in which Manika organized her collection. As long as all god images in her possession were handled with respect, and as long as all of them were occasionally addressed as mediators of divine transcendence, there was no contradiction. Again, the notion of love as a mutual process of merging was central to her understanding and treatment of the artefacts. It was only through her caring ritual attention that she could realize herself as devotional Hindu, and that the divine could manifest itself as active protecting force. She indicated that this responsibility prevented her from buying many more new god images: 'The kids must look after them after I have gone, and that is quite a task. That is why I have started giving some away to friends and relatives.'

She reiterated the significance of a respectful attitude when pointing at a wooden Ganesh, bought at the St George's market in Belfast (fig. 8.4). She explained that she had first displayed him in her office, and after some time had taken him home. 'But it is not yet at the place where I want it. It is too heavy so it cannot be hung up on the wall. It might fall. I need to find the right place so that it is taken care of well.'

Networks of Families and Friends: Circulation, Transition and Care

Her reference to the St George's Market alluded to the objects' social lives as crafted commodities that were embedded in concrete histories of manufacture, trade, exchange and religious appropriation. Transit and transition through family networks had increased their emotional efficacy. This was clearly illustrated when Manika lit a candle in front of the small temple-like structure that framed the centrally placed deities. This *mandir,* she said, had belonged to her parents and had been manufactured out of plywood in 1982 by a Gujarati friend of her parents. He had used 'bits of colourful sticky paper' to decorate the wood, 'to make the *mandir* beautiful'. Part of the decoration consisted of a *yantra,* a symmetrical diagram with religious connotations and power (see also fig. 8.3).

Figure 8.4. Wooden Ganesh, bought in Belfast. Photo: Maruška Svašek.

When her mother had passed away, Manika had taken the *mandir* to her own house. As noted earlier, it was the central piece in her *puja* room. The fact that this was the actual *mandir* that had been used by her parents for so many years was important to her. It produced a sense of authenticity that did not stem from the fact that it was a unique design, but rather followed from its habitual ritual use by a previous generation. Repetition, in other words, had increased its emotional value and appeal. The incorporation of the *mandir* in her own home evoked memories of her deceased parents and of herself during her younger years; it also linked her own recurrent acts of worship to those of her parents. Using the *mandir* in her own *puja* room fed her imaginary of a continuous genealogy that bridged the gap between the living and the deceased, allowing her to symbolically mark their relatedness. Other artefacts also reminded her of the physical absence of loved ones, whether dead or alive. Some had belonged to her parents or parents-in-law; others were presents from relatives and friends in Northern Ireland and India. Taking good care of the inherited and gifted gods was a double-act of spiritual and social belonging and affection, an opportunity to overcome spatial and temporal distance.

Deceased kin were also present in the *puja* room in the form of photographs. Lighting a candle and directing prayers to these images further framed the room as a site where Manika experienced connectedness with a reality that was both human and sacred (fig. 8.5). While interaction with the photographs stimulated embodied memories of specific human beings,

Figure 8.5. Lighting a candle in front of photographs of deceased kin. Photo: Maruška Svašek.

engagement with the idols projected an abstract, omnipresent transcendence within her body as a felt presence, described by her as 'energy' or 'vibrations'. In both cases, she felt a duty to connect with absent realities through the ritual maintenance of an active care relationship. Some artefacts in the shrine mediated care relationships with living kin. One of the bronze items had been given to her by her son, who had bought it during a trip to India. The maker of the artefact had combined the sacred symbols of *Om* and *Swastik* in a single design (fig. 8.6). Placing the artefact on a plate of offerings (*tali*) to the gods, her son's gift became part of her own gesture of loving devotion, mediating feelings of gratefulness. 'It is more of an ornament, but it still has religious meaning,' she said. 'Using it means saying "thank you for being present, for looking after us".'

The shrine also included several wedding cards of relatives; appropriated in the *puja* room, they became indicators of sacred family values. Manika explained that whenever a family member gave her such a card, a common tradition in India and the different Hindu diasporas, she would 'place it in the *mandir* to invite the God to come', an act which would 'bless the newlyweds'. At some point in the future she would remove the card, and possibly keep it somewhere else as a 'souvenir', where it would lose some of

Figure 8.6. Bronze standard depicting the symbols *Om* and *Swastik*. Photo: Maruška Svašek.

its affective intensity. Two other wedding gifts placed in the shrine were a small painting of Ganesh in a plastic frame, and a painted text referring to him, the 'Lord of all beings'.[12] Widely regarded by Hindus as the remover of obstacles, Ganesh is understood to be an active agent of successful marriage (Courtright 1985: 4). Directed at the receivers of the gift, the card did not only mediate his sacred presence, but also revitalised affection between the newlyweds and the invitees. Ganesh's presence also brought responsibilities. This has had unexpected results. While paintings and prints of Ganesh had been popular wedding gifts in Northern Ireland five years earlier, the trend had stopped, because 'it was hard if people got them and would not respect them, and where to put them all?' The problem of 'sacred waste' (Stengs 2014) underlines the need to explore the emotional consequences of the 'thingness' of material realities.

Connected (Sacred) Spaces

The material mediation approach can be stretched not only to include the revitalization of relationships with God, (deceased) kin and friends, but also to analyse diasporic engagements with distant homelands. As Patrick Eisenlohr (2006: 12) noted, 'diasporic situations often motivate people to engage in practices intended to overcome the sense of spatio-temporal remove that is at the heart of many diasporic experiences'.

In Manika's *puja* room, numerous objects and photographs related to specific Hindu temples in India, the United Kingdom and the United States. This turned her home shrine into a spatial node in an imagined sacred network that stretched across the globe. The artefacts materialized multiple temporalities. First, they represented notions of divine timelessness and omnipresence. Second, they indexed space/time-specific manifestations of the divine. Third, they were a reminder of family histories of transnational mobility, a visible, material proof of the back-and-forth movements to India by Manika and her relatives. A photograph of the Vaishno Devi temple, for example, had been taken by Manika's husband while visiting this temple some years earlier. On return, the couple had placed it in the *puja* room in Northern Ireland. 'We go almost every year', she said, 'walking thirteen miles in the hills to reach there. Last time my husband walked in the snow.' The temple, located in the state of Jammu and Kashmir, is dedicated to Mata Vaishno Devi and attracts devotees from all over the world. Its holy shrine, located in a cave, consists of three natural rock formations (*Pindies*) that represent the Goddesses Kali, Lakshmi and Saraswati. Followers of Vaishno Devi Mata see them as the manifestation of the combined spiritual strength of all three deities, a force who, manifested as a mother (Mata), calls her devotee 'children' to come to her. According to the temple authorities, those who receive the call 'are bound to visit the Mother to receive Her unbounded love and blessings. The Trikuta Mountain where the Shrine is located and the Holy Cave are the gateway to the dimension of Super Consciousness'.[13]

This authoritative claim sheds an added light on the improvisational dynamics in Manika's *puja* room. The visual reminder of their pilgrimage was not just any souvenir, but actively projected the voice of a powerful religious institution into their private space (Waghorne 2004; Eisenlohr 206). Ritual practices in Hindu temples and home shrines, in other words, should not be imagined as a 'private hermetically-sealed off domain of aesthetic contemplation', since the objects involved 'inhabit a public (and political) world' (Ramaswamy 2003: xv). They are part of what Meyer has called 'sensational forms', defined as

> relatively fixed modes for invoking and organising access to the transcendental, offering structures of repetition to create and sustain links between believers in the context of particular religious regimes. These forms are transmitted and shared; they involve religious practitioners in particular practices of worship, and play a central role in modulating them as religious moral subjects and communities. (Meyer 2011: 29–30; see also Meyer 2006)

Hindu sensational forms have not only been appropriated and distributed through the activities of Indian migrants, but also through the mobility of India-based *gurus* and *swamis*. Especially since the 1960s, many have travelled extensively between India and Indian diasporic settings, influencing the formation of Hindu subjectivities abroad. This process was also visible in Manika's *puja* room, which contained a photograph of Sri Swami Gopal Sharan Devacharya, a Vaishnavite priest who has strong links to the Hindu temple in Belfast. When I met him in 2011, he had come over for the 30th Anniversary Celebrations of the Indian Community Centre for the annual consecration ceremony, a series of rituals where Bagwan is invoked to reinvigorate the power of the temple space. Leading many of the rituals and answering questions from the Belfast congregation (both adults and children), he was clearly regarded as a highly respected and knowledgeable religious authority. His presence in the form of a photograph in Manika's home altar can be understood in multiple ways. On the one hand, it positioned her as a friend and follower of the Swami.[14] On the other, it also highlighted the appropriating activities of the Swami himself who, from 1980 onwards, has promoted Hinduism abroad, establishing a growing network of ashrams and temples. *Hinduism Today* described him as someone who started 'a far-reaching and influential global mission', who was 'the force behind the construction of 72 new temples worldwide' and who has 'successfully reached out to devotees in Canada, America, the UK, Germany and elsewhere, inspiring, consoling and guiding each one'. In so doing, he 'cultivated and nurtured an international following that is wide and influential, and this only by his early thirties'.[15]

The Affective Pull of Vrindavan: Mediation and Remediation

Manika's *puja* room contained a photograph of the main deity of the Radharamana temple in Vrindavan (fig. 8.7), the place where the transnationally operating Swami Gopal Sharan built his first ashram.[16] Radharamana is believed to be a manifestation of Lord Krishna, who made his appearance in Vrindavan as *svarupa* in the early sixteenth century.[17] As with the photograph of the Vaishno Devi temple, the picture mediated multiple temporal perspectives.[18] Pointing at the picture, Manika told me that this was the place where 'Lord Krishna has been raised', which made it into a powerful sacred and affective site that was of historical and religious relevance.

Manika talked with a loving voice about the child Krishna, expressing motherly feelings. These feelings were also invoked, she said, when exchanging views with a poster print of him in her *puja* room, or when reciting

Figure 8.7. A photograph of the main deity in Radharamana temple. Photo: Maruška Svašek.

sacred texts about him. The stories, first produced in ancient texts such as the *Harivamsha,* an appendix of the *Mahabharata,* have been remediated in comic books and television programmes aimed at children, who easily identify with the naughty lovable god-child.[19] References to Krishna as adolescent have also circulated widely on the Internet. The website of the Radharamana temple claimed, for example, that 'Lord Krishna Himself played and swam with His cowherd boyfriends' in the Yamuna, a river that encircled Vrindavan; 'He also sported in its waters with the beautiful gopi damsels of Vraja.'[20] Collapsing time and claiming the uniqueness of the locality, the website stressed that the deity's presence can still be felt; 'it is said that Lord Krishna never leaves Vrindavana', and therefore the town 'continues its position as a transcendental place and certainly anyone who goes there becomes transcendentally purified' (ibid.). Written in English, the claim to offer transforming religious experiences intended to reach and draw in Hindus from all over the world.

Devotees who have access to the Internet do not have to travel anywhere to see Radharamana. Anyone entering the home page of the temple website is confronted with three consecutive photographs of the deity, taken from the same angle, forming an alternating series projected as a continuous loop. As noted earlier, Manika had incorporated a black-and-white photograph of the deity in her home shrine, which enabled her to sense spiritual connectedness to Radharamana through repeated ritual performances of care, involving visual and tactile engagement. Internet technology provided other opportunities to mediate a sense of a connected Hindu social body. The sequence of alternating photographs creatively built on notions of repeated *darshan.* Moreover, the alternating images enabled a long-distance view of the actual social life of the Radharamana icon. Taken at different times inside the sacred shrine, they showed the deity in different outfits, which indexed a social life of active devotional attention by priests.[21] The website, produced by the temple organization, also provided additional visual impressions of the local setting 'in action'. Clicking on a 'Gallery' icon, viewers can gain access to over one hundred photographs of the deity and priests engaged in ritual activities. They also offered views of the temple buildings and the sacred river, the one in which 'Lord Krishna once played'.

While Internet-mediated '*darshan*-by-proxy' does not necessarily lead viewers to an experience of inner divine presence (Hawkins 1999: 148), the Radharama website does, however, urge distant viewers to become truly engaged, calling them to explore the website and 'join and participate in the Service in the Sri Sri Radha Raman'. The technology of digitally circulating images offers an instant and widely shared port of visual access to sacred objects located in India. This makes digital mediation radically different to the production and purchase of artefacts and pictures in India and their transit to *puja* rooms abroad. For diasporic Indians, easy access through cyberspace to places of worship like Vrindavan may stimulate a desire to get on a plane to visit specific temples. What seemed to count most of all to Manika was her urge to engage actively in Hindu tradition-making, through whatever media. Exposing her children to Hindu ways of being a good person, she aimed to build on her family legacy but did so with an open mind, accepting her children's idiosyncratic improvisations: 'I'm lucky that my parents, my parents probably knew 100 per cent of their religion. Maybe I've only taken on 75 per cent. My children probably know 70 per cent or 50 per cent of it. I don't know what the next generation would know. It's a learning process.'

Conclusion

The perspective taken in this chapter understands creative appropriation as a relational process in which individuals act and react in the context of evolving material and social surroundings (Ingold and Hallam 2007: 7). Creative appropriation, in other words, is partially conditioned by wider social, economic and political fields in which communicative interactions and material mediations are always, in various degrees, regulated, controlled and contested (Svašek 2010).

At the start of this chapter, I asked what Manika's engagement with Hindu imagery could reveal about her experiences as a migrant living in Northern Ireland. We have seen that her appropriation of various technologies of mediation, from *puja* worship to watching televised stories about Hindu mythology, had one thing in common: an urge to make absent realities present, to be intimately linked not only to God, but also to faraway people, places and times. Artefact-centred rituals in the home shrine offered performative contexts in which gods, kin, her guru and the homeland were given affective presence. Repetitive practices and performances of love and respect were informed not only by affective and religious regimes, but also by playfulness and individual preference. Repetition, in other words, was not an act of mindless copying, but rather an improvisational process in which tradition was being made. Interacting with a variety of objects, she created a presence not only of a divine force, but also of absent relatives and a distant homeland. Her very personal urge to transcend multiple distances must therefore be understood as an integral part of her transnational predicament.

The combined perspectives of transition-transformation and material mediation offered a useful analytical framework to explore the creative and affective dimensions of diasporic tradition making, and showed how Manika, in interaction with different artefacts, experienced and performed different notions of transnational self; as Hindu worshipper, linked to a larger social body of worshippers located in India and across the world; as member of a transnational family with roots in India; as pilgrim who, through her own trajectory, connected sacred places in India with her own *puja* room. The analysis drew specific attention to the embodied sensorial and emotional intensity of her routine engagements, and the ways in which these framed and evaluated different artefacts and images. Her emotions ranged from overwhelming feelings of joyful passion, to a sense of duty to look after the gods, to fear of inadequacy. Buying, inheriting and spatially arranging individual objects, appropriating them in performative contexts of worship, she valued them in various ways. God-images became actively sensed immanent gods; pictures became admired sacred landscapes; and so on. This allowed her to position herself as an active Hindu.

The focus on material mediation highlighted how specific images were mediated and remediated through different technologies. The belief that the divine was both formless, timeless and everywhere, *and* yet manifested in concrete form, provided an interesting perspective on the reappearance of similar images in different times and places. The repeated appropriation of god images within and across media was not negatively valued as act of 'uncreative copying', but rather positively celebrated as opportunity to personally worship anywhere, anytime. Overcoming spatial and temporal distances, god images were not only materialized as portable items, but also appeared through digital transmission. This allowed migrants like Manika to creatively address the improvisational limitation of living outside India.

Material mediation did not take place in a power vacuum, but was partly controlled by those who had the power and authority to produced and control specific sensorial forms. This implies that practices of worship, wherever in the world, cannot be analysed without attention to their embeddedness global networks of religious mediation.

Maruška Svašek is reader in anthropology at the School of History and Anthropology, Queens University, Belfast. Her main research interests include material culture, art, migration and emotional dynamics. Major publications include *Anthropology, Art and Cultural Production* (2007), *Emotions and Human Mobility: Ethnographies of Movement* (2012) and *Moving Subjects, Moving Objects: Transnationalism, Cultural Production and Emotions* (2012). She is co-editor of the Berghahn Books series Material Mediations: People and Things in a World of Movement.

Notes

I would like to thank Amit Desai, Alexandra Grieser and Birgit Meyer for their very useful comments to an earlier version of this chapter.

1. One Hindu lady whom I interviewed said that she had not been brought up in a devotional tradition and rather practiced meditation.
2. In earlier work (Svašek 2007), I outlined a theory of 'aestheticization' to conceptualize a dynamic process whereby artefacts and images in transit are (sensorially, emotionally) experienced by individuals and groups of people as specifically significant, valuable and powerful objects.
3. Gayatri Mantra is an important mantra in Hinduism and inspires wisdom. It means 'may the Almighty God illuminate our intellect to lead us along the righteous path'. The mantra is also a prayer to the sun, the 'giver of light and life'.
4. In the last two sentences, God is directly addressed as 'You', as a present entity that guides and inspires: 'We meditate on You (*dhimahi*); May You (*yah*) inspire and guide (*prachodayat*) our (*nah*) intellect (*dhiyah*).'
5. This is why Weibel (2011: 34) called religion a 'medium of absence,' meaning that divine presence must be effected through mediation.
6. With regard to the dynamics of sociality, Manika told me that numerous relatives and friends had copied images of Hindu deities on their phones, which had inspired her to do so as well. In terms of economic incentives, the success of mobile phone technology is partly a story of production costs and affordability; the relatively low cost has stimulated the worldwide spread of this technology, allowing for idiosyncratic uses. As to the political dimension of digital *darshan,* the emerging tradition has been stimulated by the widespread appearance of Hindu sacred imagery and gurus on television and the Internet, a phenomenon that has normalized and authenticated viewers' electronically mediated feelings of spiritual connectedness (Upadhyay and Robinson 2011; Hawkins 1999).
7. Her grandfather came over in the early 1950s, first settling in England and then relocating to Northern Ireland; her grandmother joined him in 1961. Her father went over in 1962, just after the birth of her brother. About three years later, her mother and the children followed.
8. In 2001, the census gave a number of 1,567. On Census Day 2011, 1.8 per cent (32,400) of the usually resident population of Northern Ireland belonged to minority ethnic groups, more than double the proportion in 2001 (0.8 per cent). The main minority ethnic groups were Chinese (6,300 people), Indian (6,200), Mixed (6,000) and Other Asian (5,000), each accounting for around 0.3 per cent of the usually resident population. A further 0.1 per cent (1,300) of people were Irish Travellers. Belfast (3.6 per cent), Castlereagh (2.9 per cent) and Dungannon (2.5 per cent) had the highest proportions of residents from minority ethnic groups.
9. In 1979, they established the Centre (*Mandal*) – then named the Northern Ireland Hindu Cultural Centre – and Temple (*Mandir*) in a former Methodist Church. The building was officially opened in 1980 (24 August) by the high commissioner of India, J. P. Singh (Kapur 1997: 227).
10. This supports Hans Belting's (2011[2001]: 5) notion that it is problematic to make a strict division between objects and imaginations as 'mental images are inscribed in external ones and vice versa'.
11. 'They are familiar with these deities; they have grown up with their worship and have experienced the benefit of their *puja*s. Some decide that their particular

natures or requirements respond to different facets of the Divine. Other Gods or Goddesses fulfil their specific needs' (Huyler 1999: 79).

12. The text on the card said, 'Ganesh Ji is the "Lord of all beings" / He is the god of wisdom / The "destroyer of all obstacles" / "The bestowal of peace" / The elephant symbolizes devotion, / Patience and truth. / Please accept this as a token of our Love. / Thanks for being part of our Special Day.' The card was also decorated with an image of 'Om'. The Ganesh in the plastic frame also included the Hindi word 'ekdanth', meaning 'one-tusked', which is one of Ganesha's names. Manika classified the framed painting as 'a modern version of Ganesh' and compared it with depictions of the deity in popular Hindu cartoons on television. Both managed to entertain as well as bring an important religious message.

13. According to the temple's website, '[the] journey to the Holy Shrine of Shri Mata Vaishno Devi Ji starts with the Call of Mata. It is not only a belief but also a strong experience of one and all that the Divine Mother sends a call to her children. And once a person receives it, wherever he is, is bound to visit the Mother to receive Her unbounded love and blessings' (https://www.maavaish nodevi.org/callofmata.aspx, last accessed 11 February 2013).

14. She had visited the Brijwasan Golok Dham ashram near New Delhi, established in 2004, and she had travelled with him and other followers to various temples in India.

15. http://www.hinduismtoday.com/modules/smartsection/item.php?itemid=5038, last accessed 23 May 2012.

16. 'Building and maintaining places of worship and ashrams is an esteemed activity in the Nimbarka Sampradaya', Swami explains. 'We have ancient temples of our sampradaya all over India. I am not involved with all of them, but in many prominent places I either belong to the managing committees or they frequently seek my advice. I think we have ashrams in every nook and corner of India! In Vrindavan, the gurus of the Nimbarka Sampradaya have more than 60 ashrams, big and small. I estimate that in all of India we have hundreds of ashrams, mostly in Uttar Pradesh, Rajasthan, Gujarat, Punjab, Bengal and Maharashtra.'

17. *Svarupa* are taken as self-manifested forms of the Supreme, not manufactured by humans, but materialized through divine power (Packert 2010: xxii). The temple's website notes that 'Sri Radha Raman's Appearance Place is in the Radha-Raman Temple, next to the samadhi of Gopala Bhatta. Gopala Bhatta Goswami erected this temple. The deity was installed on the full moon day in the month of Vaishaka (April–May) in the year 1542. This event is celebrated every year by bathing the deity with milk and various other items. Gopala Bhatta Gosvami's other shalagram-shilas are also worshiped in the temple. The samadhi of Gopala Bhatta is located next to Raman's appearance place in Radha-Raman Temple' (http://www.radharaman.org/?go=history&view=vrin davan, last accessed 25 July 2012).

18. It represented the frozen moment when the photograph had been taken, the historical time of her travels to the shrine and the mythical past of Krishna's birth, a sacred temporal dimension that connected her to all devotees of this particular deity.

19. See Doniger (2009: 477).
20. http://www.radharaman.org/?go=history&view=vrindavan; last accessed 14 May 2012.
21. As Cynthia Packert (2010: 58, 59) has noted, ornamentational changes create a 'sense of ever-renewing wonder' in devotees; the 'beauty of seeing such changes over an extended period in the environment of the temple is that they culminate in an overall experience of joy'.

References

Anheier, H. K., and Y. R. Isar (eds). 2010. *Cultural Expression, Creativity and Innovation*. Los Angeles: Sage.

Appadurai, A. 1990. 'Disjuncture and Difference in the Global Culture Economy', *Theory, Culture, and Society* 7: 295–310.

Baym, N. K. 2010. *Personal Connections in the Digital Age*. Cambridge: Polity.

Belting, H. 2011[2001]. *An Anthropology of Images: Picture, Medium, Body* (translated from German). Princeton: Princeton University Press.

Brosius, C., and M. Butcher. 1999. *Image Journeys: Audio-Visual Media and Cultural Change in India*. New Delhi: Sage.

Brosius, C., and U. Hüsken (eds). 2010a. *Ritual Matters: Dynamic Dimensions in Practice*. New Delhi: Routledge.

———. 2010b. 'Change and Stability of Rituals: An Introduction', in C. Brosius and U. Hüsken (eds), *Ritual Matters: Dynamic Dimensions in Practice*. New Delhi: Routledge, 1–28.

Davis, R. H. 1997. *Lives of Indian Images*. Princeton: Princeton University Press.

Doniger, W. 2009. *The Hindus: An Alternative History*. Oxford: Oxford University Press.

Dyczkowski, M. S. 1987. *The Doctrine of Vibration*. Albany: SUNY Press.

———. 1992. *The Stanzas on Vibration*. Albany: SUNY Press.

Campanella, T. J. 1998. 'Eden by Wire: Webcameras and the Telepresent Landscape', in N. Mirzoeff (ed.), *The Visual Culture Reader*. London and New York: Routledge, 264–278.

Courtright, P. B. 1985. *Ganesha: Lord of Obstacles, Lord of Beginnings*. Oxford: Oxford University Press.

Eck, D. L. 1998. *Darshan*. New York: Columbia University Press.

Eisenlohr, P. 2006. *Little India: Diaspora, Time, and Ethnolinguistic Belonging in Hindu Mauritius*. Berkeley: University of California Press.

Fuller, C. J. 1992. 'The Camphor Flame', in *Popular Hinduism and Society in India*. Princeton: Princeton University Press.

Fuglerud, O., and L. Wainwright (eds). 2015. *Objects and Imagination: Perspectives on Materialization and Meaning*. Oxford: Berghahn Books.

Gell, A. 1998. *Art and Agency: An Anthropological Theory*. Oxford: Clarendon Press.

Hall, S. (ed.). 1979. *Representation: Cultural Representations and Signifying Practices*. London: Sage.

Hallam, E., and T. Ingold (eds). *Creativity and Cultural Improvisation*. Oxford: Berg.

Hawkins, S. 1999. 'Bordering Realism: The Aesthetics of Sai Baba's Mediated Universe', in Kajri Jain (ed.), 2007 *Gods in the Bazaar: The Economics of Indian Calendar Art*. Durham and London: Duke University Press.

Huyler, S. P. 1999. *Meeting God: Elements of Hindu Devotion*. New Haven: Yale University Press.

Ingold, T., and E. Hallam. 2007. 'Creativity and Cultural Improvisation: An Introduction', in E. Hallam and T. Ingold (eds), *Creativity and Cultural Improvisation*. Oxford: Berg, 1–24.

Jain, K. 2007. *Gods in the Bazaar: The Economies of Indian Calendar Art*. Durham: Duke University Press.

Keane, W. 2006. 'Subjects and Objects: Introduction', in C. Tilley et al. (eds), *Handbook of Material Culture*. London: Sage, 197–202.

Kapur, N. 1997. *The Irish Raj: Illustrated Stories about Irish in India and Indians in Ireland*. Vancouver: Greystone Books.

Hannerz, U. 1992. *Cultural Complexity: Studies in the Social Organization of Meaning*. New York: Columbia University Press.

Meyer, B. 2006. 'Religious Sensations: Why Media, Aesthetics and Power Matter in the Study of Contemporary Religion', inaugural lecture, Vrije Universiteit, Amsterdam, 6 October.

———— (ed.). 2009. *Aesthetic Formations: Media, Religion and the Senses*. New York: Palgrave.

————. 2011. 'Mediation and Immediacy: Sensational Forms, Semiotic Ideologies and the Question of the Medium', *Social Anthropology* 19(1): 23–39.

————. 2013. 'Material Mediations and Religious Practices of World-making', in K. Lundby (ed.), *Religion Across Media: From Early Antiquity to Late Modernity*. New York: Peter Lang, 1–19.

Miller, D. 1987. *Material Culture and Mass Consumption*. Oxford: Basil Blackwell.

Miller, D., and D. Slater. 2000. *The Internet: An Ethnographic Approach*. Oxford: Berg.

Morgan, D. 1998. *Visual Piety: A History and Theory of Popular Religious Images*. Berkeley: University of California Press.

————. 2009. 'The Look of Sympathy: Religion, Visual Culture, and the Social Life of Feeling', *Material Religion* 5(2): 132–155.

Northern Ireland's Statistics and Research Agency. 2011. Statistics Bulletin.

Northern Irish Assembly. 2011. 'Migration in Northern Ireland: A Demographic Perspective', Research and Information Service Research Paper NIAR 246–11.

Packert, C. 2010. *The Art of Loving Krishna: Ornamentation and Devotion*. Bloomington: Indiana University Press.

Pinney, C. 2001. 'Piercing the Skin of the Idol', in C. Pinney and N. Thomas (eds), *Beyond Aesthetics: Art and the Technologies of Enchantment*. London: Bloomsbury Publishing, 157–180.

————. 2004. *Photos of the Gods: The Printed Image and Political Struggle in India*. Oxford: Oxford University Press.

Pope, R. 2005. *Creativity: Theory, History and Practice*. London: Routledge.

Ramaswamy, S. 2003. 'Introduction', in S. Ramaswamy (ed.), *Beyond Appearances? Visual Practices and Ideologies in Modern India*. New Delhi: Sage, xiii–xxix.

Svašek, M. 2007. *Anthropology, Art and Cultural Production*. London: Pluto.

———. 2010. 'Improvising in a World of Movement: Transit, Transition and Transformation', in Y. R. Isar and H. K. Anheier (eds), *Cultural Expression, Creativity and Innovation*. Los Angeles: Sage.

——— (ed.). 2012a. *Moving Subjects, Moving Objects: Transnationalism, Cultural Production and Emotions*. Oxford: Berghahn Books.

———. 2012b. 'Affective Moves: Transit, Transition and Transformation', in M. Svašek (ed.), *Moving Subjects, Moving Objects: Transnationalism, Cultural Production and Emotions*. Oxford: Berghahn Books.

Stengs, I. L. 2014. 'In Conversation: Sacred Waste', *Material Religion* 10(2): 235–238.

Spyer, P., and M. M. Steedly (eds). 2013. *Images That Move*. Sante Fe: SAR Press.

Upadhyay, S. P., and R. Robinson. 2011. 'Globalization, Mass Media and Proliferating "Gurus"': The Changing Texture of Religion in Contemporary India', in Prashant Kumar Trivedi (ed.), *The Globalization Turbulence: Emerging Tensions in Indian Society*. New Delhi: Rawat Publications, 159–179.

Waghorne, J. P. 2004. *Diaspora of the Gods: Modern Hindu Temples in an Urban Middle-Class World*. Oxford: Oxford University Press.

Weibel, P. 2011. 'Religion as a Medium: The Media of Religion', in B. Groys and P. Weibel (eds), *Medium Religion: Faith, Geopolitics, Art*. Cologne and New York: Distributed Art Publishers, 30–43.

9

'THE EYE LIKES IT'
NATIONAL IDENTITY AND THE
AESTHETICS OF ATTRACTION AMONG
SRI LANKAN TAMIL CATHOLICS AND HINDUS

Stine Bruland

This chapter explores the only remaining non-violent religious relationship in Sri Lanka: that between Tamil Hindus and Tamil Catholics. In May 2009, the Sri Lankan army ended the civil war in the country, completely destroying the Liberation Tigers of Tamil Eelam (LTTE). The victory of the Buddhist, Sinhalese majority over the Tamil minority has allowed an ideology of Buddhist Sinhalese supremacy to flourish on the island. This ideology is expressed in two concepts, that of Sri Lanka as *Sihadipa* (island of the Sinhalese) and of Sri Lanka as *Dhammadipa* (island of the Buddhist way), together comprising the understanding that Sri Lanka is an island given by Gautama Buddha to the Sinhalese as a place where Buddhism shall be protected (Hennayake 2006: 48). The politicization of religion is as strong as ever. Both Muslims and Sinhalese Christians are under attack from hardline Buddhist monks and other Buddhists: attacks and boycotts of Muslim stores, as well as attacks on churches and mosques – even an attempt to kill a pastor, and a Buddhist monk's self-immolation – are just some of the violent incidences in Sri Lanka since December 2009. The year 2012 also saw the establishment of the organization Bodhu Bala Sena (Buddha's Army) by a group of Buddhist monks, targeting Muslims in particular (*Asian Tribune* 2013; Groundviews 2013). At the moment of writing, there are clear signs

that these extreme and violent ideas have developed widely among the Sinhalese Buddhist population. The extensive violent attacks on Muslims in
Aluthgama in June 2014, including murders, did not only involve a small
hard-line group of Buddhist monks, but also mobs drawn from the wider
Sinhalese Buddhist population. In addition, before the war came to an end,
Wahhabi Muslims attacked Sufi Muslims in the East-Province. The Wahhabi's are strongly opposed to the Sufi's openness towards Hinduism as well
as Christianity, and the tensions between the two Muslim groups have remained severe. Furthermore, the Tamil and the Sinhalese Catholic churches
are seen as strictly separate and both parts seem to prefer not to change this
situation.

These recent violent developments evidence a situation in which ethnic
identity and religious identity are becoming increasingly conflated. In the
midst of these violent religious conflicts, the Tamil Hindu–Tamil Catholic
relationship stands out as the single non-violent one, being characterized
rather by harmonious coexistence. In this chapter I explore why this is so,
starting from aesthetic practices that are shared between the two religious
communities. I look at the enthusiasm and effort among Tamil Hindu and
Catholic devotees to decorate their god(s) with flower garlands, saris or
robes made from saris and the performance of *arati* – clockwise circulation of
incense, ghee (clarified butter) or camphor flame. I take a material approach
in which I recognize the power of religious aesthetics and its affective appeal
during moments of worship. I argue that commonalities and similarities in
the aesthetic materials and practices of Tamil Catholicism and Hinduism
produce a broader Tamil national identity. This common Tamil national
identity is reproduced both in the practices of Tamil Catholicism and in
those of Tamil Hinduism. My approach directs attention to the ways in
which concrete practices, emotions and sensations shape religious experience in ways that lead to the religious self being included in the larger national community. Both Tamil Catholicism and Hinduism include a cultural
understanding and a conception of the self that is broader than the religious
and ethnic identities found among Sri Lanka's Buddhists and Muslims.

I argue that the dynamics between religious aesthetics and ethnic identity
found in the worship practices among Tamil Hindus and Tamil Catholics
can be fruitfully analysed from a perspective that foregrounds the material
of religion and the power of aesthetics in religious practice. Such a material
approach recognizes that the way we experience and understand our world
is not merely centred on the human subject, but includes our interaction
with our material surroundings and materials (cf. Damsholt and Simonsen
2009; Ingold 2007a; Svašek 2012). Materials, objects or 'things' are active
and have agency (cf. Gell 1998); they are processual, relational and performative, rather than just fixed˙ and passive (cf. Ingold 2007a). Materials

are performed in the mutual interaction with humans; humans act out the materials by acquiring, using and sensing material objects and their material surroundings, and in the same process materials act on humans, affecting our experience of the action, place, ritual and so on (cf. Damsholt and Simonsen 2009; Ingold 2007a). This perspective includes our material environment as an essential aspect of our experience and understanding of the world. Vital to this understanding is the ability of materials to affect the senses, evoking emotions and feelings in interaction with our sensing body (Kapferer and Hobart 2005). In this chapter, I therefore argue for a need to consider the sensations and emotions produced in interaction with materials as vital aspects of people's religious experience (cf. ibid.; Meyer 2010) and also of the self as a Tamil religious person. Thereby, a material approach opens up a perspective that allows us to grasp on which grounds materials and sensorial practices come to be shared across religious divisions.

The empirical material and arguments I am about to present are based primarily on ethnographic fieldwork among Tamil Hindus and Tamil Catholics from Sri Lanka living in Paris. The fieldwork explored Tamils' religious practice with attention to use of objects. For three months in 2010, I lived with a Catholic family, joining them for visits to friends, family and neighbours, shopping and masses in the Tamil church. Of special importance was my inclusion in a circle of prayer among the Tamil neighbours. Simultaneously I spent a similar amount of time with Hindu families in their homes, and accompanied them during prayer in the temples, and when they went shopping, visited friends and relatives and performed rituals. Both the Catholic family that I stayed with and the Hindu families were relatives of Tamil families I knew from a former period of fieldwork in Oslo in 2008. In addition, part of the ethnographic material on which this chapter is based was gathered during my fieldwork among Tamils in Jaffna, Sri Lanka, in the course of 2012.[1]

Contextualizing the Tamil French Diaspora and Religious Activities

Tamils started arriving in Paris in the early 1980s. Today, France is currently home to a total of 100,000 Sri Lankan Tamils,[2] the majority living in Paris and its suburbs (Etiemble 2004). The country is only one of the many European and North American destinations where about one-third of the prewar Tamil population of Sri Lanka have sought a better future away from the effects of the conflict between the government of Sri Lanka and the Tamil Tigers that began in 1983 (cf. Fuglerud 1999).

The majority of Sri Lankan Tamils are Hindus, while 16.7 per cent are Christians, primarily Roman Catholics (Jacobsen 2008: 118). Official statistics of the Tamils' religious belongings in Paris do not exist, but Tamil Catholics in France themselves estimate that they are between nine and ten thousand people, which is about 10 per cent of the whole Tamil population in France. In Paris, two Sri Lankan Tamil Hindu temples are found in Petit Jaffna in La Chapelle, the commercial centre of the Tamil community in Paris,[3] and a third is found in La Courneuve. These temples attract mainly Sri Lankan Tamils. A Sri Lankan Tamil Catholic church has been established four metro stops from La Chapelle in Belleville, with a Tamil priest conducting services exclusively in Tamil. Tamil Catholics seldom go to other masses, preferring Tamil services. Religious rituals are also all conducted within the Tamil social network. This pattern extends throughout Tamil social life in Paris: Tamils remain a self-contained group and events such as birthday parties and family visits are conducted solely with other Tamils. It is within this context, firmly set aside, socially and institutionally, from the French community, that the majority of Tamils in Paris practice their religion.

Religious Diversity and Violence in Sri Lanka

Being an ethnic minority in Sri Lanka, constituting 18.2 per cent of the population in 1981, the Tamils share the country with the Sinhalese majority comprising 74 per cent in 1981 (Tambiah 1986: 4), who are mainly Buddhist, with a small Christian population of 6.5 per cent. Furthermore, 7 per cent of Sri Lanka's population is Muslim (Carter 1979). Although a Tamil-speaking group, the Muslims are not considered, nor do they consider themselves, as 'Tamils', but as 'Muslims'; they are thus neither Tamil nor Sinhalese: Muslims are effectively an ethnic as well as a religious group. Until recent years, Catholics, Hindus, Buddhists and Muslims commonly made pilgrimages to the same shrines, regardless of the religious tradition associated with them; the religious motive of the pilgrimage appearing to have obviated any potential political conflict (cf. Carter 1979; Roberts 2005). This sharing of pilgrimage sites seems to have ended as religion became increasingly entwined with politics and violence escalated.

On December 6th 2009, more than a thousand Buddhists attacked a Catholic church in the town of Crooswatta in a Sinhalese area, destroying the altar and religious statues, and attempting to kill the pastor (Catholic News Agency 2012). In December 2012, the *Vatican Insider* reported that about fifty cases of attacks by Buddhists on Sinhalese Christian communities of different denominations had taken place during the year, many of them by robed monks. In April 2012, Buddhist monks and other hardliners stormed and firebombed a mosque in Dambulla. According to the *BBC* (2012) one monk addressed the crowd and proclaimed that the attack on the mosque was a victory 'for those who love the race, have Sinhalese blood and are Buddhists'. Several Muslim stores have also been attacked. In May 2013, a monk set himself on fire outside the holiest Buddhist shrine in Sri Lanka – the Temple of the Tooth – in Kandy, in protest against the *halal* system and assumed conversion of Buddhists to minority religions. He later died of his injuries. Many of these actions were fuelled by the organization Bodhu Bala Sena (Buddha's Army). The organization was established in 2012 by a group of Buddhist monks, who target Muslims in particular, promoting an anti-*halal* campaign, arguing that propagators of foreign religions should leave the country (*Asian Tribune* 2013). By mid-2014, Bodhu Bala Sena's ideology and practice of violence had spread from this small group of extreme Buddhist Monks to most Sinhalese Buddhists. June 2014 became a violent month in the town of Aluthgama. Sinhalese mobs attacked Muslims, their stores, mosques and houses. Several Muslims were killed in these attacks.

These developments represent another turn of the screw in the politicization of religion in Sri Lanka and the establishment of Theravada-Buddhism as the core of legitimate citizenship as defined by Buddhist activism. The exclusion of Tamils, and now Muslims and Christians, from postwar social and political participation and engagement demonstrate a progressively more constricted relationship between national and religious identity. A similar politicization of religion has taken place among Sri Lankan Muslims. The Middle East–founded Wahhabi groups strongly oppose the more open and moderate Sufi Muslims. They accuse Sufi sects of wrongly interpreting the Quran and teachings borrowed from Hinduism. In October 2004, a mob of extreme Wahhabi Muslims, armed with clubs and machetes, attacked and burned the mosque in the town of Kattankudy (Tamilnet 2004a). Tamilnet (2004b) also reported that six hundred Sufi followers were forcibly converted to Wahhabism under threat of violence. The attack was a product of a long conflict between the two Muslim groups. Two years later, a mosque and about forty homes of Sufi followers were attacked by a similar mob, driving the Sufi followers out of the town (*The Sunday Times* 2006). In July 2009 a conflict between a Sufi sect and Wahhabi Muslims in Beruwala caused two deaths, whilst over 40 people were injured, and 132 arrested (Colombo Telegraph 2013). Thus, Wahhabi Muslims exclude Sufis from a common Sri Lankan Muslim identity and rather seek alliance with a Middle Eastern religious identity.

These violent attacks and conflicts caused by religious contradictions stand in stark contrast to the situation in the Tamil areas in Sri Lanka, mainly in the north and east. Here, religious divisions seldom cause tensions between Tamils in everyday life. Tamil Catholics and Tamil Hindus co-reside side by side, both within the same villages and in Hindu and Catholic villages bordering each other. Hindu temples and Catholic churches, as well as their respective small shrines, are plentiful throughout the landscape, and also often exist side by side in the same villages. Both church and temple bells peal across the landscape, calling people to prayer or *puja,* and both Hindu and Catholic religious processions move peacefully through the streets, regardless of whether the houses they pass are inhabited by Hindu or Catholic families. Moreover, the majority of Hindu Tamils I have met in Paris, Oslo and Jaffna had memories of attending church on occasional Sundays or Tuesdays, finding prayer in another religious shrine no obstacle, but rather desirable, especially prayers to the Mother Mary and St. Anthony.[4] Catholics in Jaffna, before and after the years of conflict, also attend the festivals of the Hindu temple in their village or nearby villages, although interpreting such festivals primarily as social rather than religious events. The two religions thus have an organic coexistence in the Tamil areas. It should be noted that a very small percentage of Tamil Christians are Protestants and Pentecostals, who are regarded as adhering more rigidly to their own religion.

Being a Catholic or Hindu in the Tamil areas of Sri Lanka thus implies a frequent interaction with people from the other religious tradition as well as observation of the other religious tradition's practices and aesthetics. Tim Ingold (2007b, 2011) understands the interplay between persons and their environments as a 'meshwork', a 'zone of entanglement'. Living and dwelling together in the same surroundings, Hindus and Catholics and their respective religious traditions becomes part of each other. I suggest that this shared religious aesthetics contributes to producing a shared common belonging and identification with the larger Tamil society.

Entry and Development of Tamil Catholicism in Sri Lanka

A few points should be made concerning the entry of Catholicism into Sri Lanka and its later development, in particular the influence of the Second Vatican Council. Catholicism was brought to Sri Lanka, especially the coastal areas, by Portuguese colonization from 1505 onwards (Jacobsen 2008). When the British took control of the island at the beginning of the nineteenth century, they invited Catholic missionaries, until Sri Lanka's independence in 1948 (Stirrat 1992). In addition to churches, the Catholic missionaries built schools that became known for 'good education', and thus gained popularity. It is recognized that Tamils from all castes converted to Catholicism, but more from the lower than the higher castes, the motive being to escape caste-based stigmas and to access better education for their children (cf. Stirrat 1992).

The Second Vatican Council (1962–1965) had a critical influence on re-ligious practices among Sri Lankan Tamil Catholics (ibid.: 43). This council recognized the cultural diversity of Christians within the Catholic commu-nity, encouraging the use of local language in the liturgy together with indig-enous customs, so that Catholics should see themselves as members of local cultures and societies – so-called inculturation. For Tamil Catholics, this meant the use of customs and cultural concepts shared by Sri Lankan Tam-ils, implicitly Hindus (ibid.), including changing the liturgy language from Latin to Tamil. Among Tamil Catholic priests in Sri Lanka, there was a small group who initiated and promoted the use of 'Tamil' elements in the Tamil Catholic church before they grew to encompass the entire church in Sri Lanka. Gradually, Tamil instruments, such as *tablas* and *veenai,* were taken into use in church music, and *arati* and flower garlands entered the mass.

Father Mari Xavior, priest in Jaffna and one of those who initiated these changes, stresses that this 'inculturation' was, and still is, important in the process of moving away from the Western form of worship that was given to them by the Europeans. Father Mari Xavior and other similarly minded priests emphasize that 'we are finding our way back to our own true Tamil culture' in the ways they practice their Catholicism as Sri Lankan Tamils. These priests invoke a common 'Tamil culture', which they claim to share with other Tamils, irrespective of religious affiliations. And in discussions, they will certainly not equate Tamil with Hindu, insisting instead on 'Tamil-ness' as a broad cultural notion that encompasses both Hinduism and Chris-tianity. This argument must be seen in relation to the Sri Lankan conflict and the position of the Tamil Tigers. The Tamil Tigers made a significant effort to create a Tamil identity that included all Tamils, regardless of caste or re-ligion (cf. Bruland 2012; Roberts 2005). Several Tamil Catholic priests have also offered support to the LTTE and the rights of the Tamils.

The historical introduction of Catholicism to a Hindu society, the conver-sion of Hindus to Catholicism and the desire to include Tamil culture within the Tamil Catholic church are unquestionably important in understanding the common ground shared by Hindu and Catholic devotees. However, while Hindu forms of worship brought into Catholicism when Hindus converted generations ago were a product of history, these practices are not performed by believers today as an historical act: the devotees are not concerned with the historical aspect when praying. Furthermore, as Roger Keesing (2012) points out, religious practitioners do not all share the same meanings and interpretations of ritual symbols. Moreover, the majority will make rather superficial interpretations, and the meaning of the symbol will depend on what the individual knows (ibid.: 406). The concern of this chapter is thus to understand how people live this similarity of practices and materials – the religious aesthetics – in Hinduism and Catholicism on the level of experience and how this experience (re)produces a Tamil national identity.

Common Aesthetics, Different Religions

Visiting Hindu temples in Paris with Sri Lankan Tamil friends in 2010, I was struck by their enthusiasm for the decoration of the Hindu gods with flowers, dresses and jewels. Both the priest and the devotees explained that these practices 'gave the gods a pleasant look', making them 'beautiful'. To my surprise, involved in a prayer circle of Tamil Catholic neighbours, I found similar practices among Paris-based Catholic Sri Lankan Tamils, who decorated Mother Mary with flower garlands and robes made of saris. Another point of resemblance was the circulation of incense in front of both Hindu deities and Mother Mary. Much effort was invested in these devotional practices, which, I was told by the devotees, made them '*santhosam*' (or happy).

One of these Catholic devotees is Malar, who has lived in the northern outskirts of Paris with her husband and four children since they came to France in 1992. Every Friday morning, Malar does her Friday morning prayer in her family's terraced house. Preparing herself and the house for prayer, she sweeps the floor and wipes the dust off shelves and ornaments. In the background, religious songs, recorded in the church of St Antony in her natal village in Jaffna, are playing. She lights two incense sticks, igniting a flame, which she then blows out. Ashes float down to the floor, leaving the incense sticks with only a dim glow. The smell of incense starts to fill the house as she moves around, holding the sticks firmly in her right hand. She goes first to a key holder with the image of St. Anthony. She moves the incense sticks five times clockwise in front of St. Antony, then she makes a horizontal line from left to right twice, and forms a cross before she finishes with two more movements from left to right. She carries on to the little shelf of statues of the Mother Mary, referred to as *Matha* (Mother) in Tamil, placed high up on the wall in the corner of the living room. The biggest *Matha* is decorated with a flower garland in plastic, a 'necklace' of flowers. Here she repeats the process of five clockwise circles, then traces horizontal lines from left to right, and a cross, and then from left to right again (see fig. 9.1).

Every Friday during the three months I stayed with Malar's family, Malar would perform the same routine with the incense. The incense sticks are essential in Malar's practice of prayer. The object initiates her prayer, and is actively used during prayer. Although incense is also used in Catholic masses by the priest, the practice of the clockwise movement is strikingly similar to

Figure 9.1. Malar circling incense clockwise during her Friday morning prayer. Photo: Stine Bruland.

the Hindu ritual of *arati*. *Arati* is a main part of every *puja*: a lamp filled with oil or ghee and often also incense or a camphor flame is moved clockwise in a circle in front of the deity.

Malar explained to me that since she and her husband got married, she has been performing this routine, and before that, her mother had done so. Malar was born in 1952 – ten years before the Second Vatican Council, thus it must be seen as a practice established within her family well before the Second Vatican Council's influence and the subsequent inculturation. Malar's strong Catholic identity is intertwined with a proud family and village identity as a Passaiyoor *makhal,* a person from Passaiyoor. Passaiyoor is a small Catholic fishing village in Jaffna where marriages are mainly arranged within the village. Talking about Passaiyoor, Malar emphasizes that all are Catholics, and that her ancestors for several generations have been Catholics: '*Amma* [mother] Catholic, *amamma* [*mother's mother*] Catholic, *amamma*'s *amamma* was Catholic, everybody, everybody, everybody are Catholics.' Other Catholics in Paris and Oslo, born in different villages in the Tamil areas of Sri Lanka, would describe the ritual of the Friday prayer in a similar manner, including the circling with incense sticks.

When asked why she prays with this movement of the incense, Malar shrugs her shoulders and says, 'It is *nallam* (good). I don't know, maybe because my mother did it and I saw it.' I asked Malar and other Tamil Catholics several times why they circled the incense. Malar's shrugging was always accompanied by a somewhat strange look, clearly showing that my question was bizarre or out of place. Others would respond in similar ways; that it is *nallam* or simply that it is what they do.

Alfred Gell (1998) argues that 'things' are 'agents', that they have social agency, operate in social worlds and possess the wills and components of social relations. In this perspective, the incense is enabled to *do* something, acting upon the person in the prayer. However, it is *Malar* who uses the incense, and who *chooses* to use it. Therefore, as Ingold (2007a: 1) argues, things are not active 'because they are imbued with agency', but because of the ways in which they continually interact with humans. Thus, the material object of the incense is performed in the mutual interaction with Malar; she acts out the incense in her movement at the same time as the incense acts upon Malar in her prayer (cf. Damsholt and Simonsen 2009). It is in this performance that the incense gains agency, provoking something meaningful to Malar, so that she chooses to use the incense in her prayer every Friday morning.

Aristotle's notion of *aisthesis* emphasizes that our understanding of the world comes through our five senses, as an inseparable whole (Meyer 2010: 743). Different materials play with different senses of sight, smell, taste, touch and sound. Thereby, materials affect how we sense our world (Kapferer and Hobart 2005). The practice of moving incense in a circle is visual, when lit it spreads out fragrance, it has a particular form that is sensed when touching it and it brings Malar's body into movement. Aristotle's notion of *aisthesis* is important in Meyer's discussion of Pentecostal understandings and experiences of the Holy Spirit. Meyer (2010) argues that an understanding of religion as aesthetics allows us to grasp the power of specific religious practices of worship and patterns of feelings to invoke and sustain particular 'aesthetic formations'. In her analysis, Meyer brings into focus the ways that aesthetics appeal to our sensing body. She argues that the authorized religio-aesthetic practices of mediating the transcendent may best be analysed as 'sensational forms' that render it sensible by appealing to the body. Sensational forms in religious practice are important because they have the power to mediate between 'the levels of humans and God (or some transcendental realm of force)' (ibid.: 750). Bruce Kapferer and Angela Hobart (2005: 4) argue that the sensing body and the feelings it creates are vital in the very production of schemes of reason and of abstract, objective knowledge. As much as rational thinking, aesthetics and its production of feelings and emotions need to be recognized as constitutive to our experience and understanding of the world (Meyer 2010).

In this perspective, Malar's use of incense sticks operates as a 'sensational form', its sensuality affecting Malar in her prayer. It is a mutual interaction between Malar and the incense sticks: the action of taking the incense sticks brings her body into a ritualized movement that, in turn, fills the house with a pleasurable smell that she senses and is affected by. Malar, then, is both subject and object of her practice. I argue, therefore, that the religious aesthetics involved in the circling of incense bridge the space between Malar and her God, producing an experience of relationship with the divine though smell, movement and sight. I suggest that this is how Malar's practice with the incense is *nallam* to her; it works. Malar depends upon this particular routine to achieve the desired experience and emotion in prayer; it is essential to her sense of herself as a religious being. This routine should not be understood as passive repetition, but as active and focused worship (cf. Ingold and Hallam 2007). The use of incense is crucial for the constitution of the relationship between herself and the divine. The incense, as material or artefact, is, therefore, a mediator of the transcendental.

Sensual practice with incense is part of both Catholic and Hindu aesthetic practice among Tamils, performed in both Sri Lanka and Paris. I suggest that the shared religious practice lies in the sensual appeal of the religious aesthetics. The sensual aspect of the incense – the movements into which it leads the devotee and the fragrance it gives – evoke a religious experience in the devotee: a transcendent engagement with the divine. Thus the shared aesthetic also transcends the religious boundaries of Catholicism and Hinduism in its efficacy in evoking religious experience.

Furthermore, the depth of experience produced by the sensual dimension of such practices is crucial: it is in its intimacy with the sensing body that the force and potency inherent in aesthetics lies (Kapferer and Hobart 2005). The practice is valued for the sensual qualities that produce the devotee's desired emotions and experiences in prayer. The same aesthetic practices, then, have been incorporated into different religions; the performance of incense in Tamil prayers constitutes an indispensable aesthetic, a sensational form that produces highly valued religious experience in the bodies of both Catholics and Hindus.

'The Eye Likes It': Emotions of Aesthetic Attraction

Flower garlands used for decoration of deities are another shared aesthetic element in Catholic and Hindu prayer. Of the eleven Catholic households I visited in Paris, ten, including Malar (see fig. 9.1) had crowned the largest *Matha* (a statue of the Virgin Mary) in their home shrine with a plastic flower garland. Flower garlands also decorate images of Hindu gods in temples (see fig. 9.2), although fresh flowers are used.

In both Catholic churches and Hindu temples in Jaffna, fresh flower garlands are also seen around the necks of statues of the saints and gods. This practice is also applied outside religion, as when an important visitor is shown honour and respect by putting a garland around his neck. In Hinduism, flowers are auspicious for the *puja* and the gods. The following discussion with Prem Sharma, priest in the Hindu Mari-Amman temple in La Chapelle, on the meaning of decorating gods with flower garlands sheds light on the importance of the sensual effect of flowers in prayer: 'When you see a beautiful thing, your mind will be happy, and it is pleasant. Everything should be in a pleasant look. This garland … it gives it a pleasant look. And you know, if you wear a garland it takes the heat out of your body, but we give it to the God, it is like to give a pleasant look. He loves that.'

The Hindu priest emphasizes the ability of the flower garlands to please the eyes of the devotees as well as to please the gods. The flowers are sensed through the eyes; it gives the devotees a feeling of *santosham (happiness)*. Meyer (2010: 756ff.) shows that 'sensational forms' must be persuasive in order to work and that this happens through shape and form. It is when sensational forms appeal to our senses and invoke emotions that they are persuasive. Bridging the gap between humans and the divine, this link is experienced as genuine (cf. Meyer 2010). The temple priest emphasizes that 'everything should be in a pleasant look', and when this happens it is, in his view, persuasive for the priest and the devotees. The Hindus I met during my fieldwork in Jaffna and Paris frequently said, when planning to go to the temple, that they would 'go to the temple to *see* God'. The act of *darsan,* or 'seeing', is important in Hindu prayer. To stand in front of the image, to see and be seen by the deity, reveals the visual understanding of the image: the deity is present in the image (Eck 1985). To 'see' is the act of worship. In this process, the devotee receives the blessing of the divine. The decoration of the gods appeals to the senses and thereby facilitates this 'seeing'.

A devotee in the same temple, a man in his early fifties who had recently arrived in Paris from Jaffna, also emphasized the sensual impact of aesthetic decoration before the evening *puja* in the Mari-Amman temple, the day before my conversation with the priest. When the temple assistant closed the

Figure 9.2. Hindu God with flower garland. Photo: Stine Bruland.

curtains in front of the *Amman* (God) to decorate the Gods for the *puja,* he said:

> They like to decorate [the Gods] with flowers. The flowers are special in our religion. And they put jewellery, and nice, good saris, silk saris, very often red colour, or pink.... We like this. The eye likes it – it makes Amman very attractive. Attraction is increasing the people, the people will come. "Oh, I was in the Amman *kovil* [Hindu temple or shrine] and saw Amman veeeeery nice." So you tell the others and more people will come.... The eyes see and we are attracted to it. It will affect prayers.

When asked, 'How does it affect your prayer?' he replied: 'Decoration makes your mind a little happy, if you go out and see a beautiful lady or man, in good clothes, you are also happy. Your mind will be a little happy, attracted to that. The same thing attracts the people; it will encourage people to pray. Watch and listen the prayers especially.'

For the devotee, the flowers, saris and jewellery, the total decoration of the gods, affects his prayers in a way that he will be more attentive to the *puja,* making him 'watch and listen'. This decoration has visual qualities; the flowers, saris and further decoration of the gods, beautifully prepared, is sensed through the body – the eye is attracted (cf. Svašek, chapter 8, this volume). As the devotees experience through their whole body (cf. Meyer 2010), this aesthetic decoration is an important part of the worship, not as isolated objects, but in what it creates in the mutual interaction with the human (cf. Ingold 2007a). Sensing the religious aesthetic, the devotees experience emotions – 'the mind becomes happy', which I interpret as a religious experience, or the act of *darsan* (seeing).

The aesthetic of the *puja* is agential, then, in attracting people to prayer: making them feel happy, thus confirming their religious belief. In more public Catholic prayers, the *Matha* is also given fresh flower garlands, draped in robes made from sari material and welcomed by the performance of *arati,* the circulation of incense, as in the practice of what I call the 'visiting *Matha*'.

The Visiting *Matha*

The ritual of the visiting *Matha* had existed in Paris for some years in unorganized form when, in October 2009, the newly arrived Sri Lankan Catholic priest organized the ritual to reach more people. Fifteen statues of the Mother Mary were distributed, one in each of fifteen districts; these 'visited' every Sri Lankan Tamil Catholic household in the district for one week each. Three statues were replicas of Madu Matha, a famous *Matha* in Madu in Sri

Lanka, believed to have special powers to cure illness (Stirrat 1982). The rest were replicas of Fatima from Portugal.[5] Many Tamils feel a great devotion towards Matha. Matha is considered to be powerful, and Tamil Catholics pray to Matha concerning the problems they encounter in their everyday life, including education, health, job and migration visa. Childless women, especially, turn to Matha for help.

The day a *Matha* was taken from the church to the first Tamil Catholic home, the priest instructed the family who received it to 'take it with flowers, incense and the light, making *arati*'. Here the complete *arati* appears, as in the Hindu *puja*. This ceremony was repeated every time a *Matha* changed household. The Catholic priest explained that, besides being a common practice in Catholic prayers in Sri Lanka, he especially wanted the people to do *arati*, because 'the people are attracted, the people are moved by that'.

In each of the four changes of households I observed, the wife in the family placed a candle together with incense and flowers on a small silver tray and circulated it three times clockwise in front of the *Matha* as it entered through the main door (figs 9.3 and 9.4).

The husband then received the *Matha*, placing her on an altar usually consisting of a table covered with blue saris, the colour of the Virgin Mary, and placed before a wall decorated with colourful flashing electric lights, bouquets of fresh flowers and lighted candles. The wife then changed the robe the *Matha* arrived in and, finally, placed a garland of fresh flowers

Figure 9.3. The *Matha* arriving at Suganthy's home. Photo: Stine Bruland.

Figure 9.4. The *Matha* with flowers, light, dress and incense. Photo: Stine Bruland.

around the *Matha*'s neck, before the family and their relations and Tamil friends and neighbours, who had been invited to receive the *Matha* on the first day, initiated the prayers of the rosary.

As in the Hindu *puja,* the ritual of the visiting *Matha* included *arati,* flower garlands and dressing of the deity. This makes the *puja* and the visiting *Matha* resemble each other in the aesthetic dimension of prayers. Although the devotional songs are dedicated to the statue of a Catholic saint, the aesthetic decorations and practices closely resemble those of the Hindu *puja.* It is after the participants in the rituals have performed or observed the performance of these three practices that they turn to emotional songs and loud prayers, moving the rosary around, creating a feeling that something very special is happening. The day the *Matha* arrived at Suganthy's home, she declared: 'I feel very happy now. You can see, on Saturday I will be very sad, because Matha is leaving. I feel that someone is in my house now. I am very happy.'

Suganthy expressed her feeling of *santosham* repeatedly during the week the *Matha* remained in her house. She also put a lot of effort into the decoration of the *Matha*: every second day, Suganthy bought her fresh flower garlands and sometimes new flower bouquets. And every day, before friends, family and neighbours came to pray in the evening, she carefully arranged the flowers in front of the *Matha,* nagging the children when they touched the decorations. Suganthy also has other *Matha* statues in her house, in the shrine in the corner of her living room. But the presence of this particular *Matha* gives her the feeling that someone special was in her house, producing greater feelings of happiness than those elicited by the other statues of *Matha* on her home shrine. I suggest that the cause for this is that the *Matha*s of the home shrine are not involved in aesthetic processes that elicit the same emotions in Suganthy. The performance of the decoration and *arati* of the visiting *Matha* activates the deity; it transforms the *Matha* from a rather 'naked', 'cold' statue of the divine to a deity they experience as present, able to listen and to fulfil their prayers. The aesthetic practices that constitute these particular experiences and emotions through their appeal to the sensing body are therefore necessary in the devotees' religious experience. This underlines the importance of 'seeing' in Tamil Catholicism, as in Tamil Hindu worship, a seeing which is facilitated by the production of particular aesthetic experiences. The same shapes and forms – that is, clockwise movement of flame and incense in *arati*, dressing the deities in beautiful robes or saris and crowning them with fresh flowers – are thus 'a necessary condition in order for the reality of power of God to show' (Meyer 2010: 749) for Hindu *and* Catholic Tamils, producing similar desired emotions in the devotees. It is, I argue, this emotional dimension of the worship that unites the

Catholic and Hindu devotees. The devotees need to reproduce these emotions to achieve a religious experience. These emotions are achieved through aesthetic practice or material objects understood as 'Tamil'.

Shared Religious Aesthetic and Tamil Identity

In the religious practices discussed above, it is the achievement of an experience of god or gods that is crucial to the devotees. Ingold and Hallam (2007: 5ff.) argue that reproduction of established traditions is not mere copying, but demands creativity. In this view, decisions and solutions are needed to recreate the tradition, as the outcome of this process is not given in advance. As I have suggested in this chapter, the devotees seek to find ways to achieve and reproduce a religious experience. Tamil Catholic devotees applying elements and practices that closely resemble those of Tamil Hindus needs to be understood as an active way of continuing to be religious and recreate oneself as a Tamil Catholic. Carrying across certain aesthetic features, therefore, is not mere copying, but rather an active and conscious process that engenders the creativity of inculturation. These religious practices are part of the meshwork within which the Tamils dwell.

To reproduce oneself as a Tamil Catholic might be seen as more important when living in diaspora. Since religious life is an area in which one is dependent upon familiar aesthetics in order to achieve religious emotions, the migrant context may reinforce creative processes of reproducing a Tamil Catholic experience, increasing the use of 'Tamil' elements in worship. Ingold and Hallam (2007) point out that human creativity occurs in mutual relation with our material and non-material surroundings. In the 'new' surroundings of the diaspora, and given the long, recently ended conflict between Tamils and the Sinhalese state, but the continuance of discrimination, aesthetically 'Tamil' objects and practices may become imbued with enhanced meanings of attachment to the distant homeland.

After the second evening of prayers in Suganthy's home, we were all served *roles* (deep-fried rice paper stuffed with spicy meat or vegetables), *vaddai* (savoury snacks) and chocolate cake. While eating, sitting faced towards the *Matha*, Suganthy's French-born 17-year-old daughter, who was studying at the lycée,[6] told me: 'I feel better now. Before the prayers I was stressed, you know, all the homework. Now I feel eased. This *Matha* is special because she comes to our house. And she is also special because she is from our homeland.' When I revealed to her that this particular *Matha* was Fatima from Portugal, she said in a relaxed voice, 'Oh, I was sure it was from our homeland.' I suggest that the total aesthetic decoration of the *Matha* – the flower garland, the other flowers, incense, lights, the sari robe and the further decoration of the alter where the *Matha* is placed, as well as her parents' welcome of the *Matha* with the practice of *arati* – makes this Matha appear Tamil, leading to it being experienced as Tamil. These aesthetic materials and practices make the *Matha* into a symbolic expression of the feeling of 'home'. This expression of feeling may intensify the devotee's attachment to the homeland and life they left or, like Suganthy's daughter, know only through visits.

Religious emotions are thus achieved and reproduced within a 'Tamil' frame. These materials and practices have aesthetic and sensorial qualities, which, I have argued, are important in the act of worship; it is the seeing, smelling and broader sensual experience of the material elements during religious practices that activate the devotee during prayer. Crucial experiences and emotions are thus realized. In this process, Malar and Suganthy reaffirm their Catholic belief and their attachment to the Tamil community. The Catholic ritual reproduces a religious and national identity, in which the two religious identities of Catholic and Hindu are experienced inclusively as a single Tamil identity. Passing this religious and national identity on to the second generation I found to be vital to parents living in diaspora.

Conclusion

By using a material approach that includes the aesthetics of the materials and the emotions they produce as active elements in our experience of the world, I have sought to craft an analysis of shared material culture and sensorial practice across religious divisions between Hinduism and Catholicism among Sri Lankan Tamils. Investigating how the aesthetic *works* in the practitioners' religious experience, I have shown that it is the achievement of an experience of God that is found to be crucial, while material objects and sensual practices are used as means to the end of producing these feelings. The appealing quality of the materials and practices used in the clockwise movement of incense (*arati*), the use of flower garlands and the dressing of the deities is their sensual form - all facilitating the experience of the divine.

This applied sensual form is neither exclusively Catholic, nor Hindu, but is experienced more broadly as 'Tamil'. Interaction between these common aesthetic elements in both the Tamil Catholic and Tamil Hindu religious traditions contributes to the reproduction of a broader and more inclusive Tamil identity and sense of belonging to the Tamil community. During worship, the person confirms his or her religious and national identity. The religious identity does not, as among the Sinhalese, exclude one from the national community, but rather includes a broader conception of religious and national identity. Analysing the religious aesthetics, how they produce emotions and feelings in interaction with the devotees, allows us to see how these materials are active and necessary elements of religious practice for believers. This opens up studies of religion and nationalism in Sri Lanka to an analysis that takes into account how religious aesthetics produce emotions and feelings essential to the devotees' particular religious experience and contributes to the production of Tamil national identity. In their worship and rituals, Hinduism as well as Catholicism thus reproduce Tamil national identity. This analysis thus also bears witness to the way this particular religious 'Tamil' aesthetic forms part of a process wherein Tamil Hinduism and Tamil Catholicism draw the lines between religion and national identity differently than is found among Sinhalese Buddhists and Muslims. In a context where other religious identities tends towards ethnification; conflating the boundaries between national identity and religious identity, leading to a correlated escalation of violence, I suggest that a consideration of the shared religious aesthetics among Tamil Hindus and Catholics is crucial to understanding why this religious boundary remains the only non-violent one in Sri Lanka today.

Stine Bruland completed her PhD thesis in Social Anthropology at the Norwegian University of Science and Technology in 2015, entitled Underneath the Margosa tree. Re-creating Meaning in a Tamil Family After War and Migration. Her main research interests are Sri Lankan Tamil families in and outside Sri Lanka, transnational relatedness, materiality and aesthetics. Her publications include the chapter 'Being there while Being here: Long-distance Aesthetics and Sensations in Tamil National Rituals' in the edited book 'Objects and Imagination. Perspectives on Materialization and Meaning' by Øivind Fuglerud and Leon Wainwright on Berghahn Books, and the article 'Nationalism as Meaningful Life Projects: Identity Construction Among Politically Active Tamil Families in Norway' in the journal *Ethnic and Racial Studies*.

Notes

1. The fieldwork in Oslo from December 2007 to August 2008 explored questions of experiences of different levels of belonging in Tamil families living in Norway. A special focus was given to generational relations between parents who migrated and their children born in Norway. The fieldwork in Jaffna in the course of 2012 explored practices of transnational family relationships. This chapter is a revised and expanded version of my article 'Transgressing religious boundaries: the power of aesthetics in Tamil Catholic and Hindu worship', *Journal of Material Religion* 9(4): 418–440.

2. This is an unofficial figure given by http://www.english.rfi.fr/visiting-france/
   20110203-sdgvsdg (last accessed 4th of February 2011). Official figures in 2002
   estimated 50,000 Tamils (Etiemble 2004).
3. Jaffna, both the peninsula and the capital city of the peninsula, is considered the
   cultural capital of the Sri Lankan Tamils. It is placed in the north of the island,
   and is, together with the East, the area with the most concentrated Tamil population on the island.
4. In Jaffna today, the church of St Anthony in Pasaiyoor is particularly visited on
   Tuesday by Hindus.
5. For more on replicas, see Rikli, this volume.
6. The lycée is the second, and last, stage of secondary education in the French
   educational system.

References

Asian Tribune. 2013. http://asiantribune.com/node/61792, accessed 8 June 2013.

BBC. 2012. http://www.bbc.co.uk/news/world-asia-17816285, accessed 8 June
2013.

Bruland, S. 2012. 'Nationalism as Meaningful Life Projects: Identity Construction
Among Politically Active Tamil Families in Norway', *Ethnic and Racial Studies*
(35)12.

Carter, J. 1979. 'Introduction', in J. R. Carter (ed.), *Religiousness in Sri Lanka.* Colombo: Marga Institute, i–x.

Catholic News Agency. 2011. http://www.catholicnewsagency.com/news/buddhist_
extremists_brutally_attack_catholic_church_in_sri_lanka/, accessed 8 June 2013.

Colombo Telegraph. 2013. http://www.colombotelegraph.com/index.php/the-wah
habi-invasion-of-sri-lanka/, accessed 8 June 2013.

Damsholt, T., and D. G. Simonsen. 2009. 'Materialiseringer: Processer, relationer of
performativitet', in D. G. Simonsen, T. Damsholt and C. Mordhorst (eds), *Materialiseringer: Nye perspektiver på materialitet og kulturanalyse.* Aarhus: Aarhus
Universitetsforlag, 1–37.

Eck, D. L. 1985. *Darsan: Seeing the Divine Image in India.* Chambersburg: Anima
Books.

Etiemble, A. 2004. 'Les Tamouls du Sri Lanka dans la région parisienne: L'emprise
du politique', *RFAS* 2.

Frenz, M. 2008. 'The Virgin and Her "Relations": Reflections on Processions at a
Catholic Shrine in Southern India', in K. A. Jacobsen (ed.), *South Asian Re-
ligions on Display: Religious Processions in South Asia and in the Diaspora.*
London: Routledge, 92–103.

Fuglerud, Ø. 1999. *Life on the Outside: The Tamil Diaspora and Long Distance
Nationalism.* London: Pluto Press.

Gell, A. 1998. *Art and Agency: An Anthropological Theory.* Oxford: Oxford University Press.

Groundviews. 2013. http://groundviews.org/2013/03/19/bodu-bala-sena-a-threat-
to-sri-lankas-future/, accessed 8 June 2013.

Hastrup, K. 2007. 'Agency, Anticipation and Creativity', in T. Ingold and E. Hallam (eds), *Creativity and Cultural Improvisation*. Oxford: Berg, 1–24.

Hennayake, N. 2006. *Culture, Politics and Development in Postcolonial Sri Lanka*. Oxford: Lexington Books.

Ingold, T. 2000. *The Perception of the Environment: Essays on Livelihood, Dwelling and Skill*. London: Routledge.

———. 2007a. 'Materials and Materiality', *Archaeological Dialogues* 14: 1–16.

———. 2007b. *Lines: A Brief History*. London: Routledge.

———. 2011. *Being Alive: Essays on Movement, Knowledge and Description*. London: Routledge.

Ingold, T., and Hallam, E. 2007. 'Creativity and Cultural Improvisation: An Introduction', in T. Ingold and E. Hallam (eds), *Creativity and Cultural Improvisation*. Oxford: Berg, 1–24.

Jacobsen, K. A. 2008. 'Creating Sri Lankan Tamil Catholic Space in the South Asian Diaspora in Norway', in K. A. Jacobsen and S. J. Raj (eds), *South Asian Christian Diaspora: Invisible Diaspora in Europe and North America*. Surrey: Ashgate, 117–132.

Kapferer, B., and Hobart, A. 2005. 'Introduction: The Aesthetics of Symbolic Construction and Experience', in A. Hobart and B. Kapferer (eds), *Aesthetics in Performance: Formations of Symbolic Construction and Experience*. New York: Berghahn Books, 1–22.

Keesing, R. M. 2012. 'On Not Understanding Symbols: Toward an Anthropology of Incomprehension', *HAU: Journal of Ethnographic Theory* 2(2): 406–430.

Meyer, B. 2010. 'Aesthetics of Persuasion: Global Christianity and Pentecostalism's Sensational Forms', *South Atlantic Quarterly* 109(4): 741–763.

Roberts, M. 2005. 'Tamil Tiger "Martyrs": Regenerating Divine Potency?' *Studies of Conflict and Terrorism* (28): 493–514.

Stirrat, R. L. 1982. 'Shrines, Pilgrimage and Miraculous Powers in Roman Catholic Sri Lanka', in W. J. Sheils (ed.), *The Church and Healing*. Oxford: Basil Blackwell.

———. 1992. *Power and Religiosity in a Post-Colonial Setting: Sinhala Catholics in Contemporary Sri Lanka*. Cambridge: Cambridge University Press.

Svašek, M. 2012. 'Introduction. Affective Moves: Transit, Transition and Transformation', in M. Svašek (ed.), *Moving Subjects Moving Objects: Transnationalism, Cultural Production and Emotions*. New York: Berghahn Books.

Tambiah, S. J. 1986. *Sri Lanka: Ethnic Fratricide and the Dismantling of Democracy*. Chicago: University of Chicago Press.

Tamilnet. 2004a. http://tamilnet.com/art.html?catid=13&artid=13277, accessed 8 June 2013.

———. 2004b. http://tamilnet.com/art.html?catid=13&artid=13303, accessed 8 June 2013.

The Sunday Times, 2006. http://www.sundaytimes.lk/061008/News/nws22.html, accessed 8 June 2013.

Vatican Insider. 2012. http://vaticaninsider.lastampa.it/en/world-news/detail/articolo/sri-lanka-sri-lankasri-lanka-20668/, accessed 8 June 2013.

10

NARRATIVES, MOVEMENTS, OBJECTS
AESTHETICS AND POWER IN CATHOLIC DEVOTION
TO OUR LADY OF APARECIDA, BRAZIL

João Rickli

In 1717, the king of Portugal appointed the earl of Assumar as governor of the provinces of São Paulo and Minas Gerais, in Brazil. The new governor was travelling around his new domains and stayed in the small city of Guaratinguetá, on the shores of the Paraíba do Sul River. All the fishermen living in the area were instructed to find fish to feed the governor and his entourage.

Fish was scarce that season and most fishermen returned to the city with nothing to offer to the governor. Three, however, were more persistent. They continued throwing their nets and, in one attempt, fished out a dark, headless statue, which they identified as a broken image of Our Lady of the Immaculate Conception. They kept the small image in their canoe and threw the nets one more time. When they hauled them again, they fished out the head of the image, pieced it to the body and continued fishing. The next time they hauled the nets, they were full of fish. The fishermen immediately understood they had found a miraculous image. They brought it with them and one of the fishermen placed it in a small shrine at his house.

The story spread around the region and people started to go to the fisherman's house to pray and worship the wondrous statue. The devotion grew, new miracles were attributed to the image and, in 1745, a small chapel was built on the top of a hill by the river to accommodate the image, which was called Our Lady of the Immaculate Conception, Aparecida.[1]

This short narrative is a version of the well-known mythic history of the apparition of Our Lady of the Immaculate Conception, Aparecida, Brazil's patron saint.[2] Throughout the centuries, the small terracotta image found in the waters of Paraíba do Sul evolved from a humble depiction of the Immaculate Conception to the powerful Our Lady of Aparecida, the cornerstone of a massive devotional cult. The figures are impressive. The so-called National Shrine, the Basilica built on a hill a few metres downstream from the place where the image was found, is bombastically introduced as the biggest Marian shrine in the world, with room for more than forty thousand people. It is located a few metres from the Old Basilica, built at the end of the nineteenth century to replace the chapel constructed in 1745 to shelter the image. Around the new Basilica, there are huge parking lots and a large building with a food court, toilets and shops called the Pilgrim's Support Centre (*Centro de Apoio ao Romeiro*). According to the National Shrine's website, eleven million people visited in 2011. This whole complex, which has been managed by the Redemptorist Fathers since 1894, is at the heart of the city of Aparecida, an agglomerate of hotels, lodges, restaurants, houses and shops that have grown up haphazardly around the old and new Basilicas over the years.[3]

This chapter investigates the entanglements between aesthetics and power in the devotional practices associated with the image of Our Lady of Aparecida. It analyses the production and circulation of images, objects and people around devotion to the saint, looking at Aparecida as a powerful 'aesthetic formation' (Meyer 2009: 6ff.) around which a plurality of subjects (devotees, clergymen, politicians, celebrities) and organizations (the Catholic Church, Catholic movements, congregations, local and national governments) negotiate their relationships, creatively producing and reproducing images, narratives and devotional practices. My main concern is to analyse narratives and movements of people and objects in order to comprehend the entanglements between aesthetics and power in the dynamics of creativity at issue in the devotion to Aparecida. The term 'aestheticization' (Svašek 2007: 9–11) offers a theoretical framework to address these entanglements. Aestheticization refers to processes in which artefacts/images are hypercognized and gain efficacy within the context of wider societal processes, undergoing a series of transformations and becoming active in different fields of power. Using this framework, I analyse how dynamics of creativity implied in the aestheticization of the image of Aparecida are determined by power relations involving multiple actors and objects.

The concept of creativity here relates to complex social processes that involve encounters and interactions between these diverse actors and objects in movement. The production, appropriation and circulation of an image trope as popular and powerful as Aparecida involves a great variety of national and transnational agents and forces within and without the field of Catholic religion. Thus, creativity implied in (1) the transformations of Aparecida's image through time, (2) the devotional practices performed at the National Shrine and (3) the (re)production of objects related to the devotion is treated here as a complex social process, in which movements of cultural agents and objects are inseparably entangled.

The abundance and effervescence of these movements are central to the devotion to Aparecida and are fundamental components of its creative dynamics. I use the notions of 'transit, transition and transformation' (Svašek 2010: 67; see also this volume's introduction) to analyse the mobility of people and objects around the National Shrine in relation to creativity. 'Transit' refers to the movements of people and objects across space and time; 'transition' to transit-related changes in the meanings, values and emotional efficacy of objects and images. 'Transformation' concerns the dynamic ways in which cultural producers relate to the changing social and material environments in which they find themselves.

This chapter is divided into three sections. The first analyses how the transitions of the image of Aparecida, which converted a Portuguese statue representing the Immaculate Conception into a Brazilian form of the Virgin Mary, reflect and act upon the political narratives of Brazil as a Catholic nation. Through the brief description of some critical events in the history of Brazilian Catholicism, it analyses how Aparecida's national character is produced in the complex interplay between the Catholic Church, the Brazilian State and so-called Brazilian popular Catholicism.[4] The second section focuses on the transit and transformations of people, objects and spiritual power around the National Shrine, describing them as the conjugation of centripetal and centrifugal forces that have the original image displayed in the Basilica at their centre.[5] The third section analyses the valuation of images and objects relating to devotion to Aparecida. It analyses attribution of value to images and objects in Aparecida as a complex negotiation between multiple forces, from the authority of church officials, who claim to be the only authorized mediators of the Aparecida's divine power, to beliefs, practices, narratives and feelings of the devotees, who create their own ways of relating to the divine through objects.

Aesthetics and the Narratives of a Catholic Nation

Lourival dos Santos (2000), in his thesis on the production of printed stamps of Aparecida, describes the different ways in which the image was depicted from 1854 to 1978, analysing its transition from a local devotional object to the most popular symbol of Brazilian Catholicism. Relying on his account and other works on the history of Catholicism in Brazil (Bruneau 1974; Della Cava 1975), I will analyse a few events in the late nineteenth century and early twentieth century that are especially important to understanding some of the transformations of Aparecida's image and its consolidation as a national symbol. Following Santos (2000), I consider the form given to the image and its attributes as inseparable from political narratives concerning the nation-state and its relation to the Catholic Church.[6]

The way the devotion to Aparecida developed through time is profoundly marked by constant tensions between local religious practices and official Catholic liturgical norms. In the second half of the nineteenth century, the period when devotion to Aparecida started to become more relevant in the national context, these tensions were part of the broader process of Romanization, the name given to the Vatican initiatives to centralize control over devotional practices and to reinforce Roman orthodoxy and the theological and liturgical unity of the Catholic Church in Brazil. Various strategies were adopted to promote unity and 'Romanize' local Catholic forms of devotion: the prohibition of some liturgical forms, investigations on the veracity of local saints and apparitions and their miracles, and attempts to control and discipline local cults, among others. The sending of missionaries from different orders and congregations committed to Roman orthodoxy was the most important way in which these strategies were brought to the local level.[7]

The devotion to Aparecida is a good example of the specific type of Catholic practice generated by Romanization in Brazil. The failure to suppress some ideas and forms of devotion led to their incorporation and accommodation into the Catholic creed, generating zones of compromise between rules and dogmas defended by the Catholic hierarchy and typically Brazilian popular forms of Catholic devotion. Analysing Aparecida's transitions as the outcome of collective, complex and constantly changing dynamics of creativity can illuminate some aspects of the tensions and zones of compromise between local and transnational forms of Catholicism.

Since 1745, the chapel at nearby Guaratinguetá had been managed by local clergymen who tended to be more or less compliant with unorthodox practices. The power of the image and its ability to perform all sorts of miracles gained regional popularity and its fame spread from Paraíba do Sul Valley to other regions of São Paulo and neighbouring states (Brustoloni 1998). In the mid-nineteenth century, the devotion had already attracted the attention and concern of the church hierarchy in Brazil. An episode presented in Santos's work (2000: 41–42) exemplifies the conflicts engendered by processes of Romanization, which sought to reorient the devotion to Aparecida. In 1851, the bishop of São Paulo, Dom Antonio Joaquim de Melo, visited the chapel and intervened in its management, admonishing the local priest and making some liturgical changes in order to purify the devotion by the exclusion of unorthodox practices. He also commanded the destruction of some prints of the image of Aparecida that he considered incompatible with

Catholic norms. In 1854, he commissioned an official and 'adequate' print of Our Lady of Aparecida from France, in which she is depicted as a white virgin wearing a rosary and a blue cloak. According to Santos, this printing gave to Aparecida's image its triangular shape, which would later become one of its distinctive attributes. It also establishes continuities between Aparecida and European images of the Immaculate Conception and Our Lady of the Rosary.

This episode can be interpreted in terms of aestheticization insofar as it reveals how the image of Aparecida, undergoing specific transitions, gained agency in the conflicts between transnational and local forms of Catholicism. On the one hand, the aesthetic qualities of the image commissioned by the bishop (a white lady wearing a Rosary and the attributes of the Immaculate Conception) stressed continuities with consecrated European forms of the Virgin Mary. On the other hand, the image does not deny to Aparecida its uniqueness as a local apparition of the Virgin Mary, preserving her name, printed on the top of the picture, and giving her one of her distinctive features – the triangular shape.

The Proclamation of the Brazilian Republic, in 1889, had important consequences for the development of the cult of Aparecida. Deeply influenced by French Positivism, the Republican constitution postulated the separation of the state and the Catholic Church, threatening to set the latter aside from the centre of political power. In this context, the investments made by the church in the organization and strengthening of the devotion to Aparecida must be understood as a means to mobilize popular support in order to maintain the position of the church as an influential player in the Brazilian political arena. Aparecida, through these investments, became a powerful symbol of Brazilian Catholicism and of the Brazilian nation.

In this sense, the history of the transitions of Aparecida's image may be considered as the slow and continuous transformation of the European Immaculate Conception, the patron saint of the Portuguese Empire, into a new autochthonous designation of the Virgin Mary, whose autochthony was reinforced by the church in its negotiations with the Brazilian State. While in earlier periods it was important to highlight the continuities between Aparecida's image and European forms of the Virgin in order to control the disruptive power of local forms of devotion, after the proclamation of the Republic it was necessary to emphasize the autochthony and originality of the image, mobilizing its popular appeal to strengthen the connection between the Catholic Church and the (imagined) Brazilian nation. In his work on Republican images in Brazil, José Murilo de Carvalho (2001: 93–94) discusses the importance of Aparecida as a feminine symbol of the nation. He argues that the consecrated French depiction of the Republic as a woman failed to become a mobilizing image associated with nationality and patriotism in Brazil. Yet the Catholic Church successfully associated the popular and powerful feminine image of Aparecida with the Brazilian nation, accepting and emphasizing her autochthony, and investing in her a certain popular sentiment of nostalgia for the monarchy and the royal family.

The ceremony of coronation of the image, in 1904, was a crucial moment in which these symbolic dimensions were articulated. A huge festival organized in the Old Basilica brought together the bishops of Rio de Janeiro and São Paulo and was widely covered by the national press. Aparecida was officially crowned 'Queen of Brazil', and a crown was definitively incorporated into the image. According to Santos (2000), it was at this time that campaigns promoting pilgrimage to the image started to refer to the city of Aparecida as the spiritual centre of the nation. His analysis shows that in the first decades of the twentieth century, Aparecida is often depicted with the background of the Brazilian map or the Brazilian flag, which was later embroidered on her cloak, together with the Vatican flag.

The culminating point of this transformative process, in which devotion to Aparecida stimulated Brazilian pilgrims to experience and claim national identity, was the ceremony in which Aparecida was declared the patron saint of Brazil, in May 1931. A large Marian congress was organized in Rio de Janeiro, gathering bishops from different parts of Brazil and authorities from the Vatican. The original image of Aparecida left her shrine and was taken by train to Rio de Janeiro. According to newspaper articles quoted by Santos (2000), thousands of people flocked to the procession from the train station to the church where Cardinal Sebastião Leme, the leader of the Catholic Church in Brazil, consecrated the nation to Aparecida. The highly ritualized transit of the image from the Basilica to the Brazilian capital city at that moment boasts its symbolic power and political efficacy, repositioning Aparecida in relation to the religious and political centre of power in the country.

This transit can be considered the critical moment when Aparecida crystallizes her position as the most important symbol articulating relations between the Catholic Church, the Brazilian state and the beliefs and practices of Brazilian Catholics. At the same time, her shrine in the city of Aparecida became the vortex of impressive movements, which I will analyse in the next section.

Movements of People and Objects:
Centripetal and Centrifugal Forces

The aesthetic and political appeal of Aparecida's image as mother and queen of the Brazilian Catholic nation also produced changes in her shrine and the city of Aparecida. In the decades that followed her consecration as patron saint, the city was remodelled to accommodate the new shrine. Parking lots, administrative buildings, toilets and food courts, as well as a range of less prestigious religious attractions, such as a large full-scale nativity scene, were added to the huge building over the years. Hotels and lodges, restaurants and shops mushroomed around the National Shrine.

The grandiosity of the complex, which oscillates between popular modesty and vulgar opulence, conveys a clear and powerful message: this is Aparecida's house, the spiritual centre of Brazilian popular Catholicism. The truth and reach of this claim can certainly be contested, especially in relation to some regionally strong devotions with their own pilgrimage sites, such as the cult of Our Lady of Nazareth, very popular in the northern part of the country, or the devotions to Father Cícero or Bom Jesus da Lapa, surely the most popular Catholic practices in most Brazilian northeastern states.[8] However, the grandiose buildings, the constant presence of Brazilian national symbols including flags, maps and coats of arms, and the flux of pilgrims from virtually everywhere in the country produce an undeniable feeling of centrality to any person visiting the city of Aparecida. The devotion to Aparecida has a clear, well-defined and carefully designed centre: the original image displayed in her golden niche in the National Shrine. The movements around this centre, therefore, are of capital importance to understanding dynamics of creativity and innovation related to the devotion to Aparecida.

In this section, I will describe some of these movements, analysing how people and objects circulate and interact in the National Shrine, and how creativity is implied in these varied interactions. I observed two main types of movements, according to their orientation in relation to the shrine: centripetal movements that converge to Aparecida's Basilica and centrifugal movements that disperse from the city of Aparecida to the whole country and beyond. I will address these two types of movements separately.

Centripetal Movements

Pilgrimages to the National Shrine, with the circulation of people and objects they trigger, constitute the core of devotion to Aparecida. During my visits to the city, I observed that pilgrimages may take a variety of forms. Some are organized by parishes or other Catholic groups, others are organized by travel agents, gathering people previously unknown to each other. Observing the parking lots, it was apparent that the majority of pilgrims arrived by coach, but many also travelled using private cars. Some pilgrimages involve physical efforts and different levels of physical pain, such as travelling hundreds of kilometres by bicycle, motorcycle, horse or simply walking to the National Shrine, sometimes carrying heavy burdens. The arrival of these pilgrims attracts a lot of attention and admiration from other visitors, prompting comments about their faith and eagerness to make sacrifices in honour of Aparecida.

The most common image used in the National Shrine to welcome and show hospitality towards pilgrims is the 'Mother's house'. Before masses or other celebrations, the priests always greet the pilgrims, saying that every child is welcome at the Mother's house and that everyone may feel at home in the National Shrine because Aparecida is the mother of the Brazilian nation. Many pilgrims I have interviewed in Aparecida also describe their pilgrimage in these terms, saying that it is good to be at the Mother's house, or sometimes that it is a filial obligation to visit the Mother every now and then. The use of this metaphor appeals to familiar emotions and feelings approximating the ideas of nation and family. The traditional image of Mary as the spiritual mother of the Catholic family is frequently associated with the Brazilian nation in Aparecida.

Pilgrimages occur throughout the whole year, but they are more intense in the few weeks before 12 October, the national holiday consecrated to Aparecida. According to the National Shrine's website, the celebration of 12 October in 2009, which was the most crowded ever, gathered 215,000 people. The daily life of the city of Aparecida is almost completely dominated by the rhythms of the National Shrine and it is hard to find anything in the city that is not somehow connected to it. A large statue of Aparecida placed on the top of a hill overlooking the city can be seen from almost everywhere. Even the garbage bins on the streets portray the shapes of church bells.

The Basilica has the shape of a Greek cross, with the main altar at its centre and four naves (see fig. 10.1). The main entrance, flanked by the Brazilian and the Vatican flags, is at the north nave. Opposite to the main entrance, at the end of the south nave, is located the niche of the image, at the base of a high column covered with a mosaic, depicting three angels. This imposing golden mural dominates the Basilica, compensating for the small size of the image, which is barely visible from most parts of the huge edifice. There are also two side-chapels, one between the west and the south naves, and the other between the east and the south naves.

The niche is positioned on a sort of mezzanine, being visible but not accessible from inside the Basilica. To approach the image, the pilgrims have to enter a lateral door accessing a one-way aisle crossing the mezzanine where the niche is located, and exiting at the other side of the south nave. This disposition allows the permanent visitation to the image, without disturbing masses or other ceremonies conducted from the central altar of the Basilica, located in the middle of the Greek cross.

Figure 10.1. View of the Basilica. Photo: João Rickli.

For the majority of people I interviewed, the visit to the original image is the most desired moment of the pilgrimage. During the visit, people gaze at the image for a while, praying silently and often touching the base of the golden column where the niche is located. Some people kneel during their prayers, but the long queues, the constant flux of people and the disposition of the place as an aisle inhibit attempts to stay for a longer time. There are also many people taking pictures with their cameras and mobile phones. Observing the exit of the aisle, I noticed a great number of devotees leaving the niche with tears in their eyes. In my short interviews with visitors to the shrine, almost all of them stressed the profoundly emotional atmosphere of the visit when I asked them about their moments in front of the niche.

Masses are another significant activity for people moving around the National Shrine and they are considered indispensable by most pilgrims and by the managers of the shrine. However, I interviewed a considerable number of people who said that they did not attend Mass during their time in the city. The National Shrine promotes six or seven masses every day in the new Basilica and one or two in the Old Basilica, depending on the weekday and time of the year. Leaflets advertising the program are available everywhere in the shrine and in hotel receptions and shops in the city. Masses in Aparecida are celebrated according to the regular Catholic liturgy. The choice of biblical texts and the main theme of the homily follow the church's official calendar. The number of priests celebrating and the number of people attending vary considerably and the masses may be celebrated in one of the side-chapels when the number of pilgrims is smaller. The nine o'clock Mass on Sunday is the most prestigious and is normally very crowded. Although there is always a reproduction of the original image of Aparecida close to the altar and the priests mention it at some appropriate moments during the Mass, its role in the celebration is minor, encompassed by the traditional liturgy, whose culminating point is the sacrament of Eucharist, the celebration of Christ's sacrifice and the redemption of humankind. After the liturgy of the Mass, which last about one hour, the so-called blessing ceremonies take place (see next section).

The pilgrimage and the diverse activities in the shrine are often described by the pilgrims as a reunion, a transformative encounter of brothers and sisters that are dispersed through Brazilian territory. During the masses and blessing ceremonies, priests often greet people and discuss the parishes, cities and states where they come from. Leaders of organized pilgrimages are invited to register their groups beforehand, so they can be included in the lists mentioned during the ceremonies, as well as receive special blessings by the priest. These references to different cities and places emphasize the centripetal movements people make to come together at the National Shrine, creating an atmosphere of unity and solidarity and enhancing the sense of belonging to a community (people often say family) of devotees spread all over the country that, at that moment, meet at the Mother's house. These are specific ways of relating devotional practice to territory and movement, creating determined modes of feeling and relating to space. Through these spatial practices, abstract political narratives about the Brazilian nation and its relationship with the Catholic faith become spatially tangible. During short interviews with pilgrims, some people referred to the pilgrimage as an opportunity to meet people from different regions of the country. They shared the experience of being at the centre, at the Mother's house, meeting their brothers and sisters coming from everywhere in Brazil. The combination of images of familial relationships and national fellowship produces a feeling of national unity around the Catholic faith. The references to space and the centripetal movements represented by pilgrimages to visit the Mother's house add a tangible spatial dimension to this spiritual national family

Together with the movement of people towards the National Shrine, the centripetal movements converging on Aparecida's Basilica include a variety of objects. The most visible and impressive demonstration of these moving objects is the *ex-voto* room, the *Sala das Promessas* (Room of Promises), also known as the Room of Miracles.[9] *Ex-votos* are objects given by Catholic believers to a saint in thanks for what they consider to be a grace or favour. Virtually any object can become an *ex-voto*. For instance, if you pray for help in your studies and you believe Our Lady Aparecida helped you finish college, you may bring your old books, notebooks or a copy of your diploma as *ex-voto*, to thank her for her help and protection. If you had a broken bone healed, crutches or even the remains of a plaster cast can be offered as *ex-voto* (see fig. 10.2).

The Room of Promises, located in the basement of the Basilica, is an impressive collection of *ex-votos* (see fig. 10.3). A great variety of objects exhibited there are organized by themes or topics, making the room look like a museum. For instance, a showcase displays bottles of *cachaça* (a typical Brazilian spirit), packages of cigarettes, playing cards, or dice (etc.), together with some letters and typed texts telling stories about people who overcame serious addictions after praying to Aparecida. Another showcase has different objects connected to pregnancy and babies, with narratives of infertile couples that had babies as a result of the miraculous intervention of the saint. The same principle applies to showcases organized around themes such as sports, music, accidents, family, profession, studies and so on. Objects donated by celebrities, such as football players, popular singers and politicians, are especially visible, sometimes accompanied with pictures of the celebrity in question visiting the shrine.

Ex-votos can be considered a way of materializing prayers, tangible signs of the devotees' faith and of Aparecida's mercy and compassion. In their

Figure 10.2. *Ex-votos*. Photo: João Rickli.

Figure 10.3. View of the *ex-voto* room. Photo: João Rickli.

transit towards the basement of the Basilica, they undergo a transition from ordinary objects used on a daily basis, into religious testimonies of faith and the power of prayer. Exhibited at the Room of Promises, they gain agency to transform the lives of those visiting the National Shrine, to strengthen their faith in Aparecida and in her capacity to perform miracles and solve people's afflictions. The collection exhibited in the room is also a way of staging Aparecida's power, a testimony to her capacity to intervene in favour of her devotees. The way the collection is displayed creates an atmosphere of solidity and permanence around the objects, showing them as persistent evidences of faith and power.

People can also offer as *ex-voto* a replica of objects or parts of the body that are related to the favour that motivates their gratitude. People can make their own replicas of, for instance, houses, cars and lorries, using varied materials and techniques. The Room of Promises exhibits a large number of statues made of plaster, carved wood, terracotta, folded wire and so on. There are also mosaics of seashells and models made of matchsticks and bottle caps. The majority of these replicas, however, are made of wax in a workshop belonging to the National Shrine. They are sold at the official shop close to the Basilica. Hearts, livers, arms, legs, breasts, heads, feet, hands and other parts of the body can be bought by the devotees and delivered at the Room of Promises.

At the back of the room there is a large counter where employees of the Shrine receive newly donated objects and store them for a few hours. According to one of these employees, everything that can still be useful (crutches, clothes, instruments) is donated to charity, while old and spoiled things are simply discarded. Items that, for some reason, are considered remarkable may join the collection exhibited in the room, replacing something that has been there for a long time.[10] Finally, wax objects are sent to a workshop where they are melted down and the wax is used to make new objects that will be sold at the shop. Unlike the objects displayed in the *ex-voto* room, these wax objects are not meant to last. They are transitory and ephemeral, their objectivity and tangibility are ready to be melted away. Their constant circulation is linked with the circulation of money between the devotees and the shrine. Buying objects that will soon be melted down is not only a way of objectifying prayers and gratitude, but also a way of making a donation to the maintenance of the National Shrine. The flux of wax and the flux of money are inseparable and the financial contribution to the shrine could be considered the most practical reason behind the circulation of these objects. However, unlike a simple donation of a small sum of money, the wax *ex-votos* also provide an aesthetic expression of the relationship between the devotees and the saint.

Centrifugal Movements

As important as Aparecida's capacity to attract people and objects to her 'house' is her ability to disperse them with her blessings and spiritual power all over the country. The words of the priests at the end of masses and ceremonies always emphasize the pilgrims' return to their homes, empowered by their experiences in Aparecida and with the mission of being testimonies of her power and grace in their own regions. The pilgrimage does not only bring the devotees to Aparecida, but it also takes Aparecida throughout the country.

The experience of pilgrimage, however, is much more than this religious process of centripetal and centrifugal movements around a spiritual centre. When I accompanied a group of pilgrims from Rio Grande do Sul in September 2011, I noticed that although the pilgrims sometimes interpret their movements in terms of religious convergence and dispersion, they also perceive their displacement in many other more prosaic ways. Very often during the four days we spent together, people were simply enjoying regular touristic experiences, through activities such as sightseeing, shopping, trying different foods or simply relaxing and enjoying a few days off. Among these varied perceptions and experiences, however, the feeling of going to the Mother's house to receive her blessing and then returning home with a renewed and empowered faith prevailed.

The ceremonies of blessing objects, which take place after masses, are completely related to these movements of dispersion from the National Shrine, insofar as they are focused on the transmission of the Aparecida's blessings to objects and bodies that will return to people's homes. In this sense, they could be seen as complementary to the convergence of *ex-votos* in the Room of Promises, in which the collection of objects is meant to remain in the shrine, testifying to Aparecida's power. While the *ex-votos* are materializations of devotees' prayers, the blessed objects materialize Aparecida's grace, becoming vehicles of her divine power.

During the ceremonies, people bring different kinds of objects to be blessed with holy water sprinkled by the priest and his assistants. At the beginning of the ceremony, the priest gives some instructions, inviting people to approach close to the altar and reminding them that no object bought in the shops around the Shrine is blessed per se, but needs to receive the blessing of Aparecida, which can only be transmitted through priests invested with the sacrament of ordination. These words of the priest, which are repeated at the beginning of every blessing ceremony, are often followed by the statement that faith and prayer are the only means to access Aparecida's power, and that the blessing of the objects is empty without true faith.

After these initial instructions and exhortations, people sing songs related to the Virgin Mary and the priest recites a long prayer, invoking the blessings of Aparecida. During the final verses of the prayer, he starts to sprinkle holy water on the devotees gathered around the altar, sometimes with the assistance of other priests or deacons. After the prayer is finished, the blessing goes on until everybody has received at least a few drops of holy water on their objects and on their bodies, while people sing the most popular song about Aparecida: a short and repetitive refrain, saying simply, 'Give us your blessing, dear Mother, give us your blessing Our Lady of Aparecida.'

While holy water is being sprinkled from the altar, people hold their objects high to receive the blessing. The objects brought by devotees vary considerably, but most are small statues and prints of Aparecida, as well as plastic flowers, key-holders and other small gadgets bought at one of the countless religious shops around the shrine. Besides objects, people also desire to receive Aparecida's blessing on their bodies. Some people put their hands up to receive the holy water, while others hold up their children. Very often, people help the sick or disabled to get closer to the altar to receive the water directly on their bodies. As in the visit to the original image, many people take pictures of the ceremony and cameras and mobile phones can be seen among the objects held up to be blessed.

A comparison between the Mass and the blessing ceremony is useful in analysing how the rituals associated with the pilgrimage are also submitted to processes of aestheticization, revealing the complex interplay between the power of the Catholic hierarchy and the people's faith in Aparecida and emotional attachment to her image. For this comparison, a few characteristics of the masses may be pointed out. First, as the celebration of Christ's sacrifice and the redemption of humankind, Christ is their central character. The altar, the crucifix and the communion wafer, all symbols of Christ's presence and sacrifice, occupy the centre of the celebration. Second, the solemnity and rigidity of their main liturgical forms reaffirms the orthodoxy of the church and the power of the priest as its legitimate and consecrated representative. Third, the ritual of communion, the culminating point of the service, is the main means of establishing feelings of the unity of church as the body of Christ. Fourth, the reading and exegesis of the Bible and the gospel play an important role as an opportunity for evangelization.

The blessing ceremony has contrasting characteristics. First, Aparecida is the central character and Christ is only mentioned in the priest's long prayer invoking her blessing. Second, the ceremonies' forms and formulas are less rigid than in the Mass and, although they respect all Catholic dogmas, they are not part of the hard core of Catholic liturgy. Third, feelings of unity and communion are not based on the Eucharist, but in the emphasis on spiritual kinship relationships: Mary as the blessing mother inviting her children to love each other as brothers and sisters. Finally, the appeal to material aspects of objects, bodies and water plays an important role in the ceremony.

The active participation of the devotees in the blessing ceremony is more visible than in the Mass. They bring their objects, they move around the altar and they sometimes touch the authorized copy of the image of Our Lady of Aparecida that is always by the central altar at the Basilica or in one of the side-chapels. The dynamics of creativity involved in the ceremony are more open to the participation of devotees than in the Mass. The colourful variety of objects shown during the ceremony breaks the repetitive flow of the priest's words. Unlike the masses, in which people's bodies only move in unison at appropriate moments, standing, sitting or kneeling, in the blessing ceremonies people move around more of less freely. Some devotees pray in remarkable ways, such as kneeling in front of the altar or touching the floor with their foreheads. Once I observed a group of pilgrims voluntarily starting a song at the end of the ceremony, and they were followed by all the others, including the priest. This sort of improvisation would not normally be welcome during masses.

The possibility of more improvisation, however, does not overcome the power of the priest, whose role in the ceremony has capital importance as the only authorized mediator between Aparecida's power and the objects to be blessed. The creativity involved in the transition of regular objects into vehicles of divine blessings is the result of the accommodation of ritual expressions of popular faith and their associated emotions with authorized Catholic sensational forms, such as sacraments, liturgies and the presence of an invested priest. Producing the sublime is a creative process in which different actors with different religious agendas take part.

Another remarkable aspect of the centripetal movements that spread Aparecida's influence from the National Shrine to the rest of the country is related to technology. The National Shrine owns a broadcasting corporation, whose main media are TV Aparecida, Radio Aparecida and the web portal A12 (www.a12.com). Every day, the most important masses and some of the blessing ceremonies celebrated in the Basilica are broadcast live through television and radio. Since the 1990s, investment in the improvement and modernization of mass media has been one of the measures promoted by the Brazilian Catholic Church in response to increasing competition from the fast-growing Pentecostal churches (see also Woets, this volume). TV Aparecida followed this tendency, evolving from a local channel into a highly professional and modern national cable TV channel. The slogan of the National Shrine's broadcasting system is an eloquent image for the centrifugal movements spreading from the Basilica: 'Aparecida's cloak covering the whole country.'

The centrifugal movements apparent in Aparecida's broadcasting system have further implications than just spreading her influence beyond the National Shrine. Technology also allows different forms of (re)mediation of the experience of the sacred. The varied ways devotees associate the image of Aparecida with technology point to the creative use of new forms of mediation. The remarkable number of mobile phones and cameras used to record the encounter with the original statue and the blessing ceremonies are ways of generating images that not only serve to register the experience of being at the National Shrine, but also create new vehicles for Aparecida's power.

The creative potential of technology is clearly acknowledged by the managers of the National Shrine, who invest in innovative forms of interaction between devotees and Aparecida (see also Svašek, chapter 9, this volume). Through the web portal, for instance, it is possible to light a virtual candle, to hear prayers and to see the niche of the original image in the Basilica in real time through a webcam. Prayers can be sent by SMS. Television screens are distributed on almost every wall or column inside the Basilica, which allows people to take part in the Mass and, at the same time, watch the television images they are used to at home. This is highly appreciated by many people I interviewed. 'It makes me remember that my family is at home and watched this same Mass', a woman told me. It also reinforces the idea of being at the centre of Aparecida's devotion: 'It is nice to participate in the masses I always watch on TV. It is a different experience to be here.'

Valuing Images and Objects in Aparecida: Authority, Authenticity and Improvisation

In this section, I discuss the valuation of images and other objects in the devotion to Aparecida, focusing on the entanglement between authority and improvisation at issue in this process. I analyse attribution of value to images and objects in Aparecida as part and parcel of the dynamics of aestheticization described in the previous sections. Valuing objects related to devotional practices also depends on complex negotiations between multiple forces: the authority of church officials, who monopolize the ability to perform sacraments and blessings, and the beliefs, practices, narratives and feelings of devotees who trust the power of Aparecida with all their faith and hope. The transcendental power attributed to objects is intrinsically connected to their aestheticization and the creative transformations that accredit them to become animated and manifest divine power, able to favour believers with miraculous interventions.

The National Shrine and the Fathers have a special authoritative position in relation to the valuation of objects in Aparecida. Being the authorized representatives of the Catholic Church, they have the mandate to organize, promote and discipline the cult to Aparecida so as to make it fit the orthodoxy of the Church and its evangelistic purposes. The presence of the Vatican flag embroidered on Aparecida's cloak and flanking the main entrance of the Basilica mark the devotion with the official endorsement of the Church. The sermons delivered by the priests always refer to the importance of the sacraments and of obedience to the norms and values of the Catholic Church. Evangelization and the instruction of devotees on correct Catholic doctrines are often mentioned in booklets and other publications as being a central responsibility of the Redemptorist Fathers in Aparecida.

As the official organization responsible for keeping the original image of Aparecida and regulating the devotional practices flourishing around her, the National Shrine has a strong influence on the circulation and valuation of objects connected to the devotion. It is in the blessing ceremonies that this influence of church officials in the production and circulation of valuable objects are most explicit. People are constantly reminded that nothing they buy or bring to Aparecida is blessed in itself and that objects ought to be brought to one of the Basilicas to receive the blessing given by the priests in order to be encompassed by Aparecida's power and mercy. In the ceremony of blessing, after the masses, the church and the priests reaffirm their position as mediators of the sacred, transforming ordinary objects into extraordinary vehicles of divine power. Similarly, the selection, organization, display and disposal of objects in the *ex-voto* room, carefully controlled by the National Shrine (Souza 2012), are aimed at framing the creative ways devotees interact with their saint through objects, mobilizing them to convey certain messages and provoke specific feelings.

Besides these explicit ways of influencing the production and circulation of objects, the National Shrine also plays an important role in the politics of authentication (Meyer, Roodenburg and van de Port 2008) around the copying of the image of Aparecida. 'Politics of authentication' refers to processes and disputes that always surround claims of originality and authenticity. The concept is an attempt to avoid the naturalization of those claims, looking at the social forces that enable objects, as well as places, habits, rituals or experiences, to claim authenticity, presenting themselves as the 'real thing'.

In Aparecida, the National Shrine produces what they call 'original copies' of the statue in the niche. These perfect resin copies of the original statue found in the river bear a seal of 'official product' and a certificate of authenticity provided by the National Shrine (see fig. 10.4 and 10.5). These

Figures 10.4. Official image with certificate of authenticity and view of images displayed in a shop. Photo: João Rickli.

Figure 10.5. A second official image with certificate of authenticity and view of images displayed in a shop. Photo: João Rickli.

expensive facsimiles of the image are sold only at the official shrine shop. The shop attendants advertise them as being made in Italy. The perfection of the resemblance to the original seems to be an important aesthetic quality of those objects mobilized by the authority of the National Shrine in the politics of authentication. Their high value, expressed in their prices and exclusivity, is linked to their official recognition as an authorized copy. The reference to their Italian origins adds some overtones to this discourse of trustworthiness, officiousness and orthodoxy.

Some of these 'original copies' occupy prestigious positions in the Aparecida cult, inspiring people's worship and devoted feelings. They are used as substitutes for the original image in pilgrimages, masses and blessing ceremonies, as well as on the main altar of the Old Basilica. Unlike the original statue, which never leaves its niche behind thick bulletproof glass, these replicas are closer to the devotees' bodies, occasionally even being touched by them. Some of them have special names, such as 'Our Lady of Aparecida, the Pilgrim', which travels around Brazil, visiting local parishes.

Contrasting with these official modes of authentication and valuation, resemblance and officiousness are lesser criteria in the immense variety of copies found in the religious shops and booths that are jumbled around the Old and New Basilicas. These comprise the absolute majority of images and objects that circulate around Aparecida's shrine. Statues in all imaginable materials (plaster, plastic, resin and wood are the most common) and sizes, prints (posters and postcards, mainly) and all kinds of objects decorated with the image of Aparecida (mugs, glasses, umbrellas, key rings, flip-flops, T-shirts and so on) are among the most common items the devotees can buy at the city. Most of these are made in China. Aparecida is depicted in many different forms with many variations of the 'blue-triangle-with-a-crown' theme: with short or long hair, with visible hands or not, white or black skin, wearing a Rosary around her neck or not and so on.

These cheap, mass-produced images and gadgets are the most common type of objects brought to the blessing ceremonies in the Basilicas. Although most of them refer somehow to the shape of Aparecida, they are not valued according to the perfection of their resemblance to the image in the niche. Their value seems to be associated with their capacity to become part of broader narratives and performances building on the relationship between the devotees and the saint. They become valuable insofar as they circulate around Aparecida together with their new owners as a token of their pilgrimage, receiving Aparecida's blessings within the walls of the Mother's house, travelling back home and, very often, becoming gifts to relatives or friends. Their transition from a simple, often cheap, commodity into a valuable vehicle of Aparecida's power with transformative potential is not a result of their level of resemblance to the original image, or the existence of an official seal and a certificate of authenticity. It is the relationship established between object and devotee, their common movements and experiences in the Mother's house, their copresence in devotional practices open to dynamics of creativity and improvisation that produce their value and efficacy.

Conclusion

This chapter analysed dynamics of creativity implied in the production and circulation of images, objects and people around the devotion to Our Lady of Aparecida. It analysed the relation between aesthetics and power implied in transformative encounters and interactions between different subjects and objects that are constantly moving around the National Shrine, in the city of Aparecida. Taking creativity as a complex social process, the chapter analysed the aestheticization of devotional practices associated with the saint as the result of the interplay of various actors, articulating popular faith, official views of the Catholic Church and national discourses.

Firstly, the chapter demonstrated how the transitions of Aparecida's image through time reflect and act upon narratives of the Brazilian nation, showing how Aparecida's national character is produced in the complex interplay between the Brazilian state and transnational and local forms of Catholicism. Secondly, it analysed the circulation of people and objects around the city of Aparecida, describing them in terms of centripetal and centrifugal movements. The description of ritual practices and discourses that take place at the National Shrine allowed the comprehension of the original image enthroned in the Basilica as the centre that orients the movement of people and objects involved in the cult. Finally, the chapter approached the politics of authentication at issue in the shrine, describing how official authority to authenticate images and objects contrasts with devotees' experiences of authentication through particular interactions with the saint.

Combining the images of a careful mother and a powerful queen, Aparecida is successful in mobilizing popular faith and devotion and the official images and practices authorized by the Catholic hierarchy. The aesthetic qualities of the image – triangular shape, dark skin, blue cloak, crown and flags – articulate important aspects of Brazilian nationhood and Catholic faith. The variety of narratives, movements and objects that orbit around her powerful image establishes the devotion to Aparecida as an official, popular and powerful aesthetic formation.

João Rickli is a lecturer at the Federal University of Paraná (UFPR), in Brazil. He defended his PhD in 2010 at VU University Amsterdam, doing research on missionary and development cooperation initiatives by Dutch

Protestants in Brazil. Recent publications include a contribution to the edited volume *Encounters of Body and Soul in Contemporary Religious Practices: Anthropological Reflections* (Berghahn Books, 2011) and articles in the Brazilian journals, *Vibrant* (2012) and *Religião & Sociedade* (2015).

Notes

1. I would like to express my deepest gratitude to Maruška Svašek, Birgit Meyer, Rhoda Woets and all the other members of the Creativity and Innovation in a World of Movement project for their collaboration and discussions on my research. I would also like to thank Maria Paula Adinolfi, André Bakker, Alexandra Grieser, José Rogério Lopes, Stella Pieve, Kodjo Senah, Irene Stengs and Marleen de Witte for their comments and suggestions.
2. This summarized version of the narrative is based on Father Julio Brustoloni's historical account (1998). Brustoloni is a Redemptorist Father with academic training in history who works at Aparecida's shrine.
3. See also the National Shrine's digital press kit, http://www.a12.com/santuario/imprensa/presskit.asp.
4. The notion of 'Brazilian popular Catholicism' refers to a large and diverse range of more or less syncretic practices and beliefs developed by Catholic believers on the margins of the official Catholic creed and liturgy. Despite its importance and frequent use in the literature on Brazilian Catholicism, seldom has the notion been rigorously and systematically defined. One of the most sophisticated and convincing attempts to conceptualize the field of Brazilian popular Catholicism is Velho's definition of 'biblical culture' (1987). For more recent developments of Velho's analysis, see Steil (1996) and Lopes (2010).
5. The decision to focus on devotional practices directly related to the National Shrine was strategic in seeking to examine the interplay between the official authorized views of the Catholic hierarchy and the beliefs and feelings of the devotees. This choice, however, does not mean that I overlook the existence of other religious and political practices linked to Aparecida, which have little or no connections to the type of process I analyse here. Remarkable examples of these practices can be found in the constant references to the image of Aparecida in Afro-Brazilian religious groups, often associated to the feminine deity Oxum.
6. Santos's analysis, which focuses on the production of images of Aparecida as a result of determined social and political contexts, was very useful in comprehending the transitions and transformations of the image in different historical times. In this chapter, however, I reinterpret part of Santos's material from a different theoretical point of view, focusing on the process of aestheticization of the image and the dynamics of creativity implied in its transformations through time.
7. For a comprehensive historical analysis of Romanization in Brazil between 1850 and 1930, see Groot (1996). Hoornaert's (1991: 129–153) book explores some of the implications of this process for the so-called popular Catholicism.
8. For a detailed ethnographic study of the devotions to Bom Jesus da Lapa and Father Cícero, see Steil (1996) and Braga (2007), respectively.

9. For an analytical account of the recent changes in the name of the room that accommodates the *ex-voto* collection, see Souza (2012: 65–70).
10. Souza's dissertation (2012) presents a detailed study of the curatorial practices in the *ex-voto* room. She contrasts the choice and disposition of the objects in the Room of Promises with documents and interviews with its managers, pointing out the connections and discrepancies between the way the collection is exhibited and the messages their curators intend to convey.

References

Braga, A. 2007 'Padre Cícero: sociologia de um padre, antropologia de um santo', PhD dissertation, University of Rio Grande do Sul, Porto Alegre.

Bruneau, T. 1974. *Catolicismo Brasileiro em Época de Transição.* São Paulo: Loyola.

Brustoloni, J. J. 1998. *Nossa Senhora Aparecida: sua Imagem e seu Santuário.* Aparecida: Editora Santuário.

Carvalho, J. M. 2001. *A Formação das Almas: o Imaginário da República no Brasil.* São Paulo: Companhia das Letras.

Della Cava, R. 1975. 'Igreja e Estado no Brasil do Século XX: Sete Monografias Recentes sobre o Catolicismo Brasileiro 1916/64', *Estudos Cebrap* 12: 7–52.

Groot, K. 1996. *Brazilian Catholicism and the Ultramontane Reform, 1850–1930.* Amsterdam: CEDLA.

Hoornaert, E. 1991. *O Cristianismo Moreno do Brasil.* Petrópolis: Vozes.

Knott, K. 2005. *The Location of Religion: A Spatial Analysis.* London: Equinox.

Lopes, J. R. 2010. *A Imagética da Devoção: a Iconografia Popular como Mediação entre a Consciência da Realidade e o Ethos Religioso.* Porto Alegre: Editora da UFRGS.

Meyer, B. (ed.). 2009. *Aesthetic Formations: Media, Religion and the Senses.* New York: Palgrave.

Meyer, B., H. Roodenburg and M. van de Port. 2008. 'Heritage Dynamics: Politics of Authentication and Aesthetics of Persuasion in Ghana, South Africa, Brazil and the Netherlands', NWO research proposal.

Santos, L. 2000. 'Igreja, Nacionalismo e Devoção Popular: as Estampas de Nossa Senhora Aparecida 1854–1978', PhD dissertation, University of São Paulo.

Souza, B. G. 2012. 'A Documentação da Fé: Fluxos, Apropriações e Enquadramentos de Objetos Votivos no Santuário Nacional de Aparecida', PhD dissertation, University of the State São Paulo, Marília.

Steil, C. A. 1996. *O Sertão das Romarias: um Estudo Antropológico sobre o Santuário de Bom Jesus da Lapa – Bahia.* Petrópolis: Vozes.

Svašek, M. 2007. *Anthropology, Art and Cultural Production.* London: Pluto Press.

———. 2010. 'Improvising a World in Movement: Transit, Transition and Transformation', in H. K. Anheier and Y. R. Isar (eds), *Cultural Expression: Creativity and Innovation.* London: Sage, 62–77.

Tweed, T. A. 2006. *Crossing and Dwelling: A Theory of Religion.* Cambridge, MA: Harvard University Press.

Velho, O. 1987. 'O Cativeiro da Besta Fera', *Religião e Sociedade* 14(1): 4–27.

11

THE ART OF IMITATION
THE (RE)PRODUCTION AND RECEPTION
OF JESUS PICTURES IN GHANA

———————◆••◆••◆———————

Rhoda Woets

Jesus pictures have successfully colonized the public and private domain in the predominantly Christian South of Ghana. In the 1990s, in a period of democratization and liberalization of the mass media in Ghana, mass-produced posters and stickers with depictions of Jesus flooded urban markets (fig. 11.1). Jesus motifs (re)appear on walls, billboard advertisements, funeral wreaths, clocks and more. Mass media allowed for a duplication and spread of Christian motifs on an unprecedented scale, reaching ever more religious believers (Meyer 2008: 103). Most mass-produced Jesus posters and objects are made in China or Nigeria and have been brought to Ghana through a network of Nigerian traders. The majority of these pictures are modelled after Leonardo da Vinci's *Last Supper* (1498), Pompeo Batoni's *Sacred Heart* (1767) or Warner Sallman's *Head of Christ* (1941). Through missionaries, and later commercial entrepreneurs, such paintings transited by means of mechanical reproduction: as they moved through time and space, their meaning, value and emotional efficacy changed in transition (on transit, transition and transformation, cf. Svašek 2012: 2–3). Locally printed and hand-painted Jesus motifs on canvas or plywood, canoes, wax-print fabrics, t-shirts or calendars are also common sights in the public arena. Visual artists and designers transform existing religious imagery by appropriating and remediating it into new forms (see Svašek 2012:5). What this means is that new depictions of Jesus, produced inside and outside Ghana's

Figure 11.1. Poster-seller, Accra, June 2011. Photo: Rhoda Woets.

borders, are constantly added to the corpus, forming a chain of reproductions that resonate with each other.

The various materializations of Jesus and their power and appeal in Ghana's social and religious settings have a lot to say about the complex relation between art and religion. In this chapter, I explore both mass-produced and handmade pictures of Jesus in urban Ghana, considering how both formally and informally trained artists remediate Jesus motifs and how Christians engage with mass-printed and indigenous representations of Jesus in processes of creativity, reproduction and appropriation. I view creativity not as an individual affair, but rather as a collective activity that takes place in a social field of producers and consumers who are bonded by social relations of power and interdependency (Bourdieu 1993; Hallem and Ingold 2007; Becker 2008). It is, therefore, necessary to take into account the constitutive relations between producers, objects and users. The focus on a single material object in its various manifestations connects producers and users in multiple spatial and social settings, shedding light on connections that would otherwise be missed.

Copying, derived from the Latin *copia,* meaning abundance or multitude, has lost its positive connotations in the course of history. Copying became associated with deception, fakery and plagiarism and was positioned as opposing the real, original, genuine or authentic. This dualism rests on the belief that it is always possible to identify the original and, hence, the imitation (Boon 2010). Marcus Boon argues in his thought-proving book *In Praise of Copying* that the dichotomization of original and copy is a false opposition that calls for deconstruction. 'Phenomena that involve copying are everywhere', he writes: 'they are a crucial factor in our ability to make sense of ourselves and the world' (2010: 9–10). Through colonialism, trade and Western economic dominance, an understanding of copying as opposed to originality spread globally. Ethnographic evidence presented in this chapter, however, shows firstly that conventional understandings of creativity and copying as mutually exclusive categories did not take firm root in workshops along urban roadsides in Ghana; and secondly that aesthetic recycling and creativity interact and operate on several levels, both in popular Christianity and art-making in the country.

Most studies of the development of an African Christology pay little attention to different materializations of Jesus in pictures and their modes of use (cf. Sarpong 2002; Stinton 2004). I regard this as a major shortcoming. After all, religious belief does not exist in an isolated discursive space; religion works and gains meaning in daily, lived practices and behaviour (Meyer 1999; Morgan 1999). The 'pictorial turn' since the late 1980s has rediscovered the relational agency of material objects and the power that pictures exert over humans (Freedberg 1989; Mitchell 2005). Objects are agents with a transformative power to influence people's emotions, moods and actions in a mutually constitutive relationship (Svašek 2012: 20). It is in this relationship that pictures evoke particular bodily sensations ranging from empathy to fear. While the production and use of Jesus pictures in Ghana takes place in a historical-social setting that stretches out beyond the local, little work has been done in this field outside Europe and the United States (see Magowan and Øien, this volume). In Ghana, religious engagement with Christian objects harks back to a long history of activity in the area, the encounter with mission organizations and the rising popularity of Charismatic-Pentecostal churches since the 1990s. A sociohistorical embedding of pictures creates a deeper understanding of the ongoing entanglement of the 'local' and the 'global' at the nexus of art and religion.

Creativity involves the human ability to make meaning of the material world through the senses. I will first highlight the social settings in which mass-produced pictures of Jesus operate in Ghana to catalyse people's creative engagement with pictures through practices of mediation, as well as the ambivalent attitude towards pictures in popular Christianity. This consideration of the setting will provide a context from which to understand and analyse the (re)production, appropriation and reception of handmade interpretations of Jesus.[1]

Engagement with Jesus Pictures in Daily Life
through Repetition and Creativity

In Ghana, approximately 70 per cent of the population categorize themselves as Christians. They belong to a myriad of churches and denominations, the fastest-growing of which are the Pentecostal-Charismatic churches that have boomed over the last twenty years (Gifford 2004; Asamoah-Gyadu 2005; de Witte 2008). Interestingly, Christians of all denominations display mass-produced Jesus posters and stickers on the walls of shops and homes, on car windows, fridges and so on.

While Jesus pictures are omnipresent in urban Ghana, they are subject to contestations indicative of religious rivalry over the appropriate media to make the transcendent visible. Many Protestants and Charismatic Pentecostals, influenced by the iconophobic stance of their religious leadership, regard the use pictures in prayer as 'idol worship' (Meyer 2011a: 1044). The understanding of 'idol' worship was used by missionaries to legitimize 'modern' Christianity as superior to the 'primitive' beliefs of Africans (Meyer 1999, 2008, 2010). Catholic missionaries brought religious pictures and statues from Europe with the aim of replacing (mental) images of local gods with a single Christian God, thereby suggesting that the two were mutually exclusive. Protestant missionaries, in turn, accused Catholic missionaries in the Gold Coast of 'idol' worship for the use of pictures and statues of saints in prayer. This notion recurs in current contestations between Ghanaian Catholics and Protestants over the use of religious objects in prayer. This does not stop many non-Catholic Christians from an attentive look or short prayer at a Jesus poster in the hall, lounge or bedroom before they leave the house, to guarantee a safe return. For some Catholics, simultaneously and paradoxically, the repetitive engagement with Christian imagery is intended to counter the constant danger of slipping 'back' into practices of 'idol-worship'. The danger of slipping 'back' into idolatry is felt as real in a society where 'traditional' religious practices might have been be pushed into the social margins but are also very much alive: both in designated spaces such as shrines, as well as in the imagination shaped by sensational pictures and stories in popular newspapers and films (de Witte 2008). As one Catholic street seller told me, in praise of his merchandise (plastic glow-in-the-dark statues of Mary and Jesus): 'These statues remind us that we should not fall back into the behaviour of our forefathers and get up at night to find ourselves worshipping trees.'

These contrasting understandings of 'idolatry' show how, in the South of Ghana, similar reproductions of Jesus pictures are subjected to interrelated, though opposing interpretations: they are seen by some as 'idol' worship and by others as a tool against such practices. The same argument can be made in relation to narratives in which popular Jesus pictures are reproduced. In such narratives, the same type of picture is used to make opposing claims that either confirm or deny the spiritual power of religious pictures. In Appadurai's (1986) terms, a single picture leads parallel, interconnected social lives. In narrative performances, people assign different roles to Jesus pictures in order to communicate different moral messages. What this means is that the narrative reproduction of the same picture does not put a stop to processes of creative engagement and appropriation. Christians in Ghana give meaningful interpretations to pictures in daily rituals, narratives and dreams as part of a creative process that involves the Christian imagination.

Let me give two examples of narratives in which popular Jesus posters are subjected to opposing interpretations. John, a man in his fifties who sold lottery tickets from a wooden booth on the streets of Accra, told me about a former 'witch' who testified in his Pentecostal church as to how she spiritually penetrated the home of a Christian woman with the intention of subjecting the woman's sleeping body to her demonic will. When the witch's eye fell on a Jesus poster on the wall, she immediately surrendered to Christ and became born again. What this means is that the Christian victim was not defenceless against witchcraft, even when fast asleep; the picture above her bed was fuelled with holy power, able to stop any demonic attack. John's story suggests that Jesus sees everything, watches over people and actively intervenes to rescue both victim and perpetrator. In the process of conversion to Christianity, local gods have been appropriated as helpers of Satan (Meyer 1999) who have the power to take possession of objects and bodies. Human bodies that are held to be possessed by demons or bad spirits become Satan's assistants as 'witches' or 'wizards'. Overall, there exists a shared popular Christianity in Ghana in which material objects, such as Jesus posters and stickers, offer some kind of spiritual protection against witchcraft.[2] The educated elite, in contrast, often associate belief in witchcraft with superstition, cultural backwardness or psychological infantilism (Assimeng 2010: 169).

Baptist Pastor Eric, a man in his twenties, conversely argued that posters of Jesus, as material objects, were never filled with spiritual power. He nevertheless did not view Jesus posters as void commodities, as he vividly illustrated with a past experience. Pastor Eric once shook hands with a church member in a town on Ghana's west coast. Instantly, as the pastor related, he received a divine revelation that showed him a mass-produced poster of Jesus in the man's living room. Pastor Eric realized that this poster was possessed and subsequently prayed intensely with the man to break the demonic spell. When the two men arrived at the house, the poster had vanished from the wall. 'The devil had taken it back', Pastor Eric explained. In the context of the growing popularity of Pentecostalism in Ghana, global commodities may not be experienced as innocent material goods, but as potentially animated and dangerous (Meyer 1998). In both narratives, popular pictures of Jesus played a role in producing evidence of God's power over Satan. In John's story, this happened through the presence of a Jesus picture in the bedroom, while in Pastor Eric's account it was rather through the *absence* of the picture. This shows how 'sameness' in terms of visual form, does not lead to a similar understanding of what mass-produced Jesus pictures mean and do. Furthermore, the fact that Christians in Ghana use cheap reproductions does not seem to detract from their persuasive, transformative power (cf. Rickli, this volume), showing the untenability of Walter Benjamin's assertion that only original works of art possess a magical aura, and that it is this quality that is lost in mechanical reproductions (Meyer 2011a: 1047).

How then are mass-produced pictures imbued with an aura? It is through active, sensorial engagement with religious objects that (new) meaning and value is created. My respondents did not consider posters to be already loaded with spiritual power when sold in bulk on the market. Rather, material objects move from the domain of the profane to the sacred through repeated modes of worship and invitation. Believers build up a personal, intimate relationship with mass-produced objects through bodily and sensory regimes of piety that involve touch, intense prayer, singing, blessing and talking to the object. Creative engagement with pictures engenders some sense of agency, just as much as it requires agency to make pictures affective and effective. One Pentecostal woman in her thirties said, for example, 'When I buy a poster at the market, it is only a piece of paper. It is through your faith that the poster works, when you believe it.'

Through constant repetition, rituals such as praying in front of Jesus pictures become internalized and 'automatically' generate wanted bodily affects such as being drawn closer to the divine. Through repeated engagement with pictures, Christians strengthen attachments to their faith, and with each other. Mary, a seamstress, told me that, much to her regret, she had to give up on her daily visits to a Mary statue in the compound of a church in central Accra. As a consequence, Mary said, she felt 'a distance between me and my God'. Sensorial experiences become familiar through repetition and create a sense of agency that enhances the experienced control over one's life and counters feelings of disempowerment (Svašek 2012: 28). When Mary became cut off from the statue that acted as a powerful medium, she lost that sense of agency. Since that day, Mary said, God had stopped sending her portentous dreams that had served her in the past as a source of direction and warning. Another example of how Christians creatively engage with pictures is when popular motifs of Jesus merge in dreams and visions from being mere material into the 'real' thing. Christians who encountered Jesus in visionary experiences and dreams always said that he looked 'as in the pictures'. Such encounters with Jesus are a remediation of the omnipresent pictures that require imagination and come with an interesting paradox. For Christians, such narratives serve as proof of the validity of mass-produced pictures scattered across city markets, while somewhat contradictorily also confirming the idea that Jesus is so holy that he can never be fully captured by human hand. What most narratives boiled down to is that material pictures sink into insignificance compared to the dazzling beauty of Jesus in dreams and reveries.

As many Christians regard pictures of Jesus as a substitute for his absent body, they require pictures that look 'true' in order to be powerful. One afternoon in June 2011, I showed Lydia, a trader and member of the Saviour Church of Ghana, a photograph of a painting carried out by the well-known painter Kobina Bucknor (1925–1972). In 1968, Bucknor painted an African Jesus majestically seated upon a ceremonial wooden stool, wearing a valuable handwoven Kente cloth and royal sandals, reserved for noble people such as chiefs (fig. 11.2). The painting was commissioned by the American Father Harold Lauck, who came to the Gold Coast in 1941 from Illinois (Elsbernd 2000:252). The 'Ghanaization' of Christ's looks and clothing in Bucknor's painting meshed well with the amendments of the Second Vatican in 1965 that called for the appropriation of local cultural practices into the Catholic Church. The painting is still on display in the interior of the Christ the King Church in Accra. Looking at the picture with a mixture of surprise and irritation, Lydia responded: 'How can Jesus be black? The devil is black!' Pictures are historically transmitted through acts of appropriation, and pictures of Jesus have been circulating in Ghana since the first European traders and missionaries set foot on the African west coast from the fifteenth century onwards. As these pictures have been present in the Gold Coast and Ghana for a long period, they have become a yardstick for what Jesus must have looked like. People want pictures of a bearded Jesus with long, wavy hair and clad in a cloth, simply because they experience such representations as historically accurate. This does not mean that they are: most popular pictures in Ghana hark back to paintings that emerged in response to particular spatial and temporal conditions in Europe and North America. Ghanaian Christians require reproductions of images that have gained worldwide popularity because recognition plays a central role in the spiritual efficacy of the image. 'As long as it looks like Jesus' was the answer I got from Christians when I inquired after their personal preferences in pictures. People reach out to the wider world and aim to connect to that world in search of social mobility and resources, which also partly explains the tremendous popularity of international Pentecostal churches. Christians in Ghana connect to a wider, global community through the use of pictures that transcend the local context and thus symbolize global connectivity (see Meyer 2011a: 1045).

Figure 11.2. Kobina Bucknor (1968), title unknown, acrylic polymers on board. Christ the King Church in Accra. Photo: Rhoda Woets.

This does not mean that an African Jesus does not strike a chord with Christians. One young man I met in front of Kobina Bucknor's painting said: 'The bible says that God created man in his own image and this painting expresses that very well.' This painting was met with praise by the young man for being, in his view, a reproduction, not of an illustrious European painting of Jesus, but of the 'African self'. This remark must be seen in light of theological discussions on the formulation of an African Christology. Some African and African American intellectuals and theologians view the portrayal of Jesus as white, and the devil as black, as a racist confirmation of white superiority (see Pobee 1992). The same painting engendered opposing sensations: while for the young man, the painting symbolized proximity, other Christians found a black Jesus in Kente cloth to be distant from them. The meaning of pictures is not fixed at the moment of fabrication and is subject to changing meanings that are 'constructed for them through human agency' (Steiner 2001: 210). As stated before, most 'ordinary' Christians are more interested in an alternative form of reproduction, one that stays close to popular material pictures.

Repetition and remediation operate on several levels in the use of, and engagement with, mass-produced pictures. In the first, pictures become affective on the condition of repeated engagement. Secondly, pictures are remediated in narratives and visionary experiences, shaped and informed by the Christian imagination. And thirdly, Christians require reproductions of familiar pictures, as recognition is paramount in generating spiritual presence and emotional efficacy.

Formally and Informally Trained Artists: In Praise or Dislike of Copying

Hand-painted pictures, as well as wooden or cement statues of Jesus, are made in workshops along the road by artists trained through an apprenticeship system. I refer to them as informally trained or wayside artists, the latter term referring to the location of production. These paintings and sculptures of Jesus are often reinterpretations of the mass-produced posters and stickers in the market place. Artists who received their training in an official art school or at the university opt for depictions of Jesus that clearly deviate from popular examples. In fact, their work is often a reaction against the mass-produced pictures that 'ordinary' Christians buy and display.

In the Ghanaian art world, formally and informally trained artists maintain distinct notions of creativity and imitation that directly and indirectly shape their work. Academically trained artists tend to discard the Jesus pictures or statues made by wayside artists as 'uncreative' or mere 'copies.' They position imitation or copying as a practice that opposes creativity. Creativity, in turn, is seen as deriving from an inborn talent to make work that is 'beautiful', original and personal, a definition that was introduced in the Gold Coast by European teachers during colonial times and taken over by the pioneering generation of modern artists (Woets 2011). To speak of wayside artists as 'uncreative' copycats, as formally trained artists generally do, must be seen as an act of social positioning that reproduces social inequalities in the local, historically constituted hierarchy of art in Ghana. As I will demonstrate, all makers of Jesus pictures in Ghana are involved in a process of creativity: the graphic designer who uses Photoshop to rearrange various Internet pictures of Jesus into a collage for a calendar, the wayside artist who meticulously replicates a picture on canvas or plywood and the formally trained artist who strives for an individual reinterpretation of conventional Jesus pictures. Creativity is a process that involves the appropriation and adjustment of existing material into new objects that serve new purposes or modes of use (Hallam and Ingold 2007). This means that sameness in form does not say much about the meaning and value that reproductions acquire in new social settings. The novelty of the end-product varies according to the artist's notions of what art is, and his or her intentions regarding the work.

I will now turn to different paintings of Jesus and their makers. At question is how artists quote from selected ideas, symbols and imagery and to what end. A related issue is how these paintings appeal to beholders, or fail to do so.

Rikki Wemega-Kwawu: Overcoming Cultural Alienation and Economic Dependency

Rikki Wemega-Kwawu (b. 1959) drew a pastel portrait of a black Jesus with naked torso in 1981 (fig. 11.3). The Jesus portrait is informed by the artist's 'Rembrandt phase', which found expression in the sharp contrast between light and dark, with light coming from a single source (*chiara-oscuro*). The portrait was commissioned by the Brothers of the Holy Cross who came to Ghana from Indiana in the United States to decorate one of the convent walls. I discussed this impressive portrait with Wemega-Kwawu in his home in Takoradi in March 2012. In April 2012, he posted a message on my Facebook wall; in an excellent summary of the arguments that he made during our interview, he wrote:

> The Holy Cross Brothers thought – and I share fully in their philosophy – that it was about time the African identified himself/herself with Jesus as a Blackman. The African continually seeing his Saviour, Jesus Christ, as a Whiteman had an adverse effect on the consciousness of his being, thereby robbing the African of all initiative to want to take his destiny fully into his hands. The African continues to look up to the Whiteman for everything, for his salvation and economic sustenance, long, long after Colonialism. It appears the African is in a state of mental stupor.

What the painter argues here is that the omnipresent pictures of a white Jesus are a remnant of colonial history. Only when people stop turning for

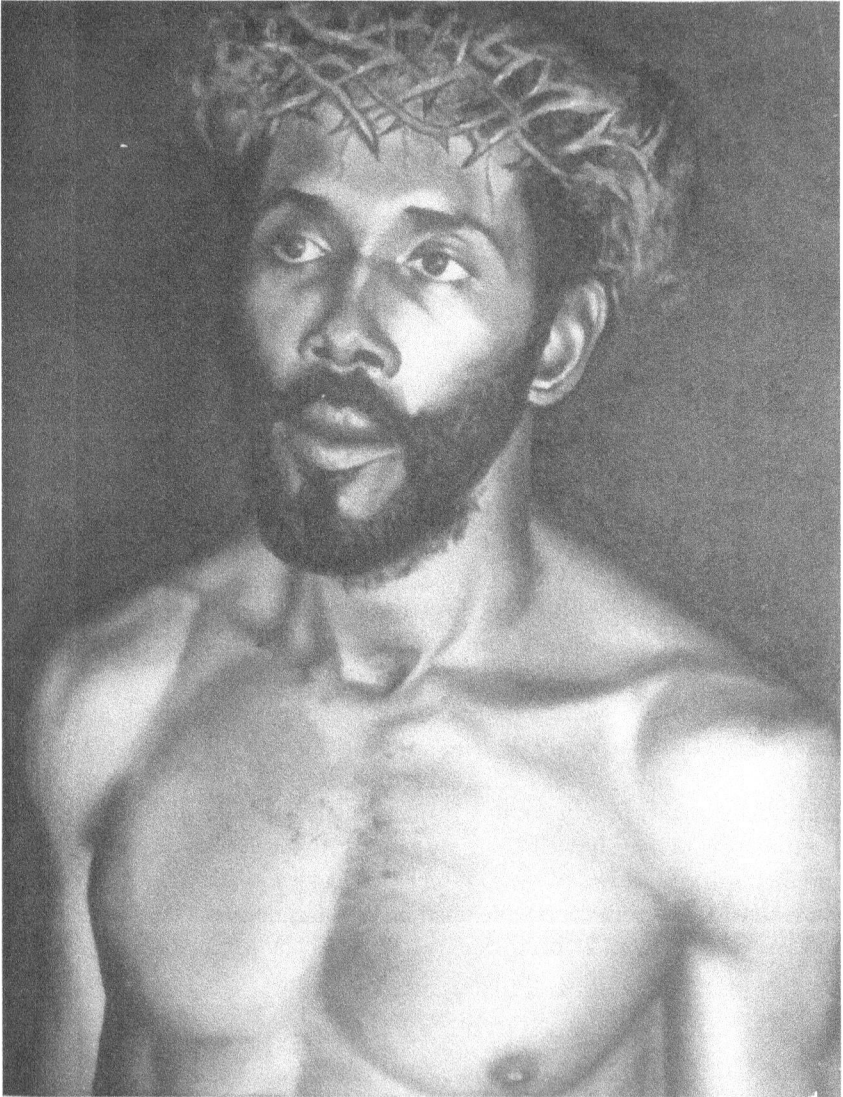

Figure 11.3. Rikki Wemega-Kwawu (1981), *What More Could I Have Done for You ... ?* pastel on pastel paper. Photo: Rhoda Woets.

assistance to a Caucasian Jesus and Western donors, seeking salvation out-side their own culture and country, he argued, will they be freed from mental colonization and become active, confident and independent. And as long as people put faith, not in themselves, but in things foreign, they will be locked into an inferiority complex. This political message was at the forefront of

Wemega-Kwawu's intentions: he is not interested in making soothing portraits of Jesus that are used to provide access to the transcendent in religious practice and desire.

Wemega-Kwawu's statement shows how feelings of cultural alienation as voiced by Kwame Nkrumah and intellectual elites in the construction of the Ghanaian nation-state resonated in Wemega-Kwawu's work. Nkrumah wanted to turn perceptions upside down by showing that Africans were perfectly capable of managing their own affairs in a modern and 'African' way. Wemega-Kwawu adapted the idea of the colonized mind to the situation of dependency on foreign loans and neocapitalist institutions such as the IMF. Wemega-Kwawu, however, did not feel the need to employ markers from 'traditional' Ghanaian culture, as Kobina Bucknor had done. The notion that Ghanaian artists should work around a shared cultural past lost its meaning for many artists after Nkrumah's downfall, after which state power shifted repeatedly between alternating military and democratic regimes.

The Brothers of the Holy Cross were so delighted with the end result that they made prints and postcards of the portrait, which were sent around the world. Wemega-Kwawu mentioned with pride that one print was sent to the Papal office in Rome. As an alternative technology of mediation, the printed postcards differed in meaning and value from the pastel drawing. The original portrait was displayed in the convent as an indigenous Christian artwork, where it remained confined to its place on the wall, only visible to the eyes of Brothers and their visitors. The postcards travelled, as Christmas cards, to a Catholic network of convents, functioning as a ritual greeting. The postcards were a means of strengthening attachments with fellow convents, marking the American Brothers as active proponents of enculturation and signalling their good taste in Christian art. The political message of enduring economic dependency on foreign loans was lost on its way to locations such as the Pope's office. Instead, recipients might have taken the postcard as representative of what Jesus looks like in Ghana. Interestingly, while Wemega-Kwawu's Jesus portrait circulated globally as a new motif, facilitated by mass production, it is not representative of the type of pictures that dominate Ghana's public space.

Wemega-Kwawu selected his friend and fellow artist Ato Mensah to model for the portrait, as his long face and beard resembled that of Jesus in conventional European depictions that had become the blueprint for Jesus's appearance for artists and patrons all over the world. In rejecting such pictures, Wemega-Kwawu needed to base his own representation precisely on those depictions that he claimed to oppose. Something else that set Wemega-Kwawu's portrait apart from conventional Jesus pictures was his model's muscular build. Wemega-Kwawu did not feel the need to adapt the torso in his portrait to the common image of a lean Jesus. Jesus was, after all, he said, the son of a carpenter and used to heavy work. Above all, Jesus showed physical strength by carrying his own cross. While Wemega-Kwawu's portrait was well received by the Brothers and the artist's friends, Roger Gocking writes of how a number of Christians were scandalized by the muscularity and nudeness of Jesus when he showed them the postcard (2009: 311). Attracted as they are by the tender, soft face in pictures that feature Jesus as a loving friend or father, they did not understand a critique of Jesus's 'feminine' appearance. Wemega-Kwawu's Jesus materialized in relation to his political and artistic ideas as well as his exchange with American Brothers in favour of indigenous representations. Many, but not all, 'ordinary' Christians are not interested in an 'original' interpretation of Jesus.

Bernard Akoi-Jackson: Imitation in Challenging the Status Quo

Visual art has a long history of continuous appropriation of materials, techniques, forms and understandings of what art is and what art should do. The idea of the individual artist who creates unique works in isolation has been undermined by avant-garde artists who claim that any work of art involves acts of citation and pastiche. The recycling of globally well-known images is a calculated critique on notions of originality and ownership (Boon 2010: 205). The acrylic painting of the Last Supper, made by multimedia artist Akoi-Jackson (b. 1979), serves as an example of copying as a form of ironic play and an artistic means of challenging established boundaries (fig. 11.4). Akoi-Jackson made this work, which was intended as an exercise in colour, as a third-year student in the Department of Painting and Sculpture at the university in Kumasi.

Akoi-Jackson's work quotes Leonardo da Vinci's world-famous fifteenth-century wall painting in a Milan monastery, appropriating da Vinci's figural arrangement with Jesus in the centre, surrounded by the apostles in groups of three, all behind a long orthogonal table in a room with three windows in the back. Jesus was given more prominence, as Akoi-Jackson made him larger than the apostles and added a halo. In the original painting, the different emotions and reactions evoked by Jesus's statement that one of his followers would soon betray him play a prominent role. In Akoi-Jackson's rendition, the facial expressions are muted, even though the open mouths seem to express surprise and shock. The figures behind the table might first appear as 'African' due to the cubistic style of the work, the decorated bowls on the table and the mask-like faces. On closer inspection, the necks and arms of Jesus and his apostles are white, suggesting that the dinner guests hide behind masks. This work may be seen as evidence for my argument that copying is part of a creative process in which an artist selects particular

Figure 11.4. Bernard Akoi-Jackson (2002–2003), *Wobole Kutu Wokpe* (Together We Sit to Eat), acrylic on canvas. Photo: courtesy Bernard Akoi-Jackson.

forms that he or she rearranges, changes, adapts or distorts in creating new meanings.

In an interview in May 2011, Akoi-Jackson told me that the coloured jumpers and abundant colours in the background symbolize the global significance of Jesus. This view was taken further by the artist in 2011 when a print of this painting served as a backdrop for a performance at the opening of an art exhibition in Accra. Clothed in a red to attract attention, the artist handed out food associated with various national kitchens: Ghanaian *yam oto,*[3] Lebanese pita bread and, in referencing the Eucharist, French wine. When objects and ritual performance move from one social setting to the next, the perceived meaning and value changes (cf. Svašek 2012: 3). Through the reproduction of the well-known religious ritual in a secular context, the artist seems to question the well-established boundary between contemporary art and Christianity, between the space of the gallery and the church. Akoi-Jackson seems to wonder if the Eucharist, as an act of sharing and social bonding, can be celebrated outside designated sacred spaces. By guiding the ritual and donning a cloth, Akoi-Jackson probes if people can become priests simply by acting and dressing up as one. Imitation operates here as an artistic strategy to discuss notions of (in)authenticity and transgress established boundaries that most people take for granted.

Akoi-Jackson's work convincingly shows how aesthetic repetition can be part of ironic play. Through imitation, the artist played with the worldview of many Christians in Ghana who experience pictures of a bearded man in a long cloth as a true depiction of Jesus. Cheap reproductions of da Vinci's Last Supper enjoy great popularity in Ghana and are sold by street hawkers and in Catholic shops. Akoi-Jackson referenced da Vinci's popular painting in showing that every picture is mediated and needs to be seen in the light of spatial and temporal dimensions. He explained that Leonardo da Vinci, being an Italian painter in the fifteenth century, made Jesus and his apostles look Italian. He subsequently played with the question of what kind of ritual food would have been on the table if Jesus had lived in Ghana, as well as what kind of ritual clothes would be worn for such an occasion. Facial paintings, as well as white cloths, are employed in rituals in Ghana where they symbolize victory and spiritual purity or sacredness.

While popular pictures comfortingly speak of what the devout viewer already knows (Morgan 1999: 150), Akoi-Jackson deliberately gives the viewers of his painting the wrong end of the stick. The artist plays with repetition, both in his painting and corresponding performance, to challenge the status quo, call into question the relation between sign and referent and thus create confusion. In popular pictures, by contrast, there is a complete correspondence between sign and referent, as the two are knit 'together in a seamless joint' (ibid.). In this painting the artist destabilizes and disturbs common conceptions of the Last Supper to which Christians in Ghana are attached. Wayside artists, by contrast, opt for reassuring pictures and statues that confirm Christian values. They do not generally seek to overturn the existing order or to challenge the status quo, as some officially trained artists do. Nevertheless, as I will now show, the boundary between formally and informally trained artists is not always clear-cut.

Wayside Artists: The Art of Quoting

Painting workshops along urban roadsides take commissions from local and foreign clients to paint signboards and portraits, to decorate cars and print banners or t-shirts. Painters advertise their workshops by lining up portraits of local and international celebrities, revealing their merit and talent to people passing by. These paintings function as advertisements that show how well the 'master', as the proprietor of the workshop is known, repaints photographs. At urban roadsides, Jesus is one of those stars of Ghanaian popular culture alongside local and international celebrities such as Barack Obama, Kofi Anan or rapper 50 Cent, to name a few. Apart from paintings, there are a number of workshops that specialize in making religious statues from either wood or wire and cement.

Before mass printing became widely available in Ghana in the 1990s, wayside painters were occasionally commissioned to paint Jesus portraits for churches and private homes. Nowadays they can no longer compete with the cheap reproductions that are sold by street hawkers. Portraits of Jesus thus mainly function as enticing advertisements for the workshop that made them. New technologies of reproduction inform the ways in which objects are shaped and transmitted (Meyer 2011b: 28). The Internet, specifically images from Yahoo and Google, provide wayside painters and designers with an endless pool of different Jesus pictures to choose and quote from, bringing ever more different depictions of Jesus into circulation. Painter Gilbert Forson downloaded Jesus pictures of his liking in an Internet café, and stored them on his phone. Digital images that circulate globally become remediated as paintings that begin life in a local workshop (Meyer 2011a: 1044). An example of a recent, popular representation that Gilbert Forson used as a motif is based on a still from Mel Gibson's 2004 film *The Passion of the Christ*. I showed a photograph of this painting, which depicts Jesus's face covered in blood, to several Christians. The majority said they were deeply touched by the painting, as it convincingly depicted Jesus's suffering. People who go through hardship strongly identify with pictures of a suffering Jesus and the inherent promise of salvation. 'Bloody' pictures, furthermore, link up with Pentecostal doctrines centred on the blood of Jesus as a powerful substance that frees people from sin and offers protection. Theological doctrines that have bloomed in Ghana since the 1990s are remediated into new representations of Jesus, and these new pictures are in turn experienced as 'true'.

The ability to copy well is considered a virtue and sign of competence for many wayside artists: they take pride in producing a clear resemblance between the original and the reproduction. However, wayside artists value work that result from their own imagination higher than paintings based on pictures taken from newspapers, magazines or the Internet. In that sense, wayside artists define creativity as the talent to paint from the mind's eye, as formally trained artists do. Wayside painter Nicholas T. Wayo emphasized in an informal talk in his studio that his aim is always to *improve* on the original picture. Wayside artists who fail to do so are not creative, he said. Wayside painters reproduce found pictures that they beautify or dramatize through their own vision; they change tones, colours, shades, backgrounds, lettering or add and remove all kinds of details. They combine different pictures to form new assemblages or create a mixture of motifs, both painted from the imagination and taken from magazines. While engaged in this process of creativity, wayside painters keep a specific purpose or a particular client in mind. In accomplishing a particular objective, wayside painters incorporate new motifs to make their work more persuasive and touching. 'Quoting' is a much better term for this than 'copying', as wayside artists use existing pictures as a starting point from which they remodel, rework and restructure the originals. While Walter Benjamin claimed that the aura of the copy was inferior to that of the original, wayside painters rather see this the other way around. Formally trained artists are also engaged in a process of quoting and recycling even though their Jesus figures are much further removed from mass-produced pictures. Wayside painters, by contrast, often strive for exactness by drawing a grid over the original picture and transfer the picture to plywood or canvas square by square.

While some formally trained artists depicted Jesus as African after Ghana's independence, in the work of wayside painters an Africanized Jesus is almost, though not quite, absent. During a visit in March 2012 to the workshop of wayside artist Kwame Akoto (b. 1950), I spotted a representation of Jesus as the *Asantehene* (Asante king) Otumfuo Osei Tutu II, who lives in a palace not far from Akoto's workshop. Akoto later donated the painting to a pastor who had successfully prayed for the painter's sick sister-in-law. What the two paintings shown in figure 11.5 share is that the

Figure 11.5. Two Christ paintings by Kwame Akoto, both made in 1990. Photo: courtesy Atta Kwami.

painter clearly worked from a conventional Sacred Heart picture to ensure recognizability. In the first painting, Akoto darkened the skin colour, added some royal accessories and traded the red cloth for Kente.

It might be tempting to link Akoto's work to Kobina Bucknor's portrait for the Christ the King Church in the heart of Accra. However, Kwame Akoto was not much interested in the issue of race; he did not say much when I asked him why he depicted Jesus as an Asante king. As an informal Pentecostal preacher, he rather told me vivid stories of deliverances in his gallery, a wooden shed filled to the brim with paintings, where he, speaking in tongues, freed people from evil spirits. I rather relate his domestic Jesus to his paintings of celebrities in Kente, examples being Obama and Queen Elisabeth dressed up as Asantehene and Queen Mother,[4] respectively. He also occasionally painted his customers fully clad as Asante royalty. The Jesus-as-Asantehene portrait speaks of matters that affect him as an artist, as an Asante and a Christian. Bucknor's painting for the Christ the King Church served a different purpose: it was a way of 'retrieving the past for the future', as the painter called it, in creating national pride and consciousness (Fosu 1993: 118). Nevertheless, the fact that both painters remediated Jesus as Asantehene suggests that they share common ground. For Kwame Akoto, a black Jesus in Kente cloth did not stand in the way of identification with a personal 'saviour' on the condition that the figure in the painting remained recognizable as Jesus. Christians who demand pictures that they experience as historically accurate might not agree with Akoto. Artists translate ideas and beliefs, shaped and informed by their religious and social background, into diverse Jesus pictures. Christians are not passive viewers but involved in a similar, reverse process: they actively translate what they see in religious pictures in (new) meaning and value. Artists and spectators are socially bonded by the artwork; scholars have to take into account this constitutive relationship in understanding how pictures are born and lead social lives of their own.

Conclusion

The influential modern artist Wassily Kandinsky, in relation to imitation in art, argued:

> For us it is impossible to live and feel as did the ancient Greeks. For this reason those who follow Greek principles in sculpture reach only a similarity in form, while the work remains for all times without a soul. Such imitation resembles the antics of apes: externally a monkey resembles a human being; he will sit holding a book in front of his nose, turning the pages with a thoughtful air, but his actions have no real significance. (2005[1947]: 3)

As a representative of modern art, Kandinsky ideally views art as a material remediation of emotions stored inside the body. In such view, a work of art is only successful when the embodied emotions of the artist are reproduced in the bodies of beholders though the gaze. Art that fails to achieve this remediation is empty and meaningless, Kandinsky argued, and no more than 'a sham' (ibid.: 7). What sets 'real' art apart from copies in a modernist definition is that underneath the surface appearance there exists an animated essence – 'a soul' – inserted there by the hand of the artist. Such a view partly overlaps with religious practices in Ghana (and elsewhere) where religious objects are seen as empty vessels to be vested with spiritual power through prayer. Objects are animated in both cases through human agency, but while modern artists attribute the inherent power in artwork to human creativity and genius, Jesus pictures are animated by divine power though human acts of prayer and looking. Furthermore, in modern art, any attempt to copy a great work of art is doomed to fail, as only the original work contains spiritual power. Such discourse is clothed in the idea of art being born out of a creative and divine force that loses its special power when copied, reducing the derivative work to the status of mere craft (Svašek 2007). In contrast, mass reproduction does not seem to detract from the power that religious mass-produced pictures have for Christians in Ghana.

In modern art, novelty was seen as the sine qua non for creativity. To position copying and creativity as mutually exclusive categories testifies of a limited view that overlooks the ways in which mimicry requires creativity and vice-versa. As I have shown, imitation is productive, both as an artistic strategy and in making religious pictures emotionally effective. Artists rearrange and repeat both mental and material pictures in new media in the process of creating new meaning. Every new representation of Jesus carries elements of older pictures and is, thus, a remediation. This process of remediation takes place in social fields that stretch out beyond the local and incorporates customers, onlookers, sellers, religious authorities and the wider networks in which they are embedded.

In Kandinsky's argument, artists reproduce intangible emotions in a material form, which, I suggest, requires both creativity *and* imitation. What Kandinsky also overlooked is that beholders will vest artwork with new meaning and value despite the intention of the artist. The paintings discussed here make it clear that artists depict Jesus in a manner that fits their own interests. This does not mean that their meaning is fixed at the moment of fabrication, as Kandinsky seems to suggest. As David Morgan argues, religious believers might see a painting of Jesus 'as an engaged signifier, not the aesthetic objects of curiosity that the connoisseur, art collector, or tourist may see' (2005: 74). Viewers engage with pictures according to their social and cultural upbringing in particular modes of looking and moral evaluation. And finally, Kandinsky argues that the imitation of past forms causes the work to lack significance and an inner core or 'soul'. I argue the opposite: through processes of appropriation and creative engagement, artists and religious believers make foreign pictures part and parcel of their own life-worlds. The fact that mass-produced pictures repeat well-known, global motifs does not mean that all Christians attribute the same kind of power and meaning to these pictures. As shown, in Ghana such pictures are subjected to various interpretations: as void commodities that can be filled with divine or demonic power, as 'empty' signifiers that mark a sacred space, a symbol that reminds people to do good and so on. We need to see such interpretations in the light of global historical processes that are articulated through local conditions. The appropriation and (re)production of Jesus pictures reflects the incorporation of Africa in broader artistic, religious and economic structures (Meyer 2008). Jesus pictures, in various forms and modes of use, are the outcome of a long history of encounters and exchanges between Africa and other parts of the worlds.

Rhoda Woets is a cultural anthropologist who received her PhD in September 2011. Her dissertation, '"What is this?" Framing Ghanaian Art from the Colonial Encounter to the Present', explores the underlying ideological premises and contestations underpinning the category of modern and contemporary Ghanaian art since its inception in colonial times. As post-doctoral researcher at Vrije Universiteit Amsterdam, she examined the circulation and appropriation of mass-produced and hand-painted Jesus pictures in urban Ghana. Her main research interests include art, material culture and religion.

Notes

1. This chapter is based on interviews, informal talks and observations with Christians of several denominations, artists and religious leaders in Accra, Cape Coast and Kumasi in June 2010 and March 2011.
2. I need to add here that there are also many Christians, of all denominations, who argue that objects cannot be powerful of and by themselves. They describe the omnipresent Jesus posters or statues as mere symbols that work as reminders to do good or that draw Jesus closer, reminiscent of the way pictures of deceased family members stand in for their absent bodies.
3. *Yam oto* is a well-known ritual food in Ghana made of mashed yam, hardboiled eggs and palm oil.
4. The Queen Mother is often not the chief's biological mother but a prestigious position in the chieftaincy system that parallels that of the chief.

References

Assimeng, M. 2010. *Religion and Social Change in West Africa: An Introduction to the Sociology of Religion.* Accra: Woeli Publishing Services.

Appadurai, A. (ed.). 1986. *The Social Life of Things.* Cambridge: Cambridge University Press.

Asamoah-Gyadu, K. 2005. *African Charismatics: Current Developments within Independent Indigenous Pentecostalism in Ghana.* Leiden: Brill.

Becker, H. S. 2008. *Art Worlds,* updated and expanded. Berkeley: University of California Press.

Boon, M. 2010. *In Praise of Copying.* Cambridge, MA: Harvard University Press. http://www.hup.harvard.edu/features/boon/In-Praise-of-Copying-by-Marcus-Boon-HUP-free-full-text.pdf.

Bourdieu, P. 1993. *The Field of Cultural Production: Essays on Art and Literature.* Oxford: Polity Press.

De Witte, M. 2008. 'Spirit Media: Charismatics, Traditionalists, and Mediation Practices in Ghana', PhD dissertation, University of Amsterdam.

Elsbernd, A. 2000. *The Story of the Catholic Church in the Diocese of Accra.* Accra: Catholic Book Centre.

Fosu, K. 1993. *20th Century Art of Africa,* revised edition. Kumasi: University of Science and Technology.

Freedberg, D. 1989. *The Power of Images: Studies in the History and Theory of Response.* Chicago: University of Chicago Press.

Gifford, P. 2004. *Ghana's New Christianity: Pentecostalism in a Globalising African Economy.* London: Hurst and Compagny.

Gocking, R. 2009. '"Who do men say that I look like?": Representing Christ and Christian Personae in Ghana', *Visual Anthropology* 22(4): 293–326.

Hallam, E., and T. Ingold. 2007. 'Creativity and Cultural Improvisation: An Introduction', in E. Hallam and T. Ingold (eds), *Creativity and Cultural Improvisation.* Oxford: Berg.

Kandinsky, W. 2005. 'Concerning the Spiritual in Art', in D. Apostolos-Cappadona (ed.), *Art, Creativity and the Sacred.* New York: The Continuum International Publishing Group Inc.

Meyer, B. 1998. '"Make a Complete Break With the Past": Memory and Post-Colonial Modernity in Ghanaian Pentecostalist Discourse', *Journal of Religion in Africa* XXVIII: 316–349.

———. 1999. *Translating the Devil: Religion and Modernity Among the Ewe in Ghana.* Edinburgh: Edinburgh University Press

———. 2008. 'Powerful Pictures: Popular Christian Aesthetics in Christian Ghana', *Journal of the American Academy of Religion* 76(1): 82–110.

———. 2010. '"There is a Spirit in that Image": Mass-Produced Jesus Pictures and Protestant-Pentecostal Animation in Ghana', *Comparative Studies in Society and History* 52(1): 100–130.

———. 2011a. 'Mediating Absence-Effecting Spiritual Presence: Pictures and the Christian Imagination', *Social Research* 78(4): 1029–1056.

————. 2011b. 'Mediation and Immediacy: Sensational Forms, Semiotic Ideologies and the Question of Medium', *Social Anthropology* 19(1): 23–39.

Mitchell, W. J. T. 2005. *What do Pictures Want? The Lives and Loves of Images*. Chicago: University of Chicago Press.

Morgan, D. 1999. *Visual Piety: A History and Theory of Popular Religious Images*. Berkeley: University of California Press.

————. 2005. *The Sacred Gaze: Religious Visual Culture in Theory and Practice*. Berkeley: University of California Press.

Pobee, J. S. (ed.). 1992. *Exploring Afro-Christology*. Frankfurt: Peter Lang.

Sarpong, P. 2002. *Peoples Differ: An Approach to Inculturation in Evangelisation*. Accra: Sub-Saharan Publishers.

Steiner, C. B. 2001. 'Rights of Passage: On the Liminal Identity of Art in the Border Zone', in F. Myers (ed.), *The Empire of Things: Regimes of Value and Material Culture*. Oxford: James Currey Ltd.

Stinton, D. B. 2004. *Jesus of Africa: Voices of Contemporary African Christology*. New York: Orbis Books.

Svašek, M. 2007. *Anthropology, Art and Cultural Production*. London: Pluto Press.

————. 2012. 'Introduction: Affective Moves: Transit, Transition and Transformation', in M. Svašek (ed.), *Moving Subjects, Moving Objects: Transnationalism, Cultural Production and Emotions*. New York and Oxford: Berghahn Books.

Woets, R. 2011. 'What is this?' Framing Ghanaian art from the colonial encounter to the present', Ph.D. dissertation. Amsterdam VU University, Amsterdam.

AFTERWORD

CREATIVITY IN TRANSITION

———◆◆◆———

Birgit Meyer

As pointed out by Maruška Svašek in the introduction, this volume is one of the outcomes of a collective research program, titled 'Creativity and Innovation in a World of Movement' (CIM). Funded within the larger scheme of the HERA research program Humanities as a Source of Creativity and Innovation, our central assumption was that 'creativity should not be measured by assessing the relative novelty of end products, a rather particular modernist construct of creativity, but rather by exploring practices of dynamic improvisation as part of ongoing processes of cultural production, appropriation, consumption and (re)contextualisation' (http://heranet.info/cim/index). In this way we sought to complicate taken-for-granted, reductive invocations of creativity and (or, better, 'as') innovation, as they are articulated in notions such as 'creative industries' and appear in the titles of ambitious research funding, such as the HERA scheme. Taken as a whole, this volume is driven by three major intersecting concerns. It engages in: (1) identifying alternative, creative practices of cultural production beyond what we called the 'modernist construct of creativity' in the spheres of craft production, heritage and religion; (2) exploring discourses and regimes of Creativity, in the narrow modernist sense, going global in the arts, fashion industries and urban development; and (3) reconceptualizing creativity in ways that are not reduced to the new, the original and the unique, and encompass the copy and imitation rather that taking them as antitheses.

Creativity-as-Improvisation: New Openings

For this critical endeavour, the path-breaking intervention by Ingold and Hallam (2007) into the study of creative practices formed a key resource (see Svašek, introduction, this volume). Their critique of mistaking a historically situated modernist and Eurocentric construct of creativity for a universal template and their plea to instead remain open to alternative creative practices in the larger framework of improvisation is well taken. In their view, the world is always in the making, with humans engaging in improvised, creative acts that do not necessarily aim at originality, but that are part and parcel of ongoing cultural production in a wider sense. They propose to transcend the typically modernist set of oppositions of original versus copy, newness versus repetition, invention versus imitation, in favour of a broader, humanist understanding of creativity that encompasses both sides of these contrasts. The merit of this perspective, as this volume shows, is that it calls attention to creative acts that occur in the shadow of a more limited take on creativity, in settings where those taking a conventional modernist approach would not necessarily expect creativity to happen.

The sphere of religion is a case in point (Ingold and Hallam 2007: 5ff.). The detailed case studies in this volume by Svašek, Bruland, Rickli and Woets show, each in their own way, how the continuation of living religious traditions – Hinduism, as well as Catholic, Protestant and Pentecostal Christianity – across space and time require practices of repetition that depend on creative improvisation and constant adaptation and transformation. This is highlighted in Svašek's analysis of how Manika, a female Hindu migrant, creatively configures her domestic *puja* room so as to be able to sense affective immanence in her Northern Irish home; in Bruland's exploration of creative inculturation on the part of Tamil Catholics in Paris, who incorporate key aesthetic features of Hinduism into their Christian religious practice; in Rickli's tracing of the transformation and mass reproduction of the image of Aparecida and the devotional practices surrounding it; or in the continuous remediation of Jesus motifs by both formally trained and street artists, a process aptly described as 'aesthetic recycling' by Woets. Their chapters serve as powerful reminders that, to invoke Rickli, 'producing the sublime is a creative process in which different actors with different religious agendas take part' and that involves thorough, sensational engagement with actual materials. So, here the broad understanding of creativity-as-improvisation offers a productive lens that is helpful in identifying the microphysics through which a sense of divine presence is generated in settings characterized by mobility and transformation (see also Meyer 2014). Another benefit of this broad take is that it engenders new possibilities for thinking about repetition and the copy as including, rather than being opposed to, creativity. This inclusive perspective is clearly articulated in Plankensteiner's transcultural account of the production and consumption of African lace. By tracing 'the movements of creative ideas and their appropriation across continents', she not only shows the making of a new 'traditional' style of dress that epitomizes postcolonial Nigerianness, but also spotlights the actual making of a new tradition. Similarly, Schneider reveals how a focus on 'creative experimentation with past cultural artefacts', such as Guaraní ceramics, offers deeper insights about the dynamics of cultural reproduction, for instance in the sphere of heritage formation. Schneider's approach also yields a perceptive, fine-tuned vocabulary with which to analyse such grounded creative dynamics, a vocabulary that may well be applicable to other settings.

In sum, a broad understanding of creativity-as-improvisation provides benefits that cannot be overemphasized in alerting researchers to the existence of creative practices, even in what may appear, at first sight, to be unlikely domains associated with the endurance of the past, such as those of tradition, heritage and religion. And yet, this broad understanding of creativity also has certain limitations that become apparent in this volume.

Creativity-as-Innovation: Going Global and Strong

To critique and reject what we called the 'modernist construct of creativity' as a scholarly framework does not imply that it is a false and flimsy construct with no reality of its own. Seeking to answer the question of what creativity, in the broad sense adopted by Ingold and Hallam, means in an era of intensifying global connections and entanglements, evokes a second pressing question about the resilience and pervasiveness of the modernist construct. How does the spread of the predominant, Western understanding of creativity in terms of artistic genius and individual originality – Creativity with a capital C – relate to other, more embedded creative practices? Pondering the case studies presented in this volume in light of these questions, I would like to offer two observations. First, Creativity has travelled remarkably well, not only as a term, but above all as a regime shaping cultural production from the onset of colonial imperialism to current neoliberal capitalism. It appears to have moved as easily from the domain of modern art to 'creative industries' as it has moved across the globe. Second, as a discourse of the new, Creativity is mobilized by various actors to mark a distinction with regard to cultural production under the aegis of tradition and repetition, yielding sets of contrasts between original and copy, art and craft, innovation and tradition in cultural production in everyday life.

While this volume takes a critical distance from such a limited notion of Creativity as a scholarly framework of analysis, it still acknowledges that Eurocentric creativity regimes are going global and impinge on cultural production along the lines sketched above. The outcry of Ghanaian fine artist Amon Kotei, evoked by Maruška Svašek at the very beginning of the introduction to this volume, testifies to the global spread of this regime and its penetration of dynamics of cultural production: echoes of his outcry from actors in the sphere of the arts and beyond can be heard throughout this book. This penetration is evident, for instance, in Øivind Fuglerud's detailed explorations of the ways in which the legacy of a Western notion of art impinges on the social production of creativity in the domain of 'indigenous art' in Canada and Norway, and in Fiona Magowan and Maria Øien's exploration of the production of 'Christian Aboriginal art' in Australia. Even more salient cases that betray the Eurocentric Creativity regime in action on a global scale are offered by Teresa Kuldova's revealing analysis of the ways in which designers profile themselves as original creators by downplaying the work of artisans as the mindless practice of craft; Kala Shreen's lucid account of the upgrading of traditional *kottan* production from 'craft' to unique, authored pieces of 'art' under the ambit of UNESCO's heritage schemes; and Amit Desai's critical discussion of the framing of Chennai as a city of arts and hotbed of creativity at the cost of marginalizing artists at work. The mantra of creativity and/as innovation spreads with neoliberal capitalism, yielding its own paradoxes and contradictions that demand to be unpacked. As many contributions to our volume show, the point is not to simply replace a problematic Eurocentric notion of creativity by a more appropriate one. After all, this notion materializes in operative regimes and hence becomes real – though not in a totalizing or uncontested manner – on the level of cultural production across the globe.

In order to understand the expansive trajectory of the notion of creativity from its emergence in seventeenth-century art (see introduction) into other spheres of cultural production, and into global arenas, it is fruitful to turn to German cultural sociologist Andreas Reckwitz's (2012) book, *Die Erfindung der Kreativität* (The Invention of Creativity). Reckwitz argues that late modern culture is shaped by an aestheticized capitalism that engages in a permanent production of the new, conveyed by sensorial-affective stimuli. Since the 1990s, a remarkable, ever-more explicit emphasis is placed on creativity in the double sense of a desire and a command: '*man will kreativ sein – und man soll es sein*' (one wants to be creative – and has to be creative; Reckwitz 2012: 10). The strong concern with creativity, from the level of personal self-making to the profiling of creative neighbourhoods, betrays the existence of what he calls, taking recourse to Foucault, a 'creativity *dispositif*'. This *dispositif* underpins personal acts and aspirations embedded in a culture of self-creation, as well as larger trends in culture and society that depend upon permanent aesthetic rejuvenation. Reckwitz traces the genealogy of this broadly shared *dispositif* to the rise of the fine arts in the seventeenth and eighteenth centuries, when *inventio* was privileged above *imitatio* and the figure of the artistic genius emerged as the ultimate human creator. With time, this figure became the performative model for personhood in capitalist modernity, thus expanding from the sphere of the arts into society at large.

Reckwitz's analysis makes a great deal of sense to me. If the framing of creativity in terms of artistic genius has spilled over from the domain of art into society as a whole, a mere discarding of modernist understandings of creativity misses the point. The 'creativity *dispositif*' of late capitalism shapes worlds of lived experience in the West, but also elsewhere, as the chapters by Kuldova, Shreen and Desai show so poignantly. Characteristic of this *dispositif*, Reckwitz points out, is the strong preference for the new, the extraordinary and the different, which are contrasted with the old, normality and sameness. He identifies an overheated 'regime of the aesthetically new' (*Regime des ästhetisch Neuen*) that is part and parcel of a radical aestheticization of social life for which the field of art served as the paradigm. On the flipside of this heavy investment in aesthetic renewal, he identifies an overstimulation of the senses, an obsession with the spectacular and overall distraction, as well as a necessary amnesia that turns a blind eye to dynamics of cultural production elsewhere and in the past, so as to maintain the illusion of newness.

Obviously, this celebration of creativity in the midst of the culture of the copy and unprecedented possibilities for technological reproduction and instant circulation is deeply contradictory, and ultimately amounts to an impossible project, as the current concerns with plagiarism in writing and scandals around copy and original in the arts highlight. Pointing out critical limits intrinsic to this regime, Reckwitz still stays – typically for a cultural sociologist – within the ambit of Western modernity. By contrast, the contributions to this volume lead right into the frontier zones of the expansion of the modernist notion of Creativity, highlighting the upgrading of crafts, tradition and heritage from a status of backwardness to the domain of creativity. In so doing, the volume offers a much-needed multisited perspective on the paradoxes and contradictions that ensue from the spread of the initially Western creativity regime across the globe.

As the volume shows, the spread of this regime comes with its own contradictions and contestations. An apt case from Kuldova's chapter that reveals these contradictions is that of the fashion designer and style guru Rajinder, who profiles himself as a 'uniquely creative individual' *and* as a custodian of collective traditional skills. While his fashion depends on traditional creativity, he derogates it as inferior in order to glorify his own creative status. The remarkable outburst of a female embroiderer in an Uttar Pradesh village, who tells a designer, 'without us, you are nobody', shows that those exploited are well aware of the appeal and costs, potential and limitations of the notion of Creativity, and may be prepared to contest it if their situation allows. Pointing out the limitations and contradictions within the operations of the creativity regime itself is one of the important achievements of this volume. It is my hope that it will stimulate more work along similar lines.

The Potential and Limits of Creativity

The wish to be creative, as Reckwitz asserts, is part of humanity. Of course, this is also the starting point of the analysis put forward by Ingold and Hallam (2007). Here it is worth noting that both Reckwitz and Ingold and Hallam argue against limiting creativity to the arts. But whereas the former argues that an artistic notion of creativity has spread throughout all do-mains of late modern society, entailing a veritable obsession with newness and originality, the latter seek to liberate creativity from this obsession and embed it in dynamics of improvisation. Clearly, there is something to be said in favour of each perspective. While Ingold and Hallam invite us to think about creativity as a human potential indispensable for the (re)production of culture, Reckwitz shows how creativity is sucked into a disciplinary re-gime that is no longer limited to the arts, but applied broadly to all aspects of being and has become fundamental to processes of self-making in late modern society, enmeshing persons in an aesthetics of the new, the demands of which are ultimately impossible to fulfil. With hindsight, the perspective offered by Ingold and Hallam strikes me as too idealistic. While it broadens the horizon of analysis by bringing to the fore dimensions of creativity that are marginalized by a reductive modernist understanding, it underplays the extent to which this reductive understanding has become a template of cul-tural production at large. The shortcoming of Reckwitz's illuminating anal-ysis is that it does not systematically address creativity outside the context of late modern, Western societies.

Our volume, then, mediates between both perspectives. It shows that as a global discourse employed to profile a particular kind of cultural pro-duction in contrast to, and often at the expense of, others, Creativity is a deeply problematic notion. Many practices that might well be understood as creative, if only one was prepared to adopt a broader take on creativity in terms of 'performative engagements with the materials that surround us' (Ingold and Hallam 2007: 3), are marginalized. Narrow, exclusivist takes on Creativity rely on problematic claims to originality that can only be sustained by indulging in forgetfulness and neglecting a great deal of cultural production in past and present contexts. So the spread of Creativity across the globe comes with its own exclusions, paradoxes and limitations. Unpacking such complex processes calls for a subtle, reflexive analysis of how various creative practices, and understandings of creativity in terms of innovation and improvisation, clash with, as well as flow into, each other in everyday life. Based on grounded case studies, this volume offers an attempt to assess the potential and limits of creativity – as a practice, a regime, a concept, a marker of humanity – in our globalized world.

Birgit Meyer is professor of religious studies in the Department of Religious Studies and Theology at Utrecht University. She has conducted research on missions and local appropriations of Christianity, Pentecostalism, popular culture and video-films in Ghana. Her publications include *Translating the Devil: Religion and Modernity among the Ewe in Ghana* (Edinburgh University Press, 1999), *Globalization and Identity: Dialectics of Flow and Closure* (edited with Peter Geschiere, Blackwell, 1999), *Magic and Modernity: Interfaces of Revelation and Concealment* (edited with Peter Pels, Stanford University Press, 2003), *Religion, Media and the Public Sphere* (edited with Annelies Moors, Indiana University Press), *Aesthetic Formations: Media, Religion and the Senses* (Palgrave Macmillan, 2009), and *Sensational Movies* (University of California Press, 2015). She is one of the editors of *Material Religion* and co-editor of the Berghahn Books series Material Mediations: People and Things in a World of Movement.

References

Ingold, T., and E. Hallam. 2007. 'Creativity and Cultural Improvisation: An Introduction', in E. Hallam and T. Ingold (eds), *Creativity and Cultural Improvisation*. Oxford: Berg, 1–24.

Meyer, B. 2014. 'Mediation and the Genesis of Presence', reprint of inaugural lecture, with a response to comments by Hans Belting et al., *Religion & Society: Advances in Research* 5: 205–254.

Reckwitz, A. 2012. *Die Erfindung der Kreativität. Zum Prozess gesellschaftlicher Ästhetisierung*. Frankfurt: Suhrkamp.

Index

Abeokuta, Nigeria, 53
Aboriginal(s), Canada, 161–63, 165
absolution, Christian, 205
abundance, 16, 269, 291
abuse, physical & sexual, 163
academics, 120, 221
accidents, 205, 277
Accra, 291, 294–98, 303, 307
Adediran, Mayo, 56, 58n29
adjustment, 39, 299
adjustment movement, 192–93, 198
advertisements, 113, 290, 304–5
advertising, 66, 74, 95, 275; *see also* marketing
aesthetic regimes, 208
aesthetics, 3, 7, 50, 54, 62–64, 71, 82n2, 167, 186–88, 209, 228, 246, 250, 252, 254–5, 262–64, 267–69, 287, 317
    Aboriginal Christian, 22, 186
    indigenous, 168, 195
    native (in Canada), 166, 172
    religious, 23, 246, 250–1, 255, 264
aesthetics of attraction, 245
affective engagement, 218, 221–22
affects, bodily, 295
Africa, 1, 7, 15, 34–35, 42–43, 45, 49, 55–56, 57n6, 58n34, 225, 309
    West, 40–1, 43, 54–55, 57n6, 12
African lace, 19, 33–59
after-empathy, 143
agbada, 39, 48, 52–53, *see also babban riga*
agency, 3, 19, 23, 27n15, 33, 42, 55, 88, 144, 165, 246, 254, 271, 278, 292, 295, 298, 308
agents, cultural, 269

aesthesis, 254
Akintola, Chief Samuel, 52
Akintola, Faderer, 52
Akoi-Jackson, Bernard, 302–4
Akoto, Kwame, 306–7
alienation, 169
    cultural, 299, 301
Allada, Benin, 40
All India Handicraft Board, 91
Alta dam, 179
altar, 193, 235, 248, 259, 274, 276, 280–81, 286; *see also* shrine
Aluthgama, Sri Lanka, 249
Anan, Kofi, 304
Ancestral connectivity, 202, 204
Ancestral Law, 187, 189–90, 193–95, 198–99, 209, 210n8, 211n10
ancestors, 1, 10–11, 72, 151, 186–87, 198, 202–4, 209, 254
Andhra Pradesh, 124, 129n7
Aneignung, 132; *see also* appropriation
animals, 43, 119, 150, 168, 174, 182n1, 187
anthropologist(s), 15, 82, 103, 163, 165, 177, 194, 221, 309
anthropology, 10, 25, 132, 153n11, 163, 209, 239
    dialogical, 144, 150
    early, 159
    hermeneutic, 144, 150
    museum, 56
    relationship between art and, 163
    salvage, 166
    social, 264
Aparecida, Our Lady of, 267–89
    as Mother of Brazil, 274
    as Queen of Brazil, 272, 287
    coronation of the image, 272

the Immaculate Conception, 267–
69, 271
the Pilgrim, 286
Aparecida, Radio, 282
Aparecida, TV, 282
Appadurai, Arjun, 2, 294
apostles, 302, 304
apprenticeship, 187, 298
appropriation(s), 4, 7, 9, 19, 21, 24,
34–35, 40, 52, 55, 88, 91, 131–35,
137, 141–7, 149–51, 152n2, 165,
220, 230, 238, 268, 291–92, 294,
296, 299, 302, 309, 313–14, 318
    art as, 212n26
    art by, 97
    creative, 218, 221, 227, 238
    cultural, 55
    hermeneutic, 131, 140
    resistance to, 132
approximation, 21, 131–33, 143–44,
146, 149–51
Arabindoo, Pushpa, 114
Araeen, Rashid, 176–77, 181
Arafura Sea, 189
arati, 246, 251, 253, 258–9, 261, 263
archaeological pieces, 134, 140, 150;
    see also artefacts, archaeological
archaeological record, 143–44
archaeology, experimental, 142
architecture, 92, 114
archive(s), 42, 45, 58n33, 76, 151n1,
212n23, 214n37
Argentina, 21, 131, 134–6, 138,
147, 151n1; *see also* nation state,
Argentine
army
    Buddha's, 245, 249
    Sri Lankan, 245
Arnhem Land, 189–91, 196, 199–200,
209, 210n2, 211n12, 211n15
ars, 73; *see also* art; skill
art(s), 9, 17, 64, 109–11, 114, 116–8,
120, 122, 124, 127, 128n5, 132,
142, 145–46, 159–60, 164–166,
168, 170–73, 175–77, 181, 308; *see
also* artwork; non-art; not-art
    Christian, 192, 195, 200, 207–8,
        210n7, 301
    commercial, 187–88, 201
    contemporary, 110, 113–5, 117,
        122, 125–27, 149
    First Nations, 159, 163, 177
    Fourth World, 159
    global, 109, 112, 116–8, 122–23,
        126

Indian, 111, 122
indigenous, 158–61, 177
modern(ist), 169, 176, 178
North-west Coast, 162, 171, 173–
    74
Norwegian, 160, 168
performance, 9, 12
Sami, 159–60, 167, 174, 177–78
tribal, 167, 177
visual, 103, 213n28, 302
Yolngu, 195, 200
Art Chennai, 109–16, 118, 122, 125–
    26, 128n1
art-craft dichotomy, 13, 18, 27n16
art-culture dichotomy, 13, 16
artefacts, 2, 8–9, 11, 13–16, 18, 20,
    22–24, 68, 87–88, 103, 139–40,
    147–48, 152n3, 165–66, 187, 219–
    220, 223, 226–30, 232–34, 238–39,
    240n2, 268
    archaeological, 134, 137–38, 145,
        152n3
    cultural, 131, 314
    religious, 2, 15, 26n6
art history/historians, 109, 116, 122,
    165, 177
art industry, 197–98
art installations, 108, 114–15, 117,
    120; *for specific installations, see*
    artworks
    multimedia, 26n9
artisan(s), 14–15, 68, 71–73, 76, 81,
    97, 100–02, 124–25, 152n3, 315; *see
    also* craftsman/men; craftsperson;
    craftswomen
artist, the, 15, 42, 70, 72, 97, 109,
    118–19, 169, 186, 202, 213n31,
    299, 308
artist(s), 7, 9, 12, 17, 20–22, 26n11,
    46, 71, 73–74, 83n6, 97, 102–3,
    107–9, 111–12, 115–17, 119–22,
    126, 132, 158–61, 168, 171, 176–
    79, 181, 186–87, 192, 195, 202,
    207–9, 210n6, 212n23, 213n31,
    213n35, 214n37, 290, 298–99,
    301–4, 307–9, 309n1, 315
    Aboriginal, 186, 188, 209
    avant-garde, 302
    Bombay Progressive, 122
    Catholic, 209
    Chennai, 112, 119, 122, 126,
        128n6
    Cholamandal, 109, 111–12, 115,
        119–20, 122–23, 126, 129n7
    Christian, 186, 209

contemporary, 12, 115, 117, 147
established, 6, 110
European, 1, 27n16
female, 201
fine, 14, 16–17, 74, 97, 315
First Nations, 161, 181
Ghanaian, 1, 301, 315
Indian, 67, 90, 110
individual, 15, 17, 68, 102, 201, 302
local, 115, 186, 210n6
modern, 168, 298, 307–8
native, 22, 181
Ngan'gi, 185–88, 191–92, 194–95, 201, 207, 210n4, 211n10, 212n21, 212n23
non-European, 16, 176
Sami, 176–78, 181
senior, 191, 201
street, 313
trained, 12, 291, 298–99, 304–6, 313
wayside, 298–9, 304–6
women, 201
Yolngu, 185–8, 194–95
artist-craftsman, 100
art market(s), 17, 22, 109, 115, 186, 194, 201, 207–8
art/artistic practices, 20, 140, 159–60, 171, 186, 189, 192, 200–1, 207–8
art production, 15, 17, 115, 187–88, 190, 201, 208–9
artspeak, 67
art world(s), 12, 110, 115–17, 165, 166, 168, 171, 177, 178, 181, 207–8, 298
Chennai, 110, 121–23
contemporary, 117–18, 122
local, 127, 160
artwork(s), 12, 14, 103, 160–61, 171, 185, 187–88, 190–92, 194, 196, 198, 200–1, 212n23, 213n2, 214n35, 307–8
Both Ways to Heal the Spirit, 205–6, 214n37
Christian, 188, 191, 207, 301
Ghost: Transmemoir, 108, 111, 115–6
Head of Christ, 291
Healing Ceremony, The, 214n37
Identidade, 145–6
Killer Whale, 174
Last Supper, The, 291, 302, 304
Parabol, 180
Passion of the Christ, The, 305

Pyramid, 107, 111, 113–14, 116
Spirit of Haida Gwaii, 174
Video Lounge, 128n6
Welcome to Country, 202–4
White Builder and Red Carpet, 116
Wobole Kutu Wokpe, 303
ashrams, 222, 235, 241n16
Asia, 7, 19, 55, 104n.1, 110, 104n1
aso ebi, 46–7, 50, 57n17; *see also* uniform
aso oke, 38–9, 50–1: *see also* textiles, narrow strip
Assumar, Earl of, 268
attachment, 262–3, 281, 295, 301
auction houses, 109
audience(s), 4–6, 10, 26n10, 100, 105n3, 108, 113, 127, 200
global, 20, 116, 124
aura, 73–74, 295, 306
Australia, 7, 185, 187, 189, 209, 315
Aboriginal, 187
Austria, 19, 34–35, 37, 41–42, 47, 55–56, 56n1
authentic, the, 158, 169
authentication, 2, 7, 71, 284, 286–87
authenticity, 16, 24, 71, 132, 231, 283–84, 303
certificate of, 201–2, 206, 213n31, 214n37, 287
authorisation, 2, 7, 22, 187, 213n31
authority, 14, 24, 80, 193, 195, 201, 207, 239, 269, 283
creative, 228
kinship-based, 188
official, 287
political, 171
religious, 22, 235
auto-analytic process, 145
autochthony, 271–72
autoethnography, 165
autonomy, 169, 200
Awolowo, Chief Obayemi, 52
Awolowo, Hannah, 52
award(s)
international, 93
Kate Challis RAKA, 212–3n28
Padma Shri, 83n7
TELSTRA art, 212–3n28
UNESCO, 93–94, 96, 104n1–2

babban riga or *babbarriga*, 39, 48, 51; *see also agbada*
backwardness, 75, 294, 316
Bagwan, 235

Balaram, Singanapalli, 75
Bal, Rohit, 73–74
banking, 35, 88
Banumbirr, 197, 200, 213n30
Banumbirr Pole, 198, 200
baptism(s), 48, 195, 202, 204–5,
    213n34
Baptist(s), 294; *see also* John the
    Baptist
bäpurru, 199
Barbeau, Marius, 165
Basilica (Aparecida), 268, 273–78,
    281–83, 286–87
Basilica, Old (Aparecida), 268, 272,
    275, 286
basket(s), 20, 87–90, 95–96, 98, 101–
    102, 196
    kottan, 87, 92, 95–96
    sculpture, 101
    silver, 89–90
basketry, 140, 153n18
    Guaraní, 133, 143, 150
Bastian, Misty L., 49
batik, 187–88
Batoni, Pompeo, 290
Bauman, Miriam-Rose Ungunmerr,
    195, 201, 205–6, 213n35
bazaars, 114
beach, 107–8, 113–15, 119
beads, 39, 94
    rosary, 205–6
beautification, 114, 223
beauty, 15, 23, 76, 145, 147, 228,
    242n21
    of Jesus, 296
    universal, 14
Becker, Howard, 6
becoming, state of, 186, 208
beholders, 299, 308; *see also* onlookers
beliefs, 24, 205, 269, 272, 283, 288n4–
    5, 293, 307
    Ancestral, 185, 189, 192
    Christian, 195, 209
believers, 23–24, 208, 235, 251, 264,
    283, 295
    Catholic, 276, 288n4
    religious, 291, 308–9
Bella Coola, B.C., 161
Belleville, Paris, 248
bells, 13, 26n7, 250, 274
belonging, 67, 72, 132, 151, 232, 248,
    250, 263, 264n1, 276
Belting, Hans, 116, 118
Benin, 40, 50, 57n12
Benítez, Karina Gabriela, 137, 152n1

Benjamin, Walter, 15, 295, 306
Beruwala, 249
betel leaves, 94
Bharatiya Janata Party (BJP), 65
bhav, 228
Biafra, 46, 48
bible stories; *see* stories, biblical
Bible, the, 281, 297
birds, 119, 150, 159, 191, 204, 213n33
Bombay, 108, 122; *see also* Mumbai
blessing(s), 24, 91, 223, 225, 227, 235,
    241n13, 256, 276, 279–83, 286,
    295
blessing ceremonies, 276, 281–83, 286
bling, 61
block-making, 68
bloggers, 76
blouses, 34–35, 37, 42
Boas, Franz, 178
Bodhu Bala Sena (Buddha's Army),
    246, 249
body/ies, 5, 24, 39, 54, 80, 82, 206,
    233, 255–56, 258, 267, 278, 294,
    308
    creativity of the, 67
    denial of the, 74
    Jesus's, 201; *see also* body of
        Christ
    sensing, 247, 254–55, 258
    social, 223, 237, 239
body of Christ, 204, 281, 296
body and mind, opposition of, 75
bone pointing, 205–6
books, 95, 134, 209, 277
    comic, 237
    inventory, 152n4
    pattern, 57n15
    self-help, 74
boom, 46, 110
    art, 110
    etching, 44
    oil, 43, 50
    tourist, 65
Boon, Marcus, 292
Boradkar, Prasad, 87
born again, 294
boundaries, 5, 13, 15, 20, 64, 81, 88,
    91, 103, 165, 264, 302–3
    religious, 255, 264n1
Bourdieu, Pierre, 69
bourgeoisie, 17
bourgeoizification, 114
boutiques, 66, 82n1, 94
Brahman, 26n14, 219, 223, 230
Brahmin(s), 91, 94, 105, 124, 127, 225

brands, 50, 55, 61–62, 69–70
Brazil, 23–4, 41, 134–35, 152n1,
153n12, 267, 269–72, 276, 286–8,
288n7
southern, 145–46, 150
bridal wear, 62
British Columbia, 21, 158–59, 161,
163, 166, 168, 171, 177–78, 181
federal Government of, 163
University of, 163–64, 177
British Empire, 1
broker(s), cultural, 62, 66
bronze(s), 15, 17, 26n13, 27n18110,
127, 219, 223, 228, 233
Brosius, Christiane, 25n4, 112–14,
128, 221
Brothers of the Holy Cross, 299, 301
Brown, Eric, 165
Bucknor, Kobina, 296–97, 301, 307
Buddhism, 245
Theravada, 249
Buenos Aires, 134, 139
builders, 170–71
buildings, 119, 237, 273
Burro, 211n.10, 213n32, 213n35
business(es), 33, 35, 45, 50–3, 52,
58n27, 66, 92, 96, 103, 117; *see also*
market
fashion, 46, 59n34
businessman/men, 38, 48, 83, 113
businesspeople/persons, 120, 125
businesswomen, 46
bust, 110; *see also* recession
Butcher, Melissa, 221

cachaça, 277
cacique(s), 149, 151, 153n17
CACSA (Central Asia Crafts Support
Organisation), 104n1
café(s), 111, 120–21, 126
internet, 305
caiman, 149
calendar(s), 17, 104n3, 201, 276, 290,
299
cambric, 43
cameras, 147, 275, 280, 282; *see also*
mobile-phones
camphor flame, 246, 253
Canada, 21, 87, 89–91, 161–63, 165,
168, 177, 200, 212n28, 235, 315
Canadian Broadcasting Corporation,
172
Canberra, 193
candle(s), 230, 232, 259, 282
canoe(s), 267, 290

canvas, 188, 190, 191, 207, 290, 299,
303, 306
capital, 68, 70, 80, 108, 110, 112, 116,
118
cultural, 73
capitalism, 314–16; *see also* neo-
liberalism
card(s)
playing, 277
wedding, 22, 221, 233, 241n12
Carvalho, José Murilo de, 271
car(s), 43, 50, 273, 278, 304
casteism, 68
caste system, Hindu, 105n5
Catholicism, 23, 250–51, 254–55,
263–64, 269, 287
Brazilian, 23, 269, 271, 273,
288n4
popular, 269, 273, 288n7
Tamil Sri Lankan, 246, 250, 261,
264
transnational, 270–71
Catholics, 191, 206, 248, 250–51,
293
Brazilian, 272
Ghanaian, 293
Tamil, 23, 245–51, 255, 259, 264,
313
causality, person-thing, 220
Cave, the Holy, 235
celebrity(ies), 268, 277, 304, 307
ceramicists, 21, 143–44, 151
ceramics, 131, 133, 135, 140, 142,
145, 149, 314
Guaraní, 138, 141–44, 146–51
ceremonies, 91, 274, 276, 279–81
blessing, 276, 281–83, 286
life-cycle, 88
naming, 48
pre-puberty, 89
chalice, 201
chanting, 220, 223
Chattopadhyay, Kamaladevi, 91
Chauhan, Samant, 65
Chennai, 108–128, 128n.1, 128n6,
315
Chettiar(s), 87–92, 94, 103, 105n5
Chettiarness, 103
Chettinad region, 87–88, 90, 92–93,
95–96, 100
chiara-oscuro, 299
chiefs, 58n32, 296
China, 17, 64, 117, 286, 290
China lace, 50
Chiriguanos, 136

Cholamandal Artists Village, 20, 108–13, 119–27, 129n7
Christ, 195, 204, 206, 276, 281, 294, 296, 299; *see also* Jesus
Christianity, 27n.17, 188–93, 195, 200–1, 204, 207–9, 210n4, 246, 251, 293–94, 303, 313, 318
  Aboriginal, 186, 194
  popular, 292, 294
Christians, 23, 24, 200, 205, 246, 248–50, 241, 291, 293–98, 302, 304–5, 307–9, 309n1, 309n2
Christmas, 192, 301
Christology, African, 292, 298
Chulalongkorn, King of Siam, 40
church(es), 8, 14–16, 22, 189, 191, 198, 204, 208, 211n19, 246, 250, 252, 259, 265n4, 274–5, 281, 293, 295, 303, 305
  Brazilian, 282
  Catholic, 246, 248, 250–51, 256, 268–72, 282–83, 287, 296
  Christ the King, Accra, 296–97, 307
  Congregationalist, 211n8
  Crooswatta, attack on, 248
  Methodist, 211n18
  New Yirrkala, 193
  Pentecostal, 282, 292–94, 296
  Presbyterian, 211n18
  St. Francis Xavier Catholic, Nauiyu, 192, 214n36
  Saviour, of Ghana, 296
  Sinhalese, 246
  Tamil, 247–48, 251
  Uniting, of Australia, 188–89, 195, 211n18
Cícero, Father, 273, 288n8
CIM Project Final Conference, Utrecht, 82n1, 128
circulation, 207–9, 230, 246, 252, 258, 268–69, 273, 279, 283–84, 287, 305, 309, 316
circumpolar cultural area, 166
citation, 302
city/cities, 20, 62–63, 78, 86, 88, 97, 108–10, 112–19, 121–22, 124–28, 128n1, 128n2, 134, 151n1, 161, 267–8, 272–74, 276, 286–87, 296, 315
  capital, 20, 21, 63, 70, 131, 136, 151n1, 153n5, 159–61, 265n3, 272
  creative, 107–9, 118, 122–24, 126
  cosmopolitan, 40

  global, 108, 112, 114, 116–18
  Indian, 108, 112–13
  metropolitan, 103
  new, 109, 116
  world-class, 108, 113–14, 128
civilisation, 75, 119, 165
clans, (Australian Aboriginal), 190, 193, 195–96, 198, 211n10
class(es) (social), 17, 40, 50–51, 68, 72; *see also* elite, rank, status
  creative, 118
  educated, 48
  lower, 64
  middle, 35, 64–65, 82n2, 112–15, 120–21, 123–25
  ruling, 40, 66
  upper, 77, 115
  working, 121
classes (teaching), 137–40, 152n3
  basketry, 133
  ceramics, 133, 137, 140, 143, 147, 152n3
  cooking, 133, 139
  pottery, 133, 139, 146
clay, 1, 139, 142–43, 151, 152n4
cleanliness, 113–4
clergymen, 268, 270; *see also* priest
client(s), 42, 45, 61, 66, 72, 304, 306; *see also* customers
clientele, 20, 121
climate, 38, 48
cloak (of Aparecida), 271–72, 282–83, 287
cloth(s), 39, 55, 68, 303–4, 307; *see also* cotton, *brocade,* damask, fabric, linen, silk, textiles woollens, yarn
  cotton, 38, 91
  Kente, 296, 298, 307
  narrow-strip, 38
  resist-dyed, 37
clothing/clothes, 33–35, 39–41, 48–49, 51–52, 54, 57n.9, 58n21, 115, 258, 279, 304; *see also* dress, garment(s), style
  festive, 33, 41
  Christ's, 296
  European, 35, 48
  Nigerian, 35, 55
  traditional, 35–36, 38, 49
coats of arms, 273
cockatoo, 204, 213n29
Cocota, Bolivia, 140
Codere, Helen, 178
collaboration(s), 14, 56n1, 74, 98, 101, 114, 147–48, 288n1

collage, 299
collection(s), 27, 38, 44, 46, 55, 56,
    57n16, 63, 78, 95, 107, 110, 128,
    140, 151n1, 152n4, 163, 230, 277–
    80, 289n10
    archaeological, 139
    art, 127
    *Artisanal: Bringing the Craft to
        the Fore,* 76, 83n11
    bridal, 76
    ethnological, 181
    ex-voto, 289n9
    historical, 137
    museum, 8, 11, 71
    princely, 16
    Robert Holmes á Court, Perth,
        213n32, 214n35
    Sami, 167 –68
    Sub-Saharan Africa, 56
collectivism, 67
collector(s), 89, 101, 110, 115, 121,
    123, 128n1, 178
    art, 108, 117, 308
colonial era, 35, 42
colonial powers, 166
colonization, 40, 190
    mental, 300
    Portuguese, 136, 250
    Spanish, 136
colour(s), 43 –47, 50, 54, 96, 188,
    206–7, 228, 258–59, 302–3, 305
    pastel, 37, 43, 46
    sacred, 62
    seasonal, 46
    skin, 307
commodification, 125
commodities, 8, 74, 89, 100, 230, 294
    void, 309
communication, 7, 35, 42, 223, 227;
    see also connectivity, internet
    artistic, 208
    cross-cultural, 205, 208
communion, 201, 281
community/ies, 124, 144, 149, 153n15,
    173–74, 178, 187, 189–90, 201,
    210n2, 212n21, 212n23, 213n30,
    225, 276
    Aboriginal, 190
    Catholic, 251
    cooperative, 121
    French, 248
    global, 114, 296
    Guaraní, 134, 147
    Haida, 173
    Indian, 225

indigenous, 148
    merchant-banking, 88
    national, 246, 263
    Nauiyu, 210n3
    Gypsy, 10
    Romani, 10
    Sami, 178
    source
    Tamil, 248, 263
community groups, 10
Congo, 19, 55, 58n32
competitiveness, economic, 118
compromise, zones of, 270
concept note, 108, 116
conferences, 124, 126, 151n1
conflict, religious, 246
congregations, 268, 270
connectivity
    Ancestral, 202, 204
    global, 296
    transnational, 2
connoisseur(s), 72, 76, 79, 308
connoisseurship, 64, 66, 79
consciousness, 119, 227, 299; *see also*
    Super Consciousness
    national, 307
Construction Industrial Development
    Board (CIDB) of Malaysia, 114
consumers, 19, 89, 94, 115, 160, 209,
    291
    conscious, 103
    ethical, 66
    international, 103
consumerism, 94, 108
consumption, 7, 17, 23, 34, 56, 86,
    93, 103, 113–16, 118, 120, 125–26,
    159, 223, 312, 314
    elite, 41
    ethical, 72
    local, 57n6
    public, 98
contemporaneity, 36, 209
content, 56n1, 66, 73, 80–81, 116,
    132, 152n2, 162, 211n13
continuity, 54, 123, 149, 208
contradiction(s), 49, 67, 70, 218, 230,
    249, 315–17
convent, 191, 299, 301
convergence, 279–80
conversation pieces, 89; *see also* items,
    curio
conversion, 249, 251, 294
controversy, 50, 132, 181
cooking, 73, 133, 139
coolamon, 201

Coomarswamy, Ananda K., 73
cooperative(s), 110–11, 119, 122, 125, 127, 186, 210n6
Copenhagen Academy of Art, 175
copy(ies), 6, 50, 142, 144, 227, 277, 292, 305–6, 308, 313–14, 316
    authorized, 281, 286
    digital, 218
    mere, 298
    original, 284, 286
    resin, 284
copying, 1–3, 50, 75, 132, 146, 284, 291–92, 298, 302, 306, 308; *see also* imitation
    mere, 262
    mindless, 2, 238
    uncreative, 239
copyright, 70, 83, 104n2, 118, 152n1
Corrientes, 134, 136–37, 151–52n1
cosmology, 186
    Ancestral, 208
    Haida, 174
    Sami, 175
    pre-Christian, 175
    Yolngu, 196
costume(s), 8–12; *see also* clothing, clothes
    Bharatanatyam, 26n7
    Kathakali, 10, 26n7
    national, 19, 33, 55
    Nigerian, 19.33, 52
    Sami, 166
    traditional, 52
cotton, 37–38, 43–44, 54, 91; *see also* cambric, sateen, voile
    printed, 43, 57n8
Council, Second Vatican, 212n22, 250–51, 253, 296
Couture, Indian, 63, 76
craft(s), 1, 7, 10, 13, 18–21, 24, 34, 50, 61, 64–81, 83n.6, 83n7, 86–87, 91; *see also* art-craft dichotomy, handicraft, *tekhne*
    Indian, 19, 65, 76
    traditional, 19, 71
crafts councils, 97
    of India, 71, 82n4, 91–92, 104n1
    World, 86, 92, 97, 100
craftsman/men, 72–73
craftsmanship, 62, 72–73
Crafts Movement, Indian, 91
craftsperson/people, 17, 19, 65–81, 88
    disempowered, 65
    idealized, 71
    impoverished, 68

Indian, 73
    savage, 75
craftswoman/women, 20, 78–81
craftspeak, 67, 80
creation, 3, 6, 17–18, 26n12, 26n14
    divine, 14
    innovative, 7
creativity, 2–3, 6–7, 13–15, 18–24, 25n1, 25n3, 41, 55, 67–82, 87–88, 109, 112–28, 142, 144, 149–50, 170, 186–87, 195, 262, 268–69, 273, 287, 291–93, 298–99, 306, 308, 312–18; *see also* talent
    artistic, 14, 15, 68, 116, 126, 145, 169, 186–8, 207, 209, 317
    as improvisation, 3, 6, 11, 21, 87, 170, 221, 313–14
    collective, 67, 73, 81, 291
    cultural, 3, 170
    dynamics of, 23, 268, 270, 273, 281, 287, 288n6
    hierarchies of, 80–81
    ideology of, 15, 18
    Indian, 71
    individual, 15, 19, 67, 71, 81, 83n6, 291
    innovation and, 41, 74–6, 87, 109, 113, 116, 133, 140, 170, 287, 315
    Ngan'gi, 187
    positioned, 21, 158, 181
    traditional, 317
Creativity and Innovation in a World of Movement project, 128, 152n1, 210n4, 288n1, 313
Cribb, Guillermo, 140–43, 152n1
Cribb, Stella Maris Muñoz de, 137, 140, 152n1
crimes of fashion, 51
critics/criticism, art, 14, 22, 108, 116–18, 126, 176, 186, 200, 207
Crosby, Marcia, 163
Cross
    Ancestral, 190, 193
    Christian, 190, 195, 212n21, 252, 302
    Greek, 274
    Stations of the, 206, 214n36
Crown, the, 163
crown, 272, 286–87
cuisine, international, 115
cult(s)
    local, 270
    of Aparecida, 268, 271, 283, 286, 287

of artistic originality, 16
of innovation, 75
of our Lady of Nazareth, 273
cult objects, 15
cult value, 15
cultivation
artistic, 119, 122
lack of human, 119
of emotional states, 228
cultural area, circumpolar, 166–67
cultural biography, 87
cultural decay, 165–66
cultural difference(s), 52, 90, 194
cultural disintegration, 166
cultural diversity, 251
cultural heritage, 92, 103, 133, 168,
210n6, 227
cultural intermediaries, 71
cultural intervenors, 93, 103
cultural politics, 159, 167
cultural production, 2, 7, 13, 18, 21,
75, 87, 92–93, 102, 125, 169, 191,
312–18
cultural zones, 117
culture(s), 9, 11, 13, 15, 17, 24, 47,
58n19, 64, 90, 93, 97, 112–3, 117–
18, 125, 131, 134, 137, 139, 160,
165, 166–70, 172–73, 177, 189,
198, 212n23, 288n4, 300, 316
African, 45, 56
dress, 47, 49
European, 15, 145
Ghanaian, 301, 304
Guaraní, 133–35, 138–39, 143,
147, 152n3
Gypsy, 9, 11–12
Haida, 172–73
Indian, 72, 103
indigenous, 21, 131, 133, 135,
146, 165, 168, 251
local, 21, 52
material, 25, 56, 103, 134, 140,
160, 167, 177, 239, 263, 309
modern, 49, 315
Nigerian, 44, 47, 54
of self-creation, 316
of the copy, 316
popular, 82, 304, 318
reproduction of, 317
Sami, 160, 162, 166–67, 175,
178
Tamil, 127, 251
tribal, 16, 64
visual, 7, 63, 124, 192
curator/curation, 8–9, 11, 13, 21, 23,

56, 82, 98, 138, 152n3, 163, 198,
207, 209, 229, 230, 289n10
customers, 19, 40, 46, 62, 66, 69, 158,
186, 195, 201, 207–8, 307–8; *see
also* clients
elite/first-rate, 61, 64
Nigerian, 42, 47
customs, 12, 191, 251, 205

Dalits, 64
Dakshinachitra tourist attraction, 20,
92, 108–9, 113, 123–27
Daly River, Northern Territory,
190–91, 202, 210n3, 211–12n19,
213n35; *see also* Nauiyu
dance(s)/dancers, 11, 26n7, 97, 189–
90, 195, 213n29, 228
Ancestral, 200
classical, 11
folkloric, 145
Morris, 11, 13, 26
of hands, 5
darsan/darshan, 223–24, 227–28, 237,
256, 258
digital, 224, 240n6
Darwin, Charles, 15
Darwin, Northern Territory, 190, 191,
213n32, 214n35, 214n37
Davidson, Robert, 159, 181
Davis, Richard, 87, 219
death, 120, 204–6, 249
deception, 291
deconstruction, 292
deforestation, 136
deity(ies), 223, 225, 227–28, 230,
236–37, 241n12, 241n17–18, 253,
256, 261
feminine, 288n5
Delhi, 19, 61–63, 72, 75, 77–78, 82n1,
82n5, 83n8–9, 93, 104n1, 110, 112,
241n14
Dehradun, 61
democratization, 64, 290
demons, 294
denominations, Christian, 24, 188,
195, 202n19, 248, 293, 309n1–2
denominational differences, 22, 186,
194–95
dependency, 77, 82, 299, 301
Derrington, Patricia, 206, 214n37–8
descent, 136–7, 147, 187
Indian, 22, 225
design(s), 1, 4, 6, 8, 12, 15, 19–22,
33–35, 38, 40–42, 45–47, 67–68, 70,
73–76, 82n2, 90, 94, 100–1, 107,

138, 147, 170–172, 178, 186–88,
190–91, 193–95, 201–2, 204–5,
209, 211n10–11, 211n13, 212n23,
213n29, 213n31, 231, 233
  Aboriginal, 193, 207
  Ancestral, 186, 190, 193, 198,
    201, 208, 211n10
  Christian, 191–92, 207–8, 210n1
  fashion, 61, 72, 81
  figurative, 45, 211n12, 212n21
  industrial, 41, 68
  innovative, 88, 104n2, 186
  traditional, 1, 76
  Yolngu, 211n10, 212n27
design companies, 140
designers, 19, 42–46, 55, 58n33, 64–
  81, 95, 100–1, 291, 315
  fashion, 19–20, 36, 50, 53, 62, 66,
    70–71, 75–6, 80, 82n1, 83n6
  Indian, 19, 74
  wayside, 305
design institutes, 76
designspeak, 67
design templates, Ancestral, 186–87,
  207
design visionaries, 74
devaluation, 74, 81; see also
  evaluation, valuation
Devanagari, 81
developers, property, 110
development(s), 18–19, 74, 76, 80,
  113–14, 125, 134, 188, 313
  artistic, 177–78, 188, 201, 210n6
  craft, 68, 75, 79, 91
  design, 42, 45, 187
  heritage, 12
  mission, 188, 190
  rhetoric of, 74; see also discourse,
    developmental
developmentalists, 78
devil, the, 294, 296, 298; see also
  Satan
devotee(s), 23, 26n14, 251–52, 255,
  261–62, 264, 268–69, 275–87,
  288n5; see also worshipper
  Catholic, 23, 246, 251–52, 261–62
  Hindu, 222–3, 227–28, 234–35,
    237, 241n18, 242n21, 251–52,
    256, 258, 261–62, 284
devotional object(s), 24, 269
devotional practices, 23, 26n12, 223,
  225, 252, 268–70, 276, 283, 287,
  288n5, 313
devotional tradition(s), 23, 212n21,
  224, 228, 240n1

Dhammadipa, 245; see also Sri Lanka
Dhuwa moiety, 193, 212n24
Dhuyu Birrimbirr, 198; see also Holy
  Spirit
dialects, 161, 210n2
diaspora(s), 262
  Hindu, 233
  Nigerian, 33
  Tamil, 23, 247, 262–63
diasporic groups, Indian, 87
difference(s), 9, 67, 70, 78–79, 121,
  124–26, 144, 151, 159, 161, 169,
  191, 211n10, 221, 223
  class, 51
  cultural, 52, 90, 194
  denominational, 22, 186, 194–95
  politics of, 137
  power, 132, 144
  similarities and, 11, 169
  small, 142–44, 150
  status, 222
  systematic, 170
dilemma(s)
  for Aboriginal art market, 207
  for Cholamandal artists, 123
  of painting practices, 195
Dilthey, Wilhelm, 143
discourse(s), 3, 6, 14, 15, 17, 24,
  27n15, 64, 69, 79, 81, 96–97, 151,
  160, 178, 194, 208, 286–87, 308,
  317; see also narrative
  art, 181, 193
  developmental, 75
  heritage, 65–66, 77, 82n4, 124
  national/nationalist, 82n4, 287
  of creativity, 13–15, 18, 312, 314
  of improvisation, 6, 25n2
discrimination, 12, 262
disempowerment, 295
dispersion, 279–80
displacement, 279
distance(s), 66, 68, 76, 79, 145, 159,
  174, 221, 237–38, 264, 295, 315
  social, 67, 79
  spatial, 35, 67, 232, 239
  temporal, 67, 232, 239
distinction, 3, 15, 19, 35, 40, 51, 64,
  71–73, 74, 78, 111, 121, 211n11,
  314
  hierarchical, 64, 69
distributors, 42, 160, 186
diversity, 7, 208, 248
  cultural, 90, 251
divine, the, 15, 23–24, 26n12, 26n14,
  185, 219, 223, 226, 230, 234, 239,

241n11, 241n13, 255–56, 261, 263, 269, 295
djalkiri, 198
djambi, 187
Djewarrpuy Yolngu, 200; *see also* Jesus, Christ
doctrine(s), 169, 186, 305; *see also* dogmas, teachings
    Catholic, 192, 208–9, 283
    Christian, 189, 204
    Protestant, 22, 208–9
dogmas, Catholic, 270, 281
dominance, western economic, 292
dove, 195, 204
Dove Communications, 214n36
drawing (*v.*), 1, 68, 120, 306
drawing(s), (*n.*), 57n16, 175
    pastel, 301
dreams, 197, 294–6
Dreamtime, 192, 211n11
dress, 19, 35–36, 38, 48–49, 103–4, 252, 260; *see also* clothing
    European, 35, 41
    local, 41, 48
    modern, 36
    Nigerian, 37–38, 47
    traditional, 39, 41, 314
    women's, 39, 50, 54
drum and drumstick, shaman, 175
Duarte, Aurelio, 151, 152n1
Dubai, 62
duodji, 175
duplication, 132, 291; *see also* copying
Durga's treaty, 226
Dutra, Eduardo, 143, 145, 150–51, 152n1, 153n12
dyeing, 68
dyes
    chemical, 94–95
    natural, 104n2

East Arnhem Shire, 189
Easter, 201
East-Province (Sri Lanka), 246
economic competitiveness, 118
economic growth, 125
economic liberalization, 65, 112–3, 124, 127; *see also* neo-liberalism
economic theory, classical, 74
economy/ies, 17, 35, 54, 98, 108, 117, 124–25, 136
    creative, 116–120
    Indian, 110, 113
    neoliberal, 118, 125
    political, 118, 125

symbolic, 117, 125, 127
    village, 124, 127
Edenshaw, Charles, 172, 181
Edensor, Tim, 118
education, 1, 10, 15, 18, 57n6, 76, 145, 164, 190–91, 213n35, 250, 259, 265n6
    art, 153n12
effervescence, 269
egalitarianism, 65
eigen, 133; *see also* appropriation, ownership
Eisenlohr, Patrick, 234
Elcho Island Arts Centre, 186, 210n6
elders, 187, 201–2
elite(s), 40–41, 51, 52–53, 64–72, 81, 82n1, 100, 110, 121, 125, 200, 294, 301
    business, 64, 92
    local, 55, 110
    urban, 66, 87
elitism, 65
eliteness, 62
embroidery, 12, 34–56, 56n3, 58n24, 58n33, 65, 68, 70, 77, 79, 82n5, 105n4
    all-over, 43, 46
    Austrian, 34, 50, 53
    guipure, 34, 38, 42, 46
    hand, 19, 34, 82n1
    luxury, 50, 61, 82n1
    machine, 37, 39, 43
    sequin, 45–46
    shuttle, 34, 56n3
    whitework, 34, 42–43, 45, 70
embroidery patterns, 44, 57n16
emotion(s), 5, 9–10, 18, 21–23, 25, 88, 103, 188, 205, 220, 222–23, 228, 230, 232, 234, 239, 240n2, 246–47, 255–56, 258, 261–64, 274–75, 281–82, 292, 302, 308
emotional efficacy, 8, 269, 290, 298
empire, 15
    Benin, 40
    British, 1
    Portuguese, 271
    Soviet, 162
encounters, 42, 132, 268, 287, 296, 309
engagement, 9, 13, 18, 21, 23, 119, 144, 224, 234, 239, 249, 255
    affective, 218, 221–22
    creative, 292, 294–95, 309
    performative, 170, 317
    religious, 229, 292

sensational/sensorial/sensuous, 9,
186, 237, 295, 313
visual, 223, 237; *see also darsan*
with artefacts/objects/matter, 9,
15, 18, 82, 298
with Hindu idols/imagery/myth,
22, 219, 233, 238; *see also
darsan*
with Jesus pictures, 293–95, 298
England, 10, 41, 225, 240n7
entanglements, 22, 58n27, 208, 268,
314
entertainment, 115, 117, 223
entrepreneur(s), 92, 108, 113, 118, 290
artist as, 118, 126
socially responsible, 96
environment(s), 8, 42, 58, 78, 95,
104n2, 119–20, 223, 242n21, 250
emerging/unfolding, 13, 221
material, 8, 13, 247, 269
mediating, 221
social, 3, 13, 269
environmentalists, 114
eroticism, 175
Errington, Shelley, 97, 212n26
essence of India/Indianness, 66, 69, 76
etchings, 188
eternity, 81
ethic(s), 66, 69, 72, 109, 116, 118, 126,
131–32, 135, 148
artistic, 122, 126
Protestant work, 189
ethnographic material, 132, 163, 187,
247
Eucharist, 195, 201, 276, 281, 303
Europe, 7, 13–17, 34–35, 40–43, 56,
64, 110, 117, 167, 212n28, 292–3,
296
evaluation, 7, 93, 104n1–2, 126, 139,
167, 309; *see also* devaluation,
valuation
evangelization, 281, 283
exchange(s), 41–42, 50, 73, 129n7,
145, 148, 211, 223, 230, 302, 309;
see also transaction
cultural, 41, 198, 208
human-material, 171
exegesis, 281
exhibition(s), 104n3, 137, 199, 212n28
Aboriginal Art and Spirituality,
214n36
*African Lace: A History of Trade,
Creativity and Fashion in
Nigeria,* 55, 56n1, 58n33
art, 98, 126, 303

art-craft, 97–98
Arts of the Raven, 77
*Benin. Kings and Rituals. Court
Arts from Nigeria,* 56
*Canadian West Coast Art: Native
and Modern,* 165
crafts, 98
East Meets West, 9–12, 26n9–10
Gali Gurruwiwi, 196
In Memórium (2002), 145–46
international, 93, 196
kottan, 86, 92, 94–5, 97–98, 100
Legacy, The, 177
Living Legends, 86, 97–98, 100–
102
national, 93
One Hundred Years of B.C. Art,
177
painting and print, 213n32,
214n35
People of the Potlatch, 177
*Primitivism in Twentieth Century
Art: the Affinity of the Tribal
and the Modern,* 169, 171
*We Paint the Stories of our
Culture,* 209
World, Paris (1867), 56n3
exhibition value, 15
exotic goods, 40
exoticization, 96
experience(s), 4–5, 7–8, 15, 23, 94, 96,
107, 121, 162, 172, 181, 186, 191,
205, 219–24, 232, 234, 237–38,
240n11, 241n13, 242n21, 246–47,
252, 255–56, 258, 261–64, 264n1,
276, 279, 282–84, 287, 294–96,
304–5, 307, 316
aesthetic, 8, 210n5, 228, 261
embodied, 3, 14
emotional, 228, 240n2, 258
religious/spiritual, 26n14, 221–24,
227–29, 237, 246–47, 254–56,
258, 261–64, 282
sensorial/sensual, 210n5, 240n2,
263, 295
Tamil, 262–63
visionary, 295, 298
experimentation, 12, 49, 125, 132,
142, 314
expert(s), 67, 71–72, 76, 79, 81,
104n2, 166, 173
expertise, 62, 68
export(s), 19, 34, 41, 50, 52–53, 55,
57n6
externalization(s), 220, 224

extinction, 96, 163
ex-votos, 276–80, 289n9
ex-voto room, 276, 278, 284, 289n10;
see also Sala das Promessas, Room
of Promises, Room of Miracles

fabric, 12, 33–34, 36–37, 39–56, 56n3,
57n14, 57n16, 188; *see also* cloth,
cotton, *brocade,* damask, linen, silk,
textiles woollens
   adire, 36–38, 50
   African, 19, 40, 45
   ankara, 37–38, 57n8
   Atiku, 57n10
   brocade, 37, 39, 48
   cambric, 43
   cotton, 43–44
   damask, 37, 39, 48, 58n23
   embroidered, 50, 53–55
   European, 40
   guipure, 44, 46
   iborun, 39
   imported, 33, 39–40–41, 49
   industrial, 33, 49, 54, 58n33
   Indian, 40
   kente, 49
   lace, 50
   linen, 40
   luxury, 19, 40, 50, 55
   sateen, 43
   shain-shain, 50
   sheer, 45
   silk, 94
   traditional, 19
   voile, 43
   wax–print, 290
fabrication, moment of, 298, 308
factory/factories, 42, 47, 52, 58
fairs art/craft, 20, 93
faith, 26n12, 126, 194–95, 274, 277–
78, 280, 283, 295, 300
   Aboriginal, 22, 205
   Catholic, 276
   Christian, 22, 185, 198, 200, 205
   in Ancestral law, 189
   in Aparecida, 278, 281
   in human progress, 169
   popular, 282, 287
faith-healer, Aboriginal, 205
family, 15, 22, 39, 46, 52, 57n17,
58n21, 61, 65, 82n2, 89, 91, 94,
124, 163, 174–75, 191, 202, 218–
19, 222, 225, 227–28, 230, 233–34,
238, 248, 252–53, 259, 261, 264,
274, 276–77, 282, 309n2

Brahmin, 91, 94
Catholic, 247, 274
   royal, 214, 272
   spiritual national, 276
   transnational, 239, 264n1
fashion, 2, 7, 18–20, 33, 43–50, 55,
57n16, 58n33, 61, 63–64, 70,
73–76, 81–82, 82n1, 82n10, 101,
103, 117, 132, 312, 316; *see also*
business, fashion, design, fashion,
designers, fashion, market, fashion,
style
   crimes of, 51
   European, 34–7, 41
   Indian, 66, 69–70, 74, 76
   international, 46, 55, 76
   Nigerian, 48–49
Fashion4Development, 58n34
feeling(s), 23, 94, 143, 200, 220, 222,
224–25, 233, 236, 239, 240n6, 247,
254–56, 261, 263–64, 269, 273–74,
276, 279, 281, 283–84, 286, 288n5,
295, 301; *see also* affect, emotion
Festivals,
   FESTAC, 49
   Fiesta del Inmigrante, 147
   Hampstead Summer, 95
Fett, Harry, 167 8
feudalism, aesthetic return to, 63
financial crisis of, 2008, 64
Finland, 162
Finnefondet foundation, 162
Finnmark, 161, 167, 179
Fiofori, Tam, 51–52
First Nations, 159, 161–65, 171, 177,
181; *see also* Indians
   British Columbian, 163
fishermen, 267
Fitzmaurice region, 190
Five Year Plan(s) (India), 91, 113
food, ritual, 304, 309n3
movements, centripetal and centrifugal,
24, 269, 272–73, 276, 279, 282,
287
Forson, Gilbert, 305
Fourth World, 159
fragmentation, social, 169
fremd, 133; *see also* Other
Fuller, Chris, 128, 223
funerals, 48, 57n17

Galiwin'ku, 22, 186, 189–90, 192–93,
195, 198–99, 207, 210n4, 211n17,
213n30
Galiwin'ku Mission, 188

gallery/ies, 14, 86, 97–98, 103, 108,
    110–11, 115, 117, 121, 128n1,
    128n5, 165, 199, 237, 303, 307
    Art Chennai, 111
    Art, of Western Australia, 213n32
    Cholamandal, 111
    Dakshinachitra, 124, 126
    Galiwin'ku, 207
    London, 197
    National, of Victoria, 214n35
    Noble Sage, London, 110
    Ottawa National, 165
    Rebecca Hossack, 196
    Vancouver Art, 177
    Worthing Museum and Art, 9
    Yale University Art, 56
Galpu clan, 195, 199
garland(s), 23, 246, 251–52, 256–9,
    261–63
garment(s), 19, 39, 41, 48, 54, 58n33,
    67, 69–70, 74, 82n2, 219, 228; *see
    also* clothing, clothes, costume, dress
    designer, 71, 74, 81
    embroidered, 55, 70
Gastaldo, Javier, 138, 152n1, 153n8
gauchos, 145
Gaup, Aage, 178
Gautama Buddha, 245
gaze, 68, 69, 227, 275, 308
Gell, Alfred, 254
genius, artistic or creative, 14, 16, 18,
    27n16, 67, 70, 73–74, 81, 97, 169,
    308, 314, 316; *see also* individual,
    creative, creativity
genre(s), 16, 18, 187, 207–8
genuine, the, 256, 292; *see also*
    authentic
Ghana, 24, 49, 57n12, 290–309,
    309n3, 318; *see also* Gold Coast
Ghanaization, 296
Ghandi, Mahatma, 91
Ghandian(s), 112, 121, 125
Gibson, Mel, 305
Gjessing, Guttorm, 166–7
Gladstone, Charles, 172
Glass, Aron, 165
globalization, 2, 35, 108
Goa, 62, 107
Gocking, Roger, 302
God, 74, 81, 147, 170, 192, 197–99,
    202, 204–5, 222, 224–25, 227, 234,
    238, 240n3–4, 255, 261, 263, 293,
    295, 297
goddesses, 222–23, 234, 241n11
    Kali, 234

Lakshmi, 219, 234
Mata Vaishno Devi, 234, 241n13
Vraja, gopi damsels of, 237
gods, 75, 81, 123, 175, 218–20, 222–
    28, 230, 232–33, 237–39, 241n11–
    12, 246, 252, 256–58, 262, 293–94;
    see also murtis
    Ganesh, 123, 218–19, 221, 223–
        24, 228–31, 234, 241n12
    Kali, 234
    Krishna, Lord, 228, 236–37,
        241n18
    Lakshmi, 219, 234
    Mata Vaishno Devi, 234, 241n13
    Vraja, gopi damsels of, 237
Gold Coast, 1, 293, 296, 298; *see also*
    Ghana
González, Elba, 138, 152n1
Goulburn Island, Northern Territory,
    118
Gove land rights case, 194, 212n25
government(s), 4, 18, 65–66, 79, 82n2,
    82n4, 91, 97, 110, 112, 117, 136,
    163, 167, 186, 191, 193–94, 210n6,
    211n19, 268
    Australian, 189, 193
    Northern Territory, 214n37
    Norwegian, 167
    of British Columbia, 163
    of Canada, 162–63
    of India, 91
    of Sri Lanka, 247
    of Tamil Nadu, 114, 127
    provincial, 137, 163
    state, 114, 127
gown, Hausa-style, 39, 41, 48
Graburn, Nelson, 158–9
grammar of social intercourse, 188
Great Britain, 34, 42; *see also* UK
Greeks, ancient, 307
Greenland, 167
Grieser, Alexandra, 239, 288n1
Guaraní, 21, 131–51, 152n3, 153n6,
    153n17, 314
    ancient, 136, 140, 142, 144–5,
        150–51
    archaeological, 133, 150
    contemporary, 134, 136–37, 140,
        143
    historical, 133–35, 147
    indigenous, 136, 140, 143
    Mbya, 134, 136–38, 147, 149,
        151, 153n4
Guaratinguetá, Brazil, 267, 270
Guinea *brocade; see* brocade

guipure; see embroidery, *guipure,* fabric, *guipur*
Gurruwiwi, Gali Yalkarriwuy, 195–200
guru(s), 22, 238, 240n6, 241n16
    Indian based, 235
    software, 113
    style, 62, 69, 316

habit(s), 232, 284
habitus, 8
Haida, 161, 171–74
Haida Gwaii, 172
halal system, 249
Hall, Stuart, 145
Hallam, Elizabeth, 2–4, 13, 20, 87–88, 118, 170, 221, 262, 313–14, 317
halo, 212n21, 302
Hancock, Mary, 124–5, 127, 129n8
handicraft(s), 27n16, 62, 70, 91–92, 96, 104n1–2, 175; *see also* craft, craftsmanship
Hannerz, Ulf, 220
harmony, 223
    inner, 219, 227
Hastrup, Kirsten, 3, 25n5, 170
Hausa-Fulani, 51
Hawthorn, Audrey, 163–4
Hawthorn, Harry, 163–4, 177
Hawthorn report, 164
healing, 204–7
health, 113, 136–7, 164, 259
hegemony, 134, 176
    cultural, 117
    structural, 137
    upper-caste, 127
Heinich, Nathalie, 100, 102
heritage, 7, 11–13, 20–21, 24, 26n8, 65–68, 71, 72, 77–80, 92, 98, 103, 123–26, 165, 171, 313–16
    Chettiar, 92
    cultural, 92, 103, 109, 133, 168, 210n6, 227
    Guaraní, 136
    Indian, 64, 66, 71, 78, 82n4
    indigenous, 133
    intangible, 79, 82n4
    luxury, 64, 66–7, 79, 82n4
    national, 65, 68
    politics of, 20, 91, 133
    tangible, 79, 82n4
    transformative potential of, 20
Heritage Lottery Fund, 11–12
hermeneutics, 132, 143–45
hierarchy/hierarchies, 40, 62, 66, 72, 81, 97, 188, 299

Catholic, 270, 281, 287, 288n5
class, 68
Hindu(s), 22–23, 90, 218–39, 240n1, 313
    Sri Lankan Tamil, 23, 245–51, 255–56, 261–64, 265n4, 313
Hindu, The, 92–93, 108, 115
Hinduism, 23, 62, 235, 240n3, 246, 249, 251, 255–6, 263–64, 313
    devotional, 128, 227
    material, 103
    Tamil, 246, 264
Hinduism Today, 235
Hindu rate of growth, 64
Hindu subjectivities, 235
historiography, 124
history, 11, 12, 19–21, 33, 35, 40–42, 47, 57n7, 57n15, 58n25, 58n33, , 68, 100, 108, 110, 122, 127, 148, 152n3, 160, 163, 168, 171, 192, 210n7, 251, 269, 271, 288n2, 291–92, 302, 309
    art, 14, 109, 116, 122–23, 125, 173
    colonial, 148, 299
    mythic, 267
    postcolonial, 57n6, 148
Hobart, Angela, 255
Hogan, Joe, 101
Holm, Geir Tore, 180
Holm, Bill, 173
Holy Communion, 201; *see also* Eucharist
Holy Spirit, 198, 202, 254
holy water, 280
homelands, 234
    traditional Aboriginal, 190, 202
    traditional Sami, 161
Homo Sapiens wood-engraving, 175
human condition, 108, 175, 181
humans, 26n14, 182n1, 187, 204, 220, 241n17, 247, 254–56, 292, 313
Hundertpfund, Heinz, 35
Hunt, Tony, 181
Huyler, Stephen, 222

iconoclash, 47
iconoclasm, 47
identity/ies, 9, 17, 41, 72, 80, 88, 90, 102, 113, 133–34, 137–38, 145–48, 150–51, 159, 164, 179, 186–87, 193–96, 200, 208, 212n24, 220, 249, 253
    Aboriginal, 161, 186, 188, 192, 208

cultural, 65, 104n2, 163, 174, 181, 207
ethnic, 177, 181, 246
indigenous, 145, 162
legal, 162
national, 4, 80, 164, 245, 252, 263–64, 272
Nigerian, 41, 49
religious, 207, 246, 249, 263–64
social, 19, 94
Tamil, 246, 251–52, 262–64
Yolngu, 193–94
identity politics; *see* politics, identity
ideology/ideologies, 7, 15, 17–19, 21, 25n2, 63–64, 68, 82, 127, 137, 153n16, 192, 309
charismatic, 69, 74
of Buddhist Sinhalese supremacy, 245, 249
of creativity/creation, 17, 21, 69, 74, 81
idolatry, 293
Igbo, 51
Illinois, 296
image(s)/imagery, 2, 4, 6–9, 11–12, 15, 18, 20, 22–24, 26n10, 35, 47, 55, 66, 69, 71, 81, 87, 92, 95–96, 102, 109, 113, 121, 124, 132, 153n17, 163, 175, 181, 186–87, 195, 198, 201, 206, 211n13, 219–20, 225, 232, 237, 239, 240n2, 240n6, 241n12, 252, 256, 267–69, 271–72, 274, 281–87, 296–97, 301–2, 305; *see also* production, image
Ancestral, 195, 198
Aperecida's, 270–72, 281, 284, 287, 288n5–6, 313
Christian, 175, 189, 207
circulating, 159, 237, 268
digital, 220–21, 237, 305
god, 26n14, 218, 220–22, 224, 227–28, 230, 237, 239
Hindu, 238, 240n6
idealized, 72, 118
mental, 240n10, 293
moving, 12, 26n9
original, 23, 269, 272–73, 275–76, 280, 282–83, 287
religious, 16, 23, 290
sacred, 22, 237, 240n6
televised/television, 226, 282
valuation of, 269, 283
visual, 6, 25n4
world-class, 122, 126
image flows, transcultural, 25n4

imaginary, 114, 120, 126, 232
imagination, 69–71, 74, 76, 108, 112–17, 122–24, 144, 171, 224, 240n10, 293, 296, 305; *see also* reimagining
anticipatory, 144
Christian, 294, 298
creative, 16
global, 122
musical, 5
Nehruvian, 113
imagined whole, 223
IMF; see International Monetary Fund
imitation(s), 2, 6, 16, 18, 201, 290, 292, 298, 302–4, 307–9, 312–13; *see also* copying
immanence, 219
affective, 222, 313
immediate, the, 220
immigrants, 41, 147, 150
Chettiar, 103
European, 147
immorality, 17, 47; *see also* morals/morality
improvisation(s), 2–7, 13, 18–19, 21–23, 25n2–3, 87, 109, 118, 125–26, 170, 171, 201, 221–22, 230, 235, 238–39, 281, 283, 287, 312–13
creative, 21, 24, 170, 228, 313
creativity as, 3, 6, 11, 21, 87, 170, 221, 313–14, 317–18
musical, 4, 6
relational, 4, 118
incense, 23, 220, 246, 252–55, 258–63
income, 22, 62, 115, 150, 210n6; *see also* money
inculturation, 251, 253, 262, 313
independence, 4, 176
Ghana's, 49, 306
Indian, 64, 91, 112, 125
Nigerian, 34–35, 39, 48–49, 52
Sri Lanka's, 250
India, 9–10, 15–16, 20, 26n13–14, 27n15, 40, 57n12, 62–81, 82n2, 82n4–5, 83n7, 83n10, 86–103, 104n1, 107–28, 128n1, 219, 223–25, 232–35, 237, 239, 241n14, 241n16
North, 62, 66, 82n1, 82n5, 224
South, 12, 20, 87, 90, 92, 96, 103, 107–10, 123–25, 127–28
Indian Act, Canada, 162
Indian Affairs, Canada, 164
Indian Community Centre, Belfast, 225, 235
Indian(s) (American), 162, 165, 200
'the Imaginary', 165

Indiana, 299
Indianness (in India), 61.64, 66, 71–72, 76, 79, 103, 125
Indianness (North American), 165
Indigenization Decrees (Nigeria), 50
indigenous people of Japan, 200
individualism, 67, 169
individual(s), 4, 11, 15, 17–20, 39, 51, 68–70, 72–73, 81, 92, 100, 102–3, 104n2, 118, 145, 160, 173, 186, 201, 208, 210n7, 220, 223, 227, 238, 240n2, 251, 302
   creative, 18, 67, 316; *see also* creativity, individual
industrialists, 108, 110
industry/industries, 18, 117, 189,
   art, 117, 197, 210n6
   craft, 50, 210n6
   creative, 18, 49, 50, 59n34, 110, 118, 313–14
   embroidery, 34–35, 42, 55, 56n4, 58n33
   fashion, 19, 58n34, 65, 69, 76, 82, 117
   music, 6, 117
inequalities, social, 24, 299
infantilism, psychological, 294
infrastructure(s), 6–8, 16, 22, 113, 126
Ingold, Tim, 2–4, 13, 20, 87–88, 118, 170, 221, 250, 262, 313–14, 317
innovation(s), 2–3, 18–20, 23, 35, 41, 50, 55, 67, 71, 74–76, 87–88, 104n2, 109, 113, 116, 125–26, 133, 140, 167–68, 170, 187–88, 209, 273, 312, 314, 318
   creativity as, 116, 314–15
inspiration, 2, 13, 16, 20, 42, 45, 46, 54, 55, 57n16, 67, 68, 70, 73, 133–34, 139, 165
institution(s), 2, 4, 7, 8, 13, 17–18, 20, 21, 92, 101, 103, 112, 113, 133–34, 137, 151n1, 160–61, 167, 171, 177–78, 189, 248
   art/artistic, 108–10, 127
   museum, 137, 163
   neocapitalist, 301
   religious, 235
Instituto Superior Antonio Ruiz de Montoya in Posadas, 138, 151n1, 152n3
intellectual property, 83n6, 118
interdependency, 19, 291
interiority, 74
International Monetary Fund (IMF), 301

internet, 35, 237, 240n6, 299, 305
interpretation, 9, 47, 81, 132, 142, 144, 150, 168, 172, 174, 185–86, 190, 194, 195, 200–1, 207, 210n5, 251, 293–94, 302, 309; *see also* re-interpretation
interpretive schemas; see schemas, interpretive
intimacy, 223, 255
Inuit, 161–62, 200
invention of tradition; see tradition, invention of
investment, 20–21, 74, 109, 113, 271, 282, 316
   emotional, 223
ironwood tree, 205
irony, 2, 79–80
Islam, 41, 55; *see also* Moslems
Italy, 14, 42, 147, 286
ITC Grand Chola, 86, 100
item(s), 10, 11, 16, 20, 22, 51, 88–90–91, 94, 102, 132, 227–28, 233, 239, 241n17, 279, 286; *see also* artefact, object
   curio, 89, 91, 103
   kottan, 88, 93
   mass-produced, 159
   original, 145
   prestige, 43, 46

Jackson, John Payne, 48
Jaffna, Sri Lanka, 247–48, 250–53, 256, 264n1, 265n3–4
Jåks, Iver, 168, 171, 174–76, 178
Japan, 16, 93, 107, 200
Jesus, 24, 198, 200–2, 212n21, 290–309, 309n2, 313; *see also* Christ
jewellery, 12, 26n7, 172, 258
   kottan, 101
Jobs, Steve, 74
John the Baptist, 202
journalists, 53, 120
Jullundur district, 224
jute, 87, 100–1

Kaivalam, 97; *see also* Worlds Crafts Summit
kala, 73; *see also* artist, craftsperson
Kandinsky, Wassily, 307–9
Kant, Immanuel, 74
Kapferer, Bruce, 255
Karasjok, Finnmark, 167, 174–75
Kathakali, 9–10, 12–13, 26n7, 26n10
Katherine, Australia, 213n32, 214n35
Kattankudy, Sri Lanka, 249

Kautokeino, Finnmark, 167, 178
Keane, Webb, 220
Keesing, Roger, 251
Kerala, 9–10, 89, 108, 124, 129n7
killer whale(s), 159, 174
kilns, electric, 139
kinship, 89, 120, 187–88, 195, 201,
    209, 211n10, 281
Kirshenblatt-Gimblett, Barbara, 98
knowledge, 12, 67, 68, 70, 76, 79, 81,
    125, 134, 137, 148, 173, 178, 187,
    195, 201, 223, 227, 235
    abstract, objective, 255
    Ancestral, 196
    artistic, 187
    embodied, 70
    expert, 76, 81
    gendered, 211n11
    'inside and outside', 187, 211n11
    internalized, 229
    religious, 188, 208
    ritual, 211n11
    shared, 187, 211n11
    specialist, 140
    technical, 42
    theoretical, 138
    traditional, 75, 179
knowledge society, 72, 76, 81
knowledge systems, 97
    Aboriginal, 195
Koodais, 96; *see also* baskets
kottan, 86–103, 315; *see also* baskets,
    kottan, jewellery, *kottan*
Krishnamachari, Bose, 108, 115–16
Krishna, Usha, 87, 92, , 97, 100
Kshatriyas, 105
Kubler, George, 144
Kumar, Ritu, 71–72, 76, 83n7
Kumasi, Ghana, 302, 309n1
Kvænangen, Norway, 162
Kwakwakw'wakw (Kwakuitl), 161

labour, 17, 35, 64, 68, 96
    individualisation of, 100, 102
    manual, 71, 73
labourer, skilled manual, 55, 97; *see
    also* craftsman, craftsperson/people,
    craftswoman
lace, 19, 33–56
    African, 19, 33–56, 57n15, 314
    chemical, 34; *see also guipere*
    China, 50
    Flemish, 58n31
    organza, 54
    Nigerian, 55

Portuguese, 55
    real, 34
    so-called, 38
    white, 35
La Cioppa, Claudio, 58n34
Lagos, 34–35, 37, 41, 46, 48, 51, 52,
    56n1, 57n14, 58n21, 58n29
Lagos Weekly Record, 48
Lahpoluoppal, Norway, 178
land, 11, 111, 119–20, 175, 190–94,
    196, 202, 204, 209
    Ancestral, 193
    politics of, 186
land-rights, 134, 162, 163, 167, 179,
    193–94, 212n25, 212n27
landscape(s), 34, 96, 165, 191–92, 250
    media, 221
    rural, 64
    sacred, 239
    urban, 114
language(s), 13, 67, 74, 81, 161, 190,
    213n31
    art as global/universal, 125, 169
    body, 5
    critical, 97
    English, 193
    Guaraní, 136–37, 153n6
    Gumatj, 193
    Latin, 251
    local, 251
    liturgy, 251
    power of, 81
    Sami, 162, 167, 179
    Sanskrit, 26n14, 27n18, 73, 227
    Tamil, 251
language group(s), 210n2–3
    Ngen'giwumirri, 202, 205
language policy, 162
Lapa, Bom Jesus da, 273, 288n8
Lapp(s), 162; *see also* Sami
    Paleolithic proto-, 167
Latour, Bruno, 27n15, 47
Lauck, Father Harold, 296
law
    Aboriginal, 192–93
    Ancestral, 186–87, 189–90, 193–
        95, 198–99, 202, 209, 210n8,
        211n10
    copyright, 83n6
    labour, 104n2
    provincial, 137, 153n6
laying of hands, 205
Leary, Father John, 192, 212n21
lecturers, 75–76
leisure, 117, 121, 125–26

Leme, Cardinal Sebastião, 272
Liberation Tigers of Tamil Eelam
    (LTTE), 245, 251; *see also* Tamil
    Tigers
Liep, John, 3, 20, 87–88
Liuzzi, Chela, 136
life cycle, 87–88
life worlds, 22, 309
liturgy, 16, 26n24, 192, 251, 270, 276,
    281–82
    Catholic, 192, 251, 270, 275,
        288n4
logo(s), 43, 61, 213n31; *see also* motif
London, 95, 108, 110, 196–197
Lopes, José Rogério, 288n1
Lowe, Beulah, 190
Lucknow, 19, 70, 77–78, 80, 82n1,
    82n5
Lustenau, Austria, 34, 45–46, 48, 53,
    57n18, 58n25, 58n29, 58n34
Lustima fabric company, 45
luxury, 19, 40, 43, 50, 55, 61, 64, 66–
    67, 70, 72, 76, 79, 82n1, 82n4, 100,
    113, 115, 128n1
lycée, 262, 265n6
Lyell Island, 173

Macdonald, Sharon, 160
machine(s), 34, 55, 56n3, 68
machinery of status, 71–72
madayin, 199, 211n9; *see also* law,
    Ancestral, objects, ritual
Madras, 88, 92, 110, 119; *see also*
    Chennai
Madras modernism, 110
Madras Movement, 111, 120, 122
Madu, Sri Lanka, 258
Madu Matha, 258
Magellan House Women's Centre,
    Nauiyu, 201; *see also* Merrepen Arts
    Centre
magic, 67, 69, 74, 81, 168, 173, 295
Maharaja(s), 61, 64
    of Rajkot, 62
MalakMalak, 190, 212n20; *see also*
    ownership, Traditional Owners
mall(s), 113, 115, 117, 147
    O2 Shopping, London, 95
    Express Avenue, Chennai, 108,
        115–16, 120
managers (of the shrine of Aparecida),
    275, 282, 289n10
mandir, 225, 230–33, 240n9; *see also*
    shrine
manufacture/manufacturers, 2, 15, 17,

19, 34–35, 40–42, 46, 47, 52, 55,
    57n18, 90, 94, 139, 142, 144, 150,
    177, 219, 230, 241n16; *see also*
    production
map(s)/mapping, 11, 153n5, 212n23,
    272, 273
Marina Beach, Chennai, 108, 113–15,
    117, 120, 125
Marrfurra, Patricia, 191, 192, 195,
    201–4, 210n1, 213n32
market(s), 2, 18, 20, 33–35, 40–41,
    44–45, 50, 52, 57n18, 64–65, 68,
    74–76, 93–96, 104n2, 110, 140,
    201, 290, 295–96, 298
    African, 33, 46
    art, 2, 7, 17, 22, 109, 115, 186,
        194, 201, 207–8
    consumer, 94, 100, 102
    fashion, 2, 7, 68
    free, 125
    global, 41, 96
    Indian, 65, 109
    luxury, 40, 72
    Nigerian, 42, 45, 50
    St. George's, Belfast, 230
marketability, 104n2, 118
market forces/demand, 6, 17, 73, 171,
    198
marketing, 56, 66, 74, 79, 103, 115,
    120, 177; *see also* advertising
market research, 46
Maroons, 158
marriages, 89, 94, 191, 253; *see also*
    weddings
Martin, Mungo, 165, 173, 181
Mary
    Mother, 23, 250, 252, 258; *see
        also* Matha
    Our Lady of Aparecida; *see*
        Aparecida
    Our Lady of the Immaculate
        Conception; *see* Aparecida
    Our Lady of Nazareth, 273
    Our Lady of the Rosary, 271
    Virgin, the, 256, 259, 269, 271,
        280
Mass(es), 192, 247–48, 251–52, 274–
    76, 279–83, 286
masterpiece(s), 86, 100–1
material(s), 3, 4, 6–8, 10, 12, 13, 15,
    18, 2o–25, 25n4, 26n7, 36, 39, 41,
    43–47, 49–51, 53, 55, 62, 66, 68,
    72, 73, 75, 81, 82, 87, 89, 91, 94,
    97, 101, 103, 104n2, 112, 115, 132,
    138, 140, 142, 145, 148, 150–51,

152n4, 160, 166, 169–71, 189–90,
213n29, 218–20, 223, 225–26, 229–
30, 234, 238, 239, 241n17, 246–47,
251, 254–55, 258, 262–64, 269,
278, 281, 286, 291–92, 294–96,
302, 308, 313, 317
    aesthetic, 246, 263
    base, 33, 43–44, 46, 54
    copyright, 118
    cotton, 37, 57n8
    ethnographic, 132, 163, 197, 247
    hand-woven, 48, 53–54
    lace, 51, 54
    male, 37–38
    promotional, 96
    raw, 19, 56
    traditional, 33, 36, 75
    visual, 189
material culture, 56, 134, 103, 140,
160, 167, 177, 263, 309
materialization, 125, 170, 239, 277,
280, 291–92, 302, 315
Matha, 252, 256, 258, 259–61, 263;
    see also Madu Matha, Mary, Mother
Máze-group, 178
McTaggart, Patricia Marrfurra, 201–2
meaning(s), 3, 6, 8, 11, 18, 20, 22, 48,
58n33, 62, 72–74, 79–81, 87–90,
103, 109, 127, 132, 144, 148, 158,
170, 173, 189–90, 195–96, 198,
200–2, 204, 208, 210n5, 211n13,
228, 251, 254, 256, 262, 269, 290,
292, 294–95, 298–99, 301, 303,
307–9; *see also* ideology
    Ancestral, 189, 190, 195, 207
    Christian, 195, 207
    multiple, 71, 80, 135
    religious, 188, 233
media, 6–8, 46, 66, 74, 92–93, 209,
221, 238, 282, 293, 308; *see also*
multimedia
    art, 191
    digital, 20
    fashion, 76
    local, 92–93
    mass, 282, 290
    print, 92
mediation, 23–24, 220–21, 224, 234,
236, 239, 240n5, 282, 292; *see also*
remediation
    material, 23, 234, 238–39
    technologies of, 238, 301
mediators, 23, 223, 230, 269, 284
meditation, 26n14, 81, 206, 240n1
Mekuye, Goodwin, 37

memory/ies, 26n8, 45, 96, 224, 232,
250
    embodied, 232
Mensah, Ato, 301
merchants, 34, 35, 40, 41, 52–53,
55, 57n14; *see also* trader, trading
houses
meritocracy, 68
Merrepen Arts, 186, 202, 205, 208,
210n6, 212n23, 213n31, 213n35,
214n37
meshwork, 250, 262
Métis, 161–62
migrant(s), 10, 20, 41, 166, 218, 238–
39, 262, 313; *see also* immigrants
    Chettiar, 89–90
    Indian, 110, 235
migrations, historical, 136
Milan, 302
Milingimbi, Northern Territory, 188
mimuy; see yam
Minas Gerais, 267
mind, 4, 67, 80, 159, 160, 168, 218,
227, 251, 256, 258, 305, 306
    colonized, 301
    open, 238
    opposition of body and, 75, 25n3
    perverse and deranged, 75
mining on Ancestral land, 193; *see also*
Nabalco
minority
    ethnic, 240n8, 248
    linguistic, 212n20
    religious, 249
    Tamil, 245
miracles, 267, 270, 278, 283; *see also*
Room of Miracles
Misiones Province, Argentina, 21, 131–
51, 151n1, 152n3–4, 153n17
Misiones Creativa design company,
147
mission(s), 22, 185, 188–89, 191–92,
206–8, 210n7, 292, 318
    Aboriginal Apostolate, 191
    Anglican, 211n15
    Catholic, 192, 207, 212n19
    diplomatic, 34
    Galiwin'ku, 188
    global (Hindu), 235
    impact upon (Australian)
        Aboriginal livelihoods, 185
    Jesuit, 21, 131, 136, 148, 190,
211n19
    Methodist, 188–89
    Nauiyu Nambiyu, 190–91

Sami, 175
Yirrkala Methodist church, 193
missionary/ies, 15, 22, 41, 57n11,
   188–94, 207–8, 213n30, 270, 287,
   290, 293, 296
   Catholic, 185, 190–91, 212n19,
      250, 293
   Methodist, 185, 189–91
   of the Sacred Heart, 191, 212n21
mobility, 7, 88, 91, 104n3, 136, 234–
   35, 269, 313; *see also* movement,
   transit
   social, 104n3, 296
Mobutu, Joseph-Desiré Sese Seko, 49
mode of life, 87
modernism, 122, 169, 176
   Madras, 110
modernity, 24, 36, 54, 71, 112, 113,
   123, 125, 169–70, 177, 179
   Western, 15, 316
modesty, popular, 273
Momodu, Dele, 54
monarchy, 272
monastery, 302
money, 26n8, 62, 73, 77–79, 127, 169,
   279; *see also* capital, income
monks, Buddhist, 245–46, 248–49
Montreal, 165
monuments, 8, 92
Moon River Store, 94, 96
morals/morality, 47, 54, 69, 72, 112,
   187–88, 193, 211, 225, 235, 294,
   309; *see also* immorality
Morgan, David, 308
Morgan, Lewis, 15
Morning Star, 195–96, 198–200,
   213n29
mosaic(s), 14, 274, 278
mosques, attacks on (Sri Lanka), 245,
   249
   Dambulla, 248
Mother's house, the, 274, 276, 280,
   286–87
motif(s), 12, 43, 45, 46, 50, 54, 90,
   143, 152n2, 158, 159, 163, 177,
   305, 309; *see also* logo, pattern
   floral, 43, 46
   Jesus, 290–91, 295, 301, 305–6,
      313
motive(s), 96, 248, 250
movement, 7–8, 10, 19, 25n4, 34, 36,
   39, 48, 49, 55, 59, 87–88, 90, 96,
   127, 170, 234, 252, 254, 255, 261,
   268–87, 314; *see also* mobility,
   transit

centripetal and centrifugal, 273,
   276, 279, 282, 287
   clockwise, 253, 263
   ritualized, 255
   translocal, 7, 24
M Rm Rm Foundation, 86, 92–95,
   102
multiculturalism, 21, 41, 145, 151
multimedia, 12, 26, 111, 302; *see also*
   media
multinational companies, 94, 114
Mumbai, 108, 110, 112, 113, 128n2;
   see also Bombay
Munn, Nancy, 204
mural, 274
murti(s), 218, 221, 223, 225, 228; *see
   also* gods, goddesses
museology, 124
Museum(s), 2, 4, 7, 8, 13, 16, 18, 21,
   56, 71, 78, 92, 110, 117, 121, 133–
   34, 137–39, 148, 150, 152n3, 160,
   163, 181, 277
   Berndt, Perth, 213n32
   British Columbian, 173
   Cholamandal, 111, 121–22, 126
   Dakshinachitra, 20, 92, 122, 125–
      26
   ethnographic, 16, 163, 169
   Ethnographic, Oslo, 166–68, 181
   ethnological, 177
   Ethnological, Berlin, 56
   für Völkerkunde, Vienna
      (Weltmuseum, Wien), 56, 56n1,
      152n4
   Government, Chennai, 110
   Madras, 127
   Musée du Quai Branly, Paris, 56,
      169–70
   Museo Provincial Andrés
      Guacurarí
   Museo Regional Aníbal Cambas
   National, of Nigeria, Lagos, 56n1
   National Taiwan, 58n32
   New York, of Modern Art
      (MOMA) , 169, 171
   Norsk Folkemuseum, Oslo, 160,
      167–68
   of Anthropology, Vancouver,
      British Columbia (MoA), 21,
      163–65, 177
   of Arts & Science, Darwin,
      213n32, 214n35
   of Cultural History, Oslo, 21, 78,
      151n1, 209, 213n32, 214n35
   of Immigration, Oberá, 147

Sami, 181
Tromsø, 166
Vancouver, 159
Voralberg, Bregenz, 56n1
Weltmuseum, Wien; see Museum
    für Völkerkunde, Vienna above
Worthing, 9–11
music, 3–6, 11–12, 25n2–3, 41, 43, 97,
    117, 145, 189, 228, 251, 277
musical instrument(s), 89
    tablas and veenai, 251
Muslims, 9, 23, 37, 68, 77, 246, 248–
    49, 264
    attacks on, 45–46, 249
    Sufi, 246, 249
    Wahabbi, 246, 249
Myers, Fred, 2, 169
mystique, power, 66, 69
mythology, Hindu, 10, 238

Nabalco mining company, 193
Nandhan, P.S., 119
Napier Peninsula, 189
narrative(s), 20, 69, 76, 112, 116, 118,
    126, 186, 196, 267–87, 288n2, 294–
    96, 298; see also discourse
    authoritative, 76, 81
    political, 269–70, 276
    visual, 228
nation(s), 33, 40, 54, 65, 78–79–80,
    113, 167, 194, 209, 274; see also
    First Nations
    Brazilian, 271–72, 274, 276, 287
    Catholic, 269, 272
    developing, 96
    imagined, 16, 271
    Sami, 179
National Shrine, Brazil, 268–69,
    273–76, 278–80, 282–84, 286–87,
    288n3, 288n5
nationalism, 18, 49, 65, 71, 264
nationhood, 21, 67, 287
nation-state(s), 56n2, 270
    Argentine, 137
    Australian, 22
    Ghanaian, 301
Native-American(s), 144; see also
    Aboriginal, Canada, art, native,
    Indian, American
Nativity, the, 195, 201, 273
natural, the, 158
Nauiyu, Northern Territory, 22,
    185–86, 190–92, 194, 201–2, 209,
    210n2–3, 212n19–20, 213n32,
    214n35–36

negotiation(s), 47, 186–87, 188, 194–
    95, 269, 271, 283
Nelson, Robert, 132
neoliberalism, 18, 67, 74, 80, 118,
    125, 314, 315; see also economic
    liberalization
Netherlands, the, 34, 82n1
network(s), 6, 22–23, 52, 56, 70, 112,
    116, 128n2, 187, 196, 230, 320,
    234–35, 290, 301, 308
    global, 222, 239
    social, 171, 248
New Delhi, 19, 62, 82n183n9, 93,
    104n1, 110, 241n14; see also Delhi
newness, 3–4, 16, 20, 25n1, 67, 109,
    112–13, 115–16, 122, 313, 316–17;
    see also innovation, novelty
newspapers, 93, 293, 305
Ngan'gi, 185–88, 191–92, 194–95,
    201–8, 210n2, 210n4, 210n8,
    211n9–10, 211n12, 212n21,
    212n23, 213n35
Nietzsche, Friedrich, 80
Niger, coast and delta, 34, 57n6
Nigeria, 19, 33–56, 56n1, 57n6–7,
    58n19, 58n23–24, 58n28, 58n33,
    290
Nigerian-ness, 34, 54, 314
Nigerianization, 49–50
Nigerians, 19, 33–56
Nkrumah, Kwame, 49, 301
node, spatial, 234
non-art, 69, 74
non-governmental organisation(s)
    (NGOs), 66, 76, 97, 102
North America, 110, 117, 167, 247, 296
Northern Ireland, 22, 218, 222–23,
    225, 232, 234, 238, 240n7–9
Northern Territory, 22, 185, 188, 190,
    209, 211n14, 211n19, 212n25,
    214n35, 214n37
Norway, 21, , 82, 158–62, 166–68,
    171, 174–75, 177–79, 181, 213n32,
    214n35, 264n1, 315
Norwegianization, 162
nostalgia, 272
not art, 194
novelty, 3, 18, 41, 45, 75, 88, 135,
    299, 308, 312; see also innovation,
    newness

Obama, Barack, 304, 307
Obama, Michelle, 46
Obasanjo, General Olusegun, 49,
    52–53

OBCs; *see* Other Backward Castes
Obebe, Chief Modupe A., Iyaloja of
  Egbaland, 45, 52–53
Oberá, Misiones, 137
object(s), 7-9, 11, 15, 18, 23–24, 43,
  49, 67–69, 79, 87, 89–91, 94–95,
  97, 100–1, 109, 126, 132, 144, 148,
  152n2, 158, 166, 169–171, 178,
  193, 210n5, 213n29, 220, 227, 229,
  230, 234, 235, 238, 239, 240n2,
  240n10, 246, 247, 252, 258, 262,
  268–69, 272–73, 276–87, 289n10,
  290–95, 299, 303, 305, 308, 309n2;
  see also artefacts, things
    animate and inanimate, 212n24
    art/artistic, 15, 68, 71, 98, 115,
      117, 118, 119, 122, 123, 124
    devotional, 23–24, 269
    ethnic, 89, 91
    exotic, 96, 103
    mass-produced, 91, 295
    material, 18, 22, 254, 262–63,
      291–92, 294
    ordinary, 278, 284
    ornamental, 89, 91, 103
    religious, 23–24, 293, 295, 308
    ritual, 89, 91, 103, 124, 199
observation, 120, 250
occupation, German, of Norway, 175
occupations, low-salaried, 136
Odulate, Toyin, 49
Okoya, Chief Alhaji Rasaq, 51
Oliveira, Daniela, 146–47
Oloris; see Queens of Lagos
O'Loughlin, Bishop, 191
om, 26n12, 223, 233, 241n12
omnipresence, 24, 218, 234
onlookers, 308; *see also* beholders
Onuoha, Louisa, 58n29
Opera Wonyosi, 50
oppression, 4, 127, 162, 165
opulence, vulgar, 273; *see also*
  ostentation
order, 73, 79, 109, 112–14, 120, 121,
  125, 189, 209, 270, 304
  hierarchical, 12, 68
orders, Catholic, 191, 212n21
ordination, sacrament of, 280
Organ, Troy, 73
organizations, 4, 11, 12, 92, 96–97,
  103, 114, 245, 249, 268, 283, 292
  craft, 87, 91, 93, 97, 102–3
  non-governmental (NGOs), 66,
    76, 97, 102
  religious, 2, 237

transnational, 82n4, 103
Orientalism, 96, 167
originality, 2, 16–17, 75, 77, 132, 271,
  284, 292, 302, 313–14, 317–18
original(s), 23, 71, 73, 97, 102, 142–
  45, 269, 272–73, 275–76, 280, 282–
  84, 286–87, 292, 295, 298, 301–2,
  305–6, 308, 312–3, 314, 316
orthodoxy, 81, 270, 281, 283, 286
auction houses, 109
Oslo, 21, 78, 82, 151–2n1, 159–61,
  166–67, 181, 209, 213n32, 214n35,
  247, 250, 254, 264n1
ostentation, 54; *see also* opulence,
  vulgar
Other Backward Castes (OBCs), 64
Other(s), 12, 120, 132–33, 143–45,
  147, 150, 220
  the craft, 66
  the indigenous, 21, 135
  the primitive, 25n2, 169
Ottawa, 165
Otumfuo Osei Tutu II, 306
outreach, 115
Ovation magazine, 46, 51, 54
ownership, 4, 40, 49, 70, 187, 213n31,
  302
Owners, Traditional, 190, 202, 204
owollulu, 204; *see also* pigeon
Oxum, 288n5

Packert, Cynthia, 223, 228, 242n21
pain, 175, 205, 207, 273
painter(s), 14, 17, 27n17, 97, 100, 111,
  175, 296, 299, 304, 306–7
  wayside, 305–6
painting (*v.*), 65, 73, 165, 187–88,
  191–92, 194–95, 199–201, 205,
  207, 211n10, 212n23, 302, 304
painting(s), (*n.*), 14, 24, 67, 90, 97–98,
  102, 104n3, 110, 132, 168, 186,
  192–93, 197, 201–8, 211n10,
  211n13, 213n31–32, 214n35–37,
  234, 241n12, 290, 296–99, 302–8;
  see also pictures. For *specific*
  paintings, see artworks
  acrylic, 188, 302
  bark, 193, 212n27
  facial, 304
painting conventions, 187–88; *see also*
  designs, painting, style
  Ancestral, 22, 186, 189, 191
painting practices, 186, 192, 195, 201,
  213n35
Pakistan, 82n5, 104n1

Paleolithic, 168
'Paleolithicum', 167
palm leaves, 88, 94, 96; *see also kottan
pandanus*, 187–88
paradox, 58n28, 62, 64, 66, 166, 177,
   293, 296, 315–16, 318
Paraguay, 134–36, 140, 152n4
Paraíba do Sul River and Valley, Brazil,
   267–68, 270
Paraná, Brazil, 140, 287
Paris, 23, 56, 56n3, 168, 169, 247–48,
   250, 252, 254–56, 258, 313
parishes, 273, 276, 286
participation, 12, 58n20, 91, 92, 102,
   122, 139, 192, 249, 281
Passaiyoor, Sri Lanka, 253
past, 3, 6, 11, 13, 36, 42, 45, 48, 49,
   67, 69, 71–73, 75–76, 80–1, 92,
   109, 112, 122–23, 124–26, 131,
   133, 135, 137, 144–45, 150, 165,
   167, 173, 177–78, 186–7, 194, 207,
   213n34, 220, 221, 295, 301, 307,
   309, 314, 316, 318
   Ancestral, 186, 192
   authentic, 65
   Christian, 186, 192
   Indian, 64, 82n2, 109
   mythical, 241n18
   royal, 64
   stuck in the, 75
pastiche, 302
pastness, 109, 122–24
pastor(s), 245, 248, 294–95, 306
patron(s), 14, 42, 47, 66, 68, 71–72,
   78, 100, 103, 121, 127, 210n6, 301
   Nigerian, 35, 42, 47, 55
patron saint, 23, 268, 271–3
patronage, 14, 15, 42, 71, 73, 87, 100,
   160, 177
   royal, 15, 72
   traditional, 16, 72
patterns, 19, 42–43, 45–47, 54, 57n16,
   58n33, 76, 88.94, 143, 147, 201,
   211n10; *see also* motifs
Pentecostalism, 250, 254, 295, 305,
   307, 313, 318; *see also* churches,
   Pentecostal
performance(s), 4–6, 8, 10, 19, 23, 39,
   42, 68, 116, 199–200, 202, 209,
   219, 222–23, 227, 230, 238, 246,
   254–55, 258, 261, 286, 294, 303–4;
   see also art, performance
   ritual, 237, 303
performativity, 10, 200
permanence, 120, 278

Persen, Synnøve, 178, 180
persona, 70–71
personhood, 14, 22, 128, 129n7, 185,
   188, 208, 316
petitions, bark, 193–94, 198; *see also*
   paintings, bark
Petit Jaffna á la Chapelle, 248
phone(s), mobile/smart, 35, 47, 147,
   218, 221, 223–24, 240n6, 275, 280,
   282, 305
photograph(s), 9, 10, 12, 13, 22,
   58n21, 58n33, 72, 93, 95, 132,
   212n23, 227, 232, 234–37, 241n18,
   296, 304, 305
photographer(s), 51
photography, 26n9, 46, 47
picnics, 95, 113
Picton, John, 42
pictures, 2, 10, 16, 22, 24, 95, 147,
   218, 239, 275, 277, 280, 290–96,
   298–99, 301–2, 304–7, 309, 309n2;
   see also paintings, photographs. *For
   specific pictures, see* artworks
   Jesus, 24, 290–309
   mass-produced, 292, 295–96, 298,
      306, 308–9
   religious, 293–94, 307–8
pigeon(s), 202–4
pilgrim(s), 239, 268, 272–76, 279, 281
pilgrimage(s), 8, 23, 235, 248, 272–76,
   279, 281, 286
Pindies, 234
pipe(s), Guaraní, 134, 138, 140, 147,
   150, 152n4
place making, 118
places of worship, 221, 241n16; *see
   also* churches, mosques, temples
plagiarism, 291, 316
plantations, 136, 190
plants, 119, 187
   medicinal, 134
plaster, 277, 278, 286
plastic, 24, 107, 180, 234, 241n12,
   252, 256, 280, 286, 293
play, 4–5, 6, 69, 117, 124, 175, 201,
   229, 237, 254, 304
   ironic, 302, 304
player(s), 11, 70, 122, 271
   football, 277
   lottery, 26n8
   musical, 4, 41
playfulness, 5, 19, 23, 177, 224, 228,
   238
playing-cards, 277
pleasure, 113–14

plywood, 228, 230, 290, 299, 306
poetry, 228
political economy, 113
   neoliberal, 118, 125; *see also*
     economic liberalization,
     neoliberalism
politicians, 38, 48, 50, 52–53, 127,
   136–37, 268, 277
politics, 17, 22, 47, 49, 50, 65, 127–28,
   137, 148, 159, 162, 185, 186, 188,
   194, 248
   cultural, 159, 167
   elitist, 66–67
   heritage, 20, 91, 133
   identity, 17, 41, 188, 194
   of art, 193–94
   of representation, 188, 209
   of authenticity/authentication, 24,
     71, 284, 286–87
   of Christian practice, 191
   of creative improvisation, 24
   of space, 20, 108, 122, 125
   of value, 3, 14
polyester, 44, 45
puja, 13, 218–20, 222–23, 225, 227–
   39, 240n11, 250, 253, 256, 258–59,
   261, 313
Pope, Rob, 2, 221
populism, 127
portrait(s), 1, 299, 301–2, 304–5, 307
Portugal, 259, 262, 267
Posadas, Misiones, 21, 131, 133–35,
   137–39, 141, 147, 150, 151n1,
   142n3, 153n5, 153n7
possession, 133, 143, 230, 294; *see*
   also ownership, Owners, Traditional
postcards, 286, 301–2
postcolonialism, 2, 18, 20, 33, 35, 41,
   54, 57n6, 132, 148, 314
positioning, social, 66, 69, 78, 92, 144,
   166, 272, 299
poster(s), 10, 24, 221, 236, 286, 290–
   91, 293–5, 298, 309n2
potlatch, 165, 177
potter(s), 21, 124, 131, 133–34, 137
potters wheels, 125, 139
pottery, 65, 133–34, 137–40, 146, 148,
   151
   ancient, 21, 145
   Guaraní, 140, 145, 148, 151
poverty, 134, 136
   of genius, 27n16
power(s), 6, 40, 50, 64, 68–69, 79, 81,
   93, 137, 171, 177, 186, 188, 198,
   205, 222, 230, 235, 239, 246, 254–

55, 261, 267–71, 278–79, 281, 283,
   287, 291–92, 301, 308–9
   Ancestral, 198
   Aparecida's, 278, 280–83, 286
   colonizing/colonial, 16, 166
   creative, 14, 74
   demonic, 309
   divine, 219, 241n17, 269, 280,
     283–84, 295, 308–9
   healing, 205, 258–9
   political, 64, 137, 271–72
   religious, 24, 230, 272
   spiritual, 24, 198, 200, 269, 279,
     294–95, 308
   symbolic, 79, 272
   transformative, 15, 292, 295
power differences, 132, 144
power dressing, 51–52
power mystique; *see* mystique, power
power relations, 19, 24, 118, 268
power station, Alta dam, 179
practice(s), 2–5, 7, 14, 16, 21, 23, 40–
   41, 46, 62, 88, 125, 133, 138, 146,
   151, 221, 246, 269, 272, 283, 287,
   292, 312, 318
   aesthetic, 22, 194, 207–8, 246,
     254–55, 261–63
   appropriating, 131–32, 134, 147
   art/artistic, 15, 20–21, 109, 116,
     127, 140, 159–60, 167, 171,
     186, 189, 192, 198, 200–1, 209,
     210n7, 211n12
   Catholic, 22, 270, 273
   Christian, 191–92, 313
   common, 46, 259
   creative, 2, 3, 5–6, 192, 313–14,
     318
   cultural, 87, 90, 132, 140, 148, 296
   curatorial, 21, 289n10
   denominational, 22, 188
   devotional, 23, 26n12, 223, 225,
     227, 252, 268–70, 276, 283,
     287, 288n5, 313
   ethical, 118
   healing, 205
   hermeneutic, 9, 21, 131–33, 151
   indigenous, 212n22
   innovative, 88
   institutional, 21
   interpretive, 21, 131–33, 153n10
   kinship, 195
   material, 145, 150
   musical, 3, 25n2, 189
   painting, 186–87, 191–92, 194–
     95, 201, 207, 213n35

political, 194, 288n5
popular, 24, 273, 288n4
pottery, 133, 137, 145
religious, 15, 19, 23, 188, 219,
    222, 228, 246–47, 250–51,
    254–55, 262–64, 270, 288n5,
    293, 301, 308, 313
repetitive, 238, 313
reproduction, 211n11
ritual, 23, 223, 235, 287
sensorial/sensual, 23, 247, 255,
    263
traditional/tradition-making, 23,
    49, 204–5, 222, 293
unorthodox, 270
visual, 151, 187, 205, 211n11
working, 18, 149
Pratt, Mary Louise, 165
prayer(s), 8, 23–24, 205–6, 220, 225,
    232, 240n3, 247, 250, 252–55, 258,
    261–63, 275, 277–82, 293, 295, 308
    Catholic, 256, 258–59
    Hindu, 23, 256
pregnancy, 277
presence, 52, 54, 120, 159, 190, 202,
    204, 218, 220, 223, 225, 229, 234–
    35, 238, 261, 273, 282, 283, 295;
    see also omnipresence
    affective, 22, 238
    Ancestral, 192
    Christ's, 281
    divine, 2, 224, 237, 240n5, 313
    felt, 233
    Ganesh's, 234
    God's, 14, 192
    market, 45, 208
    physical, 39, 222
    spiritual, 200, 298
    visual, 224
present, the, 3, 6, 12, 45, 92, 122–24,
    131, 133, 135–37, 140, 144, 158,
    166, 167, 169, 177, 181, 186–87,
    194.309, 318
preservation, 26n12, 72, 103, 137,
    139–40, 193
president(s),
    of Merrepen Arts, 202, 213n35
    of Nigeria, 48, 52–53
    of the USA, 46
    of the World Crafts Council, 86,
    92, 97
prestige, 43, 46, 53–55, 62, 64, 69,
    72, 88, 93–94, 112; *see also* luxury,
    status
Price, Sally, 158, 169

price, 34, 40, 67, 102, 104n2, 110,
    125, 132, 171, 286
priest(s), 303; *see also* clergymen, pastor
    Brahmin, 124
    Catholic, 191, 192, 205, 251,
    252, 258, 259, 270, 274, 276, ,
    279–83
    Hindu, 225, 228, 237, 252, 256
    Tamil, 248, 251
    Vaishnavite, 235
primitive, the, 15, 159, 168–69
printing, 187, 271, 305
prints
    lithographic, 173
    wax, 41–43, 57n8
private sector, 48, 113
processions, 114, 250, 272
production, 3, 7, 8, 14, 16–17, 19–24,
    34–35, 41–46, 50, 52.55–56, 64,
    68–71, 74, 82n1, 87, 91–92, 96, 103,
    104n2, 108–9, 112–13, 116, 124–
    25, 140, 144, 160, 186, 191, 194,
    207–8, 220, 240n6, 255, 261, 264,
    268–69, 283–84, 287, 288n6, 292,
    298, 314–15; *see also* manufacture,
    reproduction
    agricultural, 57n6
    art/artistic, 15, 17, 108–9, 115,
    127, 166, 171, 187–88, 190–91,
    201, 208, 209
    capitalist, 169
    ceramic, 134, 140, 145
    craft, 20, 86, 136, 312
    creative, 7, 24
    cultural, 2, 7, 13, 18, 21, 75, 87,
    92–93, 102, 125, 169, 191,
    312–18
    fashion, 19
    heritage, 11, 98
    image, 3, 16
    industrial, 34, 42
    kottan, 87–88, 93, 95–96
    mass, 45, 301
    material, 3–4, 7, 15, 18, 21, 24, 66
    modes of, 112
    poetic and mythological, 134
    social, of creativity, 160, 315
    visual, 3
profane, the, 24, 295
progress, 67, 75–76, 80, 169
property, 13, 110, 120
    cultural, 134
    intellectual, 83n6, 118
Protestant(s), 22, 189, 195, 206, 208–
    9, 250, 288, 293, 313

Protestantism, 175
proto-Lappish population, 166
psychological infantilism, 294
public domain/sphere, 186–87
publicity, 93; *see also* marketing
punishment, ritual, 191
Punjab, 219, 241n16
Punjabis, 61–62, 66, 68, 70
purity, 66, 304

quality, 1, 21, 35, 40, 62, 66, 68, 71,
    77, 79, 82n1, 83n6, 102, 104n1-2,
    169, 263; *see also* craftsmanship,
    style
    aesthetic, 20, 100, 105n3, 286,
        295
Queen Charlotte Islands, 172
Queen Elisabeth, 307
Queen Mother (Ghana), 307, 309n4
Queens of Lagos, 51

race, 168, 249, 307
racism, 147, 298
rajdhani, city of rulers, 63; *see also* city,
    capital, Delhi, New Delhi
Ramaswamy, Visalakshi, 87, 92–93,
    100
rank, 2, 12, 40, 79, 82; *see also*
    class[es], status
rationality, 114, 225; *see also* reason
rationalization, 149
reason, 27n15, 255; *see also* rationality
reception, 86, 194, 223, 290, 292
recession, 110; *see also* bust
recognition, 9, 22, 65–66, 79, 93, 162,
    165, 193–94, 208, 286, 296, 298
recombination, 87–88
recontextualisation, 97
recovery, 110, 164
recreacíon, 140
recreation(s), 64, 134, 137, 141, 143
recuperation, 137, 139–40
recycling, 302, 306
    aesthetic, 292, 313
Redemptorist Fathers, 268, 283
redemption, 206, 276, 281
referent, 304
Reid, Bill, 168, 171–74, 177
reimagining, 117
reindeer, 162, 174, 175, 181
reinterpretation(s), 36, 48, 189, 195–
    96, 298, 299
regime(s), 8, 123
    aesthetic, 208, 316
    affective, 23, 225, 238

bodily, 24, 295
political, 2, 49, 301
of Creativity, 312, 314–18
of piety, 295
of value, 2, 18
religious, 23, 219, 235, 238
religion, 7, 13–15, 18, 22, 26n14, 189,
    209, 238, 240n5, 245–46, 248, 249–
    52, 264, 268, 292, 312–14
    art and, 291–92, 309
    and nationalism, 264
    as aesthetics, 254–6, 258
    politicization of, 246, 249
religiosity, 22–23, 188, 192, 194–95,
    202
religious affiliation; *see* affiliation,
    religious
relinquishment, 133
remediation, 18–19, 25n4, 224, 236,
    296, 298, 308, 313
renaissance, 15, 40, 166
Renault, 110
Renne, Elisha, 54
renunciation, 62, 204, 13n34
repetition, 3–6, 8, 67, 75, 97, 232,
    235, 238, 255, 293, 295, 298, 304,
    313–14
replica(s), 138–39, 142–43, 258–59,
    265n5, 278, 286; *see also* copy,
    reproduction
representations, 3, 14, 72, 123, 145,
    186, 208, 220, 291, 296, 305
    indigenous, 291, 302
reproduction(s), 2–3, 6, 13, 16, 18, 24,
    25n4, 86, 94–95, 97, 125, 211n11,
    262–63, 276, 291, 293–94, 296–99,
    303, 305
    cheap, 295, 304–5
    cultural, 314
    mechanical, 290, 295
    mass, 308, 313
    mindless, 97, 100
    techniques/technologies of, 138,
        305, 316
resemblance, 252, 286, 305
resistance, 4, 114, 132.137, 165
resources, 162–63, 167, 179, 296
respect, 11, 52, 77–78, 93-94, 97,
    104n2, 146, 188, 198, 200, 210n6,
    219, 220, 222, 227, 230, 234, 235,
    238, 256, 281
responsibility, 104n2, 118, 181, 228,
    230, 283
restitution, 148, 151
resurrection, 195

retailer(s), 34, 67, 89–91, 94–96, 103
revelation, 81, 186, 294
revivalism, 71
rhinestones, 44; *see also* Swarovski
    crystals
rich, 14, 40, 46, 50, 52–53
    the new, 62
    the old, 61–62
rights, 118, 134, 162–63, 167, 179,
    187, 194, 196, 200, 211n11, 251
    collective, 22, 188
    land, 134, 162–63, 167, 179,
        193–94, 212n25, 212n27
Riksantikvar, 168
Rio de Janeiro, 113, 272
Rio Grande do Sul, Brazil, 140,
    153n12, 279
rites of passage, 89; *see also*
    ceremonies, life-cycle
Ritter, Helmut, 45–46, 57n15–16
ritual, 7, 8, 13, 20, 23, 56, 88–89,
    91, 98, 103, 124, 187, 189–91,
    195, 199–200, 202–5, 209, 210n4,
    211n11, 213n29, 222–23, 225, 227,
    230, 232–33, 235, 237–38, 247,
    251, 254–55, 258, 261, 264, 272,
    281–82, 284, 287, 294–95, 301,
    303–4, 309n3
    Catholic, 263
    Christian, 192, 203, 205
    Hindu, 223, 225, 253
    Ngan'gi, 203
    religious, 248, 303
Rojas, Liliana, 137–40, 142–43, 146,
    150, 152n1
Rolls-Royce Phantom II Star of India, 62
Romanization, 270, 288n7
Room of Miracles, 276; *see also* ex-
    voto* room, Room of Promises, *Sala
    das Promessas*
Room of Promises, 276–78, 280,
    289n10; *see also ex-voto* room,
    Room of Miracles, *Sala das
    Promessas*
rosary, 205–6, 261, 271, 286
royalty, Asante, 307
Rudder, John, 190, 198, 213n30
rulers, 40, 48, 63, 70; *see also* class,
    ruling
rupture, 123

sacraments, 195, 282–83
sacred, the, 24, 223, 225, 282, 284, 295
saffron (colour), 62
Saffronart auction house, 109

Sahlins, Marshall, 40
Said, Edward, 96
saint(s), 256, 261, 268, 270, 276, 277,
    279, 284, 286, 287, 293
    patron, 23, 268, 271–3
    St. Anthony, 250, 252, 265n4
    St. Fatima, 259, 262
    St. Frances Xavier, 192, 213n35,
        214n36
St. Gallen, Switzerland, 34, 42, 55
Sala das Promessas, 276; *see also
    ex-voto* room, Room of Promises,
    Room of Miracles
sales-agents; *see* agents/agencies, sales
sales strategy, 66; *see also* marketing
Salish, 161
Sallman, Warner, 290
salvage, 164–65, 177
salvation, 26n14, 166, 299, 300, 305
Samekomiteen, 167
sameness, 295, 299, 316
Sami, 159–62, 166–68, 171, 174,
    175–81
Sami Community College, 175
Sami parliament, 181
sandals, 107, 296
San Ignacio Miní, Argentina, 136
Sanskrit, 26n14, 27n18, 73, 227
Santa Ana, Argentina, 21, 132–34,
    148–49, 151, 152n1, 153n15–16
Santa Catarina, Brazil, 140, 145–46
Santa Cruz, Bolivia, 140
Santos, Carmen de los, 134, 148, 150–
    51, 152n1, 153n15
Santos, Lourival dos, 269–72, 288n6
São Paulo, 268, 270, 272
Sápmi, 179
Saraswati, 234
sari(s), 62, 68, 77–78, 86, 102, 104,
    246, 252, 258–59, 261–62
Satan, 294–95; *see also* devil, the
savagery, 75
Savio, John Andreas, 168
schemas, interpretive, 79
science(s), 69, 167
    social, 143
Scotland, 93–94
Scott, James, 200
sculptors, 14–15, 17, 27n18, 111, 122,
    142, 153n8, 175
sculpture(s), 1, 97–98, 101, 120–21,
    123, 127, 175, 178, 193, 298, 302,
    307; *for specific sculptures, see*
    artworks
sculpture park, 111, 120

Second Vatican Council, 212n22, 250–51, 253
self/selves, 20, 66, 223, 246–47
    the African, 297
    the religious, 246
    transnational, 238
self-creation, 220, 316
selfhood, 71, 94
self-immolation, 246
self-making, 315, 317
self-reliance, 65
sensation(s), 18, 23, 24, 113, 222, 246–47, 292–93, 298, 313
sensational forms, 235, 254–56, 282
senses, the, 24, 228, 247, 254, 256, 292, 316
sensuality, 186, 255
sensuous engagements, 186
sequences, 5–6, 144
serigraphy, 188
servant(s), 62–63
sex, 40, 47, 175, 209
Shadbolt, Doris, 171–72, 177
Shapiro, Roberta, 100, 102
Sharma, Prem, 256
Shepherdson, Rev. Harold Urquhart, 189, 192
shilpa, 73
Shilpa Shastras, 15
Shiraz Café, Cholamandal, 120–21
Shittu, Mobolaji, 43, 57n15
shopping, 117, 247, 279
shopping malls; *see* malls
shrine(s), 22–24, 225, 227, 234–35, 241n13, 241n18, 248, 250, 258, 261, 267–87, 293; *see also* altar
    Buddhist, 249
    home, 22–23, 220, 222–24, 227, 228–29, 233–35, 237–38, 256, 261
    Marian, 268
    National, 268–87, 288n2–3, 288n5
    Shinto, 107
Siberia, 167
silver, 20, 82, 87–88
silversmiths, 10, 88–91
Simmel, Georg, 169
singers, popular, 277
Sinhalese, 245–46, 248–49, 262–64
Skidegate, British Columbia, 172–73
Sierra Leone, 41
Sihadipa, 245
skill(s), 1, 10, 11, 14, 15, 17, 20, 26n13, 34, 55, 66, 70, 73, 76, 79,

81, 82, 86, 97, 102, 109, 120, 126, 187
    traditional, 96, 316
    weaving, 92–93
skilled observation/vision, 120, 144
smugglers, 58n25
social body; *see* body, social
socialist(s), 17, 64, 112
social life, 87–88, 102, 174, 237, 248, 316
socialites, 100, 103
sociality, 14, 121, 188, 193, 240n6
social production of creativity, 160, 315
Social Sciences; *see* sciences, social
society, 17, 21, 34, 39–41, 46, 69, 92–93, 97, 126, 134, 170, 293, 316
    creole-white (Argentina), 137, 144, 149, 151
    Hindu, 251
    knowledge, 72, 76, 81
    Kwakiutl, 165
    immigrant, in Misiones, 147
    Indian, 72
    majority (Argentina), 136–37, 144, 149
    modern, 169, 317
    Nigerian, 47, 52, 58n19
    Norwegian, 179
    Tamil, 250
    white (Canada), 165, 171
solidarity, 50, 276
song(s), 189–90, 195, 200, 213n29, 252, 261, 280–81
soul, 61, 76, 107, 213n29, 222, 308–9
sound, 5–6, 12, 26n9, 26n12, 54, 220, 223, 254
souvenir(s), 91, 233, 235
Soyinka, Wole, 50
Sozzani, Franca, 58n34
space(s), 7, 9, 20, 35, 52, 68, 87–88, 91, 95, 97, 102, 113–15, 117–19, 121–22, 125, 171, 207, 222–23, 234–35, 255, 269, 276, 290, 293, 313
    city, 20, 114, 118
    discursive, 292
    empty, 54
    exhibition, 9, 26n10
    gallery, 111, 117, 124, 128n5, 303
    global, 64, 72
    improvisational, 230
    museum, 11, 117, 124
    politics of, 122
    public, 22, 114, 128n6, 159, 218, 301
    private, 22, 235

ritual, 89, 103
  sacred, 234, 303, 309
  spectacular, 117–18
  temporal, 126
  urban, 20, 108–9, 114
speaking in tongues, 307
speaking nearby, 144
spectacle, 49, 113, 115, 120, 181
spectacular, 115, 117–18, 127, 316
spectator(s), 98, 115, 307
spirit(s), 65, 68, 195–96, 205–6,
  214n37, 294, 307
Spirit, Holy; see Dhuyu Birrimbirr,
  Holy Spirit
Spyer, Patricia, 6
Sri Lanka, 23, 104n1, 245–64
Sri Swami Gopal Sharan Devacharya,
  235
stagnation, 75; see also stasis
Stallabrass, Julian, 117
Stanley, Owen, 191
Star of David, 198, 200
stasis, 67, 75; see also stagnation
state(s), 48, 49, 55, 91, 103, 113–14,
  123, 127, 129n7, 133–34, 140, 145,
  153n6, 153n12, 162, 167, 193, 234,
  270, 271, 276, 301; see also nation-
  state
    Australian, 194, 210n6
    Brazilian, 269, 271–73, 287
    Canadian, 165
    Norwegian, 167
    Sinhalese, 262
Stations of the Cross, 205, 214n36
statue(s), 14, 22, 24, 152n3, 256, 278,
  284, 293, 304
    of Aparecida, 274, 280, 282, 286
    of Hindu gods, 218
    of Jesus, 293, 298, 309n2
    of Mary, 8, 252, 256, 258, 261,
      267, 269, 293, 295
    religious, 248, 293, 305
status, 9, 11, 14, 40, 50–51, 53, 55, 63,
  66, 69, 70, 72–74, 93, 100–3, 123,
  159, 171, 182n1, 194–95, 222, 308,
  316, 317; see also class[es], prestige,
  rank
    art/artistic, 102, 112, 194, 207
    artist's, 15, 17, 186
    global, 113, 115, 118
    social, 39–41, 88, 93, 97, 103
status quo, 79, 302, 304
Steedly, Mary Margaret, 6
Stella's Canteen, Cholamandal, 121
stereotypes, 11, 147

stitch density, 43, 46
stool, ceremonial wooden, 296
storage, 88, 98, 103
stories, 11, 86, 90, 132, 187, 195, 198,
  205, 237, 277, 293, 307
    Ancestral, 186–87, 192, 198, 201,
      211n10–11
    biblical, 191–92, 195
    Christian, 189–90, 192, 198
    design, 195, 201, 213n31
    televised, 227, 238
structure(s), 17, 52, 54, 108, 139, 161,
  176, 195, 209, 235, 309; see also
  infrastructure
    social, 161, 195
    temple, 219, 130
student(s), 4–5, 10, 75, 110, 111–12,
  139, 142, 145, 151, 162, 302
studio(s), 14, 67, 100, 121, 179, 305
style(s), 1, 4, 10, 16–20, 61–62, 116,
  143, 152n2, 168, 177, 186–88, 207,
  211n13, 213n35, 302
    abstract Ancestral, 191–92
    art/artistic, 195, 201
    figurative, 191–92
    naturalistic, 191–92
    Western, 191, 193
style(s) clothing, 34, 36–39, 46–48, 50,
  54–55, 57n9, 57n15, 76; see also
  fashion, suit
    African, 35–36, 49
    antique, 64
    classic, 38–39
    contemporary, 50, 54
    European, 35, 41, 48–49
    Hausa, 39, 41, 48
    Indo-western chic, 64
    local, 39, 41, 48
    new, 39, 41, 47
    Nigerian, 49, 55
    Royal chic, 64
    traditional, 36, 39, 314
style guru(s); see guru, style
subject(s), 20, 25n2, 27n15, 63–64, 74,
  88, 103, 118, 235, 246, 255, 268,
  287
    colonial/colonized, 15, 166
    research, 131–32, 135
subjectivity/ies, 4, 6, 8, 22, 25n2,
  27n15, 88, 220, 235
    emotional, 88, 103
subject-positions, 176
subordination, 223
suit
    European, 38, 41, 48

Mao, 49
men's, 39, 44
Western, 49, 51
woman's/lady's, 38, 46
Super Consciousness, 235
superiority, 15, 97, 27n16, 298;
see also dominance, hegemony,
supremacy
superstition, 15, 294
supremacy, Buddhist Sinhalese, 245
Suriname, 158
svarupa, 236, 241n17
Swarovski crystals, 44, 50, 62, 68
Swastik, 233
Switzerland, 34–35, 41–42, 45, 55,
58n25
Sydney, 213n32, 214n35
symbol(s), 48, 64–65, 72–73, 88, 151,
163, 175, 190, 204, 233, 251, 269,
271–72, 291, 299, 309, 309n2
Christian, 189, 204
national, 177, 270, 273
symbolic economy, 117, 125, 127
symbolism, 41, 48, 50, 54, 79, 81, 100,
158, 178, 191, 201–2, 204, 213n29,
232, 241, 263, 272, 296, 298, 303–4
visual, 192, 195
sympathetic intuition – see
Nachempfindung

Tahiliani, Tarun, 76, 83n6, 83n11
tailor(s), 10, 67–68
Takoradi, Ghana, 299
talent(s), 14, 27n16, 95, 173, 298,
304–5; *see also* creativity
Taller Municipal de Artes Brasanelli,
133–34, 148
Talwan village, 225
Tamilness, 251
Tamil(s), 121, 127
Sri Lankan, 23, 110, 245–64
Tamil Catholicism; *see* Catholicism,
Tamil
Tamil Catholics; *see* Catholics, Tamil
Tamil diaspora, 27
Tamil Hinduism; *see* Hinduism, Tamil
Tamil Hindus; *see* Hindus, Sri Lankan
Tamil
Tamil Nadu, 11, 20, 27n18, 86–87,
91–92, 102, 114, 124, 127, 129n7
Tamil Tigers, 247, 251; *see also*
Liberation Tigers of Tamil Eelam
taste(s), 37, 40, 46–47, 53–55, 62, 67,
71, 76, 159, 186, 228, 254, 301
bad, 54, 61

elite, 68
taxonomy, 171
Taylor, Luke, 187
teachers, 1, 136–40, 143, 145, 150,
175, 190, 213n35, 298
teachings, 189–90, 192, 195, 249; *see
also* doctrine, ideology, theology
tekhne, 73; *see also* skill
technique(s), 1, 10, 12, 21, 34, 44,
46, 68, 70, 75–76, 104n2, 122,
134, 140, 143, 148–49, 150, 158,
166, 168, 178, 187, 278, 302; *see
also* knowledge, embodied and
knowledge, technical
art/artistic, 109, 145
ceramic, 137–39
craft, 97, 104n2
embroidery, 19, 34–35
indigenous, 135, 151
innovative, 187–88
makeup, 9, 12
mystification, 67, 74, 80–81
production, 43, 104n2
traditional, 10, 139
weaving, 54–55, 86
technology, 42, 160, 189, 223, 237,
282; *see also* machines
media/mediation, 6, 301
mobile-phone, 224, 240n6
production, 42, 56
reproduction, 305
templates,
aesthetic, 187
Ancestral, 185, 209
design, 185, 187, 207
Temple(s), 22
Courneuve, La, 248
Hindu, 11, 15, 26n13, 219, 222,
225–28, 230, 234, 237–38,
240n9, 241n14, 241n16,
242n21, 247–50, 252, 256
Mari-Amman, 256, 258
of the Tooth, 249
Radharamana, 236–37, 241n17
Vaishno Devi, 234–36, 241n13
temporality/ies, 109, 123, 125, 234
territory, 162, 167, 276
textile(s), 9, 33–34, 36, 40–46, 50,
54–55, 57n12, 58n31, 72, 76, 92,
103; *see also* cloth, cotton, *brocade,*
damask, fabric, linen, silk, woollens
embroidery/embroidered, 38, 41,
43, 97
hand-woven, 43, 50
local, 50, 54

texts, 9, 10, 153n6, 167, 190, 193,
    221, 224, 234, 237, 241n12, 277
    anthropological, 144
    biblical, 26n12, 275
    sacred, 237
    Sanskrit, 27n18
    Tamil, 27n19
Tharoor, Shashi, 64
theatre(s), 9–10, 115
Thiagarajan, Deborah, 125
theology
    Aboriginal, 185
    Christian, 199, 209
thing(s), 2, 6–7, 26n12, 40, 54, 79,
    87–88, 94, 96, 109, 132, 142, 148,
    218, 220, 246, 254, 256, 279; *see
    also* artefacts, objects
    material, 23, 220, 223
    the real, 284, 295
thingness, 234
Third World, 113
time(s), 1–2, 7, 9, 10, 12, 14, 21, 24,
    25n4, 63, 74, 77, 87–88, 96, 100,
    104n3, 108, 113, 116, 122–24, 142,
    148, 163, 167–68, 171, 173–74,
    224, 227, 230, 237–39, 241n18,
    269–70, 282, 287, 288n6, 290, 313,
    316
timelessness, 14, 57n14, 76, 81, 218,
    234, 239
Times of India, 93
time/space compression, 35
Toronto, 165, 172
totem-pole project, 164
touch, 24, 68, 228, 254, 261, 275, 281,
    286, 295
tourism, 117, 125, 149, 209, 279
    eco-, 134
tourist(s), 20, 65, 108, 114, 124, 140,
    145, 158, 168, 181
Townsend-Gault, Charlotte, 159, 181
trade, 34–35, 40–42, 50, 52–53, 55,
    57n6–7, 58n25, 64, 163, 230, 292,
    307
    textile, 57n12, 58n31
trademark, 159, 177
trader(s), 40, 69–70, 78, 291, 296; *see
    also* merchant
trading houses, 34, 52
tradition(s), 2, 6, 10–11, 13, 16, 19–20,
    22–24, 26n7, 36, 49, 54–56, 67, 72,
    74–76, 78–79, 112, 122, 165, 175,
    212n22, 219, 223, 233, 238, 240n6,
    314, 316
    clothing, 35, 40, 49, 55

cultural, 48, 165, 170
devotional, 23, 212n21, 224, 228,
    240n1
diasporic, 222, 238
established, 88, 170, 262
hermeneutic, 143
Hindu, 73, 220, 238
Indian, 12, 72, 75, 122, 227
invented/invention of, 33, 48,
    56n2
living, 177, 313
local, 35, 48, 54, 208
lost, 92, 164–65
Nigerian, 35, 40, 49, 54–55
recreation of, 140, 175, 262
religious, 14–15, 23, 221, 248,
    250, 263, 313
traditionalism, 19, 71, 74, 82n2
training, 9, 42, 175, 288n2
    art, 187, 298
    design, 75–76, 100
trance, 81
transactions, 148; *see also* exchange
transcendence, 17, 25n2, 219, 230,
    233, 235, 237, 255, 283
transcript, public and hidden, 200
transformation, 66–67, 87–88, 94,
    102, 108–9, 112, 114, 122, 126–28,
    133, 172, 187, 196, 204, 208, 220,
    268–71, 283, 288n6, 290, 313
    spiritual, 213n34, 228
transit, 7, 11, 18, 23, 24, 88–89, 103,
    230, 240n2, 269, 272, 278, 290
transition, 7–9, 11, 16, 22–23, 24, 88,
    91, 96, 98, 103, 125, 168, 220, 230,
    269–72, 278, 282, 286–87, 288n6,
    290, 313
transit-transition, 238
transition-transformation, 8–9, 22,
    220, 223, 228, 238
transnational, 2, 7, 22–23, 35, 41, 65,
    82n4, 103, 118, 219, 234, 236, 238–
    39, 264, 264n1, 268, 270–71, 287
transubstantiation, 69
transvision, 144
tree, ironwood, 205–6
trend agency/ies, 46, 58n34
trend scouting, 46, 55
trickle-down effect, 117
Trikuta Mountain, 235
Trinh, T. Minh-Ha, 144
T-shirts, 286, 290, 304
Tulsyan, Sanjay, 108, 111, 115, 126–
    27, 128n1, 128n5
tsunami, Indian Ocean, of 2005, 107–8

Turkish embroiderers, 19, 34, 55
turmeric holders, 90–91

UNESCO (United Nations
  Educational, Scientific and Cultural
  Organisation), 76, 82n4, 92, 315
    Seal of Excellence Award, 86,
      93–94, 96, 104n1–2
    World Heritage Site, 136
UK (United Kingdom of Great Britain
  and Northern Ireland), 9–10, 13,
  26n8, 87, 95, 235
unanimity, 200
uniform(s), 48, 50, 57n17; *see also aso
  ebi*
uniqueness, 2, 96, 117, 237, 271
unity, 169, 173, 192, 204–5, 222–23,
  270, 276, 281
universality principle, 169–70
universe, 26n12, 26n14, 40, 187, 224
University/ies, 179, 298
    Comunitária Regional de
      Chapecó, 145–46
    Ibadan, Nigeria, 57n6
    Kumasi, Ghana, 302
    National, of Misiones, 137–38
    of British Columbia (UBC), 163–
      64, 177
    of Capetown, 1
    of Oslo, 167
    Queen's, Belfast, 10
Untouchables, 64
Urbefolkning, 162
urns, Guaraní funerary, 135, 138–40,
  142–43, 145, 152n3
USA (United States of America), 87
use, modes of, 292, 299, 309
Uttar Pradesh, 80, 241n16, 317

Vaisnava samhitas, 219
valuation, 15, 69, 74, 103, 207, 227,
  269, 283, 286; *see also* devaluation,
  evaluation
value, 3, 6, 8, 10–13, 16–18, 22, 25,
  53, 62, 66–70, 72, 74, 81, 82n1,
  82n4, 88, 96, 100, 103, 104n2–3,
  109, 115, 118, 123, 137, 171, 186–
  87, 207, 210n5, 227, 232, 239, 255,
  269, 283, 286–87, 291, 295, 299,
  301, 303, 305, 307–8
    cult, 15
    economic/monetary, 105n3,
      128n3, 208
    exhibition, 15
    politics of, 14

regimes of, 2, 18
semiotic/symbolic, 41, 73, 81
use, 73, 166
values, 3, 17, 24, 88, 100, 114, 186,
  188, 191, 269, 283
    Christian, 191, 304
    competing/clash of, 24, 54
    family, 233
    Hindu, 225
value systems, 54, 78, 81
Vancouver, 21, 159, 161–63, 174, 177
Varma, Ravi, 16, 102, 110
Vastokas, Joan, 165
Vatican, 248, 270, 272, 274, 283
Vatican Council, Second, 212n22,
  250–51, 253, 296
Venkatesan, Sowmhya, 92, 100
vermillion holders, 87, 90–91
Verstehen approach, 143
vibrations, 223, 233
Victoria, B.C., 171
video(s), 26n10, 108, 124, 128n6, 189,
  318
village(s), 20, 65–66, 77–78, 86–88,
  93–94, 96, 124–25, 127, 129n7,
  136, 249–50, 252–54, 317
    abandoned, 164–65
    Cholamandal artist's, 20, 108–11,
      113, 119–22, 125–27, 129n7
    Ghandian, 121
    Indian, 91, 103, 112
    Passaiyoor, Jaffna, 253
    real, 71
    Santa Ana, Misiones, 148
    Sompting, West Sussex, 13
    Talwan and Phillaur, Jullundur,
      225
Villalba, Paulito, 149, 153n17
Vinci, Leonardo da, 14, 290, 302, 304
visionaries, design, 74
visions, 109, 125, 295
visualization, 225–26
Vorarlberg, Austria, 19, 34–35, 41–42,
  45, 48, 54

Wakashan, Northern, 161
wangarr, 199
waste, sacred, 234
Wayo, Nicholas T.
weaving, 19, 34, 40, 54–55, 65
    kottan basket, 86, 88, 92–94, 96,
      100–2
weavers, 10, 65, 101, 124
    kottan, 87, 92–94, 97, 100–3
Weber, Max, 143, 153

weddings, 47–48, 57n17, 77, 89, 225
wedding cards, 22, 221, 233
wedding gifts, 234
Welcome to Country ceremony, 202, 204
Wells, Rev. Edgar, 193–94
Wemega-Kwawu, Rikki, 299–302
West, the, 70, 95, 110, 316
Whisnant, David, 92–93
Whitehead, Christopher, 160
wild man, 119
wisdom, 75, 240n3, 241n12
witchcraft, 294
Witte, Marleen de, 92, 288n1
wonyosi, 50
workshop(s), 4, 6, 10, 12, 61, 67–68, 78, 82n1, 100, 108, 125, 133–35, 139–40, 142–44, 148–51, 179, 278–79, 292, 298, 304–6
World Crafts Council, 86, 92, 97, 100
World Crafts Summit, 86, 92, 97, 100–1; *see also Kaivalam*
worldview(s), 81, 188, 208, 304
worship, 15, 23, 26n14, 189, 192, 206, 219, 221–24, 227, 229, 232, 235, 238–39, 240n11, 241n16–17, 246, 251, 254–56, 258, 261–64, 267, 286, 295

Hindu, 222, 23, 261, 264n1
idol, 293

Xavior. Father Mari, 251

Yamuna River, 237
yantra, 230
yapepó, 135, 139, 141–45, 152n3; *see also* urns, funerary
yam, 201, 309n3
yam oto, 303, 309n3
yarn, 34, 38, 43–44, 50, 54
Yirritja moiety, 193, 212n24
Yirrkala, Northern Territory, 188, 193, 198
Yolngu, 185–201, 206–7, 210n2, 210n4, 211n9–12, 212n27, 213n30, 213n33
yopará, 135
Young, James O., 132, 152n2
Yoruba, 39, 41, 47, 50–51, 54, 57n9, 57n17
yuta, 187; *see also* innovation

zardosi, 101, 105n4
zone of entanglement, 250
Zukin, Sharon, 117